D0845790

Colonial immigrants in a British city

International Library of Sociology

Founded by Karl Mannheim

Editor: John Rex, University of Warwick

Arbor Scientiae
Arbor Vitae

Colonial immigrants in a British city

A class analysis

John Rex and Sally Tomlinson
with the assistance of
David Hearnden and Peter Ratcliffe

Routledge & Kegan Paul
London, Boston and Henley

First published in 1979
by Routledge & Kegan Paul Ltd
39 Store Street, London WC1E 7DD,
Broadway House, Newtown Road,
Henley-on-Thames, Oxon, RG9 1EN and
9 Park Street, Boston, Mass. 02108, USA
Set in 10/11 Times New Roman
by Ronset Ltd, Darwen, Lancashire
and printed in Great Britain by
Lowe & Brydone Ltd

British Library Cataloguing in Publication Data

Rex, John
Colonial immigrants in a British city. –
(International library of sociology).
1. Handsworth, Eng. (West Midlands) – Foreign
population   2. Social classes – England –
Handsworth, W. Midlands
I Title   II. Tomlinson, Sally   III. Series
301.4'51   JV7695.Z6H/   78–41177

ISBN 0 7100 0142 8

To Marcus Nyerere Henry

Contents

Tables

Figures

Acknowledgments

The research work on which this book is based was financed through a grant made in the first place to John Rex, Wyn Lewis and Valdo Pons by the Nuffield Foundation. Our first debt is to the foundation who provided generously for what was a very large-scale and prolonged study, and helped us in every way to fulfil our commitments, despite the pressure of an unprecedented inflation in 1974–5. We are especially grateful to Miss Pat Thomas for the sympathetic way in which she responded to our problems.

Valdo Pons left Warwick University on being appointed to a Chair in Hull shortly after the grant was made, and his share of the supervision was undertaken for a year by Dr Martin Legassick. Wyn Lewis advised us on all statistical matters up to the summer of 1976 and we are grateful for the help which he gave us. After that we were immensely lucky to be able to call upon the services of Peter Ratcliffe who supervised the processing of our data and helped us on all the technical issues on which we were amateurs.

The full-time research staff consisted of Sally Tomlinson, who worked on the project for four years, and David Hearnden and Pervaiz Nazir, who worked on it for two. The work reported in this book is largely that which was carried out by the two authors and David Hearnden. Pervaiz Nazir will be publishing his own findings on the Pakistani community independently, but he did contribute to the formulation of our problem and by finding Asian interviewers. We are grateful to him and to his chief Pakistani interviewer, Mr S. Quareshi.

If our theoretical and anti-positivist inclinations lead us to insist that the survey work which we undertook was not the whole of our research, it was none the less a very important part of it and certainly one of the parts which required the most skill and determination. We took a long time before entrusting the task of drawing up a questionnaire and administering it to NOP Market Research Limited, but there can have been few such arrangements between sociologists and a market research organization which have worked out more happily. John O'Brien gave generously of his time and experience and organized the team of interviewers with a vigour and efficiency which we wish we could see matched in academic life. We must also add, however, that his work was made much easier by Irene Hickling who was a thoroughly professional supervisor of the interviewing team, and by an interviewing staff who took on board what must have been one of their most difficult interviewing assignments without demur, and despite suggestions from the police and others that such interviewing in a multi-racial area in the inner city might be positively dangerous.

We decided to code the data and analyse it ourselves and learned much in the process. The ethnomethodological joke that, if your data start talking to you, you code them to keep them quiet, may have some truth in it, but the fact of the matter is that all of us did handle the data directly and did not forget what was tucked away from sight by the codes. We hope that our understanding of those individual answers and meanings has informed the judgments which go to the making of a book such as this. Amongst those who helped us with the coding were Alyson Burberry, Mike Stacey, Valerie Jackson, Ann Oliver, Lynne Julian-Jones and Sue Tomlinson. It was a pleasure working with them and, under David Hearnden's direction, they kept well up to time.

Since David Hearnden is not formally one of the two authors of this book it is perhaps appropriate to point out that for long periods during the survey he took charge and did so, not like a new graduate, but like a research worker with years of experience. For the first three years we were also helped by Val Brown who was much more than a secretary and identified herself completely with our work. And, finally, completing the team, was Iris Host, who came in at what was a very awkward time for us and typed our book again and again. She also looked after us as any senior secretary should do, sorting out our confusions and seeing to it that nothing went wrong. It is hard to imagine this book as having seen the light of day without her.

The authorship of the final text has been the responsibility of John Rex and Sally Tomlinson jointly except for the first appendix in which John Rex continues the theoretical line of argument which he began in his book *Key Problems of Sociological Theory* and continued in *Discovering Sociology* and *Sociology and the Demystification of the Modern World*.

The maps in the book were produced for us by our consultant cartographer, Mr M. B. Stedman, Department of Geography,

University of Birmingham, whose willing help we gratefully acknowledge.

We have to thank many officials of the Birmingham Corporation for help, most especially in the housing, education and statistics departments. The Birmingham Manpower Services Commission and the Youth Employment Office also gave us every help, as did the local Community Relations Committee. Many other teachers, social workers, policemen, councillors, community workers and trade unionists also spent time in telling us how they saw things at the grass roots and generally educating us, as only those who are truly involved can. If we sometimes criticize the perspective of any of them or put it into a larger one, we should also like to say that, since Britain made little preparation for the arrival of about a million New Commonwealth immigrants, it was this new cadre of professionals and enthusiastic amateurs who had to bear the brunt of the problems and devise their own solutions *ad hoc*. There is a real virtue in this close contact with reality which sociological theorists and even researchers cannot claim for themselves.

Our last word of thanks goes to Ivan Henry of Barbados and Birmingham. Ivan was doing his own research but found time to make a critical contribution to the study. He also succeeded in maintaining a dual commitment to his fellow West Indians in Handsworth and to the scholarly life. We ask him to accept the dedication of this book to his son because he, after all, is what it is all about.

John Rex
Sally Tomlinson

1 Class analysis and colonial immigrants

Whatever may be the value perspective of the sociologist – and it should be made clear here that this study does have a value perspective – the particular contribution which sociology can make within the field of race relations is this: to note the types of social relations which arise both between individuals and between groups when a society is multi-ethnic or multi-racial or the changes in those relations which occur as a result of the immigration into the society of an alien minority. It is precisely this descriptive and analytical task which is necessary if political action is to be rationally pursued. If it can be shown that certain ethnic and racial minorities suffer disadvantage, precise sociological descriptions of this disadvantage will enable political groups to take action to rectify it. If it is shown that there are conflicts of interests between minority and majority groups, sociological analysis will suggest ways in which conflict may be pursued or resolved. If, again, it is shown that minorities are being forced to pursue goals which are not their own because of some forced policy of assimilation, it will be possible to devise strategies for achieving multi-culturalism. Objective sociological analysis by no means prevents political action; it prepares the way for it.

In the sphere of race relations and political action it may none the less be objected that the very process of selection of structural problems for analysis from the welter and flux of ongoing social relations itself involves value judgment. With this we can but agree. Yet, it is possible through reviewing the range of structural problems which have been dealt with by sociologists to go beyond a single perspective, uncritically held, to approach a problem from several different perspectives. This is not to claim, as it is sometimes misleadingly suggested Karl Mannheim did, that free-floating intellectuals have a privileged insight into objective truth.[1] It is to suggest that the institutionalization of sociology as a discipline makes

1

possible a certain degree of movement between perspectives and, hence, a move along the road to objectivity.

One perspective on the analysis of social structure in modern industrial societies is that which derives ultimately from the sociology of Émile Durkheim.[2] Locating the principal structural process in modern industrial societies as that of the social division of labour, this tradition fails to distinguish differences of class, privilege and power from differentiation of essentially complementary social roles and occupational functions. All forms of differentiation are seen as being complementary in their normal forms and simply pathological or anomic in their abnormal forms. The notion of differentiation which is perceived to be unjust and which consequently leads to conflict is excluded from this perspective.

Unrealistic though such a perspective might be, it is one which is adopted on a general theoretical level in what is usually called structural-functionalism[3] and on the empirical level in the study of race relations when a host-immigrant framework is adopted.[4] The structural-functionalism model is perhaps useful as a kind of conservative utopia which has explanatory significance in so far as conservatives realize their social aims. The host-immigrant framework is more misleading, in that it takes the realization of the conservative utopia for granted, and assumes that the fate of immigrants is to be judged in terms of their absorption into a society thought to be without class conflict.

Most empirical sociology in modern industrial societies, however, does not start from such unrealistic perspectives. The central theme of nearly all such sociology is the study of the class structure. The problem in using such sociological models as the model of the majority society within which minorities occur, however, is to eliminate a number of systematic ambiguities which are involved in the use of the concept of class.

The most central usage of the term 'class' in European sociology[5] at least is that which derives not so much from Marx himself as from orthodox Marxist usage.[6] According to this usage social class derives from men's relationship to the means of production. On the one hand this leads to an economic analysis based upon the creation, expropriation and distribution of surplus value produced by workers who have sold their labour power. On the other hand it leads to an account of the sociological development of social classes as 'classes-for-themselves' which eventually become the principal historical agents in the transition from one stage to another.

As a model for the explanation of the development of capitalist economies and as a political model for explaining changes within the structure of these economies, Marxist sociology has only remained tenable through the explicit or implicit introduction of subsidiary hypotheses. Thus what usually passes as Marxist analysis is little more than some sort of class analysis, based upon a recognition of the fact that there are differences of interest arising from differential control of property, and that it is in the pursuit of such differentiated interests that men unite for purposes of political conflict.

This more generalized perspective of a quasi-Marxist sort is the one used in his earlier formulation of the problem of class, status and power by Max Weber.[7] According to this, any differential control of property produces different market situations, and these market situations are what Weber means when he speaks of class situations. Unlike Marx, Weber believes that although class situations in different markets may become interconnected and merged, they need not necessarily do so, so that, instead of the single all-embracing class struggle in which society becomes divided more and more into two great warring camps, one finds a multiplicity of classes. Moreover, since Weber had rejected the labour theory of value and its attendant theory of capitalist crisis in favour of marginalist economics, he did not see class struggle as a process in which rising classes sought political hegemony in order to establish a new social order. Rather he saw them as relatively permanent conflict groups, whose jockeying for power was in the nature of things. Thus if any work deserved to have written on its title page, 'All history is the history of class struggles', it is the section of *Economy and Society* which deals with the city (Weber, 1968, vol. 3, ch. 16).

Much of the analysis of what is commonly called class differentiation, particularly in Britain, however, does not deal solely or even primarily with market positions, but with status and power. Probably in Britain this is true, primarily because the revolutions of the seventeenth century were never completed and the society retained strongly aristocratic elements within its new bourgeois structures. In the USA similar approaches can be found, primarily amongst conservative sociologists and those who have been struck by the social and political pre-eminence of the white Anglo-Saxon Protestant upper strata of New England (Warner, 1942).

What these approaches are concerned with is not so much class, as what Weber distinguished as a separate analytic element, namely status. This concept refers to distinctions made between people, who, as a result of these distinctions, live within relatively distinct cultures and societies, between which mobility is restricted. It is sometimes said that these distinct cultures and societies form a graded hierarchy, but such a judgment is usually based upon the perceptions of those groups who think of themselves as upper-class. The actual relations between groups within such a 'system' is a complex matter, and each group shows partial resentment of, and partial adjustment to, the system so long as it lasts.

3

The study of status-systems by sociologists has usually been carried out from the perspectives of those who had some reason to resent the system, most usually by those who have experienced some mobility, but found further opportunities blocked. There has been little in the way of a systematic conservative sociology which states explicitly the social distinctions made between classes and the optimum degree of mobility and of ideological persuasion necessary to ensure the legitimacy of their position, though such a sociology could be envisaged. Equally there could be, and to some extent there actually is, a sociology of the lower status groups, which negates the notion of graduation and that of the desirability of mobility, and simply sets out to make explicit the values and patterns of social relations which characterize the life of such groups. It seems clear, then, that the analysis of the status order of an advanced industrial society, like that in Great Britain, is likely to be many-faceted, even if this analysis is not confused, as it often is, with the questions of class struggle and political conflict.

The concept of a status order as we have been discussing it, however, does assume some degree of social and cultural closure of groups. Each is to some extent a community in itself and may even be capable of acting collectively. Clearly Weber thought of status groups as on the one hand having their own distinct styles of life and on the other as capable of seeking political hegemony, whether or not the status group was also a class. But this concept is only imperfectly realized in most societies. If, on the one hand, the concept of status group merges with that of estate, which implies actual legal closure of the group, it merges on the other with the notion of continuous status gradation. It is this concept, which, as much as any other, has preoccupied British sociologists of liberal and social democratic persuasions.[8]

There is curiously little discussion in the literature of the sociology and social psychology of a system of social gradation of this kind. One of the few who have discussed it is O. C. Cox (1948). As he sees it, writing as a 'Marxist', the concept of 'social class' which, together with political and economic class, succeeded the closed estates system of medieval Europe, referred not so much to actual groups, but to a set of concepts, which individuals kept in mind as a reference point, in judging their own advantages and disadvantages vis-a-vis other individuals. This is an interesting notion which is, of course, also implicit in the concept of relative deprivation popularized by Merton and others (Merton, 1957).

Most usually in the empirical tradition of British society, gradations in the quantitative variations of social attributes of individuals have been taken as tell-tale signs of the structure of a malign social order. Such gradations were of interest to committed egalitarians, whose ideal was the total elimination of differences of income, education and other advantages, and to liberals who, while rejecting such notions of total equality, were none the less interested in promoting equality of opportunity. These traditions thus had wide appeal and were particularly useful in monitoring and promoting the degree of equality or equality of opportunity experienced by different groups.

If, however, social class in the pure Marxian or the Weberian sense, social status groupings, and continuous social gradation may all be viewed as analytically separable elements of 'class structure' (using that term in the loose sense), there is one other element which is related to all of them and which is a primary source of motivation for those who are interested in studying social class. This is the unequal availability of political power. C. Wright Mills (1959a) and Ralf Dahrendorf (1959) in particular have treated this as a factor in itself, having a priority over all others in the struggle between groups in society. It must, however, be seen as a factor in all the other models which we have discussed above. For Marx, classes are essentially groups seeking political hegemony. The Weberian conception of market classes involves essentially power to dispose of resources and to deny them to others, thus enabling the propertied to compel the actions of others against their will. Status groupings in the closed sense are groups which can impose or seek to impose their dominance on a whole society. Finally the unequally distributed attributes considered in studies of social gradation include the control of resources and, through this, the control of the actions of other people.

It should be apparent from the above, therefore, that when we are considering the relationship of a minority to the majority in an advanced industrial society, and we define 'the majority' as participating in a 'class structure', we are referring to something very complex, and that very complex 'something' will differ in different societies. Since the comparative sociology of advanced industrial societies is so little developed and so ideologically distorted, however, we have to develop our own *ad hoc* account of what is specific about the British, as compared particularly with the American class structure, which has too often been used as a basis for sociological generalization.

An often fruitless argument goes on between American and European sociologists about the relevance of Marxism. American writers are inclined to assert that Marxism was simply wrong in its theory of classes in capitalist society, because American experience has not accorded with Marxist predictions. *Per contra*, European Marxists have been inclined to dismiss American writing about social class as mere ideology, representative of American false consciousness, implying that sooner or later underlying class formations of the European sort would become evident. We take the view here that there are structural differences of an important kind between American and British society, and that it is important to clarify these, particularly if we are concerned with the problem of the relationship which exists between minority groups and the class structure.

The first point to be noted about American society is the degree to which industrial conflict has been contained within the bounds of industry, without becoming the basis of a national labour movement, or of a class struggle in the Marxist sense. True, the labour movement is to some extent associated with the Democratic Party politics, but the association is by no means complete, and labour is reduced to being one amongst many lobbies which seeks influence and whose support is sought during electoral contests. The characteristic philosophy of American trades unions is that of business unionism. Such business unionism is by no means lacking in militancy. Indeed, American unions are often far more aggressively militant than their European counterparts. But the associations which men form in their industrial conflicts simply do not structure their whole lives to the extent that industrial conflicts do in the case of the European workers.

A second and related feature of American life is the role of the ethnic community in providing a primary form of identification for the majority of individuals, and also a means through which the individual negotiates with and protects himself against the main society. These individuals obtain jobs through ethnic associations, at least in the early stages of migration, look to ethnic leaders as their economic protectors in work and in business, and, finally, obtain political leverage in the society through their own ethnic political bosses. It would be an exaggeration, of course, to say that the ethnic group was the average American's trade union and political party, but it certainly is the case that ethnicity is a sufficiently important countervailing factor to prevent the emergence of a single, united and class-conscious working class.

A possible basic structural model of American society drawn from the observations in the previous paragraphs would be one in which capitalist enterprises, free of most of the aristocratic restraints to be found in European contexts, drew upon a seemingly endless supply of immigrant labour, so that, instead of an ethnically homogenous society being divided into classes by the bargaining of the labour market, one had a society of gradually assimilating immigrants. In the first stage of immigration, ethnic associations formed the communal and protective framework for the immigrant's life. In due course, however, given the almost boundless resources of the continent and the open frontier, workers not merely assimilated to being American workers, but reached all kinds of positions in American society as capitalists, managers, clerks, frontiersmen and store-keepers as well.

Ethnic associations provided the basis for communal action and protection before, during and sometimes after, mobility. In particular the ethnic group constituted a bloc of votes, which could be mobilized on behalf of a political candidate, who was, in turn, obligated to his voters. Thus each new immigrant group bought its way into American society.

If the reality of American society was something like this, however, this was not its myth. The myth was that of an open, individualist society. Every one of the 'huddled masses of the poor' who came into American society was seen as capable of upward mobility, and for all there was equality of opportunity. The American Dream was a dream, not of equality, but of open and fair competition, so that trades unions and class struggle were not necessary, except perhaps for the immediate business of settling one's wages.

For some 10 per cent of the population, however, neither the model of immigrants buying their way in, nor that of the open society, were true. The open capitalist society of the North and of the cities was superimposed on the slave plantation economy of the South, and as the plantation economy was superseded, its slave population became redundant, except in so far as they could compete as an immigrant group with other immigrants in the new capitalist economy. Very largely they failed, and they finished up in inferior jobs, homes and schools, and at worst they became a ghetto population of unwanted, unemployed people.

Sociologists noted that American blacks did not undergo assimilation into the class system as immigrants did. Lloyd Warner (1942), already quoted here as an analyst of the American status-system, suggested that while whites and blacks alike were stratified in terms of a three-class pyramid, there was a caste line between black and white, such that even though the number of rich blacks might increase, this would lead to a tilting rather than a breaching of the class barrier. The Civil Rights Movement of the 1950s and early 1960s, and the riots of the middle and late 1960s, may now have partially changed this. Civil Rights legislation and affirmative employment have enabled more blacks to attain middle-class status, and there seem to be some signs that a black voting bloc can now exercise political leverage, albeit late in the day, such as was once exercised by immigrant groups. The result of these changes is that although the majority of blacks remain in the ghettoes or in positions of disadvantage, the society as a whole is committed to, and has set up institutions aimed at, healing the racial breach in American society, and at enabling black men in principle to be men with equal rights in a capitalist society.

These few paragraphs are by no means intended to provide a general sociology of American life. They may, however, be seen to paint the contrast with the sociology of British life as we see it.

The first point to notice about British society is simply that it has had and still does have a class-conscious working class, and that its politics are conducted in class terms. This by no means implies that every British worker is in some sense a Marxist, any more than the widespread belief in the American Dream in America implies that every worker believes that he lives in a land of individual opportunity. But the existence of classes is something which people believe in and there is at least a large minority of the population who admit to being 'working'-class. The question is, what does this mean, and what does it mean for an outsider to gain admission to this working class?

First of all, working-class membership implies a belief in the importance of trades unions and of industrial bargaining, rather than the hope of mobility, as the major means of securing justice in one's employment. But this is by no means all, for trade unionism also has a political arm in the Labour Party, and that Labour Party provides one of the two alternative governments of this country. Not merely is it in a position to interfere with the operations of the free capitalist economy in the workers' interests, but it has also succeeded, through the creation of welfare services, in providing the worker with a social wage over and above the wages which he obtains from his employer.

Around working-class trades-union and political activity, there has grown an alternative value system to that of capitalist individualism, based on the central values of solidarity and mutual aid. Whereas a worker in a society largely constituted by incoming immigrants turns to his ethnic group for aid, a working-man in a homogeneous society turns to his industrial workmates. This culture of social solidarity also interacts, of course, with regional culture, and, since the political ruling classes and the employers tend towards a common national culture and mode of speech, regionalism itself becomes somewhat identified with class. The British are largely ethnically homogenous, but class divisions lead to a confrontation between two cultures or between a national ruling-class culture and a multitude of local or regional ones.

Politically the working class expresses itself primarily through the Labour Party, and, as a result of the pressure and the legislative acts of that party, it has been able to ensure the commitment of both parties to not straying too far from a mixed but managed economy, from the maintenance of full employment and collective bargaining over wages, and from the maintenance of certain minimal standards of welfare.

There is a dispute over the meaning of these political developments. Some American writers refer to them, not as changes in the nature of capitalism, brought about by working-class pressure, but rather as the inevitable attributes of an industrial society at a certain stage of development (Lipset, 1960; Bell, 1960). Others like Marshall (1950) in Britain and Schelsky (see Dahrendorf, 1959) in Germany have argued that they have led to a situation in which the existence of social benefits makes common citizenship a far more important basis of allegiance than purely class solidarity. Marxists divide between those who see welfare rights as a gain by the working class on the way to a new social order and those who see them as a means for preserving capitalism (Saville, 1957; Hatch and Thompson, 1958; Wedderburn, 1965).

The view taken here differs from all of these others in that it recognizes that welfare rights are won as a result of class conflict and are dependent upon the maintenance of working-class strength. Yet, paradoxically, it is precisely the existence of these benefits which at least temporarily stabilizes capitalism as a social system and alters the orientation of the working class towards it. Given that the modified system yields rights as the result of conflict, it is essential that the solidarity necessary for the successful pursuit of that conflict be maintained, but at the same time possible to accept the system, including the opportunity which it offers for social mobility for individual workers, and still more for their children, as though the system was not merely a class system but a status-system.

Parsons, who writes about status in terms of the distribution of rewards in an individualistic and competitive system, has noted that in the lower reaches of the system there is a tendency for the goal of success to be replaced by the goal of security (Parsons, 1954). What we are suggesting here makes a reverse point about working-class ideology. Whereas this ideology normally focuses on the struggle for security, there is a tendency, when overall security is won, for those who have that security to recognize the legitimacy of the mobility aspirations of some of their members, in what has after all become a more just society.

In any case, however, we should not reify ideological concepts too much. There is a sense in which class solidarity amongst working-class people in Britain is a real political fact and is thought to be so by many workers and their families. The idea makes sense of their experience particularly, but not solely, at work. But to be a member of a class, if the term membership can be correctly used at all, is very different from being a member of an army or any well-defined organization. Any particular individual who may be affected by the idea of class, and who, in terms of Marxist sociology, should count as a member, will only partially conform to the norms which

9

'membership' would seem to imply. Individuals seek promotion at work, they send their children to so-called grammar schools in the hope that they will gain superior employment, they are affected by the individualistic ideas of the market-place and the media, they may put their loyalty to their local football team before loyalty to their class, and some of them may on occasions vote for the party of what orthodox class members would call 'the enemy'.

This diffuseness of class-influenced behaviour, however, is not solely due to some kind of moral weakness. If the Weberian point is taken, it is not simply the case that industrial bargaining is the central point in men's lives, and that class-consciousness and class conflict of a society-wide kind develops around the core. Rather we should expect that there are certain central situations involving bargaining, over resources, the attainment of rights, or the acquisition of mobility opportunities, in which differentiation of class privileges exist, and that class-conflict experiences in one sphere need not necessarily coincide with, or overlap with, those in another. In particular we should expect that there will be industrial class conflict, conflict over the ownership, allocation or use of housing, and conflict over the allocation of educational opportunities. Furthermore we might expect that, because of the overlap between generational and class conflict, the actual experiences of the young in entering the labour market may be distinct from those of their parents, and there may be times in which conflicts between the population and the forces of law and order may occur independently of purely industrial conflict.

Marxism as a system of theoretical explanation will not rest content with this pluralist account of class conflict. It sets itself to trace the relationship between investment in housing and education and capital investment in industry, which is thought to be the necessary centre of the whole system, because that is where surplus value is created and appropriated (Castells, 1977). Moreover, educational agencies and the forces of law and order are seen as the result of the operation of the ideological state apparatus and the repressive state apparatus of capitalism (Althusser, 1971). We do not wish to deny these propositions absolutely here. What we do say is that they have been asserted rather than proved. It is necessary in the first instance to describe and analyse the separate arenas of class conflict before we can go on to show their degree of dependence. So far as we can see there is a considerable disjunction between some of these conflicts (e.g. as has been pointed out elsewhere (Rex and Moore, 1967), housing-conflict takes place independently of industrial conflict) and, if there is some more remote connection between them, both in their subjective perception and in their objective structures, it has yet to be shown.

It should be clear by now, in any case, that what is involved in the encounter between immigrant minorities and a society such as the British one, is by no means simply a process of absorption of immigrants into a unitary social system. The system is basically a capitalist one, and produces a division between the culture and associations of those who direct the system, on the one hand, and those who organize to defend their interests within it, on the other. Moreover, although there is more subjective awareness in Britain than in most other societies of the interdependence and unity of various situations of class conflict, it is still the case that actual behaviour is situationally determined, so that there is a multiplicity of separate experiences of class conflict. Finally, we should note that individuals in the same situation may have differing perceptions of it, and differing degrees of allegiance to their class or status position. Individuals may be exploited yet satisfied, they may have unrealistic or even sometimes realistic aspirations to mobility, they may be motivated by nationalist or royalist identifications as well as by identification with a class position, and finally, they may be aware of their relative disadvantage *vis-à-vis* other class members as well as of their disadvantage as compared with opposed classes.

Even if we speak of assimilation of immigrants into the working class, therefore, the empirical demonstration of that assimilation or non-assimilation is not easy, since there is no single position of participation in, or identification with, the working class which can act as a reference point. None the less, it will be significant if we can show how, in relation to any of the major indicators of class membership, the experience of the average member of an ethnic minority is different from that of the average native-born worker.

Assimilation of ethnic minorities, however, will depend, not merely upon the positions to which they are to be assimilated and the degree to which those positions are closed against all outsiders. It will also depend upon the positions from which immigrants have come. Thus a migrant from one region of England to another will already have had experiences of many of the roles and the conflict situation which he is likely to encounter in his new workplace and home, and he will be seen by his new workmates and neighbours as one who is ready for and entitled to full participation in their own class struggles. At the other extreme is the immigrant who comes from a society in which work-roles and the housing and educational systems are so distinct from those in Britain that he will have a considerable way to go before he gains full entry into the new situations. He may, it is true, be forced very directly into conflict by the brute reality of the situation, but he may also find that his struggles are seen as distinct from those of native-born workers and residents, and that his own ethnic organizations are more suited to the kind of action which he has to pursue than are the organizations of the natives.

11

This is of some importance when one considers the comparison which is made between Britain's immigrants and those of Europe on the one hand, and immigrants and minorities in the USA on the other. There are a number of variables in terms of which these immigrant minorities may be compared. The minority may or may not speak an alien language, it may or may not have moved from a system of production quite different from that of the country of immigration, or it may or may not have experienced the rule of the metropolitan country to which migration takes place.

Castles and Kosack (1973) have emphasized the similarity between the functions of immigrants in their country of settlement, and conclude from this that there is nothing very distinctive about the position of West Indian and Asian immigrants in Britain. However, this overlooks the distinctiveness of the positions from which they have come. On the latter point, we have found that many Europeans are inclined to emphasize the relative advantages which West Indian and Asian immigrants to Britain enjoy in relation to possible assimilation, as compared with their southern European and north African counterparts in north Europe. This view is based upon the belief that knowledge of the English language and the British system of government are available to Britain's immigrants before departure and that they are therefore less foreign than Europe's other immigrants.

Yet immigration is a more central political issue in Britain and it is necessary to consider why this is so. A first answer might be that the fact of colour-prejudice makes the crucial difference. The relatively light-skinned Spaniard, Moroccan or Turk is not the object of colour-prejudice in Europe, and would not be in Britain, compared with the black and brown immigrants from the West Indies and Asia. But this is surely not the whole answer.

Colour-prejudice is not by itself a sufficient explanation of anything. We must ask how colour-prejudice arose. The answer to this must surely lie in the experience of colonialism, both for the colonialist and the colonized. The fact of the matter is that the West Indian immigrant to Britain, like the black American migrant from the Deep South to the American cities, comes from a culture, a society, and an economy which was historically based upon the slave plantation, and his image, like that of the American black, still carries the stigma of slavery. On the other hand, the Asian immigrant comes, not from a New Britain overseas, but from the sub-continent in which an imperial system was imposed on older empires, which rested ultimately upon the exploitation of the peasantry. The transition from the status of a Bangladeshi peasant in Sylhet is, sociologically speaking, one of something like equal distance to that which must be made by a West Indian descendant of a slave when he moves to being an industrial worker in Britain.

Of course, the interrelation between the British system of stratification and that of Britain's colonial dependencies is far more complex than this crude dichotomy between the capitalist industrial system, on the one hand, and plantation and peasant economies, on the other, suggests. Colonial social structure embodies many different occupational and social positions, including not only those of slave and plantation worker and peasant, but also those of freeman, coloured and mestizo worker, poor white, urban *petit bourgeois*, settler, trader, purchaser of crops, chief, religious functionary, government official and so on, and to some extent immigration involves the immigration of these groups from colonial towns to the metropolis, together with a migration of the poorest groups. It is also true that some of these migrants will find the transition to metropolitan roles qualitatively different, if not easier than, others. None the less, this does not alter our main point that immigration from colonies to metropolis involves many difficulties not shared by the immigrant workers of north Europe. True, the colonial experience of Algerians and Moroccans may have more in common with that of British colonials, but here the geographical as well as the historical and cultural closeness of the countries surrounding the Mediterranean littoral may act as a countervailing factor.

A major problem in the analysis of British class structure, even before the arrival of immigrants from the former colonial societies, concerns the relationship between the relatively straightforward class structure or class struggle in metropolitan society and that which prevails in the imperial social system as a whole. Oddly enought, this is a problem which has hardly been discussed in British sociology. The suggestion which we would make is that the two parts of the system, metropolitan and colonial, have been separated from each other by a caste-like barrier, and that, despite the class struggle which goes on between classes in the metropolitan sector, these classes unite in the exploitation of, and in defence against, any threat from segments or groups within or from colonial society. This notion, of course, conflicts with any simplistic Marxist expectation of the unity of the international working class, though not with the more general notion that class formation arises from men's relation to the means of production. The relevant 'means of production' here is the imperial system as a whole.

There is, of course, some equivalence between the concept outlined here and Lloyd Warner's theory of class and caste. Warner's early formulation, however, suggests a static caste system. In the light of the developing Third World Revolution which has gone on since Warner's time, we have to note that groups and segments within formerly colonial societies are now seeking to liberate them-

13

selves or alter their position and that this may bring them into severe conflict with the less secure groups and classes in the metropolis. What one finds, then, is not a caste system but a new form of class struggle with ethnic dimensions.

Against this background we may approach the study of immigrant assimilation in Britain by asking the following questions. How far do immigrants on the average enjoy the same rights as their fellow workers and neighbours in British cities? How far is the group-consciousness, sense of identity and group attachment of the immigrant minority still organized on an ethnic or colonial basis, and how far have individual members transferred their attachments to class and status-based British groups? How far is the maintenance of ethnic group identity compatible with the attainment of equal rights; that is to say, is it possible for the immigrant to gain acceptance and equality of treatment, while at the same time preserving a distinct social and cultural identity? And, finally, how far does the class-consciousness of the British social classes exclude the immigrant as a potential member?

Since no one would disagree with the proposition that class conflict in the labour market is a prime determinant of a working-man's total life situation, we should begin by considering the evidence on the employment of immigrants. Ideally this should include knowledge of employment before migration, of his degree of commitment to his country of origin, including his aspirations to mobility there, and of the degree to which he sees his stay in Great Britain as temporary, before we even begin to turn to the evidence on assimilation into the British working class or acceptance into any other part of the class structure.

The history of colonialism in the West Indies has many features which are different from that of colonialism in the Indian subcontinent. Basically this difference turns upon the fact that the West Indies became far more totally dependent, culturally speaking, on Britain than did the Indian territories. Thus West Indians would seem, on the face of it, more likely to regard migration to work in Britain itself as a migration which involved crossing no cultural boundaries, and which might be conceived of simply as economically advantageous job mobility, akin to the urban migration of American blacks from the Deep South. We should expect, therefore, that West Indians would not see their migration simply as temporary, since there would be little chance, relatively speaking, of putting to use in the West Indian context any capital or skills which they had acquired in British cities. This, however, is a matter of hypothetical speculation only, and needs to be tested against the actual evidence of the extent to which migrants maintain their links with their homelands, send remittances home, or have plans to return temporarily or for holidays.

14

By contrast, Indian, Pakistani and Bangladeshi migrants have often been seen as temporary sojourners in the country of their migration. They have come from socio-economic systems in which, although the overwhelming majority of the population live in abject poverty, there are, or at least appear to be, opportunities for economic and status advancement for those who accumulate capital. If this is true, we should expect the primary interest of the worker during his migration to be one of accumulating wealth at any cost in the hope of an eventual return home. Again, however, this is all a matter of prima facie supposition and the actual evidence which we have to consider regarding return to the homeland may give an altogether more complex picture. As we shall see, during the last hundred years of Empire, Indians played a number of different roles throughout the Empire from Fiji to British Columbia, and when migration to Britain occurred, there were established patterns amongst migrating Indians of living permanently in the Indian diaspora.

In any case, of course, one should expect that, even though there might be a majority tendency in any particular immigrant group to become committed to British society, some might wish to return; while on the other hand, even though another migrant group might regard itself only as temporary, some members will form attachments which tend to make their stay more permanent. Thus, while some adult immigrants might still think of return, their English-educated children may be more attracted by economic opportunities in Great Britain and more likely to stay. Some immigrants may become secularized in urban society, so that they find it increasingly difficult to meet the traditional demands of their home culture. Some will find that the class structure of British society provides opportunities for them which are not available to other immigrants. And, finally, there may be paradoxical developments, as when the children of immigrants aim to return to their parents' home, precisely because they have developed aspirations to acceptance and mobility in British society, but have been frustrated in these.

Much of the data which we have are necessarily set out in terms of a comparison between average West Indian and average Asian (particularly Indian) immigrants. Ideally, of course, these groups should be further sub-divided in terms of their class situation in their homeland, their exposure to British education, their position in the British class structure, and, according to a number of different indices, the perceived permanence of migration. Unfortunately, so far as the survey work reported below is concerned, the numbers in each sub-group, drawn in class terms from our sample, are too small for us to make significant generalizations from them, but we have attempted wherever possible to break down the wide distinction

15

between Asian and West Indian into smaller groupings.

In what now follows we are concerned, by referring to our empirical studies, to indicate some of the major structural questions which we shall be asking. The answers which we arrived at are described in chapters 3 to 6.

The first index for comparison between different immigrant groups and between each of them and their equivalents among native workers is that which indicates how far they can enter employment at all, and it is clear that, overall, black workers are at some disadvantage in this respect. The prime problem, however, is not whether or not immigrants obtain jobs, but what sort of jobs they obtain. Here evidence on West Indian employment up to the early 1960s (Peach, 1968) suggests that West Indian workers tended to go to jobs and to areas where they were not in competition with local workers, and this was probably even more true of Asians. This conclusion fits well enough in general terms with the theory of dual or split labour markets (Doeringer and Piore, 1971). According to this theory it is normal in industrial society for two distinct labour markets to develop. One is open to candidates who have contacts (indeed it may not strictly speaking be a market at all, but simply a system of internal promotion within an organization) and who, when appointed, have long tenure, a great measure of trade-union protection, welfare benefits, high wages and also possibly some degree of humanization of their relations with their employers. In the other labour market all the opposite conditions hold. There is a frequent rotation of employees, much short-term and part-time employment, little in the way of welfare benefits, poor trade-union protection and a tendency for work to be regarded purely as a matter of disutility, a means of earning money to be used in more significant life contents. Thus, at the heart of modern industrial society, in the employment relation itself one finds something which may have more general validity, the notion of a working class which has won a secure contractual relationship with those who run the economy, and an 'underclass'[9] which enjoys no such security but which sees the economy as an alien system with which one has necessarily to communicate in order to earn a living. It is perhaps also worth noting that so far as employment is concerned, women workers share the immigrants' situation, but, because of their familial links, they remain related to mainstream working-class positions in a way in which immigrants are not.

It is not possible, of course, to classify workers precisely according to whether they are in the privileged or underprivileged sector of the labour market, because jobs do not come with labels on them. It is, however, possible to classify workers according to a number of related indices such as unemployment history, number of hours worked, frequency of shift work, job satisfaction and so on. From these indices it will be possible to see the extent to which immigrant workers are confined to the underparts of the labour market. It is also against this background that the relevance of more orthodox comparisons of occupational and industrial classifications have to be assessed.

Trade-union membership is another matter of some importance. It signifies two things in particular. On the one hand it indicates whether or not immigrants are being employed as blacklegs to under-cut native working-class standards. On the other hand it shows the extent to which immigrants have affiliated themselves to the core organizations of the working class. Such evidence as there is has not shown an unwillingness on the part of immigrants to join trades unions. On the contrary, Castles and Kosack, for example, have shown from a review of the evidence on immigrants in industrial disputes that immigrants have not merely used trade unionism for their own purposes, but have been very active in industrial conflicts in which the interests of all workers are threatened. On the other hand, they show that unions have not always been active and effective in dealing with purely immigrant grievances.

If it is shown that immigrants are often members of the major general unions, the significance of this evidence is not always clear. Immigrants may be members of these unions and satisfied with them in general terms. But the union may not have been subjected to a very severe test. A general union may, in fact, cover both sections of the labour market referred to above, but devote its major energies to the defence of its more privileged members. This will leave its less privileged members satisfied provided that they are not asking too much. It might even be the case that in giving its privileged members security the union gives the underprivileged a certain vicarious satisfaction in being members of such a powerful organization. The crunch comes, however, when the workers in the underprivileged sector demand improved conditions in their jobs, stricter control of their own elected shop-stewards and, by no means least important, a willingness on the part of the unions and its shop-stewards in the privileged sector of the labour market to permit mobility and pro-motion. In the chapters which follow the population of workers which we describe is in relatively underprivileged employment, is relatively strongly unionized, but on the whole has not yet pressed the unions to a point at which their willingness to give immigrants their full protection is tested. We have not, ourselves, been able to carry out a plant-based study which might have given some detailed indications of the sorts of problems likely to be encountered, but we have reviewed some of the evidence on industrial disputes in the region which centres on these issues.

17

One particular facet of the employment problem, however, is that which concerns the fate of immigrant-descended children when they leave British schools and enter the labour market. There they are affected by three sets of factors. One is that, since industrial rationalization is often accomplished by a reduction in the labour force through early retirement of other workers, fewer and fewer jobs are available for the young in these rationalized industries. A second factor is that all immigrants find themselves disadvantaged in the labour market. A third is that the children of some immigrant groups suffer disadvantage in schools which puts them at a further disadvantage in the labour market. Little wonder, then, that 'immigrant youth unemployment' gives such cause for concern. Little wonder also that unemployed young immigrant workers are amongst the most alienated and militant elements in the total working-class population.

The population with which we have been dealing, in focusing our study on the Handsworth area of Birmingham, is a working-class population, and we have little evidence, therefore, of the experience of middle-class immigrants from the New Commonwealth. Obviously professional men and women such as doctors and teachers face quite different problems of acceptance, on which we offer no evidence here. Significantly, however, very few West Indian and Asian professional men live in Handsworth. More common are shop-keepers, but here we should be careful to distinguish between those who have simply succeeded as British shop-keepers, and those who service ths immigrant community.

One further overwhelming factor to be borne in mind in assessing the degree of assimilation or integration of immigrants is, of course, that, even though most of the population which we have studied is stably employed, this by no means implies that they have attained equality with their British peers, or that there is no discrimination. There are many industries and occupations in which discrimination has not been reported, simply because it is so taken fot granted on all sides that immigrants do not apply. This is not merely true of middle-class occupations, but also of whole industries employing unskilled and semi-skilled workers. Thus in giving evidence to the Parliamentary Select Committee on Race Relations and Immigration Employment on behalf of the Race Relations Board, Sir Roy Wilson referred to: 'the dock industry where it is well-known that in some areas of the industry it is extremely difficult for anyone who is not a member of a docker's family to enter into this type of employment' (Select Committee on Employment, 1974, vol. 2, p. 44). This may be an extreme case, but clearly it would be possible for immigrants to be an underclass in the employment situation without any evident protest, simply because facts like that mentioned by Sir Roy

Wilson were taken for granted.

One last point to be noted about the field of employment is that it is not one which is directly affected by government action in the way that housing and education are. On the whole, governments do not create at least long-term permanent employment. They may stimulate the economy to reach overall levels of employment and they try to improve skills and match supply and demand of labour. They also intervene, when other means have failed, to regulate industrial disputes. In contrast, in the sphere of housing in Britain, local government creates and manages a large part of the housing stock, and, in the field of education, provides the overwhelming majority of the schools.

Still less does officially provided race relations machinery affect the employment situation. The evidence presented to the Parliamentary Select Committee by the Race Relations Board shows that the number of cases of discrimination proved either to the satisfaction of internal industrial machinery or to the Board itself was insignificant. The Board itself did not believe that this number gave any indication of the extent of discrimination or disadvantage. Thus the location of discrimination and disadvantage involves studying far more than reported cases of discrimination. It involves the study of the consequences of thousands of acts, which, whatever their intent, are discriminatory against immigrant populations in their effect.

What we are concerned with in the study of employment amongst immigrant workers and their children is their relationship to three different possible social structures or social functions. We are concerned with any continuing link with the socio-economic system and the class and status structure of their country of origin. We are concerned with the extent to which their average fate in the British labour market approximates to that of their British peers. Finally, we are concerned to discover whether there is any tendency at all for the formation of specifically immigrant underclass groupings marked by a separate fate and by the emergence of incipient immigrant labour organization. Subsequently to answering these questions we should also ask whether, as in the case with British trades unions, there is a tendency for immigrant workers' organizations to become the core of more comprehensive political and cultural groupings.

Related questions may now be asked about housing. We must assume that immigrants have left houses and homes, kin-networks and villages in their country of origin and that there may be considerable variation in the strength and permanence of the linkages they sustain with these people and places. At one extreme would be the case of the man who has sundered his links completely and now sees Britain as his home. There will be many whose transition is not complete, either in the sense that their dependents have not yet been brought to Britain or that they still maintain links with a second home in the country of origin. But at the other extreme is the man whose ultimate goal is return to the homeland. Of course, nearly all immigrants have some myth of return, but some maintain living links with the kinship system, the villages and the economy of the homeland. It is also interesting to notice that for most immigrants a return to a house and a home may be a more important goal than a mere return to the economy.

Within Britain there are many different types of housing, many different types of tenure, differing – and sometimes conflicting – scales of desirability of types of housing and tenure, different groups of people seeking housing and differing degrees of access to differing parts of the housing stock. It was this set of variables which led Rex and Moore in a previous study of a Birmingham ward to introduce the sensitizing concept of 'housing-class' (Rex and Moore, 1967). What it was meant to do was to show that in the allocation of houses to people, differing groups had differing degrees of power in claiming what they wanted through the allocation system, and that the detailed analysis of this particular form of resource allocation did not totally coincide with job allocation and distribution in the labour market. This assertion still seems well worth making despite the considerable literature which has accumulated concerned to refute or, more profitably, to refine and clarify, the status of the housing-class concept (see Rex, 1971, also note 1 to chapter 5).

Of particular relevance here is the comparison which we should be seeking to make between the position of the immigrant and the position of the native British worker. Some British workers in the upper sections of the labour market gain, together with job security, the sort of personal reputation of income security which enables them to obtain loans through building societies to buy relatively expensive and spacious houses in the suburbs. A majority of such workers, however, together with those from the underside of the labour market, will obtain houses and flats to rent from the City Council. Compared with the USA such publicly provided housing for rent does not carry a stigma. If any stigma does attach, it attaches to those, who, in the process of house allocation, are thought to be worthy of only the least desired forms of housing, or who are provided for by an alternative system to that of the building societies and the local authorities, particularly through special publicly provided mortgages and through some charitable housing associations.

One critic of the concept of housing-class (Haddon, 1970) suggested that it confused the question of access to the system of housing occupied with the type of housing actually occupied. This seems on reflection to be an unreasonable criticism since the type of housing occupied is a very good indicator of the strength of its occupants in the housing market. In fact there are a number of types of housing to which those whose access is weakest must have resort. They include the less-desired houses and flats for rent provided by the Council, and owner-occupied houses which are either exceptionally cheap, often because they are not freehold properties, or which, while not eligible for a normal building society mortgage, do qualify under special arrangements for a local authority mortgage or perhaps for a second mortgage from some deviant source. It seems to be the case, given the distribution of rights amongst the population which is imposed by the building societies and the councils, that a group of individuals, who actually occupy different types of housing, have it in common that the particular choice which they have made was forced on them by their exclusion from more normal forms of housing. It may also be the case that those who turn to alternative allocation systems such as those of the housing associations, form part of the same class. We discuss these possibilities more fully in chapter 5.

There is, however, one important complication to note here. This is that amongst the neighbours of those who are forced into underprivileged forms of housing, there are some who are there by choice, basically for reasons of traditionalism.

Thus, even though his home is in an area which has in effect become recognized as an area for the underprivileged, a man may still prefer to go on living in Handsworth or some similar place because of the sentimental associations which it has for him. He will resist demolition and redevelopment and, if he has to be re-housed, will choose areas thought generally to be of low desirability, because he wants to maintain what he can of traditional and sentimental links with the area. In a curious way, when suburban housing is a valued ideal, the British traditionalist who opts and wants to keep his roots where they are has some similarities with the man who rejects housing and status mobility because his roots are in another country. We might even say, for example, that Handsworth is the traditionalist working-class Englishman's Bangladesh.

Turning again to those who live in underprivileged housing by exclusion rather than by choice, we should notice a further element in their situations. This is that, by being where they are, they are excluded from the prospects of an improving housing situation later. The worst small slums are scheduled for demolition and their inhabitants for rehousing in council houses, but once an area has been classified as an improvement area and an individual has a whole house in it, there is no such hope. He may benefit from such policies as improvement schemes which enable him to install a bathroom,

21

but, hygienic though this may be, the newly installed bathroom may simply be a consolation prize, and a symbol that the occupant has no hope of new decent housing. Moreover, similar problems exist amongst council tenants in some areas. Some councils permit transfers from worse to better estates for those who pass necessary housekeeping-standard tests. In these cases the transfer system may permit normal native whites to move upwards away from the non-white immigrants, whom one would then find to be more concentrated on the worst estates than elsewhere. Alternatively transfers may not be permitted, in which case tenants may be offered a choice between less desirable accommodation quickly and better accommodation after a longer waiting period. The choice forced on a man in a desperate housing situation may thus mean that he is committed for the foreseeable future to live in inferior accommodation.

Interestingly, this discussion of the underprivileged parts of the system of housing allocation has dealt so far with owner-occupation and with council tenancies. It has not referred to what was the major issue in Rex and Moore's Sparkbrook study, namely the question of multi-occupied lodging-houses and, more generally, of private housing for rent. Of the latter we should want to say that it exists at all levels of the housing system, but that as a part of the housing stock available to poorer-paid workers it has continued to decline in importance. Either the houses have been sold to owner-occupiers or they have been purchased by the Council and eventually demolished. On the other hand, multi-occupation flourishes, and does so because it continues to be a *de facto* policy for supplementing accommodation for the homeless. Obviously the fate of the tenant of a multi-occupied lodging-house is the fate of the man who has least power of all in the housing market, and, compared with him, our owner-occupiers of houses in improvement areas and the tenants of council properties in undesirable areas are well off indeed. We should say that there is a housing-class difference between these two groups since the latter has obvious rights of access to mortgages, improvement grants and rented tenancies. But this should not disguise the fact that these rights have created a new intermediate underprivileged class between the homeless and the tenants of lodging-houses on the one hand and the normal working class on the other. In describing the members of the population of the Handsworth area who have been forced to live there by the constraints within which they have had to choose, we could still be describing a housing underclass, distinctly disadvantaged, compared with the average working class.

So far as the lodging-house owners are concerned, there may be some reason for modifying the position adopted by Rex and Moore in their Sparkbrook study. There it was asserted, perhaps too

22

strongly, that the lodging-house keepers were themselves an under-privileged group trapped by the system. This was stated as a corrective to the view of those who were deceived by the statistics into classifying this group as owner-occupiers and landlords and imputing to them all the characteristics of those groups. As against this, some writers such as Davis and Taylor (1970) pointed out that the landlords were not forced to act as they did, but did so for commercial reasons, that is for profit. That this is so need not surprise us. What may be more important, however, is not that the landlord chooses to act out of greed, but that he chooses as he does because his whole housing enterprise is conceived of as part of a life-orientation which is focused abroad (Dhaya, 1973). In saying this, however, we would not wish to overlook the truth of the Rex-Moore thesis, which is that for some, at least, lodging-house owner-ship is a strategy forced on them because there is no alternative available. We should add, too, that at the scale on which we have observed the phenomenon, it is not a major capitalist profit-seeking enterprise. Very few indeed of those whom we studied in the Handsworth area, for example, were buying a second house.

One other point which deserves comment, looking retrospectively on the Rex-Moore study, is that relating to the waiting period of five years before an applicant could go on the active housing waiting-list. It is sometimes suggested that this is no longer relevant, since, given the institution of tighter immigration control of 1962, 1965 and 1971, most immigrants are now qualified for housing because they have been here five years. Unfortunately, during those five years plus the years necessary to acquire residential points, many immigrants have made housing arrangements, such as taking council mortgages on old houses in improvement areas, which disqualify them from rehousing by the Council. This effect of the five-year rule was not temporary. Its effect has been to place many thousands of immi-grants permanently in the position of housing inferiority.

Implicit in all the discussion above has been the recognition of a superior housing position available to the normal native working class. This is something which has been fought for and won largely through the provision of council housing by the Labour Party. But the Labour Party is not simply a housing-class party. It is a party based upon industrial trades unions, many of whose councillors are actually nominated by trades unions. This is one of the effects of the class organization of politics in Britain. The parties arise to dispute over major questions relating to the economy, and, in particular, to industrial struggles, but it is to these parties that the task of housing allocation is assigned. Thus the industrial working class, representa-tive very largely of the privileged sections of the working class, and certainly of the native-born, also provides the organizational frame-

23

work for the pursuit of housing rights.

In these circumstances what is likely to happen to the immigrant in his struggle for housing? There is no basis in underclass trade-union organization for fighting over housing in local politics. The industrial organizations to which the immigrants belong are simply the legitimate unions of the British working class, and, in particular, the general unions. If they fail to represent the housing interests of the immigrants in the City Council, the immigrants will not be represented at all.

At the same time the considerable importance of kin, neighbour-hood, and housing organization in the immigrant community should be noted. A Marxist perspective would lead one to believe that the transition from a class-in-itself to a class-for-itself involves the development of social bonds and group-consciousness amongst fellow-workers of a sufficient strength to provide a framework for communal and political activity. But the bonds which an immigrant worker establishes with his working-class comrades through the unions are specialized and weak, whereas the bonds which he establishes with his ethnic group, his kin, his neighbours, and those who share housing grievances, are strong.

The conclusion which we would draw from this is that the immigrant workers may not be merely separately an underclass in the spheres of employment and housing (and also possibly in other spheres yet to be discussed), but that the putting together of all these conflict situations into one class situation is less likely to rest, as it does in the case of the native working class, on industrial trades unions, and more likely to rest upon neighbourhood activity. The notion of the 'brothers-on-the-block' is a central notion amongst West Indians in Britain as it is in the USA, and, amongst Asians, kin-organizations are a prime focus of trust. They are more likely to provide the means of group action than any industrially-based grouping (see chapter 8).

If, however, jobs and housing are two of the great means by which life-chances are dispensed in a modern urban-industrial society, the third means is the educational system. Schools provide for public rather than private and idiosyncratic socialization of children into their society. At the same time, too, that they inculcate moral orientations, they also dispense skills and knowledge differentially amongst different groups of children. Schools also act as selection agencies determining who knows what and who does what in later life. For the children, they decide whether each particular child enters the ruling, the ruled, or intermediate sections of society. For the parents they help to determine their own class situation, since the mobility chances of those parents' children are themselves a part of the important goods which life in a particular social position has to offer.

24

There is no more startlingly important feature of the social structure of an urban area like Handsworth than a variety of types of
primary socialization to which its inhabitants have been subject.
Some have never been to school and have been prepared for life
purely by family, kin and village groups. Others have been subject to
training in a school system with a different pedagogic method and
to a syllabus widely differing in content from that in English schools.
They may have been subject to diverse religious influences. Increasing numbers, on the other hand, will have been educated in
part or wholly in English schools, and in a variety of different situations produced by the reactions of British society to the coming of
immigrants. Moreover, the impact of their education will depend on
how far it is regarded as a centrally, morally valid process, or only
as an instrumental means for children, who are at the moment in the
society, but will not finally be of it.

All this would be perplexing enough for immigrant parents and
their children were the English educational system simply a unitary
thing, but it is not. The school system represents a complex system
of crossroads and there are many different destinations which may
be sought by those who understand the signposts and who have the
means to proceed along any particular road.

When the fabled *Empire Windrush* set sail for Britain and initiated
the modern black immigration, the educational system was still
fairly simple.[10] The 1944 Education Act had introduced 'secondary
education for all', but its implementation had ensured that there
would not be one but three types of such education. The crucial
thing, therefore, was the eleven-plus examination which was the
sole means of determining whether a child became a 'grammar',
'technical' or 'modern' child. At least, this was so for those who
relied upon the State for their education, though there was also of
course a private system with which the grammar schools had to
compete in placing their pupils in the upper reaches of society, and a
'direct grant' system which produced a hybrid type of school
allowing both for an inflow of selected working-class ability and
some of the superior methods of the private sector.

One says this was fairly simple, but only in order to emphasize
that it was nothing like as complex as the system which eventuated
when Labour politicians set out to reform it. The most radical
conception of all, of course, was one which would have involved the
creation of the unitary system through the abolition of selection
and of the public/private distinction. But this was never seriously
contemplated by decision-makers, whose own position depended
heavily upon their public-school, direct-grant or grammar-school
education. The private sector was to stay and all types of hybrid
such as the direct-grant school were to disappear. The concentration

25

of effort would be on comprehensivization in the state sector. There, at least, there would be a unitary system – or so it was hoped.

Two factors, in fact, prevented this transition to a unitary pattern in the state sector. One was the continuing struggle for political control of the system by the Conservative and Labour Parties. The other was the problem of creating a transitional system which would be necessary during the fifty years or so during which the facilities for a fully comprehensive system would be provided. Conservative governments and local councils did their best to preserve those central mobility agencies, the direct-grant and the grammar schools, and everywhere, in Birmingham as well as anywhere else, the system was compromised. Rather than allowing the children, as it was said, to become a shuttlecock of party politics, a half-cock system was devised as the two parties moved towards an agreed compromise. At the same time, in the absence of new comprehensive buildings, local authorities established campuses with grammar and modern components, or consortia, which grouped schools together, so that, within the group, a child would have the full range of opportunities, even though the individual schools were miles apart.

Surprising numbers of middle-class and even working-class British parents looked on the new system with dismay, saw that the status struggle in education had become stronger than ever, and put their children into a newly invigorated if highly expensive private sector (though even money alone was not enough here, since progress to the heights depended upon knowing how to enter the private 'prep school' system and the common entrance examination for fee-paying schools). But for most the question was one of placing one's bets upon a particular comprehensive school or a still surviving grammar school.

The choices to be made with the state sector were more subtle than they had ever been before. Parents of bright children wanted to know whether their children would be streamed. Parents of duller children hoped that they, too, would at least have a chance of taking 'O'-level General Certificate of Education examinations. But head-masters were uncommunicative about these things. Parents have had perforce to put their children into schools without knowing whether they will be socialized to the norm of their age group in terms of ability, class style and mobility chances, or whether they might slip upwards in the grammar stream. And many have been disturbed by what they hear of liberalizing, modernizing tendencies, which are not a necessary part of comprehensivization, but have often been tacked on to it. Thus the choices were subtle, but they had to be made completely in the dark. Head teachers who won their way to command-posts within the new system talked of 'educating the whole child' and not worrying too much about certificates.

It is a curious thing that Americans, who have never succeeded in establishing a public housing system without stigma, have been so much more successful than the British at keeping stigma and class divisions out of their educational system. Hence it is likely that these observations will hardly be understood by many of those who read them there. It therefore has to be emphasized that in the final quarter of the twentieth century in Great Britain, education has a class-selective role more complex than ever before. This, despite, or perhaps because of, the reforming and reformist (i.e. non-revolutionary) zeal of the Labour Party.

The secondary system of which we have spoken, however, represents only the beginning of this complexity. In principle things should have become clearer in the primary sector, because, selection having disappeared, there is a common task for all primary schools, viz. that of enabling children to perform well in the secondary sector. But, if the requirements of the secondary sector are unclear, the curriculum of the primary schools will be equally so. And very often in schools where preparation for the eleven-plus has been the *raison d'être* of the syllabus, there is now total uncertainty as to what can or should be achieved.

Given this system, a cynic would say that there is only one wise choice for an immigrant parent. This is to put his child into a prep school straight away and preferably to make him a boarder, so that he is not too much affected by his home. One such case came to light recently and was much publicized on British television and, more interestingly, on the radio. A young West Indian orphan had been adopted by rich English parents and put through the system. On radio, at least, he was indistinguishable in accent and manner from any other English public-school boy. Sadly, when asked what he wanted to do by way of a career, he said that he wanted to go to the West Indies and help his people.

This young man was the exception who proves the rule. The rule for the West Indian immigrant is that his parents will seek for him the same opportunities as are available to the children of the organized British working classes. As we have seen, the future is hazardous and uncertain even for the latter. It is doubly so for the immigrant parent. Slightly different considerations, however, prevail for those parents, predominantly Asian, who can see the instrumental value of English education as such. The subtle differences between different types of English education have less meaning in India, and to have any secondary education while in Britain might put any returning immigrant at an advantage.

The crucial question then becomes that of primary education, because a good training there will ensure that the child is in a better position to negotiate the hazards of the secondary system. Here one

27

would expect a continual and anxious negotiation between parents and teachers. One would expect the parents to be asking whether the signs of progress are there and, if not, why not, and there is some evidence of a belief in the West Indian community that schools in England are too liberal and informal when compared with their West Indian counterparts. On the other hand, one might expect that teachers who fail should counter accusations by references to objec-tive tests, which put the blame for any failure on the genetic endow-ment of children. But these are prima facie presuppositions only. The evidence which we have does not show total dissatisfaction on the part of parents, nor total discrimination against immigrants through testing. The empirical reality is, as always, more complex.

Education, however, is not solely concerned with social selection. A further problem concerns the cultural and moral aspects of socialization. Many English working-class children find themselves moving in school in a more middle-class world than they are used to at home. They may be changed by this system, they may successfully learn to be culturally bilingual, or they may simply fail in school through an inability to make the necessary adjustment. Another possibility, or range of possibilities, however, may be introduced by the fact that the school has no clear culture of its own, and that the same may be true of individual homes. The child who goes from a clear encapsulated working-class culture at home to an equally clear middle-class one in school is obviously a limiting case only.

Of all children involved in our study, the alternative of cultural bilingualism is most available to the children of Asian immigrants. Most of them have as a reference point a home culture based upon a distinct system of morals, language and religion set within a kinship structure. Parents and religious organizations will do all that they can to strengthen this culture. So far as English children are con-cerned, there are no such alternatives. They confront the school system with class and regional accents and the bits and pieces of a class and regional culture which survive in an urban mass society. The West Indians have the most difficulty of all. Their cultural history is one in which originally African culture was nearly com-pletely destroyed by slavery, in which they were offered an inferior position within a variant of English culture, and in which they began to develop their own culture of defiance and revolt. It is from this complex cultural situation in West Indian homes that West Indian children come to encounter the culture of the schools.

The voice of liberal reformers talking about the curriculum in these circumstances becomes somewhat confused. Some see even English working-class speech and culture as something which brings disadvantage, which must at all costs be countered with training in the language and culture appropriate to the learning situation, that

28

is, the culture of the middle classes. Others argue that such education is not relevant to the problems of children in the disadvantaged areas, and that a special and different type of education should be offered in these schools. Finally, there are a few, who, while holding the view that middle-class type education is irrelevant, argue that the alternative should not be special education for the disadvantaged, but education rooted in working-class culture and relevant to the creation of an alternative kind of society.

It is against this background that some features of West Indian education have to be considered. The West Indians are aware that they are at a disadvantage compared with the Asians, because of the strength of the Asian culture, and at a disadvantage compared with the white working class who, despite their cultural differences from their teachers, none the less do share with those teachers the fact of being English. The Asians indeed have even succeeded in getting partial recognition for the teaching of their own religions in school. The point is therefore made that West Indian children should have education in Black Studies as a kind of equivalent.

The usual argument for Black Studies education is that it provides the black child with self-respect which enables him to compete on equal terms with the white. But, just as the suggestion that working-class children should be provided with an alternative education is beset with dangers in that what they may be offered may be inferior, so also the idea of alternative education for West Indians may result in discrimination against them. On the other hand, the authorities are likely to fear Black Studies, because, even more than working-class culture, it is likely to involve subversive and revolutionary elements.

Should West Indian parents be pressing simply for equality of opportunity for their children or should they be asking for an education which respects their own cultural distinctiveness? Both claims are made. Unfortunately, where attempts are made to meet them, which are not under the control of sociologically well-informed West Indian parents, they are likely to get the worst of both worlds, that is to say, unequal opportunity on the one hand and a less than respectful and serious treatment of their culture on the other.

Of some importance here is the related question of the political effect of multi-cultural education on white British children. One of the claims which is made by African, Caribbean and Indian scholars is that the teaching of traditional imperial history gives no understanding of West Indian and Asian people except as inferiors. A multi-cultural educational programme could include a project to reform text-books and syllabus content to take account of this.

Apart from this, however, the recognition that immigrant children require special treatment raises doubts in the minds of native white parents. To many of them, all black children of immigrants have all the problems imaginable, and the more black children there are, the less will be the opportunity, so they would say, of their own children's educational needs being met by hard-pressed teachers. To have immigrant children in one's child's school at all, therefore, is to lower one's own children's chance of mobility, both because the teachers have less time, and because, in a status-competitive society, to have been to a school where there are large numbers of black children is itself to lose status.

Thus there developed in England in 1965 a demand for bussing which was reflected in the Government White Paper on Immigration of that year.

At no point is the relative disadvantage of West Indian and Asian children in Britain *vis-à-vis* American blacks more obvious than in this debate about bussing. In America it was proposed by black civil rights leaders as a way of ensuring that black and white children had true equality of opportunity. Blacks were to be given the opportunity of attending the best white schools, there was no such movement and no such proposal in Great Britain. The demand for bussing was articulated by those who felt threatened, demanding the thinning out of the black population. Interestingly, the most obvious way of thinning out was not suggested, namely through suburban rehousing, because here the cost of having black neighbours counted too much as a debit.

Turning away from the three main areas of political discrimination, now we should say something about the political organization of the immigrant community. Here we should consider four related aspects. One is the existence or non-existence of a Civil Rights Movement which claims equal rights in terms of a shared value system. The second is the development of paternalist initiatives by British political parties. The third is the development of a solidary ethnic unit insisting on its own identity and claiming justice without absorption or assimilation. The fourth is the growth and political articulation of white hostility to West Indian and Asian immigrants as such.

A key fact, which too many comparisons between the USA and Great Britain overlook, is the absence of the first of these elements. There is no supreme court to which civil rights cases can be taken, and in any case, the most powerful popular movement is that which demands that blacks or immigrants should have less rather than more rights than they otherwise have. What was suggested was that for the first time there should be two levels of British citizen with different rights. If there was a period in US history which paralleled this period in Britain, from the point of view of the direction of progress, it was the period in the Deep South between Reconstruction and the Plessey *v.* Ferguson decision. Blacks could at best fight not to be deprived of rights. They could not hope to win new ones. Even the abortive attempt by Dr Martin Luther King to start a British Civil Rights Movement in the form of the Campaign Against Racial Discrimination foundered (Heineman, 1972) and the subsequent arena of activity of its former members was in the Labour Party within which an essentially paternalist initiative to combat racism and racial discrimination was pursued.

The crucial difference between the discussion of immigrant rights and of working-class rights lay in the fact that they were not based upon bargaining between equals. The earliest attempts by the Government to deal with immigrant problems were through the National Committee for Commonwealth Immigrants, which consisted of prestigious non-party political figures drawn from British society on the one hand and leaders of minority elites on the other. Later, this body, which was still quasi-political, was, however, superseded by the Community Relations Commission which, although it increasingly employed black staff, defined its tasks primarily in social work terms. Meanwhile, the new Race Relations Board was set up to introduce law into race relations, but in terms quite unlike those in the USA because its task was conceived as conciliation, and because there was nothing like the National Association for the Advancement of Coloured People (NAACP) to provide the black lawyers who would argue cases before it.

A plethora of other organizations arose within the white community, and to some extent within the immigrant communities themselves, which were concerned with these paternalistic purposes and with ironing out the difficulties experienced by immigrants. Together these came to be known by government, by political parties and by immigrant organizations alike as 'the race relations industry'. Thus, finally, when Parliament set up a Select Committee to take evidence on immigrant problems, this industry was available, together with the more regular government departments, to provide it with an overview of the problems of immigrants.[11]

The vast majority of immigrants were passive victims of these processes and the most that they could do in the early 1960s was to collaborate with those who, albeit in paternalistic ways, were concerned with their problems. But by the early 1970s a new phenomenon was evident. Militant immigrant organizations were being formed, and, if they had no mass membership, received at least compliance and passive support from the minority of the population.

The new groups were much affected by international trends, and brought to the definition of their situation not merely the militancy of an underclass in British society, but also definitions derived from the Third World's conflict with the rich industrial nations. One heard talk of violent armed struggles, even of war, from black

31

leaders. Much of this was rhetoric, or in Sorel's precise use of the term, myth (Sorel, 1961). Just as the myth of the general strike was less important as a prediction or as a strategy than as a belief system making for the solidarity and, hence, the capacity for action of the working class in Europe, so the myth of the race war or of a revolutionary conflict between the Third World and the First, or between black and white, served to unite black groups.

One can detect three types of black groups which are not part of the compliance machinery of paternalism. There are ideological groups which address themselves to the ideas of Fanon, Garvey, Marx, Cabral, Guevara, Debray and Mao. There are groups organized around personalities of young leaders skilled at provoking and dramatizing the conflicts between black and white. And one also encounters groups organized around housing, educational and employment issues which also fall at the militant end of the militancy/compliance continuum.

Quite consciously black groups address themselves to the relationship between the revolt of the Third World and the blacks, and that of the working class organized around Marxist programmes. Very few consciously and deliberately oppose Marxism. What they do, however, is equate their own struggle with the Marxist class struggle, rather than see it as subordinated to the struggles against capitalism of the native working class, or the international working class. Amongst West Indians, however, the black struggle and the Communist struggle may become increasingly identified, as Cuban influence in the world increases, and, since Marxism is now itself indigenous to the politics of the Indian sub-continent, one may expect that some of the variations between compliance and militancy amongst Asian groups will be stated in terms of conflicts within Marxism. What is clear is that more militant definitions of the situation are now available to West Indian and Asian immigrants than were available ten years ago, whether these take the form of ideologically conscious Black Power groups, groups formed for the purpose of possible or actual conflicts with the police, and with white racists, or groupings of young Asians going on Trotskyist marches against Fascism in defiance of their elders.

All of this bears on the question of the conscious relationships between immigrants and the class structure. As we have seen, social class is a fact for the British worker in the sense that a political party and, more widely than that, a political movement has grown up based upon trades unions in industry but capable of fighting for the rights of workers in relation to housing, the education of their children and other welfare services. Overall this movement has guaranteed for its members certain minima in all of these fields. At the same time is has produced a more or less conscious sense of class membership in a large part of the population.

The immigrant worker does not enjoy all of these benefits in the same degree. His fortunes in the housing market or the labour market and the fortunes of his children in the schools are less happy than those of his native-born white peers. He affiliates to workers' organizations, but they do not constitute a focus for his life in the same way as they do for the native-born. He will possibly regard his sojourn in Britain as temporary, but, even if he does not, it is less likely that work relations will become the central focus around which other relationships, norms and ideas cohere. Far more likely, as the focus of organization and identification which transcends institutional boundaries and provides truly communal solidarity, will be the neighbourhood and the defence of that neighbourhood against the world outside. Particularly acute and central in the consciousness of the immigrant community will be the lot of the young unemployed. They have reason for resentment against an educational and economic system which has yielded them little. And, spending their time on the streets as they do, they find themselves in conflict with, and feel themselves harassed by, the police. In a situation which is by no means as peaceful or orderly as that of the ordinary British worker in his relations with his employer and the State, instances of violence which occur take on a peculiar, symbolic importance, representing in themselves the whole of the conflict between black immigrant underclass and normal society.

On the other hand, the organization of the immigrants as a class is not fully understood only through its relation to metropolitan class structure. The immigrant still has links with his own homeland, and if he is forced into a reactive militancy this may come to be defined, not in metropolitan European terms, but in terms of the Third World Revolution. The actual relationship of immigrant workers and the class structure may therefore be one of uneasy compromise between different institutions, different societies and different revolutionary projects.

We may attempt to represent the relationship diagrammatically somewhat as shown in Figure 1.1.

The underlined items represent the core of class and ethnic group formations. The arrows represent the pulls on immigrant group formations which prevent the immigrants from forming what in quasi-Marxist terms we might call an underclass-for-itself. In other words, there is some tendency for the black community to operate as a separate class or an underclass in British society, but it is pulled away from this both by the affiliation in terms of interests to the working class, and by the continuing pull of the economy, society and culture of the homelands, as well as of the Third World Revolution.

Consideration of our data as a whole led us more and more to

33

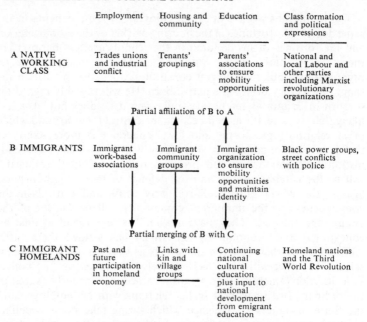

FIGURE 1.1   *Social and political orientations of immigrant communities*

the conclusion central to our final chapter that, whatever the degree to which immigrants managed to win through in British society as measured by traditional indices of life-chances, their position was still affected by the developing racial hostility which was articulated from the late 1950s onwards in white politics. Thus a truer reflection of the class–race conflict would be attained by modifying Figure 1.1 as shown in Figure 1.2.[12]

What we have done in this chapter, however, is to set out hypotheses only. In the substantive chapters which follow we present a number of different types of evidence and argument which should serve to confirm or refute the structural account which we have suggested here.

In chapter 3 we look at a particular 'inner-city' area of Birmingham, namely Handsworth, which is quite commonly thought of as the race relations capital of the Midlands. In chapters 4, 5 and 6 we consider what is happening in the three major areas of resource allocation and social conflict, namely employment, housing and education, by looking at general policy discussion, at official statistics and at our own survey evidence drawn from the four wards commonly called Handsworth. The last of these three chapters inevitably passes

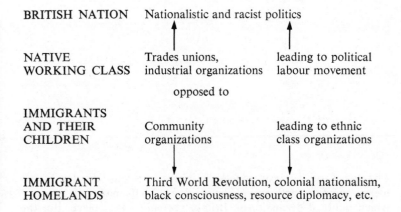

FIGURE 1.2   *Class and race conflict in contemporary Britain*

beyond the mere statistical description of life-chances to the discussion of moral education, political socialization and group
formation. The same theme is pursued in chapter 7 in which some
highly tentative data drawn from a sample of West Indian and Asian
youth are used to suggest possible differences of social and political
commitment amongst the younger generation who have been partially
educated in England. Chapter 8 then discusses the mobilization of
individuals in social, cultural and political groups in what is,
inevitably, a situation of severe social conflict.

Our final chapter attempts to pull together the threads of this
empirical argument. That question then leads to a broader one, in
which Britain's Asian and West Indian populations are looked at,
not simply in terms of whether they are included in or left out of the
British class structure, but of how they relate to wider conflicts in
the post-imperial era.

There are two appendices. One of these, which is of considerable
importance to our mode of analysis, sets our conception of the
political sociology of race relations. The other outlines the actual
research procedures used.

Before turning to this empirical material, however, we begin by
considering the way in which the definition of race relations in
British politics has changed between 1945 and 1978.

35

2 British political ideologies and the race question

The structural analysis suggested in the previous chapter by no means coincides with any of the ideological self-images[1] in terms of which political discussion in Britain normally takes place. But the fact of the matter is that these self-images are now very much under strain as a result of the settlement in Britain of a million or so West Indian and Asian immigrants and the response of the native-born to that immigration. What we see now is the growth of a widespread pragmatic racialism backed by new guiltily acknowledged racist theories together with frantic attempts to rationalize these practices in terms of the old ideologies.

The old ideologies to which we refer are those of conservative imperialism, liberal individualism and international socialism. It is necessary to understand what was involved in these if we are to make any sense of the debates which went on in the 1950s and the 1960s as the size of the West Indian and Asian settlement increased. The actual contingencies which the settlement created produced responses which were, perhaps, latent in the structure of British society, but which were at odds with these ideologies. In such a situation the main task of a sociologist might well be to demonstrate the nature of the 'real' structure of British society precisely through a demonstration of the inconsistencies of ideological explanations and the proferring of alternative sociological explanations.

Of course, one should not assume that these ideologies are merely distortions or mystifications of reality. Conceivably the society could have been changed in the direction suggested by the ideologies and the latent structures referred to above repressed. Thus, we are bound, in the course of this discussion, to raise moral and political questions about the failure of politicians who had the power to influence events, and to practice what they preached. None the less, what seems to be the case is that during this period there was a slow and painful abandonment of ideals in the face of rising racial tension. Notions which would have been dismissed as morally disgraceful by nearly all parties in the early 1950s became the unspoken ground assumptions of the most respectable politicians and leader writers by the end of the 1960s.

The ideology of conservative imperialism was itself a late development of empire. In earlier periods politicians and academics alike had been frankly racist and chauvinist as they proposed and justified colonial adventures and conquests (Bolt, 1971; Kiernan, 1969). By the inter-war period, however, the moral dilemmas of empire had been resolved in terms of a new and comforting set of doctrines such as those of the white man's burden and the dual mandate. Central to these doctrines was the belief that, within the British Empire, the claim *Civis Brittanicus sum* was a claim which entitled a man to quite definite rights before the law. This did not, of course, mean equality of life-chances amongst citizens, and was quite compatible with the subsidiary notion that colonial natives must keep their place. But it did imply that, in some sense, all men had the same basic *legal* rights, and this became an underlying assumption of discussion amongst respectable conservative politicians and lawyers.

Liberal individualism was a more radical doctrine. It may indeed have originated as a justification of possessive individualism (McPherson, 1962) but, even if it did, it took on a life of its own and became the basis of social reform. In the early twentieth century this led to recognition by liberals of the left that the fundamental liberal notions of freedom of contract and equality of opportunity could only be assured through considerable state intervention (Hobhouse, 1951; Beveridge, 1944). Thus liberalism as a domestic doctrine in the metropolis passed from a stage of simple Social Darwinism to something which was hard to distinguish from socialism.

If, however, liberalism had to change its nature in order to cope with the problems of developing industrial society in Britain, it was placed under far greater strain in dealing with the problems of colonialism and imperialism. Faced with these a minority maintained their liberal principles and became radical anti-imperialists. Most, however, either abandoned their liberalism altogether or compartmentalized it, keeping it as a doctrine for domestic metropolitan consumption only. The real problems were to arise when colonial men appeared on the metropolitan scene. Compartmentalization then would no longer be possible. The question which would arise would be whether or not these colonial immigrants were entitled to the same rights as the working-man in the welfare state. Reformist left liberalism was surely committed to the view that they were.

Socialist doctrine in Europe became attached in the mid-nineteenth century to the politics of the labour movement. It was

37

the means whereby the labour movement transcended the notion of mere business unionism. Labour leaders came to argue that their claims rested not merely upon their power in the labour market but upon the notion that an injustice brought about as a result of the superior power of the employing classes had to be rectified. Moreover, if this prevented the stronger workers' organizations pursuing their own claims at the expense of the weaker in a single country, it also implied a degree of internationalism because the claims of justice could no more allow the exploitation of foreign and colonial workers than it could of weaker groups within a country. The working-man, it was said in labour and socialist circles, had no country.

It is important to recognize that, whatever other divisions existed between utopian and Marxist socialism, there was no difference over this. In one of his early and most moving statements on the nature of the proletariat, Marx had referred to it as

> a class which is the dissolution of all classes, a sphere of society which has a universal character because its sufferings are universal and which does not claim a particular redress because the wrong which is done to it is not a particular wrong, but wrong in general (Tucker, 1972, p. 22).

Thus, whatever other pressures there were on the labour movement, the pressure of socialism was towards the acceptance of a notion of universal rights.

The conception of universal human rights, which was, then, shared by idealistic conservatives, liberals and socialists, became especially prominent in political thinking in the period just after 1945. The Allied nations had recently defeated Nazi Germany whose doctrines of racial supremacy were at odds with all three of the ideological traditions which we have discussed. This was a period in which bodies like UNESCO were earnestly drawing up declarations expressing what was thought to be the common conscience of mankind on matters related to human rights and race (Kuper, 1975). Yet, as we shall see below, the ideas which UNESCO sought to outlaw survived, and became more and more influential as the common conscience adapted itself to changed circumstances.

In order that we should understand fully the social structure within which the problems of our own empirical research are situated, it is essential that we should understand these ideological changes. They will serve as an index of underlying structural changes. It will be useful, therefore, to begin with a chronology of events connected with race relations in Britain during the period 1945–77 which will provide us with a framework for sociological discussion.

Chronology of events relating to black immigration and race relations in Britain 1945-77[2]

1946　Report by Colonial Office on poor economic prospects in Jamaica.

1947　End of Overseas Volunteer Scheme to encourage West Indians to work in Britain.

1948　S.S. *Empire Windrush* brings 492 immigrants from Kingston, Jamaica, to London. Followed by S.S. *Orbiter* and S.S. *Georgia*.

1948　British Nationality Act distinguishes between citizens of Independent Commonwealth and citizens of the United Kingdom and the colonies.

1949　Summer. Attack by whites on a black men's hostel in Deptford.

1949　Colonial Office working party on possibility of employing colonial workers in Britain.

1950　Private member's bill to outlaw discrimination in public places introduced by Reginald Sorenson MP. Not passed.

1952　McCarren-Walter Act restricting immigration from West Indies to USA. Passed.

1956　London Transport Executive establish liaison with Barbados Immigrant Service.

1956　Private member's bill to outlaw discrimination in public places introduced by Fenner Brockway MP. Not passed.

1955–60　Total number of immigrants from West Indies, India and Pakistan is 219,540. (Jamaica 96,180, rest of Caribbean 65,270, India 33,070, Pakistan 17,120, plus others.)

1958　23–30 August. Racial brawls in Nottingham public houses.

1958　September. White youths attack black people and houses in Notting Hill, London. Lord Justice Salmon passes severe sentences on white youths.

1958　Institute of Race Relations set up.

1959　James Callaghan MP, Labour spokesman on colonial affairs, urges Government to introduce legislation to outlaw discrimination.

1960　Standing Conference of West Indian Organizations set up.

1960　Withholding of passports held illegal by Indian Supreme Court.

1960　Birmingham Immigration Control Association and Southall Residents' Association set up to oppose immigration.

1961　Conservative MPs in West Midlands urge control of Commonwealth immigration. Committee of Afro-Asian-Caribbean organizations set up to oppose legislation.

39

1961–June 1962   Sharp rise in immigration from West Indies, India and Pakistan.

1961   October. Conservative conference calls for the control of Commonwealth immigration.

1961   Hugh Gaitskell, leader of the Opposition, indicates that Labour will oppose legislation for immigration control.

1962   July. Commonwealth Immigration Act introduced making entry subject to holding of employment vouchers.

1962   Commonwealth Immigrants' Advisory Council set up to advise the Home Secretary.

1963   Death of Hugh Gaitskell. Harold Wilson elected Leader of Labour Party. Commits Labour to support for Fenner Brockway's bill on Racial Discrimination.

1964   Vouchers under Commonwealth Immigration Act now restricted to category A for people with special skills and category B for those with pre-arranged jobs.

1964   Election victory for Labour, but Peter Griffiths, Tory candidate in Smethwick, wins seat from Patrick Gordon-Walker on basis of clear anti-immigration campaign. Fenner Brockway also defeated at Slough.

1964   November. Harold Wilson, Prime Minister, calls Peter Griffiths a 'Parliamentary leper'.

1964   December. Campaign Against Racial Discrimination set up following visit to England by Rev. Martin Luther King.

1965   February. Malcolm X visits England. Racial Adjustment Action Society formed.

1965   April. Race Relations bill published.

1965   Home Secretary appoints committee on immigration appeals.

1965   May-June. Ku-Klux-Klan groups active in the Midlands and London.

1965   8 July. Richard Crossman MP notes in his diary that 'we can't digest the numbers [of immigrants] who are now arriving in the Midlands'.

1965   July. Department of Education issues circular 7/65 recommending that no school have over 30 per cent immigrant children.

1965   2 August. White Paper on Commonwealth immigration reduces number of vouchers annually to 8,500 of which 1,000 are for Malta.

1965   October. Change of government policy defended at Labour Party conference by Robert Mellish MP who predicts violence in his constituency if immigrant workers get housing priority.

1965   October. First Race Relations Act passed. Soskice accepts

Conservative proposal to substitute conciliation for criminal sanctions. Act sets up Race Relations Board and National Committee for Commonwealth Immigrants (NCCI).

1965 October. Archbishop of Canterbury appointed chairman of NCCI. Hamza Alavi and David Pitt of CARD join the committee. West Indian Standing Conference disaffiliates from CARD.

1965 November. Mark Bonham Carter appointed chairman of Race Relations Board.

1966 March. General election. Labour returned with increased majority. Labour regains Smethwick. Andrew Faulds, new MP for Smethwick, declares 'we've buried the race issue'.

1966 23 May. Roy Jenkins, Home Secretary, envisages extension of Race Relations Act to cover employment and housing. Also posits a society based upon cultural diversity and mutual tolerance and expresses fears of consequences if second generation is not given full opportunities.

1966 Autumn. Political and Economic Planning report on Racial Discrimination. Street Committee report on possibility of anti-discrimination legislation.

1967 January. Representatives of the Trades Union Congress, the Confederation of British Industries and Nationalized Industry present joint statement to Minister of Labour opposing the extension of anti-discrimination legislation to employment field.

1967 February. NCCI conference on racial equality and employment. The general secretary of the TUC, Mr George Woodcock, declines invitation.

1967 7 February. Enoch Powell writes in *Daily Telegraph* that whites are having to leave homes as blacks move in.

1967 9 July. Enoch Powell writes in *Daily Express* of race problem exploding and urges that dependents should be kept out.

1967 June-July. Universal Coloured People's Organization set up as a Black Power organization. Invites Stokeley Carmichael to visit England.

1967 18 October. Enoch Powell declares that it is 'monstrous that a loophole in the 1962 Immigration Act should lead to an even greater influx of coloured immigrants from Kenya'.

1967 December. Collapse of CARD after conflict within executive committee.

1967 December. Formation of Joint Council for the Welfare of Immigrants.

1968 January. James Callaghan succeeds Roy Jenkins as Home Secretary.

1968   February. More speeches by Enoch Powell and others
drawing attention to possibility of large immigration of
Kenyan Asians. Callaghan introduces new Commonwealth
Immigration Act which distinguishes between British citizens
who are 'patrials' and those who are not and applies the
voucher system to British citizens. Act passed within a week.

1968   April. Second Race Relations bill published.

1968   20 April. Enoch Powell's major speech on immigration,
speaks of a nation heaping up its own funeral pyre, and he,
'like the Roman, sees the Tiber foaming with much blood'.

1968   21 April. Heath declares Powell's speech to be racialist
in tone and drops him from shadow cabinet.

1968   23 April. March of 1,500 London dockers to Westminster in
support of Powell.

1968   23 April. Second reading of Race Relations bill.

1968   26 April. Second dockers' march joined by Smithfield
meat porters.

1968   April-May. Pro-Powell marches in provincial centres.

1968   Black People's Alliance formed at Leamington Spa
conference.

1968   29 April. James Callaghan announces that Ministry of
Social Security will repatriate any immigrant family wanting
to return home.

1968   September. Eighty resolutions on immigration tabled for
Conservative Party conference.

1968   October. Race Relations Act passed. NCCI to be
superseded by Community Relations Commission.

1968   December. Parliamentary Select Committee on Race
Relations and Immigration established.

1968-9   First report of Parliamentary Select Committee on the
problem of coloured school-leavers.

1969   Edward Heath urges that the Government should take
steps to halt all immigration.

1969   February. Ban on entry of male fiancés from
Commonwealth wishing to marry.

1969   February. *Colour and Citizenship* published reporting
findings of the survey of race relations set up in 1962.

1969   Institute of Race Relations sets up two research
programmes, one in London dealing with international race
relations problems, the other headed by Nicholas Deakin at
Sussex to be called the Joint Unit for Minority and Policy
Research.

1969   Enoch Powell proposes a ministry to deal with repatriation.

1970   Spring. Outbreak of 'Paki-bashing' in London.

1970   June. Conservatives win general election.

1970   United Kingdom Immigrant Advisory Service set up.
1970   Parliamentary Select Committee report on immigrant
        housing.
1971   New Immigration Act replaces Aliens Restriction Act of
        1914 and Commonwealth Immigrants Acts of 1962 and 1968.
        Right of abode restricted to 'patrials'. Others to obtain a
        work permit and to register with police.
1971   Home Office sets up its own Race Relations Research Unit.
1971   Social Science Research Council's Race Relations Research
        Unit set up in Bristol.
1971   Census data provides estimate of the coloured population
        of Great Britain as 1,385,600 of whom 555,400 were born in
        Great Britain.
1972   March. New radical leadership takes over Institute of Race
        Relations after attempt by old committee to dismiss the
        director of the overseas research programme, Hugh Tinker.
1971–2 Select Committee report on relations between immigrants
        and the police.
1972   4 August. Newspapers report possibility of expulsion of
        Ugandan Asians.
1972   6 August. David Lane, minister reponsible for race
        relations, says that Britain is an overcrowded island and that
        very difficult problems would arise if more immigrants came.
1972   16 August. Enoch Powell predicts national catastrophe
        following influx of immigrants.
1972   September-October. Approximately 27,000 Ugandan Asians
        arrive. Some 21,000 pass through special camps during the
        following year. Certain areas which are already heavily
        settled by immigrants are termed 'red areas' and Ugandan
        Asians are urged to go elsewhere.
1972   Strike of Asian workers at Mansfield Hosiery Works,
        Loughborough.
1973   May. Martin Webster, National Front candidate, saves his
        deposit in the West Bromwich by-election.
1972–3 Report of Select Committee on immigrant education.
1973   May. National Front puts up twenty-six candidates in the
        local council elections at Leicester.
1973   Paul Storey, aged 15 of Handsworth, Birmingham,
        sentenced to two concurrent sentences of twenty years for
        assault and robbery. Two immigrant youths sentenced with
        him for shorter periods.
1973   Pakistan secedes from the Commonwealth.
1973   Standing Conference of Asian Organizations set up.
1974   February. *Race*, the journal of the Institute of Race
        Relations, changes its title to *Race and Class*, emphasizing its

43

new radical and Marxist orientation.

1974 February. Labour forms minority government after general election.

1974 April. Roy Jenkins, as Home Secretary, announces amnesty for illegal immigrants who entered Britain before 1 January 1973.

1974 May. Asian workers at Imperial Typewriter works at Leicester go on strike.

1974 Select Committee report on immigrant employment.

1974 Department of Education produce report on *Educational Disadvantage and the Needs of Immigrants.*

1974 June. Second PEP report on the extent of racial discrimination

1974 Husbands and fiancés of New Commonwealth women allowed to settle. Change in immigration rules (Cmnd 5715).

1974 Pyramid selling scandal. Sales organization which recruited specifically immigrant sales staff exposed. Entry into this sales organization often obtained through loan financed by second mortgage. A number of secondary banks involved in giving loans.

1974–5 Select Committee report on the organization of race relations administration.

1975 Black Parents' Movement and Black Students' Movement set up in North London.

1975 White Paper on racial discrimination proposing new bill.

1975 September. White Paper on race and housing (Cmnd 6332).

1975 PEP report on racial minorities in public housing.

1975 Race Relations Board seeks an injunction against National Front member Robert Relf for offering his house in Leamington Spa for sale to English people only.

1976 3 February. New Race Relations bill published. Proposes to include in its definition of discrimination acts which were discriminatory in effect though not in intent. Also proposes the merging of the Race Relations Board and the Community Relations Commission in a new body to be called the Commission for Racial Equality.

1976 March. Second reading of the Race Relations bill.

1976 March. Callaghan elected leader of the Labour Party and Prime Minister.

1976 April. Enoch Powell, speaking at Cambridge, describes mugging as a racial crime.

1976 April. Warrant issued for the arrest of Robert Relf. Arrested a fortnight later.

1976 5 May. *Daily Telegraph* discloses a secret Foreign Office report on the administration of immigration in India.

Hawley's report apparently at odds with the views of Alex
Lyon, former junior minister at the Home Office, dropped by
Callaghan in March. Hawley sees immigration arrangements
in India as too generous to immigrants; Lyon, the opposite.

1976   15 May. Demonstrations on behalf of Relf, on hunger
strike, outside Winson Green prison, Birmingham. Counter
demonstration by black groups.

1976   24 May. Powell, in House of Commons, quotes figures
from the Hawley report, not yet published. Sees the situation
in inner cities coming to parallel that in Belfast.

1976   May. Press reports of four Malawi Asians temporarily
accommodated in four-star hotel by West Sussex Council.

1976   Summer. Reports of both black and white vigilante groups
organizing. Callaghan appeals for 'race calm'.

1976   4 June. Eighteen-year-old Gurdip Singh Chaggar stabbed
to death at Southall bus-stop. Sir Robert Mark of Scotland
Yard says motives not necessarily racial.

1976   8 June. Home Secretary and Mark Bonham Carter visit
Southall.

1976   13 June. Race Relations Act becomes law.

1976   17 June. Peter Walker, minister and former member of the
shadow cabinet, but no longer in Mrs Thatcher's shadow
cabinet, makes racially liberal political speech calling
attention to unequal opportunities and bad conditions in the
sphere of immigrant employment and housing.

1976   21 June. Robert Relf released from gaol after widespread
protest at his continued detention.

1976   July. Third reading of Race Relations bill.

1976   July. Dr Coggan, Archbishop of Canterbury, says there
must be defined limits to immigration.[3]

1976   21 July. William Whitelaw, speaking at Leicester and
referring to immigration, says, 'The British Empire has now
paid its debts.'

1976   30 July. David Lane, Conservative MP for Cambridge,
appointed to head new Community Relations Commission.

1976   Notting Hill carnival leads to clashes between blacks and
police. Sir Robert Mark denies that police had been
provocative.

1976   17 September. Minister for the environment announces
shift of resources towards inner cities. William Whitelaw calls
for major programme in inner cities as a means of defusing
racial tensions.

1976   October. Mr Justice Gwynne Morris, sentencing six West
Indian youths for robbery in Brixton, suggests vigilante
groups to protect local women from muggers.

1977   21 January. Powell refers to enclaves of foreign lands in British cities and envisages conflict on the scale of civil war.

1977   Document from six major cities to Secretary for the Environment urges him to implement plans for inner city. Summary of the Department of the Environments' Inner Area Study published.

1977   March. Select Committee report on the West Indian Community.

1977   31 March. By-election at Birmingham Stechford, owing to Roy Jenkins's departure to head the European Commission. Won by Conservative. National Front candidate beats Liberal into third place.

1977   10 May. Office of Population Census and Surveys (OPCS) figures published. Coloured population said to be 1.77 million, or 3.3 per cent of total population.

1977   13 June. Commission for Racial Equality begins work.

1977   15 June. Government White Paper on the inner city published.

1977   19 June. Peter Walker MP calls for positive discrimination in favour of young blacks to combat truancy.

1977   June. Fighting between police and pickets at Grunwick Laboratories in East London. Strike there initiated by immigrant worker but immigrants are both amongst strikers and those continuing work. The managing director of Grunwick turns out to be Anglo-Indian.

1977   5 July. Minister for Education, Shirley Williams, announces that she will set up an enquiry into the educational under-achievement of West Indian children.

1977   8 August. National Front march in Lewisham, an area of heavy immigrant settlement. Demonstration attacked by counter-demonstration organized by Socialist Workers' Party.

1977   15 August. Prime Minister suggests that police should ban demonstrations by 'extremists'.

1977   15 August. Birmingham Ladywood by-election in area covering part of Handsworth produces clashes between Socialist Workers' Party and other anti-fascist groups and National Front outside a National Front meeting.

1977   18 August. Labour holds Ladywood seat with reduced majority. National Front with a vote of 888, as against the Labour vote of 8,222, beats Liberal into fourth place. Socialist Unity candidate, who is himself an immigrant, gets 534 votes; James Hunte, known for his exposure of the pyramid selling scandal, gets 336, and the Socialist Workers' Party candidate 152.[4]

1977   29–30 August. Clashes between police and black youths at end of Notting Hill carnival.

1977   30 August. *The Times* publishes an interview with John Tyndall, National Front leader, and itself argues that the National Front must be demythologized and revealed as a movement of misguided individuals rather than as the creation of evil men.

It is important that the chronology of events should be kept firmly in mind in considering the research findings we shall report in later chapters. Too often, contemporary discussion about race relations proceeds as though nothing had yet happened and that what has to be discussed is how a present position of equal rights between men of different colour can be maintained. What we now propose to show in analysing the bare record of events is that crucial decisions have already been taken and that the status of a black or brown immigrant from the Commonwealth, if not of all black or brown men in Britain, has already been declared to be different from, and inferior to, that of the native-born British citizen. Moreover, even if such discriminatory treatment depends not upon legislation only, but upon tides of public opinion, we would suggest that, although these tides flow in a racist direction, they rarely ebb. Hence we shall argue that the overall import of these events is that, as the problem presented by immigration from the so-called New Commonwealth has become clear, the choices made within British politics have been such as to make Britain, more than most countries in the world, into a country marked by racialist practice and racist theory. This is a strong point of view but one which we believe to be justified by the historical record. It is only against this background assumption that we are able to make sense of the events and the data which we still record.

It will be convenient to review that table of events in terms of the strains to which the three ideologies which we have outlined were subject during the twenty-nine years since the passing of the British Nationality Act of 1948. The Conservative imperialist ideology lingers on in the residual idea of a common Commonwealth citizenship, but within this common citizenship, different classes of citizens are created, each having different and unequal rights. The liberal human rights ideology leads to legislation against racial discrimination but this legislation itself is modified and weakened so as to be adapted to a variety of vested interests. Finally, the socialist ideal of the brotherhood of all working-men, though it survives in the ritualistic utterances of trade unionists and labour politicians, is coupled with the belief that immigrants are potential blacklegs, who will undercut the price of labour, and take an unfair share of the welfare rights which have been won in the course of bitter working-class struggle.

47

Turning first to the idea of common citizenship, it is interesting to notice that this is far from a simple idea when it is debated in British politics. British law has no simple notion of the rights of citizenship following from membership of some national entity (Dummett, 1976). The key notion instead is that of a British subject, and before 1948, at least, what characterized British subjects, whether in the United Kingdom, in the Dominions or the Colonial Empire, was the common allegiance of all who lived there to the person of the British monarch. This meant that citizenship for all those involved implied duties rather than rights, but it also meant there was no distinction made between those of His Majesty's subjects who lived in the British Isles and those who lived abroad. Amongst other things, it implied freedom to migrate within any of His Majesty's territories.

It is instructive to go back to the debates about British citizenship which went on in Parliament and especially in the tradition-conscious House of Lords at the time of the British Nationality Act's passing in 1948. The legislation was introduced by the Labour Government as a consequence of the passing of new citizenship legislation in Canada. When the Canadians established their own citizenship, the meaning of the wider common status of British subject became unclear. The new Act therefore declared that there were basically two kinds of Commonwealth citizens or British subjects, citizens of the independent Commonwealth countries on the one hand and citizens of the United Kingdom and the Colonies on the other. The Conservative Party was far from happy about this. Attaching as they did an almost mystical significance to the notion of a tie of personal allegiance to the monarch implied in the term 'British subject', they did not like the idea of citizenship at all. Quite explicitly, moreover, they opposed the idea that some of His Majesty's subjects should not have the right to settle within the British Isles.

It should be noted, however, that the new legislation involved two distinct classes of people who were Commonwealth citizens, but not natives of the British Isles. On the one hand there were citizens of the independent Commonwealth countries, including especially Canada, South Africa, Australia and New Zealand. On the other, there were His Majesty's colonial subjects in the Caribbean, Africa and Asia, who were mostly non-white and who lived in dependent colonial territories. The Conservative opposition to restriction on free movement, of course, was based especially on their desire to protect the rights of the first of these two classes, but, stated in general terms, it was bound to apply equally to the inhabitants of the Colonies, particularly when these Colonies achieved independence and were legally indistinguishable from the territories of the old White Commonwealth.

During the 1950s, as first West Indian, and then Asian settlement began to be evident in the major cities of England, there was increasing hostility to the settlers from their white working-class neighbours. The British working class had accepted the notion of common citizenship so long as it was purely theoretical, but when it seemed that black men from the colonies were to be treated as their equals, or rather that their own position of superiority *vis-à-vis* the blacks was not to be recognized, they became seriously concerned. Sporadic outbreaks of violence culminated in open attacks on blacks in Notting Hill and Nottingham in 1958 and became reflected in campaigns to control 'coloured' immigration.

The agitation for immigration control was resisted by the Conservative Governments of Churchill, Eden and Macmillan before 1959, but the pressure was increased during the period 1959–62, when immigration increased rapidly after a few years of decline, and when it seemed that Asian immigration, particularly, might increase out of all proportion. Eventually, after sustained pressure for control culminating in a mass of resolutions on the agenda of the Conservative Party, Mr R. A. Butler, in 1962, introduced an Act to control not 'coloured' but Commonwealth immigration.

Since the demand amongst Conservative supporters was for control of coloured immigration and the Act covered Commonwealth immigration there were bound to be anomalies in this Act. On the one hand it applied to new and old, white and coloured Commonwealth alike, so that, although it was not part of the intention of Parliament, Australians and Canadians were affected equally with West Indians and Asians. On the other hand, those who had originally shared with the native-born British the status of citizenship of the United Kingdom and the Colonies were now singled out for separate and discriminatory treatment, except for those who were to find their territories becoming independent and who did not automatically acquire any new citizenship (e.g. many Asians in East Africa).

These anomalies led to further pressure for legislation of a kind which was bound to be more and more racially discriminatory. Any attempt to be lenient in the application of immigration rules in a way which would help Australians and New Zealanders opened up the prospect of limitless illegal Pakistani and Indian immigration, while, as pressure on the Indian and Pakistani secondary colonialists in East Africa mounted, there was a demand that, whether or not they had citizenship of the United Kingdom and the Colonies as well as passports issued by the British Government, these 'East African Asians' should be subject to immigration control.

The passing of the 1968 Act to restrict the inflow of East African Asians had very considerable implications for race relations in Britain. Control was now to be applied not merely to citizens of the

49

independent Commonwealth who had an automatic right to citizenship in another country, but also to some citizens of the United Kingdom and the Colonies who were distinguished from the native-born British only by their birthplace. The nature of this distinction was made quite clear, in that so-called 'patrials', who had parents or grandparents who lived in Britain, were excluded from the new forms of control.

Clearly the Act of 1968 went a long way in the direction of distinguishing *de facto* between white and coloured citizens.

The principle of patriality was taken still further in the Act of 1971. This Act did three things: it extended the patriality exemption not only to those who had no citizenship in the independent Commonwealth countries but to those who did; it reduced the rights of those who were still subject to control, but who, under the Act of 1962 as interpreted in 1965, were able to obtain labour vouchers, by making their entry conditional upon a particular employment; and when it came into full force in 1973 it introduced more severe punishments for those who had entered the country by evading immigration control.

Probably it could be said that the Act of 1971 went as far as it was possible to go in satisfying the immigration control lobby, without actually giving up the notion of Commonwealth citizenship, and, within that, the notion of citizenship of the United Kingdom and the Colonies. The new discriminatory practice was established but was still surrounded by the mists of ideology. At this stage, however, a new realism gripped the Conservative Party. The Conservative spokesman on home affairs declared that the British Empire had now 'paid its debts', a phrase which could only be taken to mean that the Rights of Her Majesty's imperial subjects no longer existed, while the Conservative Party political centre produced a pamphlet asking for three distinct citizenships to be established, for the native-born British, for overseas British (e.g. the East African Asians), and for the citizens of the few remaining colonies (Deedes 1968). By this time, moreover, Labour thinking was moving on similar lines and the Green Paper on nationality issued by the Labour Government in 1977 (Home Office, 1977) conceded the main points of the Conservative political centre pamphlet.

Of especial importance in the evolution of Conservative policy from the concept of a unified to a divided British citizenship, have been the policies advocated in the speeches of Mr Enoch Powell. His role was particularly important because before 1964 he had been recognized as the arch-advocate of the imperialist ideology. He had opposed the British Nationality Act of 1948 on the basis of an almost mystical belief in the unity of the British Empire and the common allegiance of all its inhabitants to the Crown. Moreover, when agitation for control mounted, he opposed any kind of discriminatory action against British citizens. While maintaining this position, however, he came more and more to the view that there should be a specific British citizenship from which West Indians and Indians should be excluded. Speaking at the time of the 1971 Act he had said:

'All the difficulties out of which the Bill arises but to which it does not refer, and those which have been, which are, and which are to come, flow from the fact that this country, alone, I think, of all countries, has never known in its law a status which defined its own people. We have never had a citizenship of the people of this country' (Dummett, 1976, p. 16),

while in another speech he had gone further:

'The West Indian or Asian does not, by being born in England, become an Englishman. In law, he becomes a United Kingdom citizen by birth, in fact he is a West Indian or Asian still' (Foot, 1969, p. 137).

One interpretation which could be put on Mr Powell's views is that he is a political intellectual deeply concerned with the logical application of certain fundamental principles. British citizenship, for him, is not a matter to be dealt with in terms of the expediency of the moment. Its essential nature has to be understood. According to this interpretation, Powell had first been content with the notion of a common allegiance to the Crown of all who were British subjects, but when that notion gave way to the notion of the rights of citizenship he pleaded for a status in law whereby the British defined who were their own people.

This interpretation of Powell's thinking has been systematically challenged by Paul Foot. According to him, although Powell did indeed hold semi-mystical ideas about British nationality in the early stages of his Parliamentary career, in practice, he became a politician deeply committed to a radical belief in private enterprise, who was not much concerned with the immigration issue, until it became apparent that it could be turned to the advantage of the Conservative Party, or, still more, to the advancement of his own political ideas inside or outside the Conservative Party (Foot, 1969).

It does seem to be the case that up till 1967 Powell did not stray far from official Conservative thinking on immigration, and that in the late 1950s, under pressure from small lobbies within his own constituency and in the West Midlands, he had shown little interest in the matter. But the situation began to change in 1964 when Peter Griffiths of Smethwick showed very convincingly that the immigration issue taken by itself could reverse national political trends. Early in 1967, reviewing a book by one of the present authors on Spark-brook, Birmingham (Rex and Moore, 1967), Powell began to give publicity to what he said his constituents were saying about the settlement of immigrants. In his Deal speech later in the year he sounded the alarm about the potential numbers of Asian immigrants from East Africa and, when he had won his point on this, turned, in his most dramatic speech (which is now known in political mythology as The Powell Speech), to the general question of halting immigration and finding ways of repatriating those who were already in Britain.

The main difference between the two interpretations given above is that one argues that Powell was mainly concerned with the issue of Britishness and that he developed his ideas differently in different circumstances, while the other argues that he simply took up the immigration issue because of the political advantage which it might bring him. But the difference between these arguments is academic only. Either Powell moved from being a consistent imperialist to being a consistent nationalist or he moved from seeking the support of orthodox Conservatives to responding directly to populist pressure. In any case he did move from an earlier Conservative position, which has not led to him being recognized as a politician of more than the second rank, to espousing doctrines with immense popular appeal. He became the most charismatic figure in British politics, at least for a while, and one who might in suitable circum-stances even be able to break the grip which the Conservative and Labour Parties had on political power.

What Powellism certainly shows is the emergence in British politics of a new doctrine and a new constituency awaiting mobiliza-tion, which has little in common with the doctrines and the move-ments of conservatism, liberalism and socialism mentioned above. This doctrine and this constituency express themselves first in the work of the Immigration Control Associations from 1959 to 1964, then in Peter Griffiths's Smethwick campaign, in the spontaneous support which Powell's speeches evoked, and, finally, in the not insignificant electoral support won by the National Front from 1973 onwards. All parties, but the Conservative Party especially, took account of Powellism in formulating their policies from 1968 on-wards, and, of more recent years, treat the threat of the National Front in elections as a serious one. It matters little in the long term whether Powell leads this new movement. The odds seem to be that, having followed his own preoccupations about citizenship to the extreme extent of having become an Ulster Unionist MP, he will cease to make such a great impact. What does matter is that a populist movement to the right of the Conservative Party has emerged which has pre-empted most right-wing positions.

The ideology of liberalism emphasizing the rights of all men before the law is not the sole prerogative of the Liberal Party. No doubt what that party says and does still provides a kind of marker for what liberalism is, but its main expressions are to be found in the liberal wing of the Labour Party. This wing by no means coincides with either the left or the right of the party but represents, within the Labour movement as a whole, a distinct axis of differentiation.

Hugh Gaitskell, leader of the Labour Party in the 1950s, was not a liberal in the orthodox sense of the term. He had made it clear in his adoption of Anthony Crosland's political theories that the idea of equality was the most important one in his political creed, and he took a militant stand against the left on the issue of public ownership. What made him a liberal, and indeed a left-winger, in his party, however, was his stand on immigration. Faced with the proposal to distinguish between the rights of one Commonwealth citizen and another, he drew attention to the fact that immigration followed the laws of demand and supply, and promised to repeal what seemed to him to be an irrational form of legislation (see Peach, 1968).

In the 1964 general election Labour maintained the liberal view that the problems which the public were identifying as racial problems were in fact problems of defective social services, and undertook to deal with the deficiencies when it was elected. Moreover, the new Prime Minister's first reaction to the Smethwick campaign was to call for the ostracism of the new member for that constituency as a Parliamentary leper, a nice phrase which indicated that an alien and dangerous element had entered British politics. It was the preservation of the liberal tradition on racial matters which seemed then to be at stake.

The question of the reactions of the working-class movement to immigration will be discussed below. Here it should be noted that, whatever changes occurred in the thinking of that movement, an essentially liberal impulse remained in the Labour Party. Of course, that impulse was expressed in vocal opposition to the White Paper on immigration, in which the party indicated its acceptance of Commonwealth immigration control in an even tighter form than the Conservative government had dared or wished to introduce. But, characteristically, even after the battle against immigration control had been fought and lost, the campaign continued for equal rights for those who were already here.

Roy Hattersley, the new MP for Sparkbrook, suggested the basis for a continued liberal policy despite immigration control when he said, 'Integration without control is impossible, control without integration is indefensible.' The Archbishop of Canterbury, Dr Ramsey, had his doubts about this, warning the Government that if the newly founded National Committee for Commonwealth

Immigrants found that the fact of immigration control itself had such an effect on the status and the image of the immigrants that integration was impossible, the committee would reserve the right to call for the ending of control. In fact, the continued agitation about control did adversely affect immigrants and eventually the National Committee went out of existence at the time of the 1968 Act. But, even allowing that control gave a breathing space for integration, evidence that the promise implicit in Hattersley's statement was fulfilled is slight.

Crucially, the fulfilment of this promise turned on the possibility of establishing institutions which would ensure equality of opportunity for the immigrant. The models to which all liberals looked were those which were to be found in the USA. There, there were examples of race relations and civil rights legislation at national and state level; there was a judicial system through which it was possible for American blacks to win their rights; and there were organizations of the black community as well as of their liberal well-wishers which ensured that cases were taken to court. The first task in Britain seemed to be the passing of an Act against racial discrimination. Such an Act had originally been proposed by Reginald Sorenson MP in 1951, and by Fenner Brockway every year since 1956. Ironically, Fenner Brockway had been defeated at Slough at the same time as Gordon Walker was defeated at Smethwick, while Sorenson then made way for Gordon Walker at Leyton, only to see him defeated again. Now, however, the Labour Party took up the bill officially and eventually made it law in 1965.

The bill had very obvious defects, which were excused mainly on the grounds that it was only a beginning and that law of any kind was better than no law, because it had a declaratory function. These defects were that the bill did not apply to the main areas where it was necessary to defend coloured people against discrimination, namely employment and housing, and that instead of making racial discrimination a criminal offence it set up a Race Relations Board with the object of achieving conciliation.

The notion of conciliation rather than one of legal process was the more unsatisfactory because of the absence of organizations which could represent immigrants effectively even before the Board. The new National Committee for Commonwealth Immigrants could not do this because its role was thought to be that of giving policy advice to the Government rather than taking up cases of discrimination, and because it was in any case an appointed body only marginally supported by immigrants. The main possibility here was that the role of plaintiff's representative might be taken up by the new Civil Rights organization founded at the suggestion of Martin Luther King. But this organization collapsed in confusion just at the moment when it might have fulfilled a useful function (see Heineman, 1972).

The collapse of CARD was part of a series of events which occurred between October 1967 and April 1968 when the second race relations bill, which extended the coverage of the law to employment and housing, was published. The National Committee for Commonwealth Immigrants had made many recommendations to the Government including one which called for the extension of the Act to these fields. Mr Mark Bonham Carter, head of the Race Relations Board, also saw the extension of the scope of the Act as one of the main changes necessary. Bonham Carter's close links with the Home Secretary, Roy Jenkins, led to this change being given priority, and a survey of racial discrimination by the organization Political and Economic Planning was commissioned,[5] with the intention of giving Jenkins and the racial liberals in the Cabinet ammunition to fight for the change, against ministers, led by Mr Ray Gunter, who were said to be opposed to it.

A new important political grouping had now come into being, both within the National Committee for Commonwealth Immigrants and within CARD. This included the lawyer, Anthony Lester, the assistant director of the Survey of Race Relations in Great Britain, Nicholas Deakin, Julia Gaitskell, daughter of the former leader of the Labour Party, and Dipak Nandy, a young Indian lecturer in English literature at the University of Kent, who now appeared as a leading member of most liberal bodies concerned with racial questions. Within CARD some of this group opposed the more militant political and Third-World oriented line being adopted by many members, and urged that the organization confine itself to the role of a civil rights organization. Eventually a group led by Nandy and Lester protested at the attempted take-over of CARD by militant organizations and, denouncing their opponents as Maoists and Trotskyists, left to fight for the race relations bill in the Labour Party conference (Heineman, 1972). Nandy was shortly to become director of an organization called the Runnymede Trust which was to put the liberal view on race questions.

Unfortunately, the passage of the race relations bill was not completed by Roy Jenkins. For the extraneous reason that James Callaghan at the Treasury had been forced into a devaluation which he opposed, and therefore wished to change jobs, Jenkins went to the Treasury and Callaghan to the Home Office. The first six months which he spent there were some of the most difficult which any Home Secretary could have faced, and it was unlikely, therefore, that Callaghan would be able to cope with them, let alone resolve them in terms of the liberal positions with which Roy Jenkins's name was associated.

As a Labour politician, Mr Callaghan was always represented as a pragmatist and as one intuitively sensitive to the mood of the trades unions as well as that of the man in the street. It is doubtful whether he would have introduced the new Race Relations Act, but there was little doubt that he would amend the original draft in a way which would satisfy the more orthodox members of the TUC. The CBI and the TUC had made a statement to the Minister of Labour in January 1967 opposing the extension of the Act to the field of employment, and the general secretary of the TUC, Mr George Woodcock, had declined an invitation to attend a NCCI conference on racial equality and employment. The first need, therefore, was for Callaghan to appease the TUC. This was done by sharply modifying the employment sections of the Act, so as to permit quotas if this was in the interest of the workers concerned, and requiring that industry's own internal machinery should be exhausted before employment cases went before the Race Relations Board. The sections on housing were also weakened, and in its final form the Act made no provision for the subpoena of witnesses or the right of the Board to call for documents.

In later chapters dealing with employment and housing we shall show that the actual achievements of the Board in the field of housing and employment were small. Arguably they were so small as to bring the Act into disrepute and to raise doubts amongst those who had argued that some law was at least better than no law. But, even if it was the aim of the law to have a declaratory or educational effect, this was made more dubious because of the dramatic events of early 1968 which surrounded and obliterated news of the Act. These were concerned with the East African Asian question and the Powell 'rivers of blood' speech.

We have already mentioned Powell's speeches. He first addressed himself to the question of East African migration in October 1967, thus opening up an issue which Jenkins had persuaded Duncan Sandys not to make a subject of public debate the year before. He continued to speak about the topic throughout these next five months, and, after another of his speeches in February, Callaghan, at the Home Office, adopting a line sharply different from that of Jenkins a few months before, introduced a new Commonwealth Immigration Act which, while exempting patrials, introduced a voucher system for East African Asians with British nationality and British passports.

Nicholas Deakin writes that 'the critics of this Act contended that it was in breach of five international covenants or declarations' (Deakin, 1969), but this was a point to be made primarily by Jenkinsite liberals. British legislation on immigration was now far more subject to Powellite, trade-union and populist pressure than it was to abstract notions of the rule of law. Nor was Callaghan much moved when told by the Archbishop of Canterbury that the bill introduced into immigration control 'a measure of injustice and indeed of bad faith, which unless considerably modified [could] do the gravest harm to community relations' and that the NCCI and its staff were 'perplexed to see how they might continue their work' (*The Times* 28 February 1968). In fact Callaghan was not much concerned whether the committee continued its work. The new Race Relations Act provided a convenient opportunity for winding it up and replacing what was a quasi-political body with a new one, the Community Relations Commission, which would not dabble in politics.

But, if the Commonwealth Immigrants Act shocked the liberals, Powell's speech of 20 April demoralized them completely, and finally discredited the Act so far as many members of the public were concerned. Not merely did Powell pass on alarming stories which came from his constituents and refer to immigrants in terms of an imagery which could only excite alarm, he also suggested that immigrants were placed in a position of privilege by the Act and that his speech, made just before the Act was passed, represented a last opportunity for an Englishman to speak. The spontaneous support which Powell's speech received meant that the publication of the Race Relations Bill in the same month was greeted with, if anything, hostility. Subsequently a series of events were given publicity in the media or deliberately staged to discredit the Act. At first these had a relatively playful character as when a paper drew attention to an 'illegal' advertisement from a porridge loving Scotsman seeking a Scottish cook. More serious, however, was the deliberate flouting of the Act by Robert Relf of Leamington Spa, who advertised his house for sale to an English purchaser only. When Relf was put in gaol for contempt of court, orthodox liberal opinion supported his release, and pro-Relf marches were opposed only by Trotskyist and Maoist groups and some immigrant organizations.

The outlook for the racial liberals in the late 1960s was not promising. As Nicholas Deakin put it, the Liberal Hour had passed (Deakin, 1970), but he himself did seem to think that the period of panic about immigration had passed and that a new period of a more constructive kind lay ahead. The three prongs of the liberal pro-gramme for the future were to be the Race Relations Board, the Community Relations Commission, and the new Urban Programme, which consisted of a new government allocation of money for the benefit of areas of urban stress. It was true that the existence of these institutions did give those concerned about racial harmony and integration a framework within which they could work, but it is still possible to argue that their actual effect on immigrant welfare or on the problem of discrimination and racial injustice was negligible.

More important than this lack of impact, however, was the fact that the new legislation was entirely paternalist in conception. The NCCI had hardly been a militant spokesman on behalf of the immigrants. The new body, the CRC, was not a spokesman at all. The Race Relations Board had to await individual complaints or to initiate investigations itself. It could not look even to a moderate body like the American NAACP to organize a systematic campaign against discrimination since CARD was no more. Clearly the CRC could do much to iron out minor problems of inter-community relations and provide technical help to those in the social services working against immigrants, and the Race Relations Act could have some effect through the knowledge that overt discriminatory action was now known to be illegal, but these institutions were not communicating with real representatives of the immigrant community at all.

Much liberal discussion after 1968 has consisted in whistling in the dark to keep up courage. But whistle the liberals did, and anyone who was concerned with race relations over the longer period became aware after 1968 of the existence of a huge race relations industry employing hundreds of workers. Amongst these workers were a considerable number of well-paid black men, usually conscious of the fact that the apparatus within which they worked was of little use to their own community, but prevented from thinking too much about this by the size of their salaries. In fact, paternalism worked, not so much by meeting the needs of the immigrant communities, but by siphoning off into welfare jobs a not inconsiderable stratum of blacks who might otherwise have been community leaders. We do not wish to impugn the integrity of the men who served in this apparatus, however. Our main point is a structural and institutional one. No organization could effectively deal with immigrant problems if its salary came from, and its loyalty belonged to, the Government.

This race relations apparatus was not improved by the contacts which many of its workers made with the USA. There, civil rights legislation, positive discrimination and affirmative employment had brought into existence a new cadre of black civil rights workers and other experts, some of them able men, others mere opportunists. To pretend, however, that the British situation was in any way comparable, was disastrously misleading. Rights won in political struggle are one thing; welfare given out to a quiescent if oppressed and exploited population is quite another. And the further refinement of the process whereby money is set aside for 'community self-help' only makes matters worse. Fast-talking operators become skilled at knowing how to apply for the money and a further stratum of the immigrant community finds itself effectively bribed into silence.

If then, Conservative imperialism gives way to nationalism and outright racialism, liberalism, unable to fight with those whom it wishes to serve, gives way to paternalism, more and more out of touch with the immigrant community as a whole. It now remains to be seen what has happened during this period to the thinking of the working-class movement. That movement, as we have said, starts with some conception of internationalism and anti-racialism. How well has that tradition stood up to the events which we have listed?

In a Conservative political centre pamphlet written in August 1968 in the aftermath of the 1968 Immigration Act, Mr William Deedes asks why Labour should have shown such hostility to earlier attempts by the Conservatives to control immigration and answers, 'One reason is that Labour's traditions of the brotherhood of man left them with no option but to take a strong stand on multi-racialism.' He might also have added that this opposition was fortified by the fact that the Labour Party was also the guardian of the liberal tradition in these matters. He is, however, certainly right in drawing attention to the fact that there was strong rank-and-file feeling in the Labour Party that, in Marx's words, the struggle for justice with the Labour Party was not merely a struggle against a particular wrong, but against wrong in general. The Labour Party cause, therefore, included a strong note of internationalism and anti-racialism.

If this was so, however, many workers outside the Labour Party, as well as some within it, saw the struggle of the labour movement as a struggle to right their particular wrongs in terms of a kind of business unionism, fortified by a strong dash of xenophobia, which was the inevitable consequence of three generations of imperialist adventures in which the working class provided the foot soldiers. Thus, along with those trade-unionists who came to profess, and indeed fight for, a kind of socialist liberalism in racial matters, there were many others who could be easily caricatured by a figure like Alf Garnett on television. To some extent these others would be attracted by extreme right-wing movements provided that they shed their unpatriotic nostalgic support for Adolf Hitler. But some were to find their way into the Labour Party and leaders of the Labour right were well enough aware that keeping in touch with the masses meant showing some sensitivity to this xenophobia. More than that, some of them actually felt it themselves. And it must also be said that this kind of response was not entirely confined to the right of the party. The left was more likely to fight Gaitskell over his attempt to get rid of the party's clause 4 on nationalization than it was to support him in his stand against the Immigration Act of 1962.

The dilemma within the Labour Party was apparent as early as the Notting Hill riots of 1958. These riots were largely the work, it is true, of young men inspired by the extreme right-wing groups, but it is significant that the first comment made by the Labour MP for North Kensington after the riots was not to condemn the violence which had been committed against blacks but to demand legislation to curb what he called 'the tremendous influx' of coloured immigrants (Hiro, 1971). Any such comment, moreover, was likely to win strong support from a small group of influential and often union-backed MPs who almost automatically abstained from voting with the party on racial issues, such as, for instance, the setting up of the settler-dominated Central African Federation.

Looking back on the 1964 election campaign, it is remarkable to notice how little the Labour Party at that time made concessions to pressure on the race and immigration issues. Mr Wilson's line during the campaign was clear. The problems, as he saw them, were not problems of race at all. They were problems of under-provided and overstrained social services in the central city areas. He therefore undertook to give special aid to those areas which amongst other things had high concentrations of immigrants. The minister charged with carrying out his undertaking was Mr Richard Crossman, the new Minister of Housing.

We shall return in a moment to the factors which actually influenced Mr Crossman's thinking on these matters. Here, however, it is important that we should notice the dramatic change in the Labour policy towards immigration between their 1964 election victory and the publication not long before the 1965 party conference of a White Paper on Commonwealth immigration. Impressed by the populist pressure which had resulted in Mr Gordon Walker's two defeats at Smethwick and Leyton, a Cabinet committee headed by Mr Herbert Bowden rushed through the White Paper with scant regard to the investigations which some of its members were carrying out on behalf of the party.[6] When the White Paper was presented to the party conference in the autumn, its principal defender was Mr Robert Mellish. Mr Mellish's speech deserves notice because of the extent to which it has absorbed populist sentiment and the carelessness with which he refers to the possibility of racial violence. The key paragraph in his speech reads as follows:

'Am I, as Parliamentary Secretary, to go to Lambeth, which has
a waiting list of 10,000 of its own people, and ask them to
give preference to the coloured people who have come in? If
you ask me to do that and say that this is a socialist approach,
I say to you frankly and fairly I shall be asking Lambeth to
create the most grievous racial disturbance we have ever seen
in London' (Rex, 1968).

Shortly after this Mr Mellish was given responsibility by Mr

Crossman for immigrant housing. This is not surprising because he accepted fully what was now the normal Labour Party thinking on these matters, namely that the immigrants were placing an undue strain on the social services. Mr Crossman, however, probably knew better than this. He saw the question of immigration almost entirely in electoral terms. Thus he writes in his diaries, which are an invaluable source both in relation to his own thinking and that of his colleagues,

> This has been one of the most difficult and unpleasant jobs the government has had to do. We have become illiberal and lowered the quotas at a time when we have an acute shortage of labour. No wonder the week-end liberal papers have been bitterly attacking us. Nevertheless I am convinced that if we hadn't done all this we would have been faced with certain electoral defeat in the West Midlands and the South East. Politically, fear of immigration is the most powerful undertow to-day. . . . We felt we had to out-trump the Tories by doing what they would have done and so transforming their policy into a bi-partisan policy. . . . On the other hand I can't overestimate the shock to the party. This will confirm the feeling that ours is not a socialist government, that it is surrendering to pressure. . . . If only we had had a Home Secretary who could have done this as a matter of principle and done it strongly and early (Crossman, 1975, p. 299).

It is clear that whatever the ideals of the Labour Party, one of its leading intellectuals, and the one moreover more responsible for the integration of immigrants than any other, had accepted that the Labour Party had no option in this matter than to accept the electoral undertow. On racial matters the Labour Party was likely after this to be responsive to, if not the actual vehicle of, populist anti-immigrant feeling. That Crossman's choice was not inevitable has been argued elsewhere (Rex, 1968), but the fact it that was made in the direction in which it was is a fact of history and one which subsequently structured the whole situation in which the immigrants found themselves.

Crossman's reaction to his mandate to give special aid to areas of urban stress as a means of taking the steam out of the immigrant problem was to insist that special aid to immigrant areas as such should be avoided because this would smack of positive discrimination which would in turn exacerbate hostility to the immigrants. At best, this could be thought of as doing good by stealth and this indeed was the inevitable trend of Labour policy after it had been decided that any pro-immigrant stand would have unacceptable electoral consequences. Of more immediate importance, however, was the notion that the problem was a problem simply of general social service provision and that the immigrants were placing an undue strain on the services.

There have been a number of academic attempts to assess the actual demand placed by immigrants on the social services. The upshot of these studies seems to be that, while overall immigrants take far less out of the social services than do their British counterparts, there are some particular services, such as education and child care, in which they present special problems and do require additional expenditure. This has not prevented the British public, according to opinion polls, from believing that the services are being milked by immigrants. One leading trade-unionist indeed seemed to suggest that this was a major cause of the perpetual economic crisis with which the Labour Government seemed to be faced. Thus, Sir William Carron, in his valedictory address to his union, had this to say:

> 'It would be interesting to obtain detailed statistics applying to the grand total that is consumed in education grants, National Health expenses and subsistence payments that became immediately obtainable by the ever-growing number of individuals who are not born in this country and in no way contribute to the fund into which they so willingly dip their fingers. As they succinctly put it, "they know their rights". It would be very acceptable to some of us if some small measure of appreciation and thanks were in visible evidence' (Rex, 1973b).

Lord Carron, as he was to become shortly after this speech, was no maverick. He was a pillar of the right-wing Labour and trade-union establishment. What he was representing in sharp terms was a commonly held view amongst working-class people that immigrants were competitors for a limited social service fund and that they were getting more than their fair share. It was quite common, therefore, to find Labour politicians arguing against positive discrimination in favour of immigrants in situations in which the immigrants were actually suffering grievously from discrimination. Nowhere is this more apparent than in the Labour Party's approach to housing, characteristically represented in the White Paper on immigration by a warning against discrimination in favour of immigrants, despite the fact that all immigrants already suffered the penalty of a five-year wait before they could even begin to qualify for points on many local authority housing lists.

The conclusion which we must draw from all this is that, whatever else the Labour Party was, it was not an organization representative of immigrant worker interests. More than this, it would seek to show in public that it was positively anti-immigrant. What then was the effect of this stance on the liberal impulse within the party and the abstract commitment to the 'brotherhood of man' which Mr Deedes rightly says to be part of the Labour Party creed?

In the first place, these anti-immigrant attitudes were likely seriously to limit any action which the party might wish to take to establish legal machinery to fight against discrimination. Thus both Race Relations Acts introduced by the Labour Party were introduced almost ritualistically, at the very times when the party was trying hardest to win electoral support by anti-immigration measures, and the Acts themselves were considerably modified in response to pressure from trades unions and local Labour councils.

Second, the feeling grew amongst those better informed Labour ministers that, if the disadvantage which the immigrants were clearly suffering according to the evidence of two PEP reports were to be dealt with, it had to be dealt with by stealth. During the course of our research, we were urged by someone with close contacts with government thinking on these matters in 1976, that the best thing we could do would be to suggest some way in which money could be spent so as to help the black population, without actually mentioning that this was the intention of the expenditure. We believe that the sudden move by the Department of the Environment to redirect aid from the suburban areas and new towns (DOE, 1977b) was intended as a move in this direction. It was supported by both parties and was justified in terms of a new ideology which suggested that racial tension, along with many other evils, was the product of some barely understood and mysterious process called 'urban blight'. Apart from the fact that this doctrine avoided any politically danger-ous suggestions of human responsibility, it was also positively mis-leading, for there is no certainty that spending money on the inner-city area will bring help to immigrants. It might simply lead to an inward migration of more privileged sections of the community, while immigrant areas continue to decay between the new thriving factories and offices.

The third way in which the liberal and socialist impulse within Labour thinking becomes diverted is that it finds an expression in the militant activities of the Trotskyist and Maoist sects which form the labour movement's far left. Significantly the Labour Party has little representation amongst students at the present time. Elections to student representative councils are commonly fought between the so-called Broad Left, an alliance of Communist and Labour supporters, the International Socialists, a group which has now formed the Socialist Workers' Party, the International Marxist Group, the Anarchists, the Liberals and the Conservatives. There has been some resurgence of right-wing forces recently, as demonstrated by Conservative victories in several unions, and the Broad Left has shown rather less taste for direct action, but all unions are under pressure from their Marxist, anarchist and, sometimes, liberal factions, to turn their backs on Parliamentary politics and to engage in direct action. No such action has more idealistic appeal than that which is concerned with opposing racialism by direct street confrontations with the forces of the extreme right, represented in 1976 and 1977 particularly by the marches of the National Front.

The Front itself is, of course, one of the more significant developments of the 1970s. Its doctrines and its methods were such that it was able to elicit reponses which Powellism could not do, and, probably, would not wish to have done. But it did succeed both in gaining working-class support and acting as pacemaker for change in Conservative Party thinking in an anti-immigrant direction. Before Enoch Powell made his most famous speech in Birmingham the Front had called for a policy which would 'preserve our British native stock in the United Kingdom (and) prevent increased strife such as seen in the United States by terminating non-white immigration with human and orderly repatriation of non-white immigrants' (*The Times*, 24 April 1968).

It recruited many working-class conservatives when the Conservative Party reluctantly accepted its responsibilities and admitted 27,000 Ugandan Asians in 1972, and subsequently its candidate was able to stand without losing his deposit in the West Bromwich by-election, while candidates in other Midlands by-elections beat the Liberals into fourth place at Birmingham Stechford and Birmingham Ladywood. Clearly the National Front had become a small but significant political force in Britain.

In this chapter we have shown how idealistic elements in the ideologies of conservative imperialism, of liberalism and of labourist socialism, collapsed in the face of anti-immigrant agitation. Thus, despite sporadic attempts to oppose first Griffiths and then Powell (Wilson had called Griffiths a Parliamentary leper and Heath had responded to Powell's Birmingham speech by dropping him immediately from the shadow cabinet), in the long run their views became the common currency of political debate. Powell indeed received even greater recognition. Again and again he was represented in the media as being one of the outstanding intellectuals in politics and his views received coverage not merely in political and documentary programmes on television, but quite commonly in religious programmes on television. Indeed, concern about the threat of immigration to the nation came to be treated almost as a sacred matter. It was therefore no surprise that Dr Coggan, the successor to Dr Ramsey, who had always fought for immigrants against racialism, saw it as part of his arch-episcopal function to call for a limitation to immigration at a time when there were few immigrants other than dependents coming into the country.

What we are saying in this chapter should need no further underlining. But in case the diverse strands of our analysis permit any other conclusion, we now repeat that by the mid-1970s, whatever the humane traditions of conservatism, the concern for human rights of liberalism, or the internationalism of the unions and labour, there was effective agreement amongst the majority of each of those parties that coloured immigration must be limited and that any special effort to help coloured immigrants to overcome discrimination was electorally unprofitable. At best, immigrants were to be tolerated, but, on the whole, the consensus was that this was a dangerous element outside normal politics and outside the normal class system. The immigrants were frequently treated as scapegoats for the economic ills which beset the community, and, if they occasionally engaged in outbursts of violence or joined in the often ill-considered attempts of the extreme left to defend them against the National Front, they were blamed as much as anyone for the breakdown of law and order.

Two factors operated against this political consensus. One was the fact that throughout the social services, in local government and occasionally amongst idealistic city councillors, particular problems were faced in terms of professional traditions, and those traditions had a life of their own, at least partially independent of the racialist storms which were blowing. The other was the defensive reaction of the black community itself.

So far as the professionals were concerned, we have to admit that looking at Birmingham some twelve years after one of us was involved in a study of Sparkbrook, we were impressed to find a new cadre of teachers, local government officers, voluntary workers and, occasionally, councillors, who were not simply dealing with problems in terms of the new national anti-immigrant ideology, but rather trying pragmatically, to solve the problem before them. They were not, of course, immune to prejudice and often used little bits of academic knowledge to justify their own discriminatory acts or the immigrants' failure. But to call them racists would be absurd. There were, for instance, teachers who, whatever their political opinions, either in general or on the racial question, when they encountered the problems of low reading age amongst West Indian children, dealt with it as a problem of low reading age and applied whatever techniques they had at their disposal to solving it. Similarly, although perhaps less frequently, there were housing department officials who defined their problems professionally in housing terms and to some extent avoided the cruder forms of discrimination. And, if this were true at local level, it was probably even more true at the level of the

65

national civil service, where the normal stiff-necked refusal of one department to understand another, and of all of them to understand or communicate clearly with their political masters, meant that there were some policy areas which were kept partially immune from racist pressure.

The above paragraph should not be misinterpreted. We do not intend to give all professionals a clean bill of health on the race question. What we are saying, however, is that the existence of professional traditions and the relative independence with which professionals and bureaucrats sometimes operate, means that we should by no means treat these professionals and bureaucrats simply as the agents of prejudice and oppression or, as popular Marxist academic jargon now has it, as part of the repressive or the ideological state apparatus. There is much scope for communication between academics and professionals, and, whatever convictions one might have about our governmental agencies being subject to political control, there is always still a fruitful possibility of an expert's paper coming up through the bureaucracy, and, by its technical expertise, blinding a hapless politician who has to translate it into action with 'science'.[7]

Our concluding introductory notes must deal with the immigrant response to the situation in which their communities find themselves. The chronology of events which is outlined above should serve to show the direction of change in this matter. From an initial posture of subservience, compliance and accommodation, nearly all immigrants who engage in political activity have moved to more and more militant attitudes, and there is little sign that this process will be reversed.

Effective immigrant organization to deal with growing discrimination and racism could perhaps be said to have begun when the Standing Conference of West Indian Organizations was formed at the instance of the West Indian High Commission after the Notting Hill riots, though there had, of course, been many immigrant organizations before that, not least the Indian Workers' Association, whose history goes back to the 1930s.

The West Indian Standing Conference was an umbrella organization which brought together numerous committees and organizations, some of them with paper membership only. At first its member organizations, where they were active, were compliant and accommodating, but very quickly after the passing of the 1962 Act, it began to affiliate more militant organizations, it broke its link with the West Indian Commission and was challenged from within by new ideologies, particularly those with a Third World and Black Power orientation.

A crucial question which the Standing Conference had to face was its attitude, first to CARD and then to the NCCI. After some hesitation it joined CARD but left when the West Indian leader, Dr David Pitt, together with the Pakistani political scientist, Hamza Alavi, who had been members of CARD's executive, joined the NCCI. They also complained that members of CARD's executive had engaged in private discussions with the Labour Party, which resulted in the use of criminal proceedings against those who offended against the Race Relations Act being replaced by the notion of conciliation machinery. Shortly after this, in any case, CARD collapsed, when a large number of West Indian organizations, some of them allegedly fictitious, joined CARD in an attempt to overthrow the liberal group which was headed by Dipak Nandy and Anthony Lester (see Hiro, 1971).

The NCCI never succeeded in establishing effective contact with grass-roots organizations but it did make contact with a new stratum of black, salaried officials who were employed by local voluntary immigrant liaison committees. When the Community Relations Commission was established, these officials became even better organized on behalf of the Government and its policies, and elite leaders from local communities were co-opted to sit on its committees.

The NCCI and the CRC are mentioned here, however, only as a negative reference point. The fact of the matter was that most effective black organizations had little to do with the CRC or its local councils or, even if they sat on the councils, they did so only as a tactical manoeuvre, More commonly the West Indians at least joined organizations with Black Power and Third World orientations. Malcolm X, the former Black Muslim leader, visited England in February 1965 and was the inspiration behind the formation of the Racial Adjustment Action Society. In June 1967 the Universal Coloured People's Organization was formed, and invited Stokeley Carmichael, the American black student leader, to speak. Many other organizations of this kind were formed and, though many of them were ephemeral, they began to explore new possibilities of independent political and industrial action by immigrants. The Racial Adjustment Action Society, for example, gave immediate support to the Asian workers' strike at Courtaulds in Lancashire. It was no longer the case that immigrants looked to the major British political parties for their self-defence. However unclear they might have been about long-term strategy, they came to be more and more suspicious of white allies and more inclined to trust their own strength.

One particular problem which faced the immigrants was that of what they should do about the National Front's demonstrations and the counter-demonstrations which they provoked. Liberal opinion amongst whites was almost unanimous in arguing that the Front's marches should be ignored rather than opposed, while the Trotskyist groups organized for their own reasons behind the slogan 'Smash the National Front'. In these circumstances some branches of the Indian Workers' Association decided to support the anti-Front marches and, whatever their organizational leaders said, young Asians and West Indians joined in these marches. It seemed that, having lost faith in the orthodox political parties, the younger immigrants felt that they had no option but to support the extreme left, though some might well have intended that they should use the left sects' activities for their own purposes, rather than for the purposes of the left.

A question worth asking is what the ordinary immigrant felt about these developments, because not all immigrants by any means were involved in organizations. The pages which follow contain much evidence on this question which divides into two streams. On the one hand are the vast majority of those who settled as immigrants between 1950 and 1965 who are concerned with their own domestic and job problems, who know that discrimination exists, but have decided to make the best of it, improving their homes and staying steadily in a job. On the other, there are the young who have been born in England or at least partly educated here. Very few of them are in organizations but many of them complain about discrimination in employment and about relations with the police, who, they say, harass them.

While many of the older immigrants represent a somewhat conservative force and were on the whole critical of the delinquency of the younger generation, we found in conversation with them that they were also very much afraid of potential white aggression. Thus, although they may not actively support the new militant political organizations they are certainly not critical of them except to complain that 'leaders' in general do not stand up for the people sufficiently.

So far as the young are concerned, they too are unlikely to belong to formal organizations, but they are increasingly race conscious and show little respect for the police. Many of them wear characteristically West Indian woolly hats, some with the Rastafari colours, and some grow their hair in Dreadlocks like the followers of Rastafari Partly these outward signs are simply signs of affiliation to a West Indian youth culture, but whether they are conscious of it or not they have political significance. The police take the Rastafari symbols to be signs of truculence and are more likely to stop and question a youth dressed in this way. Naturally enough, with youth unemployment high and an absence of a feeling of the legitimacy of police authority, a fair number of them do become involved in crimes against property and crimes of violence.

It must surely be expected that, with all the idealisms centring around the idea of racial equality having collapsed, with a paternalistic system established for the administration of race relations, and with overtly racist organizations being allowed to march into immigrant areas, blacks will prepare to defend themselves. If a judge in Brixton sentencing blacks for robbing white women calls for the setting up of vigilante squads, then blacks, faced with a long catalogue of violence against black men and women usually coupled with an assurance from the police that the violence is not necessarily racist in intent, are likely to form their vigilante squads too.

The battles which take place in the streets today are largely symbolic. Moreover, even if the percentage of blacks in the total population reaches 7 per cent by 2000, as the best estimates suggest, there can be little hope of a black revolution. The street battles are, however, a symbol of something, namely that black immigrants in Britain have, in the course of political debate, in the treatment of topics connected with them in the media, and in the statements of public officials, been stigmatized as an inferior group. Many, of course, will find their way into the working-class mainstream, despite all the abuse which a growing racism may heap upon them. But others will fight, even if they lack all hope, and that fight will go on, until, integrated into the main community or not, they will win respect for themselves, and the ordinary legal, political and social rights of Englishmen.

We do not simply wish to end this chapter on a note of rhetoric. It is therefore important to emphasize that, in speaking to politically articulate West Indians in organizations, we found that the language which they used was far more violent and the attitudes they expressed more militant than anything we have suggested here. It seems reasonable therefore to suggest that, if present definitions of the immigrant and the black Englishman prevail amongst the native population, we may expect to see continuing and deepening conflict, even if the contemporary militant leaders of the immigrant organizations seek, in a 'statesman-like' way, to damp down the hostility. This was the implication of the events in Notting Hill at the summer carnivals of 1976 and 1977. It is against this background that we undertook our study of racial discrimination and race relations in Birmingham.

3 Handsworth—the population and social structure of a multi-racial area

Given our view of the way in which class-conflict situations occur within any of the major institutional systems through which resources and life-chances are allocated, it might be thought that we should now continue directly to a discussion of employment, housing and education. First, however, we propose to begin with a discussion of the populations of different ethnicity who inhabit a particular part of the city. We do so for three reasons. The first and the least of these is that the collection of survey evidence leads naturally to the study of a sample population sharing a common locale. The second is that we believe it to be the case that the race relations problem in Birmingham was perceived above all as a problem of conflict between peoples living in the same neighbourhoods. Finally, we believe that the differential distribution of various demographic, economic, cultural and social characteristics in the different ethnic populations says something about the kinds of class and other groupings which were being formed within each ethnic community.

Handsworth, however, is not simply a particular stretch of urban territory which we happen to have chosen for our research. It is a symbol of areas of black, and particularly West Indian, settlement in Birmingham and possibly of black immigrant settlement in Britain as a whole. Obviously there are some areas of greater immigrant concentration in London, such as Brixton, Ealing or Willesden, but arguably, since these are part of the main metropolitan area of Great Britain, they are subject to some special circumstances which make them atypical. While Handsworth and Birmingham are provincial, on the other hand, it is hard to conceive of a scenario in the development of race relations in Britain in which they do not figure importantly. Certainly one could say that outside London, Handsworth is one of Britain's race relations capitals.

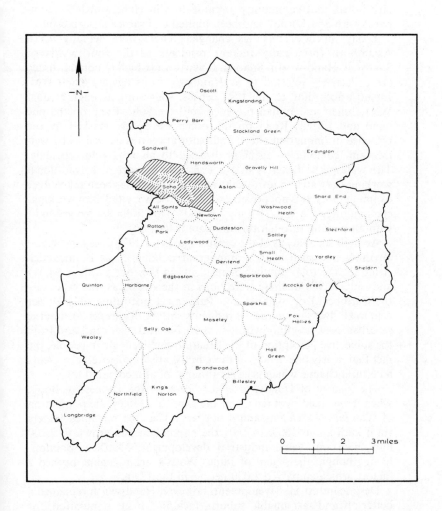

FIGURE 3.1 *Ward map of the City of Birmingham (excluding Sutton Coldfield) indicating the survey area*

Handsworth's importance has increased in the race relations field since the early 1960s. At that time Rex and Moore were attracted to Sparkbrook as a representative immigrant area in the twilight zone or the zone of transition. They saw it as typifying particularly the lodging-house phenomenon and problems of conflict and community organization in such an area. Handsworth they referred to as a characteristically West Indian area as compared with Sparkbrook which was mixed, but Pakistani and Irish dominated. They also noted that community organization in Handsworth as compared with Sparkbrook had been limited and rather unsuccessful.

Today much of this has changed. There were actually 9,116 Asian-born (principally Indian) residents in the four wards of Sandwell, Handsworth, Soho and Newtown (which in popular usage are collectively referred to as Handsworth) as against 8,880 West Indians, according to the 1971 census, suggesting a roughly equal West Indian and Indian presence, and the Soho Road on the one hand and Lozells Road on the other are clearly marked by the presence of immigrant shops and cultural centres as well as by welfare and community agencies directed to an immigrant clientele. The widespread belief is that a considerable part of a traditional working-class area in north central Birmingham has been taken over by immigrants. It is not possible to visit those two citadels of working-class culture, the West Bromwich and Aston Villa soccer grounds, without passing through this immigrant territory.

Actually an analysis of the census figures for 1971 does not suggest anything like such a great immigrant dominance as is imagined. After all, the total number of residents in the four wards is 94,087 and only 17,996 of these were born in the Americas (i.e. especially the Caribbean) or in India and Pakistan, constituting only 19 per cent in all. But the number of residents with both parents born in the so-called New Commonwealth was 29,740 or 31 per cent, and from the subjective perception of the situation by Birmingham people, the fact that nearly one person in three in the area is coloured represents a cultural change which is easily thought of as a coloured take-over.

The history of Handsworth goes back to the Domesday Book, when it was held by a tenant of the Lord of Dudley. Its population in 1086 was '14 villains and 4 bordars'. The area remained largely rural until about 1800. In 1801 the population had grown to 2,200 and there was some industrial development. Matthew Boulton, having bought the patent of James Watts's steam engine, opened a factory which employed 1,000 people in the 1790s.

Despite industrial development, however, Handsworth remained a better-off and fashionable suburb, including in its population, for example, wealthy jewellers from the jewellery quarter immediately to the south. But with the development of the tramway, working-class

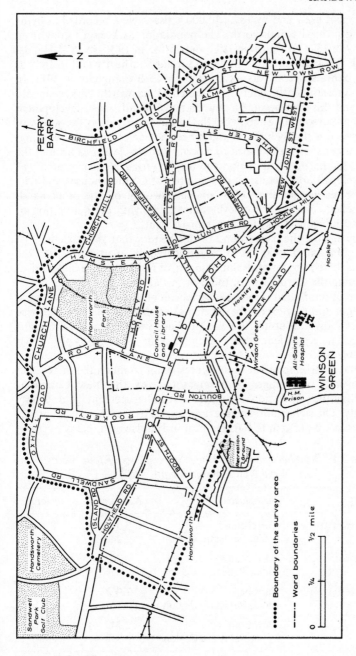

FIGURE 3.2 *The survey area*

settlement grew and by 1890, 10,000 artisans were recorded as living in and around Handsworth. The population as a whole grew from 14,359 in 1871 to 68,610 in 1911 and 75,145 in 1921. In 1874 Handsworth was constituted as an urban sanitary authority and in 1888 as an urban district. It was incorporated into Birmingham in 1911. In 1904 Victoria Park, later to be called Handsworth Park, was laid out, and this area became a new centre of middle-class development in villas surrounding the park. In the inter-war period the whole of the area was finally built on and it became one of the main working-class inner suburbs attached to a better middle-class area around the park. In the post-war period the neighbouring Newtown area was redeveloped and a considerable number of Council houses and flats were built in that area. Most of Handsworth, on the other hand, was scheduled, not for redevelopment (implying the demolition of the old housing stock) but for improvement.

It is against the background of this history that the settlement of immigrants after 1950 has to be considered. At the time of the 1951 census there were insignificant numbers of residents born in America, including the Caribbean, in India or in Pakistan. In 1961 the distribution of immigrants from the Caribbean on the one hand and India, Pakistan and Ceylon on the other, was as shown in Table 3.1. These figures show that up to 1961 West Indians were the main immigrant group. The equivalent figures taken from the 1971 census are shown in Table 3.2.

What is striking about these figures is not so much the increase in the overall percentages of immigrants from the New Commonwealth in the population, since the West Indian percentage rises only slightly. The significant increase is amongst Asians whose percentages rise from 1·3 per cent to 7·65 per cent in Handsworth, 1·2 per cent to

TABLE 3.1   *Numbers and percentages of residents of four wards born in the New Commonwealth – 1961*

Ward	Birthplace	Numbers	% of total
Handsworth	Caribbean	2,307	8.4
	India, Pakistan, Ceylon	349	1.3
Newtown	Caribbean	302	1.0
	India, Pakistan, Ceylon	356	1.2
Sandwell	Caribbean	1,027	3.6
	India, Pakistan, Ceylon	167	0.6
Soho	Caribbean	2,749	10.5
	India, Pakistan, Ceylon	732	2.8

Source: Census of Population 1961, County Report, Warwickshire.

TABLE 3.2 *Numbers and percentages of residents in four wards born in the New Commonwealth – 1971*

Ward	Birthplace	Numbers	% of total
Handsworth	America	3,291	11.1
	India	1,461	5.3
	Pakistan	655	2.35
Newtown*	America	599	4.8
	India	411	3.3
	Pakistan	336	2.7
Sandwell	America	2,086	7.3
	India	1,337	4.7
	Pakistan	140	0.5
Soho	America	2,904	11.3
	India	4,333	16.8
	Pakistan	443	1.7

Source: Census of Population 1971, County Report, Warwickshire.
   *The total resident population in Newtown had declined from 30,198 in 1961 to 12,377 in 1971 due to slum clearance.

6 per cent in Newtown, 0·6 per cent to 5·2 per cent in Sandwell and 2·8 per cent to 18·5 per cent in Soho.

We may conclude from these figures that while the four wards were a largely white working-class area in 1951, by 1961 two of them were marked by the presence of a significant West Indian minority, while by 1971 West Indians and Asians were present in almost equal numbers, with Asians representing nearly one in five of the population in Soho ward. It was during the latter decennial period that Handsworth became regarded as a problem area. By this time, taking account of children born to New Commonwealth immigrants, the population percentages of New Commonwealth immigrants and their children for the four wards were:

Handsworth	32·5 per cent
Newtown	16·6 per cent
Sandwell	20·0 per cent
Soho	48·0 per cent

Suddenly, then, 'Handsworth' (meaning the four wards) had become a 'black' area in the eyes of Birmingham and the terms 'black' or 'immigrant' came to mean 'undesirable', combining all the characteristics of both West Indian and Asian areas considered to be problematic.

We drew a sample of 300 West Indians, 300 Asians and 300 whites from the 128 enumeration districts in the four wards with the highest

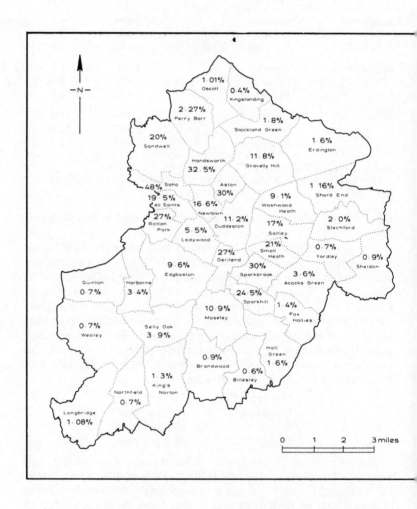

FIGURE 3.3   *Birmingham immigrants with both parents born in the
New Commonwealth, as a percentage of total enumerated
ward population 1971 Census*

concentrations of immigrants, together with a sample of 100 white and 100 immigrant council tenants in Newtown. Ninety-five of the immigrant council tenants were West Indian and 5 Asian. There were 42 white, 27 West Indian and 14 Asians in the main sample in council properties. The methodological problems involved in the construction of these samples are discussed in Appendix 2. Here it should be noted that after comparing our tables with tables which allowed a weighting, because of the different types of sampling used in the main sample and the council sample, we found that there was little difference in the percentages obtained. We therefore decided simply to aggregate the numbers for each group drawn from the main sample and the council house sample except in the case of our chapter on housing where the two samples are discussed separately.

In the total sample we found that 83 per cent of West Indian respondents had arrived between 1954 and 1962 while 65·25 per cent of Asian respondents had come between 1960 and 1968. These figures confirm the picture of the area becoming West Indianized in the 1950s and the supplementation of the West Indian presence by Asians occurring in the 1960s.

We found these people in 1976 in what were basically four types of housing in the area. There were houses which were simply left to themselves by the Council because they were structurally perfectly adequate, although some of them might be registered as in multiple-occupation. There were a few remaining houses in redevelopment areas still awaiting demolition and some in housing action areas likely to be demolished. There were an overwhelming majority in improvement areas and in housing action areas which were not scheduled for demolition and which, although on the whole in poor repair and of poor appearance, were envisaged as suitable for improvement. Finally there were council-built dwellings.

The immediate striking difference which appears from the survey data is the age structure of the immigrant as compared with the native-born population, shown in Table 3.3.

Over 50 per cent of our white respondents were 60 and over,

TABLE 3.3   *Age of heads of household in sample by ethnic group*

	West Indian	Asian	British
16–34	16·2%	34·8%	13·3%
35–59	73·6%	60·6%	36·0%
60–74	8·4%	4·6%	36·7%
75 or more	0·5%	——	14·0%
refused	1·3%		
N	395	305	400

whereas only 8 per cent of our West Indian and 4·6 per cent of our Asian sample were over 60. Handsworth like many similar inner-urban areas, has a population consisting of elderly white residents living amongst younger black people. If, moreover, one leaves out of the white sample those in council properties, the percentage who are over 60 is even higher. Thus, although it is often said that Handsworth is a black ghetto it is worth noting that there are probably as many elderly (60+) white people living in these inner areas as there are black immigrants of all ages. Clearly the term 'ghetto' is inappropriate though. What we have is a part of the city where several different categories of people are concentrated. Rex and Moore drew attention to the fact that problem people along with immigrants were concentrated in the twilight zone in Sparkbrook. In Handsworth, although no particular effort was made to find problem people, it would seem that the white population had not gravitated there because they had problems. They were simply the native-born population who had aged while staying where they were, though they may, of course, have been subject to negative selection, the unsuccessful remnant who remained while the successful migrated to the suburbs.

The other side of the same coin, of course, is the high proportion of West Indian and Asian immigrants who are in the age-group 25–59. In both groups about 86 per cent of the heads of households in our sample were from this age-group, whereas only 46·5 per cent of the white householders were.

In terms of marital status there are sharp divisions. Amongst the West Indians 73·9 per cent are married while 11·4 per cent are divorced or separated. Amongst the Asians no less than 91 per cent are married. Amongst the whites 58·5 per cent are married and 21·56 per cent widowed. Some 31·75 per cent of British household heads, 21·8 per cent of West Indian, but only 2·6 per cent of Asian are females. The percentages of households in each group which consist of a couple with children are 61·36 per cent for the West Indians, 68·8 per cent for the Asians and 26·3 per cent for the whites. Of all white households, 20·5 per cent consist of a single person. Table 3.4 gives the household structures for the three groups.

The mean household size amongst West Indians was 4·713, amongst Asians 6·366 and amongst whites 2·64. The percentage of families having more than two children was 50·5 per cent amongst the West Indians, 49·7 per cent amongst the Asians, and only 7·3 per cent amongst the whites. Asian households were larger partly as a result of having more children and partly as a result of having more adult relatives attached to the same household. More striking, however, than the large Asian family was the small white one. In over 72·8 per cent of the families whose heads were interviewed amongst

TABLE 3.4 *Household structure of sample by ethnic group*

	West Indian	Asian	British
Single person or couple with no children	11·9%	13·1%	49·0%
Single + children	17·2%	2·9%	12·8%
Couple + children	61·3%	68·3%	26·3%
Other	9·6%	15·7%	12·2%
N	395	305	400

the whites there were no dependent children. Inevitably this means that, although the highest percentage of immigrants in a ward's population is 48 per cent in Soho, percentages of children in school whose parents are immigrants are very high indeed, in one primary school as high as 94 per cent.

One further factor of the family structure of immigrants in Handsworth which deserves mention is the comparison with the population described by Rex and Moore in Sparkbrook. Although it is true that the categories of divorced and separated and single persons are larger amongst West Indians than other groups and there is a minority of single-parent families, the rate of marriage amongst West Indians is high and the West Indian family seems to have moved towards an English norm. Amongst the Asians, on the other hand, since 68·3 per cent of all households consisted of a couple with children, there seems to have been a considerable change since 1964 in Sparkbrook, where there were very few Asian children and a great many households consisting of groups of single men.

Clearly this population had transcended, not merely the special problems which led to the rush of migration between 1960 and 1962, but some of the more general problems of family strain undergone by migrant populations. We are talking now of fairly well-established migrant families. Moreover, in answer to our question as to whether any of the householders had children, spouses or parents still wanting to immigrate into Britain, we found that there were only 18 children and 6 parents amongst the West Indians, and 44 children, 5 spouses and 25 parents amongst the Asians, i.e. a total of 98 dependents still to come to 700 households consisting of about 3,600 people.

The economic statistics were roughly in accordance with what one would have expected from the demographic ones. Table 3.5 shows the percentage of each group in our survey who were working, unemployed or retired. The two facts worth noting in this table are the high percentage of retired people and widows amongst whites, and the rather higher rates of unemployment amongst immigrants.

TABLE 3.5 *Economic activity of householders in sample by ethnic group*

	West Indian	Asian	British
Working	77·5% (306)	77·7% (237)	49·4% (197)
Not working	19·0% (75)	19·3% (59)	13·3% (54)
Retired	3·3% (13)	1·3% (4)	29·5% (118)
Never worked	0·3% (1)	1·6% (5)	7·8% (31)

The 'social class' of our respondents is shown in Table 3.6. The West Indian and Asian class distributions are very similar except for a slightly greater likelihood that an Asian worker will be in the skilled working class C.2. On the other hand, nearly a quarter of all whites are in the white-collar groups A/B and C.1 compared with only 6 per cent for both immigrant groups.

A total of 26 per cent of all West Indians and 21·9 per cent of Asians had worked in agriculture before coming to Britain, while 20·7 per cent of West Indians and 36 per cent of Asians were too young to have worked. Moreover, 55·9 per cent of West Indians and 39·3 per cent of Asians had fathers who worked in agriculture. Only 20 per cent of West Indians and 6·5 per cent of Asians had worked in manufacturing before migrating, and the equivalent percentages for their fathers were 10·1 per cent and 13·4 per cent. Amongst the white sample, on the other hand, 44 per cent had fathers who had been in manufacturing employment. These figures and those for social class show that the white population has larger family experience of manufacturing industry and has risen to the higher class positions. For many immigrants, manufacturing employment is a new experience and they have, on the whole, gone into jobs requiring the lower grades of skill.

For what it was worth we asked all respondents what their personal

TABLE 3.6 *Social class* of householders in sample by ethnic group*

	West Indian	Asian	British
A/B	1·0% (4)	0·9% (3)	9·3% (37)
C.1	5·0% (20)	5·2% (16)	15·3% (61)
C.2	32·2% (127)	38·3% (117)	34·3% (135)
D	59·0% (233)	51·8% (158)	28·5% (114)
E	1·0% (4)	0·3% (1)	10·5% (42)
Never worked	1·8% (7)	3·4% (10)	1·8% (7)
Refused	(0)	(0)	0·3% (1)

*Standard Market Research categories.

income was, and 16 per cent refused to answer or did not know, but 79·2 per cent of West Indians, 81·6 per cent of Asians and 90·25 per cent of whites did answer. We discovered that 55·9 per cent of West Indians, 53 per cent of Asians and 71·4 per cent of whites were earning below £2,500 per year at a time when the average weekly wage for men and women was £46, or £2,392 per annum. Clearly the immigrants, in all groups in the area, came below the national average. The low earnings of whites, of course, are explicable in terms of their age and household structure.

The fact that the members of different ethnic groups are at different points of their life cycle means, of course, that there are considerable differences of interest between the groups. The younger immigrant groups, for example, are likely to be interested especially in the schools which are available for their children and in their proximity to work, whereas these are less important requirements for the elderly whites who are more likely to be interested in peace and quiet and the prestige of the area. Not surprisingly, therefore, when we turn to the answers given by members of our sample to questions about their relationship to their actual homes and to the area, we find sharp divergence of response.

The first striking fact which emerges from these answers, however, is not entirely one of divergence. We found that no less than 92·8 per cent of our white sample had been in the Birmingham area for 20 years or more and that only 7 of the 400 had come in in the last 3 years. On the other hand 26·8 per cent of the West Indians and 11·6 per cent of the Asians had been in Birmingham for 20 years or more, and 91·4 per cent of the West Indians and 86·6 per cent of the Asians for 10 years or more. It would seem, therefore, that book titles like *The Newcomers* and *Dark Strangers* are no longer entirely appropriate. Nor is sociological analysis in terms of the host/ strangers hypothesis. We are discussing white, West Indian and Asian Birmingham burghers for all of whom Handsworth really is home.

The ties of the members of all three samples are, moreover, not merely with Birmingham in general but with north central Birmingham (i.e. suburbs adjacent to Handsworth) in particular and with their present homes. Some 31·2 per cent of the West Indians, 36·6 per cent of the Asians and 50·9 per cent of the whites had lived in their present houses for 10 years or more, while only 7·3 per cent of the West Indians, 10·4 per cent of the Asians and 8 per cent of the whites had moved in from outside north central Birmingham in the last 10 years.

We asked immigrants from overseas both why they had come to Britain and why they had chosen the particular area, as well as whether they were satisfied with conditions in Britain and in the area.

In the case of the whites we asked simply about their satisfaction or dissatisfaction with the area and what its major problems were.

A large number of the immigrant samples, 33·4 per cent of West Indians and 46·6 per cent of the Asians, came because of the better economic prospects here as compared with their homeland, while 19·4 per cent of West Indies and 25·4 per cent of the Asians came because they were joining members of their families already here.

When we asked immigrants whether they had found life better or worse than they expected we obtained the responses shown in Table 3.7. It would seem that whether because their expectations were lower or because they had better experiences, far fewer Asians were even slightly disillusioned by the experience of migration. On the other hand, asked the more general question whether they were satisfied or dissatisfied with their life in Britain, 68·1 per cent of the West Indians and 88·8 per cent of the Asians said that they were satisfied.

All respondents were asked what they most liked and most disliked about Britain. About 40 per cent of the West Indians and Asians mentioned employment, wages and living standards as reasons for satisfaction, and 8·1 per cent of West Indians and 9·1 per cent of Asians mentioned the benefits of the welfare state. An interesting minority of 9·4 per cent of the West Indians and 9·1 per cent of the Asians, however, chose the answer 'individual freedom'. So far as dislikes were concerned, 43·3 per cent of West Indians and 25·5 per cent of Asians mentioned the weather, while 16·5 per cent of the West Indians and 38·3 per cent of the Asians said they liked everything. Only 13·4 per cent of the West Indians and 10·6 per cent of the Asians mentioned racial prejudice.

On the face of it these figures suggest a population which has either accepted or transcended the difficulties which beset immigrants, although we should remember that there is a dissatisfied minority in both ethnic groups, and that, since these were householders who had migrated themselves, it was always possible that their children might give different answers. To this point we shall return in a later chapter.

We felt that an important question to be put to the immigrant

TABLE 3.7 *Satisfaction with life in Britain amongst sample by ethnic group*

	West Indian	Asian
Better than expected	17·5% (69)	36·7% (112)
Worse than expected	42·3% (167)	8·8% (27)
As thought it would be	23·3% (92)	21·3% (65)
Don't know	17·0% (67)	33·1% (101)

groups concerned their intentions to settle permanently and their interest in the affairs 'back home'.

A rather surprising set of answers were given to the question, 'How interested are you in the news and politics of your country of birth?' The answers given are set out in Table 3.8.

Contrary to our expectations, the Asians gave more negative replies than the West Indians and this was so even in the case of a sub-sample of Asians interviewed by Asians. The same tendency was confirmed when we asked West Indians and Asians whether they wanted to go back to their own country or stay in Britain. Of West Indians, 65·3 per cent wanted to go back and only 19 per cent definitely wanted to stay in Britain, while amongst the Asians only 26·2 per cent wanted to go back, while 47·2 per cent definitely wanted to stay. Finally, when asked whether they had definite plans to return, more West Indians than Asians amongst those who had said they wanted to go back, said they had plans.

It might seem surprising in the light of all this that 67·8 per cent of Asians had been home since migrating while only 46·3 per cent of West Indians had. In fact, these various figures taken together indicate the different attitudes of the two groups to their homelands, to migration and to the country of migration. The Asian is committed permanently to being a migrant. He does return more for visits, but he is aware that his economic survival is tied up with life in Britain. The West Indian, on the other hand, is more likely to regard migration as an unfortunate necessity and his migrant status as temporary. He visits his homeland less, but is more likely to want to go back for good.

Questioned as to why they had come to live in the Handsworth area, 30 per cent of West Indians and 42·6 per cent of Asians said that they came because it was convenient for school or work or because they wanted to be near friends or relatives; 16·3 per cent of West Indians and 25 per cent of Asians said that they moved there because they liked the area. On the other hand, 18·1 per cent of West Indians felt that they had no choice but to accept a house for pur-

TABLE 3.8 *Interest in affairs of homeland amongst sample by ethnic group*

	West Indian	Asian
Very interested	15·4% (61)	14·4% (44)
Fairly interested	39·5% (155)	26·8% (82)
Not very interested	33·4% (132)	37·7% (115)
Not at all interested	10·1% (40)	17·7% (54)
Don't know	1·5% (6)	3·2% (10)

chase or rent in the private sector, and another 16 per cent felt that they had no option but to choose the council property in which they lived. Less than 5 per cent of Asians admitted to choosing their house under constraint in any way.

These figures do not, however, suggest that Handsworth was in fact an ideal area freely chosen as a home by large numbers of immigrants. Most people, when asked why they live where they do, are likely to give an optimistic account of their reasons. What is perhaps a most interesting point here is that 34 per cent of West Indians did feel that they acted under constraint. Here, as in many other matters, the Asians seem to have lower expectations and to accept constraints without noticing them, perhaps as an inevitable part of the privations of immigration.

Only 16·2 per cent of the West Indians and 11·8 per cent of the Asians expressed positive dislike of the area. Of those who expressed a positive liking for the area, the majority thought of Handsworth as providing a quiet and friendly environment, convenient for work and having good amenities. Reasons for disliking the area were varied, and 45·6 per cent of the West Indians and 54·7 per cent of the Asians could not find any particular cause for complaint. A minority of about 12 per cent in both groups were prepared to accept that the presence of coloured immigrants was a reason for disliking the area, although in the main these were West Indians complaining about Asians and vice versa. Another 12 per cent of the West Indians and 9 per cent of the Asians noted high levels of violence, crime and juvenile delinquency, although the element of juvenile delinquency was less prominent in Asian responses, possibly because their own children were less frequently in trouble.

We may now compare the responses of whites to the last few questions about the area since they are significantly different. Those who had moved house in the last ten years most commonly said that they did so because of convenience for work, to be near friends or relatives, or simply because they were born in the area. A minority of slightly less than 20 per cent said that they had no choice but to accept the rented council property offered, but very few felt that they were acting under constraint in choosing private property for purchase or rent. Thus, whereas the West Indians did feel to a significant degree that their housing choice was constrained, and the Asians probably were glad to have what they could get because of low expectations, the whites are attached to the area for traditional reasons only.

Altogether 41·8 per cent of whites, as compared with 27·8 per cent of West Indians and 16·3 per cent of Asians, were thinking of moving from the area, and the majority of these said they wished to do so because of the deterioration of the area. Of whites 46·5 per cent as compared with 16·2 per cent of West Indians and 11·8 per cent of Asians said that they disliked the area. This does not seem to be a factor strongly associated with social class, moreover, since while the percentage of them disliking the area who were from the skilled and semi-skilled working class was higher, so was the percentage of these groups liking the area.

Very striking, however, was the difference in the first mentioned reason for disliking the area. Of the whites 24·5 per cent mentioned physical deterioration of the area due to coloured people and 35 per cent merely said there were too many coloureds. Referring to amenities, moreover, whites were significantly less satisfied with shopping facilities, the schools and the quietness and safety of the area than the immigrant groups. All in all we can say that while Handsworth provided a relatively satisfactory and acceptable home for West Indians and even more so for Asians, the whites found many features of their changing environment and situation unacceptable, and a large minority were thinking of moving either to other Birmingham suburbs which were predominantly white or to other places in the Midlands. (None actually envisaged emigration from Britain.)

We asked our respondents how they thought the races got on with each other in Birmingham and obtained the replies shown in Table 3.9.

Clearly, while the West Indians, and to an even greater extent the Asians, think the races get on well, only 31 per cent of the whites were prepared to make this statement in an unqualified way. These figures, however, could be deceptive. The question asks the respondents to reflect not on the other groups but upon the relations between groups, and a negative response might seem to involve criticism of their own group. We do not know from these questions what West Indians and Asians thought of the whites and it is interesting that while 59·5 per cent of whites saw coloured immigrants as the most problematic factors for the area, only 37 per cent actually said that there were problems in race relations without also affirming that the

TABLE 3.9 *View of race relations amongst sample by ethnic group*

	West Indian	Asian	British
Races get on well	47·8% (189)	65·2% (199)	31·0% (124)
Races get on well but some problems	25·3% (100)	13·4% (41)	25·0% (100)
There are problems in race relations	16·0% (63)	7·5% (23)	37·0% (148)
Don't know	10·8% (43)	13·7% (42)	7·0% (28)

races got on well. What we may perhaps conclude is that there was more hostility between the races than is reflected in these figures, but that it was also asymmetrical in that the whites were far more inclined than the immigrants to see the existence of the opposing groups as giving rise to problems. This would imply that West Indians and Asians were actually unaware of, or were concealing from themselves, the extent of the hostility which was being directed against them.

The final set of indices which we have of the characteristics of the people of the area relate to religion and politics.

Religious affiliation is recorded in Table 3.10.

There is a surprising difference here between the British and West Indian Christians, in that although one might have expected a predominance of Nonconformist church membership in a white working-class area, a very high proportion of the population identified with the established church. Amongst the West Indians, on the other hand, what one might call orthodox Nonconformity predominated while Church of England membership and Pentecostalism represented minority trends. We did not include Rastafarianism as an option here and this may have been an error. On the other hand, Rastafarianism is a pervasive cultural phenomenon which might have overlapped with these categories. We believe that although, culturally speaking, it is very important indeed, actual membership of the Rastafarian church is small. The break-down of Asian religious affiliation shows that the Asians are a varied group, and though Sikhs are the predominant group, 58·7 per cent are not Sikhs. For the Sikhs the temple is an extremely important meeting-place. There is also a Hindu temple in Heathfield Road in Handsworth, but Hindu religion is practised as much at home as in the

TABLE 3.10 *Religious affiliation of sample by ethnic group*

	West Indian		Asian		British	
No religion	12·4%	(49)	1·7%	(5)	5·0%	(20)
Buddhist	0·3%	(1)	0·7%	(2)		(0)
Muslim	0·3%	(1)	19·3%	(59)		(0)
Hindu		(0)	32·1%	(98)		(0)
Sikh		(0)	41·3%	(126)		(0)
Church of England	22·3%	(88)	2·6%	(8)	73·6%	(295)
Methodist/Baptist	37·7%	(149)	0·6%	(2)	7·3%	(29)
Pentecostal	17·0%	(67)		(0)	1·3%	(5)
Roman Catholic	4·3%	(17)	0·9%	(3)	8·3%	(33)
Other	5·8%	(23)	0·3%	(1)	4·5%	(18)
Refused to answer		(0)	0·3%	(1)		(0)

temple. There is a main Birmingham mosque but a number of houses have been converted for use as mosques.

The question 'Which political party does most for people like you?' produced the cynical response 'none' from 32 per cent of the British and 27·8 per cent of the West Indians but only 18·3 per cent of the Asians. The Asians produced the largest group which looked to the Labour Party (49·8 per cent), while the British produced more Conservative (25·3 per cent) and Liberal (5·3 per cent) supporters than either the West Indians or Asians. Of West Indians 5·1 per cent looked to the Conservative Party and 0·8 per cent to the Liberals. Of Asians 0·3 per cent looked to the Conservatives and none to the Liberals. The West Indians who looked to the Labour Party constituted 35·2 per cent of all West Indians, and compared with only 21·8 per cent of British who looked to Labour.

The differences in voting between the groups were even more marked. Altogether 69·8 per cent of Asians, 63·0 per cent of West Indians and 36·0 per cent of the British sample had voted Labour in the October 1974 general election, whereas 3·0 per cent of West Indians, 3·2 per cent of Asians and 33·3 per cent of the British had voted Conservative. Only 3 West Indians and one Asian had voted Liberal as compared with 31 (7·8 per cent) of the British.

In the local election the Asians were twice as likely to have voted than the British, who were rather more likely to have voted than the West Indians. Of those who did vote, two-thirds of West Indians voted Labour, three-quarters of Asians voted Labour, but only a little more than one in three British. More than 50 per cent of the British votes cast went to the Conservatives.

The two things which stand out from these figures are, first, that the Asians are politically highly active and that they look to the Labour Party more than the other groups do to help them; and second, that, although the percentage of Labour voters is higher than the percentage of Conservatives amongst the British in the general election, there is a substantial Conservative vote in this group and an overall majority vote in local elections.

It would seem as though the Labour Party can expect better support from the immigrant populations in Handsworth than it can from the whites, and that the Conservatives can rely upon the white British particularly in local elections. We did not, however, ask the immigrants whether they would look to immigrant representatives to look after their interests, and there were no minority candidates other than the National Front candidate in general and local elections. The National Front candidate only received one vote from our sample at the general election and two at the local election which we studied, and only one West Indian and one Asian suggested that the Communist Party was the best party for his group.

Some possible voting options were concealed by these figures, however, and they were used in the Ladywood by-election in August 1977. These were support for Trotskyist parties and for immigrant candidates. These appeared as real competitors for Labour votes, taking perhaps one in four or five of its immigrant vote, while the Conservatives began to lose something like an equivalent vote to the National Front, a trend not yet evident in our study.

'Handsworth', according to Gus John (Humphry and John, 1971),

is in many ways a typical inner-city suburb, once prosperous, now on the decline, and multi-racial. In the eyes of many of its older residents, that decline is associated with the number of black immigrants, although the facts do not support that view. To the blacks on the other hand, Handsworth is a second-class area . . . Handsworth is not unique or peculiarly nasty, but it is in many ways typical of the inner areas of our major cities.

Earlier, John had described Handsworth from the point of view of West Indian youth, emphasizing police harassment and the high level of racial tension, and had been rebuked by the *Birmingham Post* (6 January 1970) as follows:

Many of the city's problems stem not from racial prejudice but from the excessive rate of immigrants in the past. The city's positive work is usually underestimated and it is positively hindered when a Harlem ghetto mentality is encouraged by ill-considered surveys.

It would seem that four separate factors are being identified here as the cause and the essence of the problem suburb of Handsworth. First, there is the ecological explanation that the problems of Handsworth are the problems of the decaying inner city. Second, there is the notion that problems arise because there has simply been excessive immigration. Third, there is the notion that the problems are problems of race prejudice and racism on the part of the white inhabitants. Finally, there is a notion of the emergence of a ghetto mentality.

So far as the first of these explanations is concerned. it is one which has played an increasingly important role in policy formation, culminating in the White Paper, *Policy for the Inner Cities* (Department of the Environment, 1977b). In fact it is a favourite explanation by racial liberals who wish to reject the notion that immigrants have brought problems with them and who are looking for rational-technological ways of solving pressing political problems. What our own study showed, however, is that there was no uniform problem of urban decay.

The development of Handsworth (in the sense of the four wards) took place over a long period and provided both large villas for the middle classes and small cottages for the workers. Today some houses have been destined for demolition, some have been converted to multiple-occupation, and many are being preserved and improved. Thus, one can distinguish at least three types of problems. First, there are the areas which have been partially demolished, leaving behind large areas of rubble-strewn space together with little islands of abandoned and boarded-up cottages. These are offensive and depressing in appearance, but can hardly be called blight, since these areas have been planned for demolition and replacement and their present condition can only be temporary.

Second, there are the areas of the larger villa-type houses such as those overlooking Handsworth Park. Some of these are known to be in multiple-occupation, but if they are, most usually they are occupied by two or three West Indian families, rather than converted into the pathological form of lodging-house described by Rex and Moore in Sparkbrook.

Finally, there are the general improvement areas and housing action areas which cover the largest part of the 128 enumeration districts from which our survey sample was drawn.

So far as the general improvement areas are concerned, these are houses which have specifically been exempted from demolition and redevelopment because they were thought to be structurally too sound to justify their elimination. The whole policy of improvement is one which has been developed since 1967 as a major housing and planning strategy designed to succeed and to complement slum clearance. It particularly affects older people who, for sentimental and traditional reasons, have not wanted to see their homes destroyed, and immigrants who, being debarred from other avenues to improving their housing situation, have been offered the chance to buy and improve one of these houses. It may be that this policy is not yet working effectively enough, because of an insufficient understanding of the system, but it can hardly be said that these areas are being simply left to decay by the authorities.

Housing action areas are, in fact, areas intermediate between redevelopment and improvement areas. Their institution seems to suggest that Government and local authorities alike are concerned not merely to institute general policies in the hope that they might statistically be proved to have some effect, but are concerned with the highly specific implementation of policies based upon a consideration of the best course of improvement on a street-by-street and house-by-house basis. Each house is to be looked at and proposals for its future brought forward within five years of the setting up of the housing action area. Again, these areas have only just been set up and some were actually declared during the period of our research. Temporarily, of course, the fact that some houses in the same streets or blocks might have different decisions taken about them means that there will be a visible contradiction between the intention of improving some houses, and consigning others to a period of boarding-up, demolition and replacement. The sense of improvement will quickly be undercut by the depressing appearance of these other houses. One must assume, however, that the intention is that the unfit houses will be replaced by newer and better ones which could have an uplifting rather than a depressing effect on the morale of the residents.

All in all one cannot explain Handsworth's reputation as a problem suburb as due to blight and decay. The area is subject to housing policies which are both comprehensive and detailed. Looking at housing and planning problems alone, our conclusion is that the physical fabric and appearance of the area is likely to improve, provided that the resources necessary to carry through improvement programmes are not denied to local authorities, so that a long transitional period has to be envisaged. Of especial importance in this matter would be, not merely the improvement of houses, but the improvement of streets through the elimination of unused sites, the improvement of paving and lighting, the control of traffic, and, by no means least important, the expenditure of extra resources on street-cleaning and refuse collection.

We say all this, however, not in order to deny that Handsworth is a place with problems, but in order to emphasize that they do not arise from defects of housing and planning policy. In fact, we cannot express too strongly our dissent from the view that the problems of declining, multi-racial, urban areas are problems of a basically physical kind. This notion is often taken over as part of a pessimistic belief that the problems of American cities are necessarily universal. In fact, there are numerous types of control over free market forces in Britain which do not exist in the USA, and physical development is not something which is beyond political control in this country.

The question which next arises is whether what is believed to constitute a problem is not the physical fabric at all, but the sorts of people who are living in the area, how they occupy their houses, how they spend their time and what they do on the streets. This certainly is what many old white residents believe. For them physical deterioration is not something which just happens. It has been brought about by immigrant settlement and that settlement is due to the fact that irresponsible governments have allowed excessive numbers of black immigrants to settle during the past twenty years.

We believe that much of the sense that the area is deteriorating arises from this source. Complaints about the physical fabric are a concealed way of complaining about neighbours. But how far are the complaints about neighbours justified?

From the point of view of Birmingham as a whole, the complaints are not justified. The immigrants are in the city because they have come to do jobs, which have to be done if the city's economy is to continue to function. The actual population of the city declined between 1951 and 1961 and again between 1961 and 1971. There should, therefore, have been no difficulty in replacing one population with another. None the less, the Handsworth area, and Soho ward in particular, was transformed demographically, gaining a 13 per cent immigrant population between 1951 and 1961 and a further 35 per cent (making a total of 48 per cent) between 1961 and 1971.

How far was the reaction of local residents to this change in population structure one of prejudice? We believe that there are several separate elements which should be distinguished in answering this question.

First, we should say that we are singularly unimpressed by the attempts which have been made to measure the extent of racial prejudice in the British population at large and in the populations of British people living far from or near to immigrants. Bagley (1970), Lawrence (1974) and others have shown convincingly how the some-what optimistic conclusions of the Survey of Race Relations on this matter were based upon quite arbitary definitions of prejudice, and we believe that the main function of such work is simply to fill ideological gaps in the arguments of liberals and racists alike. What British people think about black colonial immigrants is not a question of what chemicals are or are not present in their heads and bodies, it is a question of the meaning which such immigrants have for them. Attitude testing, if it is to have any significance at all, must be based upon an understanding of such meanings.

Crucially, British people confronted with immigrants from what used to be the Empire, cannot but be expected to react to them in terms of the roles which the immigrants used to fill. This is not a matter to be established by some naively designed attitude test. It is a matter of history and of logic. It is part of the situation of the British working class that it has lived, particularly during the period of the second British Empire from 1880 onwards, in a world in which the British economy and British life were structurally related to the economies and societies of the Colonies. No Englishman concerned with his own reputation during that period would have wished to become confused with a colonial native, and, if this was true in general, it was true particularly in Birmingham where the populist politics of Joseph Chamberlain's local political caucus were combined with the advocacy of imperialism abroad. All of these attitudes, moreover, could only have been strengthened by the experience of conscript soldiers who took part between 1945 and

91

1965 in a series of colonial wars, including those in Malaya, Kenya, Aden, Suez and Cyprus. The whole of this imperial experience from Chamberlain down to Anthony Eden and beyond was built into the consciousness and the very language of the people of Birmingham, and only a liberal or socialist optimist of the most unrealistic kind could expect that other ideological conceptions of an anti-racist kind could act as a sufficient counterbalance to neutralize those beliefs.

The assimiliation into British society of colonial immigrants, then, was bound to be a traumatic experience for lower middle- and working-class people, simply because they were likely to feel destatused themselves, through having to accept these people as equals, as fellow workers and neighbours. In work, some sort of status line could be drawn with black colonials doing the dirty work, but status lines could not be so easily preserved when black men presented themselves as neighbours. To live with the blacks raised the possibility that one might be classified with the blacks for status purposes, which was a terrifying threat for those whose status had become insecure anyway as they were left behind by educational, industrial and urban change.

Such feelings, of course, were common amongst working people in many areas of Birmingham as in other cities. But for the people of Handsworth there was an additional grievance. It was this: other people such as those on some of the better council estates or the better residential areas of private housing had protected themselves by discriminatory action from having black neighbours, and in some areas blacks had simply forced their own way in by buying and converting property. But in the case of Handsworth, the council had actually encouraged the blacks to settle, by offering mortgages as an alternative to other forms of housing provision. Taking it for granted that having black neighbours was a burden anyway, the whites of Handsworth felt that they had been unduly put upon and called upon to bear more than their appropriate share of the burden.

Our thesis is that the deterioration which white residents in Handsworth came to see about them, was not an accelerated physical deterioration due to the misuse of buildings by black immigrants, but simply a deterioration of the area due to the fact that there were what were thought of as inferior, black, colonial men living there. This, we believe, was a more important factor than that of cultural differences or differences of house-keeping standards or, simply, strangeness.

We should, of course, recognize that cultural differences did exist. The Asians spoke different languages and ate different food and the West Indians had their own rather boisterous style of social life. But we cannot accept some other allegations as proven, as, for example, that immigrant tenants looked after their property less than their white neighbours. So far as we could see, some did more than the whites, some the same, and some less. There seemed to be no explanation of the virulence with which the strangeness and cultural differences were perceived, therefore, other than that of the place which it was thought appropriate for colonial men to occupy in an imperial structure.

In short we feel that the explanation of the situation which existed in Handsworth in terms of the prejudice of white residents is inadequate for two reasons. On the one hand the concept of prejudice begs all the important questions and we would suggest that the analysis of culture and belief, systems and attitudes, has to be shifted from the level of psychology to that of the sociology of knowledge. On the other we would suggest that decisions which produced racial confrontation in Handsworth were not made by the people of Handsworth at all, but by those who were in a position from which it was possible to influence the allocation of resources over the city as a whole. The white people of Handsworth were no doubt the agents through whom racial confrontation came to be pursued, but they were themselves victims of the system, called upon to cope with a cultural and social situation which most of the decision-makers in their outer-ring suburban homes did not have to face.

Lastly, we should note the point made by the *Birmingham Post* about Gus John's book creating a ghetto mentality. The same could be said of statements by many of the West Indian leaders. It is certainly the case that in the twenty-five years since large-scale West Indian settlement began, there has been a characteristic set of problems, of forms of behaviour and of political postures which is no part of West Indian culture itself but which results from the West Indian encounter with English society. This has to do with lack of success within the schools, with youth unemployment and with encounters with the police. Whether this is caused by discrimination by teachers and employers and harassment by the police or by genuine cultural differences and misunderstanding, it is none the less a very real set of problems, which West Indians are trying to articulate and deal with. Simply to dismiss it as part of a mischievous attempt to create a ghetto mentality is to run away from an important part of the total problem of Handsworth.

Having dismissed these four over-simplifications of Handsworth's problem – that it results from urban blight, from excessive immigration, from prejudice on the part of the white residents, or from the inculcation of a ghetto mentality by black leaders – we should now conclude by suggesting our own analysis of the kind of confrontation which exists in the area.

Basically, what we wish to suggest is that Handsworth has not one population but three, and that, since each of these populations has different goals and would wish to put available physical and commercial resources to different uses, there is bound to be conflict. The three populations are, of course, the old white residents, the West Indians and the Asians.

The white residents are where they are for traditional reasons. Their goals are quite literally conservative ones. They have reached a stage in their lives when they want social recognition, secure enjoyment of their homes and neighbourhood, and peace and quiet. Instead of being able to achieve these things, however, they find that their neighbourhood has been chosen as the primary place to house the black colonial workers who have been brought in to fill gaps in British industry. They find what they regard as their social space occupied, at a time when they most want to use it, by people who seem alien and hostile. The area seems suddenly to have become crowded and noisy and violent and to have actually gone down-hill physically. For such people day-to-day life is hard to bear at all, and many of them retreat into a conservative or reactionary utopian fantasy about Handsworth as it used to be.

The West Indians are workers from a stagnant colonial economy which can no longer support them. They come from Jamaica to England, despite its terrible climate, simply because there are jobs here, but none in Jamaica. They are, in the first place, not merely willing to become assimilated, but a people who regard themselves as a part of Britain. Hardships they expect, as all immigrants do, but what they do not expect is systematic discrimination and open hostility on the part of the English. This is what they do encounter, and, as the PEP studies and our own survey shows, they do not fully realize the extent to which they are discriminated against and hated. The shock and disappointment is something which they suppress and they work hard and save so that they can buy their own houses and create their own community. The desire to integrate may weaken with time as they come to create their own communal organizations and institutions. The young, particularly, know that they are under attack, and the need to defend the community becomes a part of its self-image. The ideologies of the group vary between a puritan conservatism of those who have survived with jobs and houses despite everything, and the extreme militancy of those who have come to believe that they are not accepted as part of British society and that the only thing to do is to prepare for confrontation on the one hand or emigration on the other.

The key to the Asians' situation is the Asian immigrant's acceptance of the inevitability of his having to live in the diaspora. There is really no better alternative available to him in his homeland and, as he has low expectations, England seems to have much to offer him in terms of a job, a home and money. His value system is not one which is linked to the idea of status-striving which will be attested to by the consumer durables and furniture which he can acquire, but much more by the values of his extended family and in the importance of maintaining its wealth and strength. If the West Indian retreats into a 'ghetto mentality' after first striving for assimilation, the Asian immigrant never envisages anything other than maintaining his own cultural and social order in a strange land. Real social relations are those of the kin-group, fellow villagers or people of his faith. All the rest is environment only. Unlike the West Indian he does not complain of discrimination, simply because his goals are such that he does not place such a high value on the goods which discrimination would deny him. On the other hand, one should not press this point too far, because there are goods which the host society has to offer, even if he does not aim at assimilation into that society. Most important among these are access to education and to well-paid employment. Thus, along with the particular goals and the particular ideology of the Asian community, there is also a common frame of reference and the basis for a political debate and for fighting for rights by political methods within British society.

Rex and Moore, in writing about Sparkbrook in 1964, chose as their title *Race, Community and Conflict*, and it was a main theme of that book that despite the obvious inter-racial conflict, particularly over the use of housing, the ultimate destiny of the immigrants was assimilation into suburban society, and a community of interests could be established by bodies like the Sparkbrook Association which had already gone far in setting goals for the whole community or at least a framework within which conflict could be resolved.

We do not think this perspective is relevant any longer. There is not even an incipient community council of the kind which the Sparkbrook Association provided. The ethnic communities are concerned with pursuing their own goals through their own separate organizations, and the attempts which have been made to set up agencies for the whole community, defined in non-racial terms, have had little response from the immigrants. The immigrants may use the services which such organizations provide, but they trust their own leaders more. On the other hand, the definitions adopted by the new agencies themselves tend to be derived from the radical and left-wing traditions of their own political culture. They express dissatisfaction with British society as such without formulating explicitly the problems of the immigrant minorities.

Since we do not see community as triumphing over conflict we have to admit that what we do see for the moment in Handsworth is the escalation of conflict and the formation of class-like groups for the pursuit of that conflict. This is not to say that every individual is mobilized already for action on behalf of his group. Far from it. There are many West Indians, for example, who still aspire to normal working-class roles and normal working-class rights in British society. Indeed, it might be argued from our data that in terms of jobs and of housing they appear to have found a home within working-class structures. We do not believe, however, that the attainment of homes and jobs, despite all the difficulties, coupled with the stigmatization of those who have attained them, will lead to the incorporation of this community into the working class. The objective situation which they face is such that they will be increasingly forced to seek a new and separate social identity and to defend their own interests.

So far as the Asians are concerned, they will not be forced back into creating a separate community organization. They have it already. What we should note, however, is that instead of this community organization gradually fading away it will continue to exist, both because it is a necessary structure for those living in the diaspora, but also because it is necessary for self-defence. Moreover, it seems likely that, if the community is subject to further physical attack, as it has been in dramatic cases like that in Southall, the present forms of organization and leadership may be thrust aside.

Finally, we are likely to see a change in the attitudes and the organizations of the whites as they become more overtly organized against their black neighbours. In the case of the West Indians and the Asians, our survey evidence still shows that most of them still believe that the races get on well together, and the notion of racial conflict is something which we predict on the basis of objective evidence of their situation. In the case of the whites, evidence is already there in their replies, of the belief that blacks have caused the deterioration of their homes and neighbourhood. However inadequately informed such a belief may be, we expect that there is a point where such beliefs and attitudes produce organization. In the case of Sparkbrook, Rex and Moore believed that the potentiality for such organization would not be actualized because of the multi-racial character and goals of organizations like the Sparkbrook Association. In this case there is no exactly equivalent community organization, and such organizations as these are drawn away from playing a conciliatory role into expressing the resentment of the white inhabitants on the one hand, or becoming formally radical in the sense in which that term has meaning in the larger society. We shall discuss some of these problems more fully in chapter 8 where we deal with the associations in more detail.

Thus, the greatest likelihood is that conflict in this community will grow, and it is at this point rather than in all the other conflicts over markets and the allocation of resources that tension will find expression. The conflict in Handsworth will, however, be important not only in and for itself but as a dramatic representation of the conflict in the whole of a society which can be seen as in the process of creating an immigrant underclass. In saying this, we may find ourselves accused of irresponsibility and nihilism and may be asked what we would do in Handsworth to put things right. Our reply would be that Handsworth itself is a symptom, not a cause, and that the sources of the conflict are to be found immediately in political decisions taken by the gate-keepers of Birmingham and British society, and indirectly in the gap which exists internationally between countries like Jamaica, India and Pakistan on the one hand, and the advanced countries like Britain on the other.

4 Black immigrants at work

However much we might wish to qualify Marxist approaches to the study of class conflict, there can still be little doubt that the social relations of production in a society, are at least one of the prime determinants of social structure. Thus, while we will go on, in the next chapter, to give an account of those social and class relations which arise out of men's relation to domestic property, in this chapter we examine the social relations of production both in themselves and in the effect which they have on racial and ethnic group relations in other areas of life.

Birmingham and the West Midlands have always constituted, since the industrial revolution, a highly important, though specialized, part of the British economy. Between 1500 and 1700 Birmingham became a thriving centre of the metal industry. Iron manufacturers migrated from Staffordshire to the Tame valley where water power was available for forges and mills. Nearby Birmingham appealed as a place of settlement because of its commercial connections and freedom from guild restrictions. Colonial expansion and the slave trade encouraged a demand for guns and the other horrific impedimenta of colonialism which the Birmingham metal industry was especially well-equipped to satisfy. As a by-product of this development a large number of small establishments producing brass toys, buckles and buttons grew up, and these, in turn, provided a base for the jewellery and precious metal trades. As these grew in Birmingham, the heavier and less-skilled metal industry settled across the Birmingham border in the more or less continuous Black Country conurbation. Birmingham naturally became not only the industrial but the commercial, financial and communications capital of the West Midlands region.

Birmingham participated to the full in the age of technological innovation, which was initiated by the Exhibition of 1851, entering particularly important new trades like machine-tool making. On the other hand, according to the *Victoria County History*, 'the lack of local demand for machinery comparable to that of the railway or textile industry had kept the engineering industry in Birmingham small in size, local in importance, and with none of the advantages of specialization' (Eversley, 1964).

Small industry continued to play its part in Birmingham in the twentieth century, and as recently as 1957, according to the Birmingham abstract of statistics, 76 per cent of the labour force was employed in factories with fewer than 100 workers. On the other hand, the one major development was motor-vehicle manufacturing for which Birmingham's skills in the metal trades had equipped it well. According to the 1971 census, the largest industrial group was in vehicle manufacturing, employing 14 per cent of the total labour force and a quarter of all those employed in manufacturing industry. Some 74,725 people worked in motor-vehicle manufacturing in 1971 compared with 70,021 in metal-goods industries making such things as bolts, nuts, screws, hand-tools, small tools and gauges, cutlery, jewellery and items in precious metals. In an industrial structure in which motor-vehicle manufacture was a principal priming element for the economy as a whole, Birmingham had an important base for industrial prosperity. Equally, of course, the threatened decline in that industry which was apparent by the mid-1970s meant that the whole urban industrial structure had a very fragile base.

As a regional metropolitan centre the distribution of occupations in Birmingham was, of course, varied, and the proportion of the total population in non-manual and administrative occupations increased.

As Table 4.1 shows, the number in the categories of employed professional workers, intermediate and junior non-manual workers, and personal service workers in 1971 was about 180,000 compared with 270,000 in the three manual categories, while amongst the latter nearly half were skilled workers. There were also nearly 25,000 employers and managers in small establishments and 14,000 workers other than professionals working on their own account. It seems fair to say from these figures that nearly every second Brummie might be classified in Marxist terms as *petit bourgeois*. Certainly one would expect that in an industrial society such as this, many of those who had worked in industry were likely to finish up in white-collar positions, and even more that, with the number of white-collar jobs available, would expect to see their children leave the factory bench for the office desk. The existence of such a movement would, of course, make the remaining heavy unskilled industrial jobs less attractive to the native-born, both in Birmingham itself and the neighbouring West Midlands boroughs.

Commenting on trends in employment in the 1960s and early

TABLE 4.1 *Economically active persons* enumerated† in area to become metropolitan district, by sex and type of occupation followed*

Type of occupation	Socio-economic group	Males	Females Married‡	Others‖	Total
Employers and managers in central and local government, industry, commerce, etc. Large establishments	1	11,890	940	1,220	14,050
Employers and managers in industry, commerce, etc. Small establishments	2	19,250	3,760	1,630	24,640
Professional workers – self-employed	3	1,780	170	140	2,090
Professional workers – employees	4	11,560	780	770	13,110
Intermediate non-manual workers	5	15,860	10,180	8,740	34,780
Junior non-manual workers	6	35,850	40,070	33,810	109,730
Personal service workers	7	2,410	15,150	5,690	23,250
Foremen/women and supervisors – manual	8	12,710	840	330	13,880
Skilled manual workers	9	116,340	6,590	3,860	126,790
Semi-skilled manual workers	10	62,370	25,690	12,440	100,500
Unskilled manual workers	11	26,760	13,420	3,680	43,860
Own account workers (other than professional)	12	11,620	1,980	820	14,420
Farmers – employers and managers	13	130	10	—	140
Farmers – own account	14	80	10	20	110
Agricultural worker	15	290	60	150	500
Members of Armed Forces	16	490	—	—	490
Persons with occupation inadequately described	17	9,640	5,660	3,700	19,000
All types of occupation		339,030	125,310	77,000	541,340

Sources: Census of Population 1971, Small area Statistics (10% sample) for Birmingham C.B. and Sutton Coldfield M.B.
  *Including out of work.
  †Strictly, persons enumerated in a 10 per cent sample, multiplied by 10.
  ‡Including separated.
  ‖Single, widowed and divorced.

1970s, the Birmingham Council's *A New Plan for the City – Employment and Industry* notes the following:

1. The gap between the demand for labour (as represented by the city's total labour force) and the resident supply has grown in recent years, as the economically active population has fallen. To offset this the contribution of in-commuters to the city's labour force has grown absolutely. At the same time the number of out-commuters from the city increased.

2. Thus gross, and to a less extent net, commuting flows increased at a much greater rate in the period 1961–66 than did the total labour force. This reflects the increased accessibility of large sections of the working population and the growing preference of many persons in the higher socio-economic and white-collar groups for homes outside the city. Associated with these trends are the problems of an increase in the average time of work journeys, and an increasing load on the transportation network at peak hours.

3. There has been a slight decline in the number and proportion of operatives in the city's economically active population, though as a proportion of all occupied persons it is still high.

4. The trends in unemployment and vacancies show that in general in the 1960s the city had a buoyant labour market with unemployed rates normally below the national average. The situation has deteriorated both locally and nationally in recent years, and, since April 1971, the unemployment rate in each month in the city has been above the national rate. The increase in unemployment nationally seems to have been the result of both technological change in industry, and a decline in the general level of economic activity. The city has been particularly hard-hit because of the preponderance of manufacturing industry.

5. There has been a disproportionately high level of demand for workers in service industry, while unemployment levels have been increasing. The difficulty in recruiting workers must reflect the occupational structure biased towards manufacturing.

There are several conclusions relevant to the theme of this book which may be drawn from their observations.

In the first place, we should note the fact that in the 1960s the labour market was 'buoyant' and the rate of unemployment below that of the nation as a whole. We might surely, therefore, expect that there was an actual shortfall in the numbers of workers available, since low unemployment rates of this kind almost certainly mean that there were jobs which the existing unemployed workers could not or would not fill. Given the overall movement towards skilled manual and white-collar jobs in the native population, one would expect that, during the 1960s, there would have been large numbers of potentially unfillable vacancies in less attractive unskilled and semi-skilled jobs. This is a gap which would have been filled by West Indian and Asian immigrants.

The contradiction between high unemployment and high demand for labour in the service industries might have a twofold explanation. On the one hand, there are jobs which a population educated for skilled manual work are unable or unwilling to do. On the other hand, there are some service jobs, as for example in transport or in the health service, which are insufficiently attractive in terms of wages and conditions to attract even the redundant and the unemployed.

A third factor to note is the change in rates of unemployment. If immigrant workers were tolerated in industry at a time when there were more jobs available than workers to fill them, this will by no means be the case with rising unemployment nationally. The trend for the Birmingham rate to rise above that at national level did not in fact continue into the mid-1970s, but the fluctuations here do suggest that Birmingham need not necessarily be able to count as being above the average in the buoyancy of its labour market.

In these circumstances it is possible that there might be a lowering of expectations on the part of workers who would otherwise have sought more skilled jobs, and a consequent increase in competition in the unskilled area. This, however, is speculation only and needs to be proved empirically. It could be that, despite unemployment, the status-striving of the established population might militate against the return to unskilled jobs. Moreover, one thing which is certain is that these circumstances would certainly tell against late entrants to the labour market being upwardly mobile.

Finally, there is the question of commuter-flows. The 'growing preference for homes outside the city' amongst the better-off, of course, relieves the central city of some of its housing responsibilities. It does not have to house as many people as work in the city. But if the housing stock was continuously replaced on a one-for-one basis, this would mean that there were more than enough houses for the present working population if overall demand for labour had not grown. The city would then become the location of housing for the lowest occupational categories.

These findings certainly help to put our study as a whole into perspective. We should expect that the immigrant population as a whole in our study consists largely of those who came to fill the gaps in the less skilled and the less attractive jobs in manufacturing industry as well as in the less skilled jobs in the service industries. They would naturally find homes in the inner-city area, where demand for old, terraced houses was relatively low, and they might well hang on to their jobs even when the job market was less buoyant. On the other hand, both because of the basis of their original acceptance and because of the declining number of better jobs, their chances of promotion might be expected to be small. One would expect a very clear clash of interest between native workers trying to protect a smaller and smaller number of jobs and an increasingly settled immigrant population looking for advancement for themselves and their children.

One should notice, then, that immigrants have settled in Britain and have found their place in British industry in very particular economic circumstances. One should also expect that their situation will change as economic circumstances change. Just what the direction of that overall change will be is difficult to specify, but the leading trends in 1978 seem to be these:

First, there is an economic depression affecting the whole of the capitalist world and no certainty that any way out of it will be found, even though one might be unjustified in seeing this as some kind of final crisis of capitalism. This depression internationally and nationally will particularly affect Birmingham as the above notes show.

Second, since the *New Plan for the City* was written, the future of the motor industry has become increasingly uncertain. Rootes, now taken over by Chrysler, in neighbouring Coventry, has been reorganized and is heavily dependent upon central government finance; British Leyland, now nationalized, is being reorganized in order to maintain even a part of its share of the market, and is also dependent on support from the National Enterprise Board; and there are minor plants like the BSA motor-cycle plant in Small Heath, Birmingham, which have had to be entirely closed. Should the crisis in the motor industry lead to something like the closure of Birmingham's British Leyland plant at Longbridge, the effect would be cataclysmic, not only in terms of the lay-off of the Longbridge labour force, but in terms of the collapse of large parts of the components industry.

Third, there is the possibility of the recovery of prosperity in Britain, through the increasing flow of North Sea Oil. This might, it is true, produce a national economic recovery, but it is difficult to see that that recovery will benefit Birmingham's industry in particular. It would hardly help the British motor industry to compete in world markets and its seems unlikely that Birmingham would enjoy any special advantages in any new industrial revolution such as it enjoyed in the nineteenth century.

This generally pessimistic picture, however, ought not to obscure the fact that different sections of the population at work might have different experiences. We have seen how, early on in the history of the West Midlands, there was a concentration of skilled work in Birmingham itself and of heavier less-skilled work in the Black Country. We have noted that in the present occupational structure there is a high preponderance of white-collar and skilled manual jobs on the one hand and a continuing minority of semi-skilled and unskilled jobs in the service and manufacturing sectors on the other. And we have noticed that immigrant labour was likely to be more readily tolerated in less attractive and dirty jobs. It may therefore be asked whether there is already, or whether there will develop, a dual labour market. In a strict sense there might be argument about this, but if we take one of the classic definitions derived from this theory it is certainly worth asking whether it applies to Birmingham. According to Bosanquet and Doeringer (1973), a distinction can be made between advantaged and disadvantaged workers and between primary and secondary labour markets:

> Disadvantaged workers are employed in enterprises where wages are low, working conditions are poor, employment is often unstable, and opportunities for on-the-job training and advancement are severely limited. By contrast, advantaged workers tend to receive higher pay, relatively secure employment and on-the-job training that leads to higher wages.

Distinctions such as these do clearly exist in Birmingham industry, although they do not necessarily all overlap with one another. Employment in the motor-car industry is unstable in that it is subject to frequent temporary lay-offs and to redundancies. Moreover, production on the motor-car production line is certainly onerous. Yet this is a highly unionized industry which pays relatively good wages. On the other hand there are factories and foundries, in which unions operate only feebly, but which give security of employment in dirty, monotonous work which is ill-paid and offers few chances of promotion. We shall see in the pages which follow how far distinctions of this kind affect the employment of immigrants and whether they may be said to have been fitted into industry through a secondary labour market. This is one part of our overall consideration of the question of whether black immigrant workers are to be thought of as part of the working class or as an underclass. The existence of distinctions of the kind mentioned here in the labour market would seem to be a necessary, although not a sufficient, condition of the emergence of an underclass.

During the 1939–45 war and in the late 1940s and 1950s, there was a shortfall in the overall labour supply available to Britain and active steps were taken to recruit labour from overseas. A Ministry of Labour Liaison Office was open in Dublin until 1954. A Polish resettlement corps was set up in 1946 under which large numbers of Poles were directed to the lower-paid sectors of industry, and European volunteer workers were recruited for a few years after 1947 with the agreement of the TUC.

In 1942 a committee on overseas manpower had been established in the Ministry of Labour to co-ordinate the movement of labour from overseas, and in the last six months of 1942, 155 unskilled West Indian men were brought to Britain and, after training, put to work in the Manchester and Liverpool areas. In the last four years of the war, 787 Indian men were trained and put to work in munitions factories.

Birmingham's first black workers were a group of thirty Asian ex-seamen who were directed by the Ministry of Labour to work in munitions factories. A few West Indians were already settled in Birmingham in 1948, but it was the general process of emigration/immigration coupled with the boom conditions in the city which made it one of the two main areas of settlement when a general migration began with the voyage of the *Empire Windrush*. Once basic colonies of settlers from Jamaica, Barbados and St Kitts on the one hand, and from the Gujarat, the Punjab and East Pakistan on the other, were established, there was a sound base for the arrival of other immigrants. Peach makes the point about West Indian migrants in general that they went where the net emigration was greater than was compatible with the staffing of local industry. This was certainly the case in Birmingham in the 1950s. So far as the upswing in Asian migration which came later is concerned, it is less certain that migration and patterns of settlement were determined by this relationship, but there was certainly no great pool of Asian unemployed in England in general or Birmingham in particular by 1965 or even 1970. There had been a gap in the labour force and it had been filled by immigrants. Our survey data, which we shall present shortly, record the quantitative and structural differences between their position and that of Birmingham workers.

Before turning to our survey data, however, we can obtain some further insight into the state of the economy by looking at the available statistics for the West Midlands conurbation as a whole.

In the first place, we are able to look at the percentage of New Commonwealth workers in the total population in each economic activity category in Britain and the West Midlands. These figures are given in Table 4.2 and 4.3.

Obviously immigrant workers form a higher percentage of the total workforce and of each economic category in the West Midlands than they do nationally.

Table 4.4 gives the rates of economic activity for each of the main immigrant groups.

105

TABLE 4.2   *Economic position of people born in the New Commonwealth* (1971 Census) – Great Britain*

	No. of people (aged 15 and over)	As % of total population in each category
In employment	607,310	2·6
Out of employment	45,855	3·4
Economically inactive	389,250	2·01
Activity not known	15,310	2·5

Source: Census 1971 Great Britain Advance Analysis.

TABLE 4.3   *Economic position of people born in the New Commonwealth* (1971 Census) – West Midlands conurbation*

	No. of people (aged 15 and over)	As % of total population in each category
In employment	49,330	7·1
Out of employment	3,430	7·8
Economically inactive	10,810	4·9
Activity not known	745	10·9

Source: Census 1971 Great Britain Advance Analysis.
   *New Commonwealth – those born in India, Pakistan, West Indies and Africa.

TABLE 4.4   *Enumerated persons (aged 15 and over) by sex, country of birth and economic position – West Midlands conurbation*

Males	West Indies	India	Pakistan	Africa	General population
In employment	15,835 (78·4)	18,450 (78·0)	13,235 (79·4)	1,810 (47·6)	604,020 (77·7)
Out of employment	1,550 (7·1)	1,065 (4·5)	785 (4·7)	140 (3·7)	39,235 (5·0)
Economically inactive	2,630 (13·0)	3,950 (16·7)	2,415 (14·5)	1,815 (47·7)	127,805 (16·4)
Activity not known	285 (1·4)	190 (0·8)	230 (1·4)	40 (1·0)	6,825 (0·9)
	20,300	23,655	16,665	3,805	777,885
Females					
In employment	9,975 (54·4)	3,190 (17·9)	260 (5·8)	925 (31·3)	409,185 (41·3)
Out of employment	1,260 (6·9)	535 (3·0)	75 (1·7)	80 (2·7)	23,020 (2·3)
Economically inactive	6,630 (36·1)	13,740 (76·9)	3,945 (88·7)	1,900 (64·3)	548,880 (55·3)
Activity not known	480 (2·6)	395 (2·2)	165 (3·7)	50 (1·7)	10,930 (1·1)
	18,345	17,860	4,445	2,955	992,015

Sources: Census of Population 1971 Great Britain Advance Analysis and Draft Table 1747, Census of Population 1971, 10% sample – specially supplied by OPCS.

These tables show the high rate of economic activity for these economic groups compared with the general population in the conurbation. Of particular interest, also, is the very high rate of West Indian female economic activity compared with that for the general population, and the very low rate for Asian women, particularly for Pakistanis.

The industrial distribution of the immigrant population is shown in Table 4.5

In a national sample David Smith (1977) noticed that immigrants were strongly over-represented in the categories shipbuilding and vehicle manufacture, textiles, and in the residual group labelled 'other manufacturing industry' as well as in transport. Men were under-represented in the service industries, but West Indian women were strongly over-represented in the health service.

Despite the predominance of the vehicle-building trade in the West Midlands, only 1 in 8 West Indian men, 1 in 6 Pakistanis and 1 in 20 Indians are employed there. On the other hand, 1 in 3 West Indian men, more than 1 in 2 Indians, nearly 1 in 2 Pakistanis and 3 out of 10 East African Asians, were employed in metal manufacture or in the manufacture of metal goods. Between a third and a half of the immigrant workers of the West Midlands appear to be working in hot, dirty industries, marked by shift work.

When we turn to occupational distribution as distinct from industrial distribution, these figures are confirmed, as Table 4.6 shows.

Both New Commonwealth males and all males have just about 28·5 per cent of their numbers in engineering and allied trades, but whereas the next highest categories amongst the general population are professional and technical workers (8·9 per cent) and 'labourers not elsewhere classified' (7·2 per cent), amongst the New Commonwealth immigrants labourers not elsewhere classified constitute 22·9 per cent, and furnace, forge and foundry workers 10·4 per cent. Clearly one-third of the New Commonwealth immigrants are working in forges, furnaces and foundries or as labourers elsewhere. This is true of less than one in ten of the general population.

Amongst women, 26·9 per cent of the general population are clerical workers and 20·15 per cent are in service industries, with engineering and allied trades third in importance at 13·7 per cent. Amongst New Commonwealth women, on the other hand, 27·1 per cent are in engineering and allied trades, 16·3 per cent in professional and technical trades, and only 12·0 per cent in the service trades. It would seem, therefore, that whereas the white woman typically becomes a secretary or a shopworker the immigrant woman works in a factory, or in a hospital, and rather less frequently in service industries.

Since these figures refer to the West Midlands rather than Birming-

TABLE 4.5 *Enumerated persons by sex, country of birth and type of industry (selected categories) – West Midlands conurbation. Census 1971, 10% sample*

	West Indies	India	Pakistan	E. Africa	General population
Males					
All industries and services	1,636	1,982	1,477	114	76,550
	%	%	%	%	%
Metal manufacture	18·5	40·5	24·2	15·8	11·0
Metal goods not elsewhere specified	14·9	14·9	22·3	13·2	12·9
Vehicle manufacture	12·6	5·3	17·1	7·9	11·8
Transport and communication	8·8	6·3	3·4	10·5	5·7
Electrical engineering	4·5	2·9	6·4	12·3	4·4
Mechanical engineering	6·1	6·3	4·6	7·9	8·8
Construction	6·05	3·6	0·3	3·5	8·2
Professional and scientific services	1·6	2·9	1·02	7·02	5·2
Females					
All industries and services	1,072	317	24	52	43,235
	%	%	%	%	%
Metal manufacture	4·2	5·9	—	1·9	4·2
Metal goods not elsewhere specified	18·0	18·6	4·2	21·15	12·4
Vehicle manufacture	6·2	3·8	4·2	3·85	4·2
Electrical engineering	6·4	2·5	—	9·6	5·5
Mechanical engineering	3·2	2·5	—	—	3·7
Distributive trades	2·7	7·3	8·3	7·7	15·9
Professional and scientific services	26·9	12·6	16·7	17·3	17·8
Miscellaneous services	3·4	3·15	8·3	—	11·1

Sources: Census 1971. Great Britain, Economic Activity Part III (10% sample) and Draft Table 1726, *Census of Population 1971*, 10% sample – supplied by OCPS.

ham, and we have no official figures for Birmingham, it might be argued that the Birmingham pattern itself is different. This may be true, but it is irrelevant to the study of Handsworth, where, as we shall see, a significant proportion of the population are out-commuters who cross the border each day to neighbouring Black Country boroughs.

So far as the unemployed are concerned, we do have figures for

TABLE 4.6   *Enumerated persons by country of birth, sex and occupation (selected categories) – West Midlands conurbation, 1971*

	West Indies	India	Pakistan	E. Africa	General population
Males					
All occupation orders	1,636	1,982	1,477	114	74,092
	%	%	%	%	%
Furnace, forge and foundry workers	8·6	16·15	5·35	2·6	3·9
Engineering and allied trades workers	29·1	24·9	32·6	34·2	28·5
Construction workers	1·2	1·1	—	—	2·98
Labourers not elsewhere classified	15·8	21·0	34·5	7·0	7·2
Transport and communications workers	8·3	5·65	3·3	5·1	6·1
Sales workers	0·7	2·7	1·6	2·6	6·3
Administrative and managers	0·2	0·55	0·3	0·9	5·2
Professional and technical workers	1·5	4·7	0·95	7·9	8·9
Females					
All occupation orders	1,072	317	24	52	42,863
	%	%	%	%	%
Engineering and allied trades workers	29·3	21·1	8·3	26·9	13·4
Clothing manufacturing workers	3·1	10·7	—	3·85	1·8
Warehouse workers, packers, bottlers	3·8	4·7	—	3·85	3·8
Clerical workers	5·1	7·6	12·5	17·3	26·9
Sales workers	1·3	6·3	8·3	3·85	10·1
Service and recreation workers	15·2	3·5	8·3	—	20·15
Professional and technical workers	18·2	9·8	12·5	19·2	9·0

Sources Census of Population 1971, Great Britain, Economic Activity Part II and Draft Table 1746, *Census of Population 1971,* 10% sample – specially supplied by OPCS.

Birmingham and for Handsworth. Here it would seem that by February 1977 in Birmingham, unemployment amongst immigrant workers had risen to about 19 per cent and was 20·1 per cent of the total unemployment, as Table 4.7 shows.

TABLE 4.7   *A comparison of general and coloured unemployment**
in Birmingham and Handsworth[†]

		Birmingham			Handsworth EEA		
		Total unemployed	*Total coloured unemployed*	*%*	*Total unemployed*	*Total coloured unemployed*	*%*
Feb.	74	14,665	1,643	11·2	1,806	462	25·5
May	74	14,918	1,571	10·5	1,649	446	27·0
Aug.	74	17,858	1,978	11·0	1,783	449	25·1
Nov.	74	No figures	No figures	—	No figures	No figures	—
Feb.	75	20,686	2,994	14·4	2,255	889	39·4
May	75	25,821	3,869	14·9	2,848	1,079	37·8
Aug.	75	40,452	6,473	16·0	4,339	1,928	44·4
Nov.	75	39,379	6,456	16·3	4,285	1,815	42·3
Feb.	76	41,664	6,854	16·4	4,802	2,060	42·8
May	76	39,719	6,644	16·7	4,862	2,036	41·8
Aug.	76	47,127	8,512	18·0	5,635	2,653	47·0
Nov.	76	No figures	No figures	—	No figures	No figures	—
Feb.	77	39,426	7,956	20·1	5,003	2,172	43·4
May	77	36,635	6,470	17·7	4,615	2,062	44·7
Aug.	77	43,738	7,923	18·1	5,422	2,535	46·7
Nov.	77	36,704	6,107	16·6	4,404	1,726	39·2

Source: Manpower Services Commission, Birmingham.
*Registered at either an employment or careers office.
[†]Handsworth refers to the Handsworth Employment Exchange Area which includes Handsworth, Handsworth Wood, Winson Green, and the parts of Hamstead, Hockley, Sandwell, Rotten Park, Ladywood, Edgbaston, Lozells and Smethwick bordering on Handsworth.

Compared with the 20·1 per cent of the total unemployed which immigrants constituted in Birmingham, the figure for Handsworth was 43·4 per cent of the total unemployed in February 1977. Since immigrants constituted about one in ten of the economically active population in Birmingham, it would seem that they were carrying double their appropriate share of unemployment.

Turning now to our own survey data, our sample may be broken down by ethnic group and employment status as shown in Table 4.8. Over three-quarters of both Asian and West Indian respondents were working, whereas less than half of the white sample were working. This is, of course, to be expected, given the age structure of the white population. What we should now do, however, is to analyse these separate employment status categories, and particularly the first two, separately.

Tables 4.9 and 4.10 give a break-down of the sample of those working by socio-economic group and ethnic origin, and 'social

TABLE 4.8   *Employment status of sample by ethnic group*

	West Indian	Asian	Great Britain
Working	77·5% (306)	77·7% (237)	49·3% (197)
Not working	19·0% (75)	19·3% (59)	13·5% (54)
Retired	3·3% (13)	1·3% (4)	29·5% (118)
Never worked	0·3% (1)	1·6% (5)	7·8% (31)
Totals	395	305	400

TABLE 4.9   *Socio-economic group by ethnic origin for sample in work*

	West Indian	Asian	Great Britain
Large firms			
Employers	—	—	—
Managers	1 (0·3%)	—	7 (3·6%)
Small firms			
Employers	—	—	1 (0·5%)
Managers	1 (0·3%)	2 (0·8%)	7 (3·6%)
Professional self-employed	—	—	1 (0·5%)
Professional employees	1 (0·3%)	—	4 (2·0%)
Intermediate non-manual			
Ancillary and artists	18 (5·9%)	4 (1·7%)	16 (8·1%)
Foremen and supervisors	—	1 (0·4%)	1 (0·5%)
Junior non-manual	7 (2·3%)	4 (1·7%)	26 (13·2%)
Personal service	—	—	6 (3·0%)
Manual			
Foremen and supervisors	7 (2·3%)	1 (0·4%)	13 (6·6%)
Skilled manual	132 (43·0%)	126 (53·2%)	65 (33·0%)
Semi-skilled manual	94 (30·7%)	62 (26·1%)	26 (13·2%)
Unskilled	41 (13·4%)	31 (13·0%)	14 (7·1%)
Own account (except professional)	2 (0·7%)	4 (1·7%)	7 (3·6%)
Farmers – employers and managers	—	—	—
Farmers – own account	—	—	—
Agricultural workers	—	—	1 (0·5%)
Members of Armed Forces	—	—	—
Occupation inadequately described	—	—	1 (0·5%)
Refused	2 (0·7%)	2 (0·8%)	1 (0·5%)
	306	237	197

TABLE 4.10   *Social class* of sample by ethnic origin*

	West Indian	Asian	Great Britain
I Professional	2 (0·7%)	—	6 (3·0%)
II Intermediate	21 (6·9%)	8 (3·4%)	33 (16·8%)
III Skilled Occupations			
(N) Non-manual	6 (2·0%)	4 (1·7%)	20 (10·2%)
(M) Manual	140 (45·8%)	131 (55·2%)	82 (41·6%)
IV Partly skilled	94 (30·7%)	61 (25·7%)	40 (20·3%)
V Unskilled	41 (13·4%)	31 (13·0%)	14 (7·1%)
Refused	2 (0·7%)	2 (0·8%)	1 (0·5%)
Occupation inadequately described	—	—	1 (0·5%)
	306	237	197

*Registrar General's classification of occupations.

class' and ethnic origin respectively. Both of these tables show a greater predominance of the lower-skill groups than in Smith's national sample (Smith, 1977). Smith's percentages of each group in the white-collar categories are whites 40, West Indians 8, Pakistanis 8, Indians 20, and African Asians 30. In our sample, percentages in these groups were whites 30, West Indians 9·6, and Asians 5·1 (these being mostly Indians). In the skilled manual category, Smith gives whites 42 per cent, West Indians 59 per cent, Pakistanis 33 per cent, Indians 44 per cent and African Asians 44 per cent, whereas our sample are distributed as whites 41·6 per cent, West Indians 45·8 per cent and Asians 55·0 per cent. In the semi-skilled and unskilled categories Smith gives whites 18 per cent, West Indians 32 per cent, Pakistanis 58·0 per cent, Indians 36 per cent and African Asians 26 per cent. In our sample 27·4 per cent of the whites, 44·1 per cent of the West Indians and 38·7 per cent of the Asians are semi-skilled or unskilled. In summary it would seem that amongst the whites there are fewer white-collar workers and something like an equivalent increase in semi-skilled and unskilled workers in our sample as compared with Smith's. Amongst West Indians our sample shows something like the same percentage of white-collar workers, but a considerable down-grading from the skilled to the semi-skilled categories. In our Asian sample, the percentage of professionals and white-collar workers is lower than that of any Asian group in Smith's table. Our percentage of Asians in the skilled manual category is correspondingly higher, while amongst the unskilled and semi-skilled category our figure is higher than for any of Smith's group except the Pakistanis.

These figures are, in fact, what we would expect in Handsworth. It is relatively speaking a lower-class area for any group, with a high proportion of retired white people. Amongst all groups, more-over, we find that, although about 60 per cent of the whole survey population are either skilled manual or non-manual workers, there is a greater preponderance in each ethnic group here of unskilled and semi-skilled manual workers. This is entirely consistent with our findings for the West Midlands as a whole, where we found a con-centration amongst whites and immigrants alike in engineering occupations, but a greater predominance than in Smith's national sample of immigrants who were labourers or foundry workers.

Allowing for the fact that in Handsworth overall occupational status and class are lower, one still has to notice the same differences between the whites and their black neighbours as are to be found in the national sample drawn by PEP. The whites differ from the Commonwealth immigrants in having higher percentages in the higher categories and lower percentages in the lower ones.

Table 4.11 gives the industrial distribution of the Handsworth sample by ethnic origin. It shows over-representation of immigrants in the manufacture of metal goods and in transport, but not in other sorts of manufacture, nor in the professional and distributive groups taken as a whole.

Turning to hours worked, Table 4.12 shows that Asians and West Indians tend on the whole to work longer hours than white British workers. Moreover, if we take only those in full-time employment (those working 30 hours or more a week) we find that whereas only 8·75 per cent of all full-time employees nationally work 48 or more hours a week, more than 20 per cent of West Indians and 30 per cent of Asians in our Handsworth sample did so.

Tables 4.13 (a), (b) and (c) present data relating to hours of work earnings, social class, and shift work by ethnic origin. Table 4.13 (a) on hours of work by earnings by ethnic origin shows that although Asians and West Indians were on the whole working longer hours, their weekly wage was not necessarily higher than that of white workers in the sample. In fact, taking the figures overall, 32 per cent of West Indians and 37 per cent of Asians were working 40 hours or more a week, yet taking home less than £50 (It should perhaps be noted, however, that earned incomes amongst our sample, with the exception of non-manual white workers, are generally low, when compared with a national average weekly wage for all full-time adult workers of £57.65 in April 1976). In order to bring their basic wages up, both Asian and West Indian workers were obliged to work considerable overtime. The extreme case was an Asian bakery worker who worked as many as 84 hours a week.

Separate analysis of hours of work by social class and ethnic

113

TABLE 4.11 *Industrial distribution of sample by ethnic origin*

Industrial Group/Order		West Indian	Asian	Great Britain
I	Agriculture	—	—	—
II	Mining	—	—	1 (0·5%)
Manufacturing				
III–	Food, fuels and			
V	chemicals	17 (5·6%)	12 (5·0%)	10 (5·1%)
VI–	Metal goods	180 (58·8%)	163 (68·7%)	87 (44·2%)
XII				
XIII–	Textiles, leather,			
XIX	bricks, pottery,			
	timber, paper,			
	other goods	18 (5·9%)	10 (4·2%)	15 (7·6%)
XX	Construction	12 (3·9%)	6 (2·5%)	4 (2·0%)
XXI	Gas, electricity,			
	water	—	—	4 (2·0%)
XXII	Transport,			
	Communication	35 (11·4%)	24 (10·1%)	9 (4·6%)
XXIII–	Distributive,			
XXVI	banking, assurance,			
	professional and			
	miscellaneous			
	services	34 (11·1%)	17 (7·1%)	54 (27·4%)
XXVII	Public			
	administration	6 (2·0%)	3 (1·2%)	11 (5·6%)
	Insufficient			
	information	—	2 (0·8%)	—
	Refused	4 (1·3%)	—	2 (1·0%)
		306	237	197

TABLE 4.12 *Hours worked by sample by ethnic origin*

Hours worked	West Indian	Asian	Great Britain
8 or less	2 (0·6%)	—	1 (0·5%)
9 but less than 30	9 (2·9%)	2 (0·8%)	18 (9·1%)
30 but less than 40	44 (14·3%)	19 (8·0%)	45 (22·8%)
40 but less than 48	161 (52·6%)	116 (48·9%)	85 (43·1%)
48 or more	64 (20·9%)	82 (34·5%)	35 (17·8%)
On holiday	21 (6·8%)	9 (3·8%)	6 (3·1%)
DK/CR/Refused	5 (1·6%)	9 (3·9%)	7 (3·5%)
	306	237	197

origin shows that in fact it is skilled manual workers who tend to work the most hours. However, despite this, as Table 4.13 (b) shows, two-fifths of skilled manual Asian workers and a third of West Indians earn less than £50 per week. On the other hand, the low incomes amongst semi- and unskilled manual white workers may be due to the fact that they tend to work fewer hours.

Taking weekly earnings by shift work, it emerges that West Indians rely most on shift work to increase their earnings. Overall, we find that a third of West Indians earning £50 or more are on shift work compared with 23 per cent of Asians and 12 per cent of white British. Yet it is also the case that those West Indians doing shift work earned no more than other workers who were not on shift work.

We asked our sample about their place of work and found that amongst the whites 42·1 per cent either worked in Handsworth itself or in the city centre (workplaces which might be thought most desirable from the point of view of local residents) compared with only 23·8 per cent of West Indians and 17·2 per cent of Asians. On the other hand, when one looked at the Black Country boroughs of Dudley, Smethwick, West Bromwich, Warley, Walsall, Wolverhampton and Wednesbury, only 13·2 per cent of whites but 28·5 per cent of West Indians and 52·2 per cent of Asians from our Handsworth sample worked there. This suggests that Handsworth was acting as a dormitory on the one hand for white-collar workers in the city and on the other for workers in the heavy industries of the Black Country.

Further to this, although both black and white workers had to commute, and the industry of the Black Country would appear to be readily accessible to the people of Handsworth, 35·3 per cent of West Indians and 20·2 per cent of Asians as against 16·8 per cent of whites had to go more than five miles to work, and 60·8 per cent of West Indians and 47·2 per cent of Asians as against 39·1 per cent of whites had to go more than three miles.

Paradoxically, despite the long hours worked, low pay, and longer journeys to work, an overwhelming majority, above 80 per cent, of all groups said that they were satisfied with the jobs they were doing, with the Asians (88·6 per cent) the most satisfied of all. Yet, whereas 27·1 per cent of the West Indians who said they liked their jobs, and 32 per cent of the Asians who said they liked theirs, could not think of any reason for liking them, there were only 12·7 per cent of the satisfied whites of whom this was true. On the other hand, more than one in three whites as against 18 per cent of West Indians and only 6·3 per cent of Asians said that they found their work rewarding.

One of the most interesting findings in this survey was that the population whom we interviewed were all relatively stably employed.

TABLE 4.13 *Hours of work, earnings, social class, shift work by ethnic origin amongst sample*

(a) *Hours of work by earnings by ethnic origin*

	West Indian			Asian			Great Britain		
Weekly earnings*	Less than £50	£50–9	£60 or over	Less than £50	£50–9	£60 or over	Less than £50	£50–9	£60 or over
Hours worked†									
Less than 40 hours	22·6	18·5	11·1	11·5	2·1	10·0	48·5	17·9	27·3
40–5 hours	50·5	60·0	46·0	57·7	54·2	38·3	30·9	56·4	43·9
46 or over	26·9	21·2	42·9	30·8	43·7	51·7	20·6	25·6	28·8
Sample size‡	93	65	63	78	48	60	68	39	66

(b) *Earnings by social class by ethnic origin*

Social class	Non-manual	Skilled manual	Semi/ unskilled manual	Non-manual	Skilled manual	Semi/ unskilled manual	Non-manual	Skilled manual	Semi/ unskilled manual
*Weekly earnings**									
Less than £50	58·3	33·6	50·5	57·1	40·0	43·0	37·3	25·9	61·2
£50–9	16·6	32·7	27·8	28·6	20·9	32·9	19·6	32·5	14·3
£50 or over	25·0	33·6	21·7	14·3	39·1	24·1	43·1	41·6	24·5
Sample Size‡	24	119	97	7	105	79	51	77	49

(c) *Shift work by earnings by ethnic origin*

	Less than £50	£50–9	£60 or over	Less than £50	£50–9	£60 or over	Less than £50	£50–9	£60 or over
Weekly earnings*									
Shift work									
Shift work	43·3	52·9	62·7	27·2	24·0	50·8	11·6	14·3	24·2
No shift work	56·7	47·1	37·3	72·8	76·0	49·2	88·4	85·7	75·8
Sample size‡									

*Average weekly income for all full-time men (21 years and over) and women (18 years and over) was £57.65 – April 1976 (*Department of Employment Gazette*, September 1977).

†Average working week in April 1976 for all full-time men (21 years and over) and women (18 years and over) was 40 hours (*Department of Employment Gazette*, September 1977).

‡Excludes those off work and those who refused or did not know hours, income, social class or shift work.

Some 68·0 per cent of the West Indians, 51·5 per cent of the Asians and 67·5 per cent of the whites had been in their present jobs for five years or more, and only 6·6 per cent of the whole sample were looking for other jobs.

Of the people in our sample, 33 West Indians, 36 Asians, and 13 whites were unemployed and looking for work, and a further 22 West Indians, 17 Asians and 20 whites were not at work for various reasons but not looking for employment. Long-term unemployment of two years was about the same for West Indians and whites but only about one-third as likely amongst Asians. One common reason for leaving a job was illness, but amongst West Indians 40·9 per cent, and amongst the Asians 53·7 per cent of the unemployed had been made redundant as compared with only 29·5 per cent of the whites.

Amongst the retired in our sample 118 out of 135 were white. Of these 35 were non-manual workers and 47 were skilled workers, suggesting that the proportions of the inhabitants in Handsworth who had been in the higher occupational groups twenty years ago was somewhat higher than it is today.

Two very central sets of questions which we asked our sample were concerned with promotion and with trade-unionism. These questions are crucial since they indicate something about the morale and the commitment of workers to their employment on the one hand and their affiliation to the working class on the other.

Almost twice as many whites (38·5 per cent) as immigrants (20·6 per cent West Indians and 21·2 per cent Asians) had been offered promotion (see Table 4.14). About one-fifth of each group said they were not interested in promotion. Promotion for whites, however, was more likely to be to a supervisory job, and although 30 per cent of the West Indians and 19·5 per cent of the Asians

TABLE 4.14 *Opportunities of promotion and type of promotion available to sample*

	West Indian	*Asian*	*Great Britain*
Whether offered promotion or not			
Yes	76 (20·6%)	61 (21·2%)	88 (38·5%)
No	207 (56·25%)	175 (60·9%)	88 (38·5%)
Not interested	85 (23·1%)	51 (17·7%)	52 (22·8%)
	368	287	228
Type of promotion offered			
Unskilled/semi-skilled job	14 (18·4%)	19 (31·1%)	5 (5·6%)
Semi-skilled job	13 (17·1%)	15 (24·5%)	—
Foreman/chargehand	18 (23·6%)	7 (11·4%)	30 (34·0%)
Other manual, supervisory	5 (6·5%)	5 (8·1%)	14 (16·0%)
To a better machine/work	12 (15·8%)	8 (13·1%)	5 (5·6%)
Shop floor – staff	1 (1·3%)	1 (1·6%)	7 (8·0%)
To non-manual, supervisory	4 (5·2%)	2 (3·3%)	8 (9·0%)
Higher management	—	—	14 (16·0%)
Other	9 (11·8%)	2 (3·3%)	5 (5·6%)
Don't know (DK)/can't remember (CR)	—	2 (3·3%)	—
	76	61	88

offered promotion had been offered promotion of this kind, usually the immigrants interpreted promotion as meaning movement from one operative's job to another.

We were very interested to find out whether those who had been denied promotion, as well as others, saw racial discrimination as a factor affecting a worker's chance of success. Over a third of the Asian and West Indian sample who had not been offered promotion believed that this was due to racial discrimination. When asked who got promotion in their industry, about 10 per cent of the immigrants believed it was for whites only, whereas only one white respondent out of 228 mentioned this possibility. A rather higher proportion of West Indians than whites, but a lower proportion of Asians than whites, had had the experience of going for an interview and not getting a job, and 31·3 per cent of the immigrants involved here (119 West Indians and 56 Asians) thought this was due to colour-prejudice.

It does seem that a substantial minority of immigrants do see their progress in industry blocked by discrimination and prejudice and it is perhaps interesting to notice that although we tend to accept that Asians are more quiescent about their jobs than West Indians, as many of them as West Indians are actually interested in promotion.

The PEP survey, *Racial Disadvantage in Employment*, noted that 'the racial minorities have certainly joined the trade unions in great numbers', and this was our own experience. Even when we excluded the retired whites from our table we found that immigrants were far more likely to join their unions than white workers. Table 4.15 gives our findings on this point.

Our findings are strangely at odds with the view common in left-wing circles that immigrants represent a form of ununionized and potentially blacklegging labour. They are, however, consistent with the view put forward by Castles and Kosack (1973) that, whereas immigrants on the whole supported the labour movement industrially and politically, they did not necessarily obtain support from it in times of crisis.

TABLE 4.15   *Trade-union membership of sample by ethnic origin**

	West Indian	Asian	Great Britain
Yes, now	270 (72·5%)	208 (71·7%)	118 (49·3%)
Yes, used to belong	56 (15·0%)	51 (17·5%)	57 (23·8%)
No, never belonged	46 (12·3%)	31 (10·7%)	64 (26·7%)
	372	290	239

*This table excludes retired, never worked and not worked in last ten years.

118

The distribution of our sample between various unions is shown in Table 4.16. Clearly from this table, the TGWU, the AUEW or TASS and the GMWU are the crucial unions for all groups, but there is a much wider range of union membership amongst whites as well as a much lower representation in the TGWU.

One may say that the general unions, and the TGWU in particular, have a large measure of responsibility for immigrant welfare in industry. In our sample, 66·7 per cent of all respondents thought the union was doing enough for them and only six immigrant workers in all thought the union should be doing more for coloured workers.

On the face of it this seems to suggest that the immigrants are in fact well protected by the trades unions. But there is some reason to suppose, as there is in the case of their support for the Labour Party, that if what we were discussing was not simply generalized support, but support for and reliance upon the unions in particular circumstances, this support might well appear more dubious.

Before we look at the question of trade-unionism and affiliations to the working class in more detail, however, we should notice that in theory the immigrant has a double protection, that which derives from the special race relations machinery set up to achieve equal opportunity for all, and that which derives from the unions.

The Department of Employment has a stated policy that there must be equal opportunity for all workers but that: 'For its policy to succeed the department needs the support of both employers and unions in industry and commerce.'

The department had two advisers on race relations in London prior to the 1968 Act. Subsequently, advisers were appointed in

TABLE 4.16   *Union membership of sample*

	West Indian	Asian	Great Britain
TGWU	131 (40·1%)	123 (47·3%)	49 (28·0%)
AUEW/TASS	61 (18·7%)	61 (23·4%)	37 (21·2%)
GMWU	24 (7·4%)	10 (3·8)%	9 (5·0%)
NUR	15 (4·6%)	2 (0·7%)	2 (1·1%)
Bakers' union	4 (1·2%)	7 (2·6%)	1 (0·5%)
UCATT	8 (2·4%)	4 (1·5%)	2 (1·1%)
ASTMS	0	1 (0·3%)	7 (4·0%)
NUPE/COHSE	17 (5·2%)	1 (0·3%)	5 (2·8%)
UPOW/POEW	5 (1·5%)	3 (1·2%)	6 (3·4%)
Other	17 (5·2%)	13 (5·0%)	45 (25·9%)
DK/CR/Refused	44 (13·4%)	35 (13·4%)	11 (6·3%)
	326	260	174

each of the Department of Employment regions. According to a press notice by the department, these officers would:

> In conjunction with Employers Associations, Trades Unions, the Institute of Personnel Management, the British Institute of Management, Chambers of Commerce, Community Relations Councils and the Race Relations Board, also seek to develop the department's policy of promoting equal opportunity in employment, and to secure the best use of the immigrant's abilities.

The TUC, while preferring not to treat race relations in industry as a special problem requiring special machinery separate from that normally involved in dealing with industrial grievances and disputes, has none the less always professed an anti-discrimination position. Moreover, in 1974, it appeared to go further than it had done previously in the course of its evidence to the Parliamentary Select Committee on Race Relations, when the General Council itself recommended the inclusion of equal opportunity clauses in union agreements with employers and the collection of statistics on employment levels of black workers.

Finally, under the 1968 Race Relations Act, it became unlawful to discriminate on grounds of colour, race, or ethnic or national origin in recruitment, training, promotion, dismissals, and terms and conditions of employment. Complaints were to be referred first to the relevant industrial machinery and, where the complainant was dissatisfied with the decision of the approved industrial machinery, appeal could be made to the Race Relations Board. The Board would then seek to form an opinion as to whether discrimination had occurred and, if it had, to seek to conciliate. It was hoped that by these means, discrimination would be reduced not only in the conciliated cases, but in numerous others in which knowledge of the Board's work would have a preventive and educative effect.

The second PEP survey discovered that there was considerable concentration of minority workers in particular industries and particular plants due possibly to discrimination but indicating at least relative disadvantage of minority workers. It backed up its evidence of disadvantage with situation tests in which actors of different ethnic origin made applications for jobs both personally and by correspondence. It concluded, as had the earlier PEP study, not merely that there was discrimination but that there was far more of it than minority workers actually complained about.

Thus, relative disadvantage exists for immigrants in Handsworth as exists in British industry as a whole. In Handsworth there were fewer immigrants in white-collar employment than there were whites, and there were far more semi-skilled and unskilled workers amongst the immigrants than among the whites. There were, more-over, concentrations of immigrant workers, not so much in the vehicle-manufacturing industry in which the PEP sample found them to be concentrated, but in metal manufacture, transport and, in the case of women, in the health service. It was also the case that in terms of occupation, while immigrants and whites were pre-dominantly represented in engineering occupations, many immigrant men were employed as labourers and foundry workers. Earnings were lower in each of the main employment categories for immigrants as compared with whites except amongst the unskilled and there, as in the other categories, immigrants worked longer hours and also did shift work more frequently.

Smith has rightly rejected the argument that research into dis-crimination through job-testing by actors overestimates discrimina-tion by sending the actors to apply for jobs which immigrants would not normally seek. He is surely right in suggesting that where it is the case that men do not apply for jobs because they realize that it is unrealistic or hopeless to do so, discrimination exists as an institutionalized fact. We need not, however, even press the point about discrimination. It seems clear from our own study that although there is some overlap between the employment of black and white workers in the skilled manual occupations, immigrants are employed predominantly in less attractive industries and in less rewarding jobs. They have been accepted as a replacement labour force only, and one in three of them is conscious that the way to promotion is barred by racial discrimination and prejudice. If they or their children were to develop aspirations to better jobs than they now seek, the extent of the discrimination barrier would quickly become apparent.

In the face of concentration, discrimination, and segregation which exists, the activities of the Race Relations Board, within the terms of the 1968 Act, have really been little less than derisory. In 1963, for example, Smith reports that there were 150 complaints relating to recruitment to employment brought before the Board. Of these there were only about 20 to 30 cases in which an opinion of dis-crimination was formed. In the 18 months from 1 January 1975 to 30 June 1976 the Board dealt with 788 employment complaints in all, and the number of cases in which discrimination was formed was still only 92.[1] Smith estimates, on the basis of his tests, that some 6,000 cases of discrimination must occur in the field of unskilled employment alone, and even in our own small sample 175 immigrant workers had been refused a job after an interview and about 55 of these believed that colour-prejudice was responsible.

Given the actual scale of the problem of immigrant disadvantage, it seems clear that the Race Relations Act of 1968 is making no significant difference. It remains to be seen whether the new Act passed in 1976 will alter this situation. The new Commission for Racial Equality is charged with dealing with the problem of disadvantage and not simply racial discrimination and it may now carry out its own investigations without waiting for complaints to occur. It is also no longer limited by a racial balance clause which hitherto has made racial quotas in employment in particular industries permissible. How successful it is in bringing about significant change remains to be seen. The earliest cases seem to show that it may do more than the Board in pursuing cases of overt discrimination but that it will hardly make any inroads into the problem of disadvantaged immigrant workers in employment.

There are, of course, three agencies which would claim to be taking positive rather than negative steps to reduce disadvantage. These are the Department of Employment, the Community Relations Commission and the Trades Union Congress. Of these, however, the Department of Employment will be mostly concerned with intervening in industrial disputes and is likely to have little impact in more general educational terms. It does not seem that the threat of withholding its services from discriminating employers has ever been seriously applied. The Community Relations Commission does propaganda work amongst employers but has success mainly in preaching to the converted over friendly lunches and dinners. Finally, the trades unions tend to be long on resolutions and short on action, as we shall illustrate in a moment.

One should not, of course, seriously expect that statutory and voluntary agencies of the kind we have been discussing are likely to be able to make much impact in a free market situation where the driving motive is profit and self-interest. Employment in Britain is not something which is to any large extent administered by the Government and local authorities as housing is, and in general terms the most that can be expected from the Government is *ex post facto* actions to rectify wrongs committed in a free market. Of course, there are nationalized industries and there are the ordinary public services, but the former operate very much like private industries, free of central government control, and very little has been done in government and local authority services to ensure a minimum employment of minorities.

A final area of possible further investigation in the field of race relations is the systematic analysis of industrial disputes. When we began our investigation it seemed to us that two of the areas in which conflict was likely to occur were the under-protection of Asian and West Indian workers in industries with a high degree of segregation, and the attempt of immigrant workers to pass from being mere replacement workers where white workers could not be found, to enter the more sought-after jobs. These issues had been brought sharply into focus by disputes involving Asian workers at the Wolf plant in Southall (Marsh, 1967) and in the Mansfield Hosiery Mills dispute in Loughborough. In both these cases Asian workers on strike identified strongly with the union but the union failed to give them maximum support and, in the second case, the issue of the promotion of Asian workers to skilled jobs was posed sharply. When the Secretary of State appointed a commission of enquiry into the Mansfield dispute the strike committee, in its evidence, isolated four main issues in the dispute:

1 The restriction on the promotion of Asian workers to knitting jobs.
2 The low pay of bar-loaders at Mansfield Hosiery compared with their pay elsewhere in the industry.
3 Reduction in the number of semi-skilled and unskilled jobs compared with an increase in the number of skilled knitting jobs.
4 The failure of the union adequately to represent its members.

Shortly after the present study began there were two further disputes in the East Midlands, at Coventry Art Castings in Nuneaton, and at the Imperial Typewriter works in Leicester.

Low wages for long hours was claimed as the main reason for their strike by Asian workers at Coventry Art Castings, Nuneaton, in December 1973. The Asian workers at the factory, which made components for the car industry, were overwhelmingly concentrated in the heavier, unskilled jobs. Over a period of five years they had built up a branch of the Transport and General Workers' Union at the factory.

On 3 December 1973, the Asian workers called a ban on overtime working in protest against the management's refusal to negotiate over a demand for higher wages. Three days later a shop-steward was dismissed and the Asian workers walked out, unsupported by white workers. The strikers received dismissal notices, and the company began recruiting outside labour to take the place of the strikers. Confrontations between police and pickets followed, and nine pickets were arrested. It took the TGWU three months to make the strike official. The strike finally ground to a halt in April 1974 after four and a half months. The majority of strikers returned to work but some preferred to take redundancy rather than return. Subsequently, two Indian workers were found guilty of assaulting a coloured police officer.

The strike at the Imperial Typewriter Company, Leicester, lasted for thirteen weeks. The dispute arose out of the company's attempts to increase production quotas without paying higher wages for

123

increased productivity. At the time of the strike, May 1974, women workers received a basic wage of £18 and men £25 for a 40-hour week. Another source of grievance was the fact that, despite the large number of Asians employed at the factory, the shop-stewards' committee was overwhelmingly white. The strikers also claimed that white workers had lower production quotas, and talks between the strikers and the TGWU convenor at the factory revealed that this was in fact the case. This meant that Asians were being denied an extra £4 a week in their pay packets.

An original walk-out of forty Asian workers was supported by a further walk-out of 500 Asian workers. The strike met with the total opposition of the local branch of the TGWU. However, with the help of the magazine *Race Today*, the Imperial Typewriter strike committee was able to mount pickets on factories, shops and warehouses belonging to or acting as agents for Litton Industries, the parent company, elsewhere in the country. The TGWU initiated an enquiry into the dispute, which backed the strikers and criticized local officials of the union. In the meantime, the strikers returned to work having secured a promise of no victimization.

There had, during the early 1970s, been similar disputes to these in the West Midlands. Disputes of this kind usually involve concentrations of Asian workers in low-paid jobs with inadequate communications between them and either their employers or unions. The employers have, in such cases, been content to use cheap labour and, indeed, to increase the level of exploitation. The workers have, on some occasions, formed branches of British unions, and in other cases, when they were already members of these unions, asked for official support. In so far as union support has not been forthcoming they have formed their own unofficial committees and have also received support from the Indian Workers' Association as well as from similar organizations of Pakistani, Bangladeshi and Kashmiri workers, although this has not led to the formation of separate Asian unions. Where 'black workshops' and 'black shifts' develop, there is usually resistance to movement and promotion from these jobs to more integrated participation in the more skilled labour force. Moreover, where there have been disputes attempting to rectify the grievances of these Asian workers, the long-term effect has been the closure of the plants concerned as uneconomic.

A further phenomenon which is beginning to be evident is that of Asian firms employing cheap and ununionized Asian labour. This has now passed the stage at which familial bonds between employer and employee make what would otherwise be regarded as exploitation acceptable, and the Asian community has once again shown that trade-union consciousness is part of its culture by organizing workers against their employers. On the other hand, such organization is likely to create divisions within the various Asian so-called workers' associations, some of whose members are, in fact, employers. In the long-lasting dispute at the Grunwick works in North London, one has what is essentially the same phenomenon, in which an industry with low profit-margins employs Asian labour and where some workers are prepared to accept a non-union shop, while others protesting against pay and conditions, strike and form a union.

West Indian labour is more dispersed than Asian and the individual West Indian worker is in some respects more like his English counterpart. The phenomenon of the black workshop is less evident and many West Indians work as individuals in ordinary factory production. They are more interested in individual promotion than are the Asians, and the disputes which involve West Indians are likely to be those which relate to individuals being made redundant unfairly, which involve conflict with other workers, supervisors or managers, which might take on racial overtones, or which concern the denial of promotion. An interesting issue in which discrimination was alleged was reported at the British Leyland plant at Longbridge in the winter of 1976.

A Birmingham community newspaper revealed that management at the Longbridge plant, with the tacit approval of some shop stewards, were preventing black (mainly West Indian) workers from gaining promotion to better paid jobs on the assembly line. It was alleged that black workers were being deliberately failed on an aptitude test which all semi-skilled workers were required to take before being up-graded, and that some white workers had avoided the test by being transferred to other departments and being up-graded at the same time. Black workers were largely restricted to semi-direct (those jobs supplying the track) and indirect (labouring) jobs, whereas white workers were predominantly in the skilled jobs. Moreover, it is estimated that 70–80 per cent of all workers at Longbridge were direct.

Those black workers interviewed by *Broadside* complained that they had received little support from shop-stewards. 'The weight of race prejudice', it was claimed, 'is invariably too much even for shop stewards, white and black, who are trying to change the situation.' Increasing frustration led some black workers to organize informal meetings outside the factory gates and token hour stoppages without the support of the works' committee. Complaints about the method and marking of the progressive tests were taken to the Race Relations Board. An investigation was undertaken. The company forestalled criticism by dropping part of the aptitude test (the wire-bending test) and promoting black workers to better jobs.

Obviously the record of industrial disputes shows that there are many potential sources of dispute which in the case of Asians involve group reaction, and in the case of West Indian and some other Asian workers, involve individuals who get involved in disputes of a racial kind. What we have not seen yet is the involvement of the young black British worker in industrial disputes. His problem tends to arise more frequently in the form of being left out of the labour force altogether.

So far, industrial disputes have not become a major focus of racial tension. That focus tends to lie more in communities and neighbourhoods and in conflicts between the young and the police. But the 'black workshop' type of dispute is a fact and the Grunwick dispute has shown that industrial disputes involving immigrant workers can spill over into street violence. It is possible, even if it is not immediately likely, therefore, that some future dispute might itself become a community issue. So far, however, there does appear to be a possibility that if the unions, and especially the big general unions, apply themselves specifically to developing policies on the problems of minority workers, the solidarity of the trade-union movement might be maintained, and, whatever the conflicts elsewhere, race need not be a factor which distorts the overall pattern of industrial relations. There is also scope for union action to overcome the incipient racial stratification of industry, if the unions are capable of representing all their members and not solely a privileged new white 'aristocracy of labour'.

5   Black immigrants and the housing system

In an important way the research on which this book is based started as a study of immigration, housing and community. Rex and Moore's study of Sparkbrook had isolated the study of 'housing-classes' from the conflicts between other interest groups in the various systems of resource allocation in Birmingham, and had seen the conflicts between groups differentially placed in relation to the control of housing as the crucial factor exacerbating if not determining racial conflict. The present study, of course, seeks to correct this over-emphasis and to see housing conflict as one amongst a number of possibly interconnected forms of class conflict. None the less, it would be misleading even in this context not to recognize that men's relation to their houses and homes is one of their most important life-interests and one around which they are likely to organize in the course of ethnic and class conflict.

A great deal has been written about the concept of housing-class since the publication of *Race, Community and Conflict*, ranging from some writings which see the concept as a crucial and path-breaking one in urban sociology, through others which draw attention to its internal ambiguities, to still others which see it as essentially diversionary, drawing attention away from the central social process of industrial class struggle.[1] Some of the literature which this debate has generated is referred to below. Here we need only briefly recapitulate the main points about the concept's use which are relevant to the analysis of Birmingham's housing system as it has changed between 1965 and 1978.

The central notion indicated by the housing-class concept was that in any city there was a stock of housing of varying degrees of desirability to which different groups of people having different characteristics had differing degrees of access. The crucial point was not that of having different possessions or even a different life-

127

style at the moment of observation, but of being able to command a certain type of tenure in relation to 'desirable' housing in the overall system of allocation. It would, however, have been nonsensical not to recognize that the actual kind of house and tenure which a man actually possessed when observed was one indicator of his power in the housing market or allocative system. Again, it is true enough that in the model of housing-class relations which was posited, the over-simplifying assumption was made that there was an agreed scale of what was desirable in terms of housing style and tenure, and that, in any actual model, particularly in a multi-ethnic society, such an assumption was unrealistic. It was important, none the less, not to allow the formulation of this more complex model to build in a justification of discrimination against minority groups, because they were held not to want what the majority wanted. Finally, because this was a variable concept only and not a description, it was never claimed that the housing-classes which seemed more relevant to explaining ethnic political conflict in Sparkbrook in the mid-1960s could be taken as a kind of inductive generalization covering all cases at all times.

One criticism, of which much was made by sympathetic critics, was precisely that we had confused the central question of access with that of life-style and actual type of house occupied. This point was made by Haddon, and Pahl built upon it in a paper given to a British Sociological Association seminar in Leeds in 1972, when he argued that if access was the criterion the following housing-classes emerged:

1 Large property-owners and capitalist speculators.
2 Smaller landlords.
3a Owners of capital sufficient to own their own houses and owning.
3b Owners of capital sufficient to own their own houses and renting.
4 Those who must rent.

It seems to me that what this attempt at a reformulation does is simply to rehabilitate the notion that money is the sole key to access and that access happens solely through markets. Not surprisingly, Pahl was to become engaged in debate with Castells about housing as a matter concerned with the reproduction of labour and with collective consumption regulated by the State.[2] Equally, Lambert, Blackaby and Paris (1975), who had started out with the housing-class concept, turned eventually to the monistic Marxist type of explanation offered by Castells.

We do not wish to dispute here the possibility of the ultimate demonstration in terms of Marxist political economy of the dependence of the housing system upon the needs of capitalism and of the industrial class struggle. We should note, however, that Pahl's formulation given above really only makes distinctions amongst the rich and the powerful, and has nothing to say about the institutions which enable some of those, of whom it might have been said that they 'must rent', actually to buy, nor of the varying kinds of renting which follow from the differential possession of political power.

What was new about the Sparkbrook study was precisely its recognition that, while established members of the locally-born working class had the security which came from actual or potential access to publicly provided rented housing, there were others who had of necessity to own, and that their ownership indicated a weaker position in the total allocative system than that of the established council renters. Socialist prejudice, however, dies hard, and this argument was difficult for many of our radical and reformist readers to accept.

One way of reformulating what Rex and Moore were trying to say in Pahl's terms is to emphasize that there are some who 'must buy' while amongst those who 'must rent' there are some who have to rent on worse terms than others.

Valerie Karn, in reviewing *Race, Community and Conflict* (and rightly criticizing it for the exaggeration of the importance of the immigrant lodging-house due to statistical error), accused Rex and Moore of concentrating attention upon a particular type of owner-occupation, that of the lodging-house proprietor, while ignoring the widespread phenomenon of non-pathological forms of owner-occupation, which not only seemed to be a preferred form of tenure amongst immigrants, but was actually furthered by the local council, who, by giving mortgages of its own generously and even disproportionately to immigrants, actually strengthened their housing-class position.

Karn may have been correct in suggesting that the multi-occupied lodging-house in Sparkbrook was not typical of owner-occupation. Indeed, we would reinforce the point by pointing out that the pathology of Sparkbrook in particular had much to do with the disturbed sex-ratio attendant on the panic 'beat-the-ban' migration of Asians in 1960–2. None the less, we would emphasize that the multi-occupied lodging-house is still a reluctantly acknowledged part of Birmingham's housing system, and, even more important, that many of the other forms of owner-occupation to which Karn refers are underprivileged housing situations of those who are forced to buy.[3]

The crux of this matter is that many West Indians and Asians, who may indeed have had a cultural preference for owner-occupation, were trapped into a form of owner-occupation, which was to represent a new bottom of the housing system, and which not merely left them with inferior houses, but actually denied them the chance of moving to the privileged rented sector. The fact was that, however hard it might be to get a council tenancy or a mortgage on suburban property, it was possible by unorthodox forms of finance (e.g. council mortgages and bank loans) to obtain inferior inner-city property for purchase. Anyone who did this thereby made himself ineligible for rehousing through slum clearance and redevelopment and probably also through the waiting-list. It is also the case that there was an unorthodox way into the privately rented sector, through gaining the tenancy of a housing association converted flat or house, but this sort of charitable, and sometimes anti-racist, activity placed its tenants primarily amongst the run-down inner-ring properties referred to above.

In a word, what Karn has done is to identify housing-classes of owner-occupiers and private renters, who, while they are clearly better-off than the lodging-house proprietors and their tenants, are none the less distinctly underprivileged classes. Denied normal access to the legitimate and desired sectors of the housing market, they have been channelled into that complex entity which comes gradually to be known as the pathological inner city.

Turning now to those who were 'forced to rent' and, indeed, to those who chose to do so, it is important to realize that amongst these, some had certain avenues closed to them which were open to their competitors. In the first place those who lacked local connections would either be denied access to private lettings altogether, or would have to pay a substantial premium to outbid the natives. But much more important was access to the public sector, and here the Sparkbrook study identified exclusion of larger houses from redevelopment schemes, residential qualifications for access to and acquiring points on the list, and discriminating actions by housing officers faced with matching qualified applicants with actual houses, particularly through offering the less fortunate applicants slum property awaiting demolition rather than council-built property.

The Lambeth Borough Council in its exceptionally well-argued case before the Parliamentary Select Committee on Race Relations, identifies six ways in which local authority policy might discriminate against racial groups (Select Committee on Race Relations and Immigration, 1971, p. 43):

(a) In devising a 'points' scheme for the allocation of housing to families on the waiting list which placed undue emphasis on length of local residence so that it prejudiced the applications of newcomers to the area who were in many cases in greater housing need.

(b) By the omission from slum clearance and redevelopment

programmes of those areas which contain large numbers of immigrant families.

(c) By the rigid definition of classes of persons who are considered to be eligible for rehousing from 'clearance' and 'redevelopment' areas which leads to the exclusion of families because of insufficient residence or because of the nature of the tenancy.

(d) In the type of property which is offered to immigrant families, leading, it is claimed, to such persons finding their own accommodation rather than accepting housing in 'short life' property.

(e) In allowing housing enquiry officers to be prejudiced in the assessment of a family's living standards, which in turn influences the types of accommodation the local authority is prepared to offer.

(f) In creating 'ghettos' in certain zones by vigorously attacking multi-occupation in areas adjacent to these zones.

The authors of the Sparkbrook study could hardly have wished the case they were making about discrimination in the public sector to be put better. Matters, however, have moved on since 1965 and housing policies as well as the available housing stock have changed. This has led some researchers, notably Lambert, Blackaby and Paris, to conclude that the whole question of the housing queue or queues is now so complicated that it can be construed as a device to mystify the applicant by the bureaucratic authorities. This has been their main reported conclusion after a study which set out to examine neighbourhood associations and housing opportunities, building upon an earlier pilot project by Lambert and Filkin on ethnic choice and preference in housing. This study, while starting from the analysis of Rex and Moore on the one hand and Pahl on the other, had suggested a move away from survey methods in the study of discrimination, towards phenomenological perspectives on the one hand and action-research (sitting-in on and helping housing advice groups in dealing with tenants who came for such advice). The upshot of all this was that while at a national level two PEP surveys, as well as the work of Elizabeth Burney (1967) and others, were serving to focus attention on and clarify issues raised by Rex and Moore, research work on housing in Birmingham moved more and more towards emphasizing the obscurity of the problem, and to helping individuals to cope with the system as it was, and at the same time to seeing how the system could be improved through what the Housing Advice Liaison Committee, with whose work Paris and Blackaby came to be associated, called 'dialogue and discussion with those whose concerns and interests in Housing Management at Bush House are similar to our own' (Housing Advice Liaison Group, 1973).

Taking into account all of these arguments and looking at Handsworth between 1974 and 1978, we suggest that analysis of the situation there and more widely in Birmingham can still fruitfully be looked at in terms of housing-classes of which the following are the most important:

1a Outright owner of house   ⎫ in suburban or desirable area.
1b Owner of mortgaged house   ⎰
2a Tenant of good post-war or inter-war council housing.
2b Tenant of inner-city council housing or housing on undesirable estates.
3   Tenant in redevelopment area with possibility of rehousing.
4   Homeless person eligible to be rehoused.
5a Outright owner of house   ⎤ in general improvement area,
    (i) freehold (ii) leasehold ⎥ housing action area or
5b Owner of mortgaged house   ⎰ other undesirable area
    (i) freehold (ii) leasehold ⎦
6   Tenant of charitable housing association.
7a Owner-occupier of multi-occupied lodging-house.
7b Tenant of multi-occupied lodging-house.

Of course some reservations may be held here about the evaluations of what is and what is not desirable built into this set of categories. That they are not the values of the present authors should be made clear at once. What is perhaps more important, however, is that they are disputed amongst the observed population themselves. We believe that there are three separate factors involved here. The first is a continuing widespread belief in the value of suburban semi-detached migration, which is shared by better-off West Indians and even Asians. The second is that the very attempt to improve the houses beyond the original redevelopment areas stigmatizes them. But the third is forced dispersal, whether of the old and retired who are attached to the inner areas for traditional reasons, or of the immigrants who may resent or be afraid of the consequences of the forced dispersal policy and influenced by a counter-tendency to stay in their own safe, enclosed and protected communities. This third factor should be taken into account, but really does not alter the fact of the existence of housing-classes (at least in themselves) since access is in effect denied to those who do wish to move.

It is now necessary to look at the way in which the new situation in Birmingham, indicated by the new account of the housing-classes mentioned above, has come about through developments in housing policy. This includes looking at two separate aspects of the problem. One is the general housing policy enshrined in the 1969 Housing Act, which succeeded the phase of slum clearance and redevelopment. The other was the new set of policies worked out for council housing, including the place of immigrants within this system.

By 1975 it was clear that the slum clearance programme which Birmingham had begun in the immediate post-war period was coming to an end. Two new problems were emerging. One was that of how to deal with the sites vacated by slum clearance, the other that of what to do about the next oldest houses. The redevelopment of clearance sites would appear to be a simple problem, namely that of knocking down old houses and replacing them with new ones. But this could not be done according to the same style or formula as that which applied in the case of council rehousing in the suburbs. Here, on these formerly overcrowded sites, there had to be a net housing gain in terms of the numbers of people per acre. This was one reason given in 1965 for not rehousing immigrants from the lodging-house areas in Sparkbrook. That sort of move would have meant that when the lodging-houses, with their intensive over-occupation, were knocked down, there would have been an actual surplus of people for whom there was no room in the new houses.

Obviously what had to be done was, on the one hand, to find more land on the outskirts which could be incorporated into the city and, on the other, to build tower-blocks or high-rise apartments. Moreover, if this was done, with the highest 'housing gain' and, one might add, the greatest gain in popularity by the Council, it had to be done by demolishing first the old red-brick, two-storey, single-family houses. In so far as this was done, the 'net housing gain' would be achieved, and there would be a surplus of space for the population of the more overcrowded larger houses.

The two positive symbols of this housing policy, taken by itself and leaving aside the question of those who would not be rehoused, were the Chelmsley Wood Estate to the east of the city, and the tower-blocks which began to spring up on the cleared inner-city sites and on the periphery.

Chelmsley Wood was built on a stretch of land won back from what had originally been thought of as a green belt, as the result of negotiations with the neighbouring authority. It was thought to be such a significant development that the Queen was brought up to open it. Unfortunately it quickly became evident that it was to be one of the least desired estates in the city. Its small shopping precinct became a kind of wind-trap, humanly deserted and littered with paper at weekends; and down some steps near the car-park, special works' buses seemed to indicate that this place was not on normal transport routes. 'Even' immigrants, as they qualified for housing, refused to go there (though since many of them worked across Birmingham's western border in the Black Country this was not

133

surprising). In the Town Hall there was still hope for the place, and when under local government reorganization the estate passed from the Birmingham to the Solihull District Council, Birmingham District saw it as essential that it should control the re-lets. Moreover, the leader of the Labour group on the Council looked forward to a future railway-line which would make the estate desirable. Up until 1977, however, this net housing gain looked like a human loss.

The tower-blocks gave as little satisfaction. Like so many housing and planning developments which went to the drawing-board in 1945, they represent a cheap and vulgarized version of what had been described in the little Penguin books on planning, housing and reconstruction at that time. But whereas the Penguin reconstruction architecture presupposed green spaces and playgrounds between the blocks as well as communal facilities within them, the actual new tower-blocks seemed to rise directly from ungrassed rubble, while, inside, circulation space was confined to not always effective small lifts and ill-lit corridors.

When the Rex-Moore study of Sparkbrook was conceived, it was thought of as the first of a series of studies in urban sociology, a study of Birmingham's zone of transition to be followed by a study of the first tower-blocks. It was suggested then that, given the dominant ideology surrounding the rehousing business, namely that social status improvement lay in semi-detached suburbia, rehousing in tower-blocks in the inner city was at best an ill-understood alternative unlikely to be acceptable to those to whom it was offered. Very quickly, in the first stage of redevelopment, the policy was modified by easing out the gaunt appearance of the tower-blocks with exaggerated cottagey types of development, but, as rehousing moved into its second stage, and the British economy deeper into crisis, even this easing out ceased. The tower-blocks now rose directly from the demolition sites and from the new network of urban motorways which made them even more terrifying islands for isolated pedestrians.

Rehousing, then, presented unexpected problems and the newly housed did not necessarily feel that they had been translated to Utopia. But their lot was significantly different from and superior to the un-redeveloped areas which now came to form the oldest portion of the city's housing stock. If, at the time of the Sparkbrook study, the city's biggest shame and anxiety had been called 'the twilight zones' now it was called the 'inner city'. According to the new mythology the inner city was the focus of all pathology, including pathological race relations. Cure the apparently intractable problems of the inner city and you would cure the problem of race relations. This was of especial interest to us because it was a brief study of Handsworth, Augustine John's *Race in the Inner City*, which became the very symbol of the inner-city problem in Great Britain.

We have already discussed the constitution of the 'inner city' which the authorities, central and local, are now blaming for all our ills, and claiming to put right. We have emphasized that it is not a problem of some natural and ill-understood problem of urban blight, but the product of definite decisions and phases of rehousing and planning policy. Briefly these are its elements.

In one part of the inner ring are demolition sites which have not yet been replaced by new housing or other buildings. Some of this land, of course, was scheduled for industrial use, but has not been taken up, partly, no doubt, because of the high cost of land, partly because of the absence of entrepreneurship and investment funds, and partly because it was the policy of the national, if not the local authorities that industry should migrate to new satellite towns. Other parts of the area, however, are scheduled for housing developments and these too are long delayed, because demolition itself may not yet be quite complete, and because there are uncertainties about the desirability of inner-city housing redevelopment anyway. The result is that the typical redevelopment area is a waste-land of rubble-strewn ash, pock-marked here and there by a house or two which, although boarded up, has escaped the bulldozer. No one looking at such sites, except perhaps an elite amongst the planners, knows for sure what the destiny of these sites will be, and to be told that one might be rehoused there one day would seem quite literally to be offered a fate worse than death. They are an eyesore and for many people they *are* the inner city.

Small Heath, two points round the inner-city clock from Handsworth, was chosen as one of three areas to be studied as a basis for the formulation of inner-city policy.[4] We have no space to discuss its problems here. It is, however, a living monument to the working-class culture of the past. In the middle of a sea of demolished sites is the Birmingham City football ground, which still brings fans from one knows not where on a Saturday afternoon, and which, unlike some other grounds, does not lack for parking space. There are very few houses indeed within shouting distance of the ground. But there is also Small Heath park, which is a fine place, which was once no doubt a playground of the local working class, and which still has cottages around it inhabited by ageing people who have no wish to leave them. Finally, there is a shopping street, populated largely by Indian, Pakistani and East African Asian shops.

The Inner Area Study Report, which includes an account of Small Heath, concerns itself on the whole with the question of strengthening the economy of the inner cities by bringing back industries and improving housing so that a better mix of population will come to live there. The old white householders have recently expressed fear that if the city's dispersal·policy for immigrants is abandoned, blacks will settle in places like Small Heath. But the Small Heath study rightly notes that the entrepreneurship of Small Heath's Asian settlers is precisely the sort of factor which will make business growth possible in an area which does not attract large-scale English entrepreneurs (Department of the Environment, 1977c).

This strange mix of problems in Small Heath is likely to be seen as typical of the inner city. It exists also in Handsworth, but there the demolition sites are less obvious. There are still terraces of houses around the West Bromwich and Aston Villa football grounds, and these, like the houses around Handsworth's park, are inhabited by West Indian and Asian workers. The limbo of the demolition sites is there, but more characteristic are the general improvement and the housing action areas.

At the time of the Sparkbrook study there was a contradiction, also evident in London, and reported in the Milner Holland report, between a slum clearance programme, going on in the old working-class terraced areas, where there was some social stability and some housing which was not all that bad, and the continuing existence of larger houses which were structurally sound, but which provided the most squalid living conditions in the city.

One possibility, of course, was the declaration of a new slum clearance programme for the 1970s. This, however, was not pursued for a number of reasons. First, it seemed to be uneconomic, although the kinds of social benefit and cost to be set for and against the operation were difficult to calculate. Another factor was a developing doubt amongst urban social theorists, planners, and politicians about the development of the whole city as some kind of extended suburban estate. This had been the theme of work like that of Jane Jacobs and Herbert Gans in the USA and of Young and Willmott and others in England. Something of the same kind of reservation was expressed in the report of the Sparkbrook study, which suggested that, properly administered by the responsible local authority, the conversion of houses to multiple occupation could provide a socially valuable element in the total urban housing system. Finally, it was clear that some at least of the old residents did not want their homes destroyed. They might not like their new neighbours, but they could be readily mobilized to direct action if necessary against the bulldozer.

Rex and Moore were consulted by both national and local politicians on this question in the light of the Sparkbrook study, being asked the policy question whether they favoured the improvement of the large old terraced houses of Sparkbrook to demolition and redevelopment. Their reply was that this policy question, like most policy questions directed to researchers, was falsely posed. If what was being implied was that improvement was being offered as an alternative to rehousing in the normal way, so that the tenants of lodging-houses would lose even those minimal rights which they had, the question was in fact not as simple or innocent as it seemed. They pointed out that a renewal policy might simply be a policy for 'gilding the ghetto', although, conscious of the appalling housing conditions, they also agreed that the gilding of the twilight zone might be better than leaving it ungilded.

Immediately after this, the Government published its White Paper, *Old Houses into New Homes* (Department of the Environment, 1968), and, for better or for worse, a new direction was set for the future development of the city's second ring. Most of the owners, landlords and tenants there would not be faced with the threat of demolition, but would be offered generous subsidies to refurbish their own houses and provide them with amenities. Under the 1969 Housing Act, moreover, the areas in which houses were situated could become general improvement areas and the council could set up schemes for improving not merely houses but whole streets and neighbourhoods.

Since it is only eight years since the setting up of general improvement areas, it would probably be unwise to suggest that a policy of this kind, which was contingent upon both local authority initiative and co-operation by the residents, has failed. Certainly the Birmingham Council adopted it with a will, and many of the streets and blocks studied by Rex and Moore in Sparkbrook, and in our own survey area in Handsworth, became general improvement areas. But there was a feeling that more urgent action was necessary, and it was this which led the Government to set up the Inner Area Studies (including that at Small Heath) on the one hand and housing action areas on the other.

Housing action areas, we assume, are expected to give greater precision and bite to the improvement policy, to deal with the worst houses in the secondary ring and bring to bear upon the situation a sense of urgency as well as compulsion. The first housing action areas were set up only in 1974 and are still in their early stages, but inspections have been carried out and houses selected for demolition or improvement. There have also been sporadic reports of resistance by local residents to possible demolition, and to negotiations and subsequent reclassification of houses and streets.

What is commonly called the inner city really refers to a secondary ring neighbourhood. It is essentially the archaeological residue of an Edwardian or late Victorian industrial working-class culture and society. It includes usually a declining number of factories; a park of some grandeur, but somehow now under-used and gone tatty; a football ground which still brings noisy and turbulent crowds onto the street, but which is essentially divorced from ordinary domestic

137

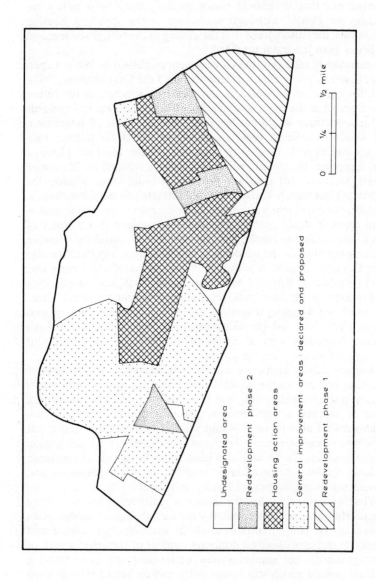

FIGURE 5.1 *Urban renewal in the survey area, 1976*

living; demolition sites, whose future has been pencilled in by planners, but which is uncertain and unknown to the local populace, some odd pockets of boarded-up houses not yet demolished; old working-class shops, some with new garish fronts as they are taken over by the supermarket chains; and, finally, the huddled, though often tree-lined terraces which actually constitute lodging-house zones, general improvement areas and housing actions areas. This is the stage set on which many native old people, hard-working immigrant adults and black minority children work out the pattern of their lives.

At the time of writing the Government's new policy for the inner cities is being worked out. It was extensively discussed in 1976 and 1977 and was the basis of a White Paper in July 1977 (Department of the Environment, 1977b). The essential new, bold stroke of this policy was to transfer to the sort of area which we have been describing the resources and the emphasis which had hitherto been directed to the new towns and the suburbs. Sites would be urgently prepared and offered to revive the industrial economy; the advance factories which had attracted industry to the declining areas such as the North East would now be built in the heart of the city; industrial improvement areas would be established along with areas of residential improvement, and a whole flow of subsidies would be organized to get entrepreneurs to act against their instincts and the natural directions of the land, labour and other markets. The policy would also take on board housing improvement, but in certain of its sections the White Paper suggests that the retired, the skilled and the semi-skilled would be encouraged to move to the periphery to make way for those who were building the vibrant new inner-city economy.

Meanwhile, despite all the arguing which attached to the inner-city policies and to the concept of improvement, private and public estates continued to be built, and those who succeeded in their occupations tended to move away from the improvement areas and housing action areas altogether. Those who remained were, as we have suggested in our regrouping of the housing-classes mentioned above, near the bottom of the heap, above only the tenants and owners of the lodging-houses. (It should be noted that there were still many of these, for between 1965 and 1975, according to the management team of the Policy and Resources Committee, some 4,000 houses in multiple occupation were registered, estimated to be occupied by some 25,000 people in 11,000 households, with a further 100 properties a year being referred to the Planning Officer for enforcement action.)

But what of those who moved? The richer amongst them made not merely a suburban move, but a move outside the city altogether.

139

Solihull became the smart district in the West Midlands conurbation' and Sutton Coldfield, while actually being included in the Birmingham District, retained its own identity as a centre for upper-class communities. Those who could went even further afield to Warwickshire and Worcestershire villages, to Herefordshire or to the Cotswolds. There was *not*, it must be emphasized, anything parallel to the subsequent inward migration of the rich and the white-collar people leading to a gentrification of the inner areas which occurred in London. At most there was an area of middle-class apartments in Edgbaston, but even that threatened to be engulfed by Balsall Heath on the one hand, and Ladywood on the other. Generally speaking, if one wanted to keep away from immigrants and council tenants, Sutton Coldfield and Solihull were safer. It should be noted that immigrants participated in these moves hardly at all. Those who did well made a more modest move such as from Handsworth to neighbouring Erdington.

The council housing stock of new houses continued to increase and the stock of slums awaiting demolition in council ownership declined in significance both as an embarrassment and a resource. The most astonishing development, however, came in 1976 and early 1977. On 23 January 1976 the chairman of the Housing Committee called for a review of the housing waiting-list. Only fourteen months before, the *Post* had reported a Birmingham MP as saying that '30,000 families were on the council list and new applicants were coming on at the rate of 200 per week'. Yet on 27 January 1977 the *Evening Mail* was able to report that there were only 10,000 'live' applicants and that, of these, not all wanted housing immediately. Little wonder that in September 1977 the Council finally responded to the pressure of the Cullingworth committee and reduced the waiting period before applicants could go on the active housing list from five years to two, and also lowered the age limit for the rehousing of single people. We believe that, in the late 1960s, Birmingham systematically exaggerated the numbers of those of its native population requiring council houses as an argument for not rehousing immigrants, and that by 1976 the figures had simply become incredible. In the mid-1970s, immigrants, who would by now have got by on the five-year rule anyway, stood as good a chance of getting an offer of a council house as whites, except that owner-occupiers in the improvement areas would not qualify anyway, and that it was possible that different kinds of offer might be made.

We must recapitulate here the stages through which discrimination against immigrants in the public housing sector has gone, because there are some aspects of this discrimination which have had irreversible consequences in segregating the coloured population,

short of some new act of positive discrimination of a kind unprecedented in Britain.

Obviously the principal barrier to the public rehousing of immigrants in the early 1960s was the period of residential qualification,
and a great many of those whom we describe in this survey living in
poor houses as owner-occupiers might well have been forced to buy
at this time. But, even amongst those who qualified, there was a
further hurdle to overcome. They had to be assigned to houses by
housing visitors whose attitudes are well summed up in the following
quotations from our own interviews:

'We can't hide the fact that people have different standards of
housekeeping. We don't want to offend people. We try to put
people in neighbourhoods where they won't conflict. After all,
some of the Asians may just be getting out of the stage where
they made curry patties on the floor. It's like the English
working class – they kept coal in the hall and donkeys in the
kitchen when some of them were put in council houses in the
twenties. It takes education to raise standards.'

'The standards haven't changed since 1969. People haven't
learned a thing. It's what we call central area standard, and
of course we are down to the dregs now. People with anything
about them have moved out and it's the Irish, the immigrants
and poor Birmingham people left – people we've moved around
into the clearance houses. Now we are having to move them to
the inter-war estates and they are turning these into slums.'

Finally, one visitor, referring to Handsworth in particular, said:

'It's a very mixed place. After the first war it was a lovely place
– Holly Road, Antrobus Road, Chantry Road – they were all
big houses with servants and huge rooms. Then after the second
world war it began to go down. A lot of Irish came and then
the West Indian people. There are still some very respectable
white people living there. Mind you, I'm not saying West
Indians aren't respectable. . . .'

It was on the basis of opinions such as these that, as our second
quotation suggests, immigrants, instead of being rehoused in council-
built houses, were 'moved around into the clearance houses'. Thus,
before about 1966 there were only a few immigrants in council-
built houses.

Some change in policy, however, was inevitable once the slum
clearance programme neared completion. Those immigrants who
were qualified in terms of residence for rehousing, and had enough
points in total, could no longer be shunted around the clearance
houses and it was necessary to move them to council estates.

141

What exactly the Council's policy was with regard to which estates it assigned the immigrants to between 1965 and 1970 is not clear. The Conservative chairman of the Housing Committee in 1968 was forced to justify the allocation of council-built houses in the inner-city area of Ladywood, and refused to change his policy, even in the face of a rent strike by white tenants there. We do not know, however, whether there was at this time any further policy of discrimination so far as suburban estates were concerned. Possibly as the second quotation above suggests, those who were sent to the suburbs were assigned to inter-war (i.e. older) estates and poorer houses. But matters might have been further complicated by an immigrant preference for the inner-city estates where they could maintain communal ties.

A wholly new situation faced the Council by 1970, however. The question was no longer one of whether immigrants should be put in council houses at all, but of how they should be concentrated or dispersed on council estates. This was a difficult policy question and one which produced cross-voting. There were 'liberals' on the race issue who feared segregation on particular estates, but others who for equally liberal reasons, opposed forced dispersal. On the other hand there were 'racialists' who wanted to prevent estates 'going down' through having too many blacks, and others who thought that it was best to concentrate immigrants in a few areas and avoid putting them on other white estates at all.

Subject to this sort of cross-cutting pressure, the Conservative-controlled Council in the early 1970s adopted the policy of 'dispersal'. The policy was that when a black family was offered a property, six properties on either side were marked 'NC' (not coloured) on the index of property. There was some confusion within the housing department as to whether the ratio was in fact one in thirteen rather than one in seven.

The new policy resulted in a reduction in the housing stock available to black families and to the stock-piling of coloured families who had asked for areas where the quota of houses available for coloured families had been reached. On the other hand, the policy could not in fact be fully applied, because, even though the housing department might have wished it, actual records of the ethnic origin of applicants were imperfect.

In effect, dispersal was very far from effective. A social development department was set up in the housing department in the late 1960s with the task of monitoring allocation procedures, policies and housing preferences. In 1975 this department undertook some research on the distribution of immigrants within the council housing stock. This showed that New Commonwealth immigrants were seriously under-represented in council tenancies based on the

142

proportion of immigrants in the total population. Immigrants formed 10 per cent of the population of Birmingham, but only 3·3 per cent of those renting council housing.

In the inner wards of Highgate, Newtown, Nechells and Lady-wood, the ratio of immigrant to non-immigrant tenants was well above the average for all council estates, while in Highgate and Nechells as a whole, as well as in small areas (enumeration districts) in all four wards, it was above the proportion of immigrants in the total population. The ratio of immigrant to white tenants in Highgate was 1 to 5·8 and in Nechells 1 to 9. In the most concentrated enumeration districts in the four wards the ratios were, Highgate 1 to 3, Newtown 1 to 4, Nechells 1 to 6 and Ladywood 1 to 4.

It will at once be apparent that, so far as certain parts of these estates of flats and houses are concerned, immigrants, far from being kept out, are actually over-represented. This by itself suggests that the problem of discrimination in the public sector has changed since Rex and Moore's Sparkbrook study. Immigrants do now get council houses, but in the inner city there has arisen a *de facto* type of segregation and even a tendency towards making ghettos of certain small areas.

On the other hand, a look at the figures for some of the outer estates suggests an entirely contrary pattern. In Primrose Hill and Walkers Heath only 19 out of 400 tenants were immigrants, in Shenley only 25 out of 610, and in Woodgate Valley 30 out of 2,754.

These figures suggest that the dispersal policy has not worked as yet. Immigrants are heavily concentrated in inner-city estates and badly under-represented on the newest suburban estates. How far is this a matter of immigrant choice and how far a matter of discriminatory application of the dispersal policy to certain areas only?

To our surprise we found that immigrants did not even mount a campaign for equality of access to suburban housing on the new estates. The social development department found that 90 per cent of immigrants interviewed preferred central areas and there was a marked unwillingness to move to estates like Chelmsley Wood. What immigrants did oppose as discriminatory was the dispersal policy itself, partly because it effectively reduced the number of offers they were likely to receive, but also because it involved the forced break-up of black neighbourhoods.

So far as the Council was concerned, it was committed in principle to the policy of overall dispersal or 'thinning out'. This could be justified on liberal assimilationist grounds and would also satisfy those more 'racialist' councillors and voters who wanted to limit the effect of the black presence. But this double and contradictory

143

justification had important consequences. It produced three kinds of situations:

1 Fewer offers of houses in central areas than immigrants wanted.
2 More offers of houses in some undesirable suburban estates than immigrants were willing to accept.
3 Few offers of houses in some desirable suburban estates which, however, might have been turned down, had they been made.

The dispersal policy was eventually challenged by the Race Relations Board and, after some confused reporting in which the Board was represented in the press as having cleared the Birmingham Council of discrimination, a committee was set up to ensure that a discriminatory policy of forced dispersal was not pursued. Since this so-called 'watch-dog' committee, including representatives of the Community Relations Council, has only recently begun its work it is too early to say whether it will effectively prevent discrimination.

The adjustment which Birmingham has made to the rehousing of immigrants in the public sector thus turns out to be somewhat different from either of the two possibilities which appeared open in 1965. At that time it appeared that either Birmingham would keep immigrants out of council houses altogether or that immigrants would make the suburban migration through the public sector. What has happened is that many of the earliest New Commonwealth immigrants have bought inner-ring property and thus withdrawn themselves from the public sector, while those who have been lucky or unlucky enough to have stuck it out, without resort to house purchase, have more frequently finished up in inner-city estates where they could maintain communal links with their property-owning kinsmen. Very few have made the suburban migration.

The problem which actually confronts us now is a different one from that which Rex and Moore may have led us to expect. There are not two groups of immigrants, one discriminated against and united by strong ethnic bonds, and another assimilated through having acquired equal rights to suburban housing. Private property-owners and renters on the one hand, and immigrant council tenants on the other, have tended to be much the same sort of individual, and, to all intents and purposes, we found very little differences in the observed attributes of those housed in the public and private sectors. It has seemed realistic to us, therefore, to treat the ninety-five West Indians in council houses and the 300 in our main sample as a single population for all purposes except when we are looking at housing conditions themselves.

The methodological problems involved here are discussed in Appendix 2. The point which we wish to make here is a substantive one. The immigrant community in Handsworth is now constituted of a number of groups in different housing situations. There is a core of private owners, either outright or with a mortgage; there are private renters either from private landlords or from housing associations; there are still some tenants of council property awaiting improvement or demolition, and there are council tenants. The proximity of the houses of all our council tenants to the improvement areas and housing action areas, however, means that they form part of one community with the inhabitants of those areas, and have shared communal institutions.

But, while we are seeking to emphasize here that being a council tenant is a less privileged status than Rex and Moore imagined, we would not wish to suggest that being an owner-occupier, or living in the private sector, represents a position of privilege for those who live in improvement or action areas. For, in spite of all that has been done to develop special policies for these areas, beyond the original renewal areas, the fact is that they contain some of the worst housing and some of the most depressed conditions for their inhabitants of all areas of the city today. We may not be talking of groups quite as disadvantaged as the Pakistanis and their tenants in Sparkbrook in 1965, but we are talking about some of the most disadvantaged housing classes and sub-classes.

In our survey we had a sample of 300 white British, 300 West Indian and 300 Asian householders in 128 contiguous enumeration districts surrounding and including Soho ward. We also had samples of 100 white and 100 New Commonwealth tenants of council properties in Newtown. We are thus able to give a closer indication of immigrant housing conditions by looking at comparisons between ethnic groups in the owner-occupier sector and the private and public rented sector.

Table 5.1 shows the distribution of our whole sample (including the 200 council tenants in Newtown) by ethnic group and tenure. It should be noted immediately here that there are more council tenants than those whom we deliberately went out to look for. Our specially selected council sample included 95 West Indians, 5 Asians and 100 white British. There were, however, another 27 West

TABLE 5.1 *Survey respondents by ethnic group and tenure*

	West Indian	Asian	British	Total
Owner-occupiers	212 (53·7%)	249 (81·6%)	165 (41·25%)	626 (56·9%)
Private renters	61 (15·4%)	30 (9·9%)	91 (22·75%)	182 (16·5%)
Council renters	122 (30·9%)	19 (6·2%)	142 (35·5%)	283 (25·7%)
Other	—	7 (2·3%)	2 (0·5%)	9 (0·9%)

145

Indians, 14 Asians, and 42 white British picked up in the general sample who were tenants of council-owned properties. For some purposes it is necessary to separate these two groups since some of the second group will be in houses awaiting demolition. Bearing this in mind, however, we may now turn to an analysis of the housing conditions of owner-occupiers, private tenants and council tenants as revealed by our survey.

We analysed the 'social class' of owner-occupiers, using the Standard Market Research classification of occupations by social class. Here we found that 19·4 per cent of the 165 white owner-occupiers were in the upper and middle classes as compared with only 0·5 per cent of the 212 West Indians and 1·2 per cent of the 249 Asians. On the other hand, 58 per cent of the West Indians, 51·8 per cent of the Asians, but only 15·2 per cent of the white British were in class D (semi-skilled and unskilled working class). The striking fact which emerges here is that a much higher proportion of immigrants in the lower social classes are forced to buy than amongst the whites. This is the other side of the coin to the under-representation of the immigrants in council houses.

Interestingly, whereas only 30·5 per cent of the Asians and 30·9 per cent of the white British had a mortgage, no less than 84·0 per cent of the West Indians had one. No less than 62·3 per cent of the Asians and 67·3 per cent of the white British owned their houses outright. It would seem, therefore, that while the large proportion of British outright owners is explicable mainly by the fact that many are old enough to have paid off mortgages, Asians have a preference for or are constrained to accept what is an unusual form of housing tenure.

Amongst those who do have mortgages or loans there are again interesting differences between ethnic groups as Table 5.2 shows.

TABLE 5.2 *Source of mortgage or loan by ethnic group amongst survey respondents*

	West Indian	Asian	White British
Bank	4 (2·2%)	34 (36·2%)	3 (5·6%)
Building society	96 (53·3%)	5 (5·4%)	32 (59·2%)
Council	58 (32·2%)	33 (35·1%)	14 (25·9%)
Private individual	4 (2·2%)	6 (6·4%)	—
Brokerage/finance company	7 (3·9%)	11 (11·7%)	4 (7·4%)
Other	1 (0·6%)	3 (3·1%)	1 (1·9%)
Refused to answer	10 (5·6%)	2 (2·1%)	—
	180	94	54

The outstanding features here are the heavy reliance of the West Indians and Asians on council mortgages and of the Asians on bank loans. This suggests that normal building society loans are less readily available to or sought by immigrants (in the case of Asian immigrants, building societies play a very small part indeed). Some 10 per cent of all the owner-occupiers had second mortgages. These included twelve who had obtained them from the Julian Hodge group, whose activities had been a special area of West Indian political concern.

Mortgage repayments were surprisingly equal as between West Indians and white British. Indeed, West Indians paid marginally less, but whereas only 3·9 per cent of West Indians and 3·7 per cent of white British paid £50 a month or more, 26·5 per cent of Asians did so, probably reflecting their preference for early outright ownership and their reliance on bank loans.

The West Indians paid higher rates than did either the Asians or white British, but it was only amongst the white British that a significant proportion of the population received a rate rebate (21·8 per cent).

Asians (47·4 per cent) were more likely to be in leasehold property than West Indians (42·1) per cent or British (34·5 per cent), and amongst those who did hold leasehold property, the Asians were more likely to have short-term leases. This may suggest that the Asians were in less desirable properties, and this is confirmed by the fact that only about 70 per cent of Asians had sole use of the three basic amenities – fixed sinks with hot water, baths and inside toilets – as compared with about 93 per cent of West Indians and 86 per cent of whites. Again, the average density of occupation for Asians (1·04 per room) was higher than that for West Indians (0·8 and for white British (0·4).[5]

Generally, Asian owner-occupiers were worse off than West Indians or white British, despite the greater frequency of outright ownership in their group. On the other hand we did not find, as Rex and Moore suggested in Sparkbrook, that they were buying second houses or sub-letting to any substantial degree. Only ten out of 249 Asians were buying more than one house.

West Indian owner-occupiers are in some respects better off than whites (e.g. in the level of their mortgage repayments and household amenities) and in some respects worse off (e.g. level of overcrowding).

The idea of general improvement areas was fairly well understood at the time of the survey. Of the owner occupiers, 55·3 per cent said that they lived in a general improvement area and actually did so, but the notion of housing action areas was still little known. Only 6·6 per cent of the population said that they lived in housing action areas and actually did so. The availability of improvement grants

147

was widely known, though slightly less so to Asians. More than a quarter of all owner-occupiers, including 31·9 per cent of all West Indian owner-occupiers, had applied for grants. On the other hand, whereas 69·4 per cent of white applications for grants were successful, the percentage for West Indians who were successful was only 26·2 per cent and for Asians 35·4 per cent. We were not able to discover why, although they were aware of improvement grants and applied for them, West Indians were less successful in getting them.

It should be remembered in assessing these comparisons that the overall living standard was low. This was the worst property available for owner-occupation in the city. The whites were there because they had stayed on while their property deteriorated. The West Indians were encouraged or constrained to go there by the kinds of housing finance available to them or not available to them. The Asians went there because they were the cheapest houses available.

Within this it would seem that the West Indians did better than other groups, but this conclusion is misleading. For a young population of economically active people with children they needed more in the way of housing than the old white population, so that it still seems reasonable to conclude that these West Indian owner-occupiers were a disadvantaged group, or, compared with comparable white groups, a housing underclass.

There was a total of 182 private renters in our sample as compared with 626 owner-occupiers. Of these, 91 were white British, 61 were West Indian and 30 were Asian. Over half of the Asians were renting from a relation, whereas 60·7 per cent of West Indians were renting from a housing association, and 53·8 per cent of white British tenants were renting from another individual. The actual number of West Indians renting from housing associations was 37. It is interesting, therefore, to notice that 95 out of 273 West Indians whom we interviewed, and who were not council tenants, got their housing through a housing association tenancy or through a local authority mortgage. This compares with 96 who obtained a building society mortgage. It would seem, therefore, that the special provision which has been made for West Indians in the private sector makes an approximately equal contribution to West Indian housing to normal building society finances. Amongst Asians, by contrast, the percentage of renters is small and the most frequent form of housing is through outright purchase.

There is nothing in the Handsworth data suggesting a parallel with the Sparkbrook situation in which the Pakistanis tended to be the landlords of other immigrant groups and of British people with problems. Only 14 out of 101 tenants renting from other individuals rented from a landlord in another ethnic group, and of the 14 landlords involved 9 were Indians, 3 were Pakistanis and 2 were British.

No West Indian was a landlord to a member of another ethnic group. There was, moreover, little record of disputes with the landlord, though West Indians and white British were more likely to have been in dispute with their landlord than the Asians.

So far as the condition of rented housing was concerned, about three-quarters of West Indians as against about 62 per cent of white British were likely to have sole use of a bath, fixed sink, and an inside W.C., though white British were more likely to have sole use of a hand-basin with hot water, and a garden, than were West Indians. By comparison, the Asians overwhelmingly had to share the amenities which they had. It should be remembered that most of these Asian tenants were heads of households occupying shared accommodation in flats or rooms which were not purpose-built. Again, however, here as elsewhere, one finds that objective lack of facilities is not accompanied by subjective dissatisfaction. Of all Asian tenants, 70 per cent, as compared with only 29·5 per cent of West Indians and 24·2 per cent of the British, expressed themselves as satisfied with their accommodation.

Of the 182 private renters, 65 said they were eligible for a council house (38 West Indians, 3 Asians and 24 white British). Some 75 tenants did not know whether they were eligible (18 West Indians, 18 Asians and 39 white British), and 42 said they were not eligible (5 West Indians, 9 Asians and 28 British).

We took owner-occupiers and private tenants together to ask whether they had applied for a council house in the last ten years. The results are shown in Table 5.3. The percentage of West Indians and British and even more so of Asians who may have been drawn into owner-occupation through failure to obtain a council house is obviously small (although one should notice that one in seven West

TABLE 5.3   *Application for council house in past ten years by survey respondents*

	West Indian	Asian	White British	Total
Owner-occupiers				
Applied	28 (13·2%)	9 (3·6%)	18 (10·9%)	55 (8·8%)
Never applied	184 (86·8%)	240 (96·4%)	147 (89·1%)	571 (91·2%)
	212	249	165	626
Private renters				
Applied	46 (75·4%)	4 (13·3%)	35 (38·5%)	85 (46·7%)
Never applied	15 (24·6%)	26 (86·7%)	56 (61·5%)	97 (53·3%)
	61	30	91	182

Indians had made such an application). In the case of private renters it is clearly the West Indians whose demand is most urgent.

Questioned as to why they had not applied for a council house, half of the private renters said they had no need, that they preferred to buy or were satisfied with their existing rented accommodation. Only a tiny minority said that they had not applied because they had been deterred by the length of the waiting-list.

Of those who had applied, 15 out of 55 owner-occupiers and 58 out of 85 renters thought they were still on the housing list. Of those who said they were no longer on the waiting-list over a third said they had withdrawn voluntarily, while 23 (29·5) per cent said they had never heard from the housing department. Of those who had applied, 69·4 per cent said that they had never been offered a house. It does not seem, however, that there is still a large frustrated demand for council housing. Out of 808 private renters and owner-occupiers only 140 had even applied for a council house in the last 10 years and only 73 thought they were still on the waiting-list. There were only 97 who said that they were on the list and who had not yet been offered a house.

One cannot conclude from all this, however, that the problem of discrimination in the allocation of council houses has not made a difference. It should be remembered that out of 273 West Indians and 279 Asians in our category of owner-occupiers and private renters, only 74 West Indians and 13 Asians have applied for council houses, even though they are in precisely the occupational and demo-graphic categories from which one would expect council house applications to be made. On the other hand it must be admitted that it is hard to disentangle the fact of discrimination here from that of ethnic choice. It would be interesting to know what the consequences would be of an active campaign by the council to publicize council housing with a view to providing immigrant families with accom-modation suited to their needs and within their incomes.

We did not find any large number of cases of exorbitant rents in privately rented accommodation. In fact, for all groups, the per-centage paying more than £10 per week was less than in council housing. Amongst Asians 13 out of 30 lived rent-free. Altogether 31 out of 142 white, 19 out of 122 West Indian and 2 out of 19 Asian tenants received rent rebates. The higher percentage amongst whites, however, is consistent with the large percentage of retired people on low incomes and does not necessarily indicate discrimina-tion in this matter.

It is hard to decide from our data whether rented accommodation is better or worse than that in owner-occupation. Marginally one could say that there is a higher density of occupation per room amongst West Indian (1·1) and Asian (1·1) tenants than among owner-occupiers (West Indian 0·87 and Asian 1·04), but the figure for white tenants (0·4) is the same as for owner-occupiers.

Private rented accommodation is, of course, a declining element in the total housing stock, but it is perhaps worth noting that 37 of the 61 West Indian tenants and 11 of the 91 white British were tenants of housing associations. It could be that these associations will gradually take over an important role from the individual land-lord, and they will undoubtedly do so more effectively, given the capacity to understand and use government and local authority finances.

Finally we come to council tenants. We had intended to study these separately and our questionnaire included a cue which led to every-one who was a council tenant answering a specific set of questions. Instead of this producing answers simply from the 100 pre-selected black and 100 white tenants, which we obtained from the housing department, however, it also 'cued in' another 83 tenants of council properties in the main sample.

Out of 200 in our main council house sample, 128 had been council tenants at an earlier address, while 45 out of 83 of the council house tenants in the sample of 900 had previously been council tenants. The remaining 72 tenants in the council flats and houses and 38 in the sample of 83 were in council property for the first time. Thus, in the present population of both the council-built houses and flats and the population of houses purchased by the council, there were more in their second (or more) council house than there were first-time renters. This gives the impression that it is quite usual for those in council housing of quality to have got there by stages. Moreover, some of those in council-built houses will want to move from their present houses to better ones by applying for transfers, and even those who have not actually got to council-built property may have been moved to their present slum homes from still worse ones.

The whites in the sample of 200 in Newtown had lived at their present address longer than blacks. Of the white tenants, 57 per cent had lived there for more than five years compared with 32 per cent of blacks. In the sample of 83 in the acquired properties, 90 per cent of West Indians and Asians had been at their present address for less than ten years, whereas 45 per cent of whites had been at theirs for more than ten years. This means in the case of acquired properties that the tenant was already in the house when it was compulsorily purchased. In the case of council-built houses, whites have been there longer, because of the lateness of the adoption of the policy of putting blacks in council houses. The council houses and flats, in fact, had a white history before blacks were put in them.

Amongst the 200 council tenants, a majority of whites came from

151

earlier council tenancies whereas the West Indians came equally from council rented and private rented accommodation. Taking all the first-time renters together, whether in the council-built properties or the demolition area, the majority had spent less than two years on the waiting-list. In the case of those who were in their second or later council house, the majority in all groups had been in council property for more than five years. Because they have been in council housing so long we did not think that survey data about their experiences on the housing list would be reliable. All in all, however, the pattern appears to be this: in the first place, before 1965, whites were moving into council-built properties as their houses were demolished, whereas immigrants rarely got council houses at all because of residential qualifications, or, if they did, they were put in demolition properties. In the second place, immigrants moved into some sort of council property in large numbers and a few moved into the council-built flats and houses. Finally, as the demolition programme reached its end, migrants moved directly into council-built houses, since some of them had only lately qualified and there were no more scheduled slums in which they could serve their apprenticeship as council tenants.

Further analysis of the first-time council renters in the Newtown council houses (i.e. those who had gone directly into their council-built properties without a prior period in any other council-owned property including demolition property) gave us some idea of the dates of application and period on the waiting-list for black and white tenants. This showed that since the period 1965–9 blacks and whites alike were not spending long periods on the waiting-list. Two-thirds of the blacks and a little more than two-thirds of the whites had had to wait less than three years.

What the figures in Table 5.4 suggest is that while the majority of the tenants of the Newtown estate (126 out of 200) were second-time renters, having graduated to their present homes via council houses in the demolition areas, there were another 76 who had gone there directly. Apart from three of them whose homes were scheduled for demolition and who were involuntarily moved into council property, these tenants came via the list. The figures suggest that by 1975 there were relatively few applications from white tenants to be mopped up, and that by this time West Indian applicants were coming on to the council list and getting council houses after a relatively brief wait. The housing situation was easier for these tenants, and we even found that the proportions of black tenants who had refused the first offer made to them (48·9 per cent) was higher than that amongst the whites (27·3 per cent).

It does seem that a considerable change was occurring in the total housing situation in the 1970s mainly owing to an easing of the total

TABLE 5.4   *Date of application and period on the waiting-list of survey respondents by ethnic group*

		Black tenants	White tenants
Applied	1973–6	20·4% (10)	9·1% (2)
	1970–2	24·5% (12)	50·0% (11)
	1965–9	34·7% (17)	27·3% (6)
	Before 1965	14·3% (7)	13·6% (3)
	Don't know	6·1% (3)	—
Total		100% (49)	100% (22)
Period on waiting-list			
Less than 3 years		61·2% (30)	72·2% (16)
3 years or more		32·6% (16)	22·7% (5)
Don't know		6·1% (3)	4·5% (1)

housing shortage. In these circumstances the housing histories of West Indian applicants depended more upon choice than upon constraint. One should not overlook the fact, however, that choice itself was constrained or, rather, conditioned by circumstances. Given that certain patterns of rehousing had been established, the later applicants chose to go where the council had previously placed people of their own group.

All of the whites in the pre-selected sample of council-built houses had been in the Birmingham area for twenty years or more. The period of length of residence of West Indians and Asians were as follows:

Less than 10 years	9 per cent
10 but less than 15 years	27 per cent
15 but less than 20 years	44 per cent
20 years or more	20 per cent

Thus the immigrants we are discussing in the Newtown estate are people 90 per cent of whom have been in the Birmingham area for more than ten years.

The age structure of the 200 tenants of the Newtown estate is shown in Table 5.5. It is interesting to notice that although there is a slight tendency for the 100 whites to be younger than the whites overall, this population is still older by far than the immigrant population of council tenants. Figures for household structure also confirm this tendency. In the sample of 400 whites, 20·5 per cent of all white households consist of a single person and 26·3 per cent consist of a couple with children. In the sample of 100 council tenants, 9 per cent consist of a single person and 39 per cent of a

153

TABLE 5.5   *Age structure of 200 household heads on Newtown council estate*

	Black		White	
20–30 years	16 ⎫		14 ⎫	
31–40 years	32 ⎬ 76%		15 ⎬ 40%	
41–50 years	28 ⎭		11 ⎭	
51–60 years	13		17	
61–5 years	8 ⎫		15 ⎫	
66–9 years	1 ⎬ 11%		10 ⎬ 43%	
70+ years	2 ⎭		18 ⎭	

couple with children. Quite naturally the council estate whites are younger than those who have stayed in the heart of Handsworth, but they are still substantially older than their immigrant neighbours.

Some 23 per cent of blacks and 37 per cent of whites in the council sample were thinking of moving. This compared with 27·8 per cent of West Indians, 16·3 per cent of Asians and 41·8 per cent of whites in the total sample. The absence of any great difference here is significant. It would seem that merely being in better housing does not increase attachment to the area and the racial tensions manifested in white attitudes in the area as a whole are reproduced in the council estates where there are high concentrations of immigrants.

Amongst comments made by white inhabitants of the post-war Newtown houses are the following:

'Lots of people have come from slum areas here, there is general rowdyism and too many coloureds' (44-year-old unemployed white van driver).

'There's too much noise from the rubbish shoot and the flipping kids and the noisy neighbours' (59-year-old white security man in tower-block).

'This block has a bad name and the lifts get dirty' (36-year-old white storeman).

'The green areas have been turned into rubbish tips and dog runs and the white people would like to see the coloureds go' (70-year-old machinist, retired).

On the other hand, blacks who express dissatisfaction are as conscious as those in the general sample that they are in a low-status area. For example, these fairly typical respondents replied:

'The rubbish shoot is troublesome, we have everybody's nuisance. We have dogs fouling outside the door and kids

154

running around' (29-year-old bakery labourer who has lived five years in the area).

'We came out of a run-down area and we'd like to live somewhere nice. I used to live in Erdington' (25 year-old quality control inspector who has lived four years in the area).

'We want a house, we would stay in Newtown if they gave us a house but we wouldn't mind going somewhere else' (34-year-old service worker).

The 200 tenants were asked whether the different nationalities got on well together. Those who chose the answer 'there are problems' formed 28 per cent of the white sample (as compared with 37 per cent in the sample as a whole), and amongst the black tenants 7 per cent (as compared with 15·95 per cent in the West Indian sample as a whole).

Taking the data on intention to move and on attitude to inter-group relations together it would seem that there is some small tendency for race relations to improve as people are rehoused. It is, however, slight, and our conclusion would be that conflict between ethnic groups continues in the inner-city council estates as it does in the general improvement and housing action areas.

Taking all of this evidence together we have asked ourselves whether it disproves two central themes in the Rex-Moore analysis of Sparkbrook. Could it now be argued that discrimination was ending and that in so far as there was conflict it was simply inter-ethnic conflict and not 'housing-class conflict' at all? Our conclusion is that this answer is oversimplified and that it does less than justice to the way in which discrimination and housing-class conflict have crystallized into a pattern for the inner city as a whole.

The assumption underlying the housing-class theory was that where men's housing situation changed, their interests and hence their behaviour would change. Hence it might be argued that, according to the theory, wholly new patterns of race relations should be expected on the Newtown estate. The first question we have to consider, however, is whether the housing situation of the rehoused black tenants has actually changed significantly in terms of access to the total housing stock.

It would seem to us that in the final phase access to the desirable post-war suburban estates is denied by the fact that such housing prevents cheap access to work and that it would leave the West Indian tenant dispersed and isolated from communal ties. Effective access to council housing, for all but a minority (whom we were not able to study during our present research), is to inner-city council houses and flats. The white and black tenants who move to these houses and flats remain effectively part of the communities from which they came. For social, cultural and political purposes they remain allied with their ethnic peers in the areas from which they have come, rather than form inter-ethnic ties or ties with the suburban council house tenantry. This, it seems to us, will be the nature of the situation for many years to come.

What we are interested in here, as the authors of the Sparkbrook study were, is not life-chances or attitudes, taken in isolation from each other, but the formation of groups and the development of group-consciousness and values amongst men as a result of the definitional distribution of life-chances. It is thus the history of a group relative to the system of housing allocation as a whole, and taken over a period of time, which leads to the formation of what we would call 'housing-classes-for-themselves'. Such classes are only likely to disappear when a change of a more fundamental kind occurs in the total housing system. We cannot imagine that a policy of merely modifying the system, so that West Indians gain access to what is, in effect, inferior housing, is a change of this kind. What is produced is the 'inner-city area' with its own council housing system alongside the improvement areas, a type of area which is as character-istic of the 1970s as 'twilight zones' like Sparkbrook were of the 1960s.

We know that in our hesitation to draw optimistic conclusions about the effect of an easing housing situation we will be accused of 'moral nihilism' by some of our reformist friends. It is therefore important that we should conclude by saying what we think would be necessary to eliminate the effect of housing-class conflict on race relations.

Crucially we believe that a situation would have to be created in which West Indians and Asians could choose their housing freely without being subject either to discrimination or to the need to use their housing situation as a resource for strengthening ethnic ties.

The ending of discrimination will not be achieved simply by allowing the West Indian applicant who perseveres with his applica-tion despite all discouragements to obtain rehousing in inner-city council housing. Nor will it be achieved through a punitive policy of dispersal. What is necessary is that the Council should actively pursue a policy, as it does with its white electorate, of making known the kinds of housing which are available, and of allowing all appli-cants the opportunity to make a fully informed choice. Such an information programme would include discussion with ethnic organizations as well as individuals about their attitudes to housing. We would be misleading our readers if we suggested that the move from deliberate discrimination and segregation to dispersal and then to the abandonment of dispersal is a policy which in any way meets

156

this need. We can only imagine housing policy as changing in the way we are suggesting as a part of a deliberate 'high profile' minority rights programme.

Paradoxically, however, even though discrimination in housing is something which immigrant leaders would oppose, it has helped to provide them with a communal resource. Just as exploitation in industry gave rise to the trade-union movement and more widely to the Labour movement amongst native British workers, so the fact of discrimination in housing has given rise to partially segregated areas, and to locally based and relatively effective communal and ethnic organizations, which are useful as a means of protecting the rights of minority groups. Thus to propose dispersal in terms of housing alone, before minority group rights have been assured right across the board, seems to minority group leaders, not so much a sound reform, but rather an attempt to weaken them politically. Thus the 'high profile minority rights programme' which we referred to in the last paragraph would have to be one which dealt with all those areas in which, at present, ethnic organizations are necessary to defend rights and not merely housing by itself.

We believe that it would be unrealistic in the present political situation to expect the adoption of this total package. Clearly the new Commission for Racial Equality set up in 1977 might see its task as lying in the carrying through of just such a programme. But the Commission has to operate in a hostile political situation in which the dominant trend is that of the anti-immigrant lobby. In such circumstances we can well understand the importance of political militancy amongst the immigrants. Such militancy is not an obstacle in the way of the Commission achieving its task. It is the essential condition of its success. Equal rights in housing are in fact dependent, above all, on effective political representation.

Our task in this chapter, however, has not been primarily to advocate change of this kind. It has been to ask what changes have occurred in the housing situation since black immigration began. Clearly there have been changes and the situation in Handsworth or in Sparkbrook in 1978 is not the same as it was in Sparkbrook in 1965. None the less, we have not been describing a smooth process of assimilation. What we have seen is the emergence of a set of housing policies, which have produced the new social phenomenon of the 'inner city'. What its destiny will be, particularly as it is affected by new and deliberate inner-city policies, must be the subject of future research.

6   Black immigrants, schools and the class structure

The focus of this study as a whole is that of the relationship of West Indian and Asian communities to British society, and, realistically speaking, that means the degree to which they are absorbed into its class structure. This includes two interrelated problems, namely the relative chances of immigrants attaining different class positions (e.g. of their becoming 'working class' or 'middle class' at least as crudely indicated by whether they enter manual or non-manual occupations), and the belief and value systems which they hold which lead to identification with particular groups and conflict with or deference towards other groups. Before we turn to the evidence which we have of the operation of the educational system locally and nationally, we should clarify these two problems further in order to indicate what questions we are posing.

The traditional preoccupation of the sociology of education in Britain has been with the selection of children from different occupational or class backgrounds for certain types of schooling. The simplest focus of all has been on the relative chances of non-manual and manual workers' children getting into and staying in state grammar schools. This, however, is only part of the problem, for a further contrast has to be drawn between the free state sector and the private or fee-paying sector. Underlying sociological studies of this kind has been the assumption that entry into selective state schools means a passport to at least white-collar employment, and that some of those who go there might also join graduates of the fee-paying schools in going on to university education and particularly to the more prestigious type of university education which in turn leads to the most prestigious and powerful jobs.

Behind the factual investigations which such studies involve has lain the egalitarian reformist judgment that it is wrong that children from the lower strata should not have an equal chance of obtaining

158

the better positions. On the one hand this concern has been with the children of manual workers entering selective schools. On the other, it has been with the chances of children from the state sector as such having equal rights of entry to prestigious higher education and jobs. The debate about and the introduction of policies of comprehensive education in the state sector has now changed the focus of concern. In principle the first of these problems should be disappearing, although it may continue in more subtle forms in streaming within schools. On the other hand, while private education has not been abolished, and both the link between the so-called Clarendon schools and Oxbridge, and the prestige and power of being an Oxbridge graduate continues, the second problem remains, and indeed raises more pressing issues of social justice, since the Clarendon schools will no longer contain 'scholarship boys and girls' paid for from public funds, but solely the children of the relatively rich.

The problem of cultural differences between classes, and of the role of schools in re-socializing the socially mobile into acceptance of the values and belief systems of the higher classes, is less often discussed in Britain. Indeed, in so far as emphasis is on the injustices of selection, it cannot be discussed, for one cannot both demand equal chances of incorporation into the upper classes and call into question their value system. Thus the main emphasis in studies of language and culture has been upon the extent to which working-class language and its usage in working-class cultural settings acts as a barrier to educational success and social mobility.

Of course there are real difficulties here. While one can imagine someone with socialist convictions opposing social mobility and the cultural processing which goes with it, the usual stance of Labour and socialist thinkers in Britain has been to treat secondary education of the more prestigious sort as educationally valuable and ideologically untainted. On the other hand the idea of a different education for the children of workers has usually been advocated by those who want to keep them in a position of inferiority.

Both the problem of selection and the problem of moral and social indoctrination have taken on a new dimension in recent years, however, with the discovery of the new poor and the disadvantaged in the inner city. Apart from the problem of differences of life-chances, life-styles and values between white-collar and manual workers, it now seems to be increasingly recognized that there are divisions between manual workers – between those who have job security and political and trade-union protection of their social rights on the one hand and those who live within 'a tangle of path-ologies' on the other. The question for many children seems to be not whether they have an equal chance of rising from the working class to the middle class, but whether through their education they

159

can at least have the same rights and cultural equipment as the mainstream working-class. Once again the suggestion occurs that these children should have a special education which is relevant to their condition.

When we turn to the study of black immigrants and the class system in education, the main focus of attention is not on the access of blacks to middle-class positions, certainly not to the public school-Oxbridge type of destiny. For those with the necessary money there is no political obstacle to entry to the super-privileged positions. The vast majority of Asian and West Indian immigrants, however, are poor workers, and for them the question is whether they will be pressed into the lowest destiny of all in the disadvantaged urban schools or whether they will achieve the same right as mainstream working-class children, that is to say the right to compete for educational success and social mobility in streamed comprehensive schools.

It may perhaps be necessary to qualify this by noting that amongst Asian professional workers and other successful immigrants who have escaped from the inner city and areas of immigrant concentration, the choices which are open are different, namely whether to stay in the state sector or 'go private'; or, more mildly, they can choose the school with the best track record in the state system. This minority might be interesting and deserves separate study. By definition, however, these individuals are excluded from our study within the Handsworth area, and the majority whom we will be discussing are those who are fighting for equal rights with the working class.

The problems facing this majority are complex and subtle. They may, as workers and the children of workers, share many of the disadvantages of the working classes. But, over and above this, they may have to face up to processes of selection subject to handicaps of language and culture and those imposed by colour-prejudice and bias on the part of the selectors. The effect of this may be that they are pushed into a competitive position equivalent to that of the new poor and the urban disadvantaged, and paradoxically, when well-intentioned schemes to help those disadvantaged come to be thought of as including immigrants *per se*, then the process of social reform itself can become a means of putting immigrants in a disadvantaged position.

So far as cultural and ideological education and indoctrination are concerned, immigrants are in a complex position. They are being subjected simultaneously to processes of socialization of the upwardly mobile and to the more horizontal process of assimilation from one culture to another. Thus an Indian immigrant worker's child taking 'A'-levels is simultaneously learning a middle-class life-style and English middle-class culture, either in place of, or alongside, his family's life-style, tradition and culture. On the other hand, a young West Indian boy who becomes a Black Power militant rejects the normal respectable middle-class and white life-style in favour of what is, in part at least, a culture of revolt.

It would be wrong to assume that all Asian immigrants are in the position of the Indian mentioned in the last paragraph or that all West Indians either aim at being middle-class Englishmen or affiliate to the culture of revolt. An Indian militant and a respectable middle-class man with a West Indian culture may also be envisaged. What we should beware of, however, is confusing cultures which are primarily the product of or shaped by political oppression, conflict and revolt, and those which are simply shaped by cultural pluralism. A recurrent phenomenon in the sphere of education and race relations is the attempt to defuse political conflict by misrepresenting it as a problem of cultural pluralism.

We noted above that there are few native, British, working-class socialists so committed that they refuse to have their children educated in a corrupt, middle-class educational system. For the immigrant, however, as for the black American, the problem is more acute. It may seem to some that to try to launch one's children into social mobility and assimiliation is to connive at the oppression of one's own people. Thus one may expect to find more strongly among immigrants (at least amongst West Indian immigrants) than amongst native workers, an opting out of the overall competitive system in favour of affiliation to a culture of revolt. On the other hand, this is likely to be a vanguard movement only, for the decision to opt out of a competitive system, when no revolutionary change in that system can be realistically envisaged, may be foolhardy.

All that we have said so far involves looking at education from a sociological perspective, a perspective which to an educationalist might seem unduly cynical. But there is no doubt that the questions of selection, social mobility and the indoctrination of the socially mobile are an important element in educational theory which it is important to abstract out. We also believe that these issues, normally recognized by educational sociologists within a British population thought of as ethnically homogenous, occur in a more acute but slightly different form when immigrants from Asia or the West Indies are concerned.

On the other hand we should be doing educationalists an injustice, and we should misunderstand the full complexity of educational problems, if we were to represent them as simple hypocrites doing a political job disguised as an educational one. There is no doubt that they approach the problems of the 'lower' classes and of immigrants in terms of what they see professionally as a purely educational expertise. This educational expertise, moreover, is institutionalized

161

in our society and is not simply at the beck and call of any political ruling class. Our problem will be to see how this educational expertise affects the total class and race relativns situation, as well as to look at the way in which it is partially shaped by political factors, and in which educational practitioners are led by bias to depart from the expertise itself.

Policy issues in education and immigration

It is with these considerations in mind that we now turn to look at the way in which the education of West Indian and Asian immigrants has been approached by educational policy-makers nationally and locally.

The problem of how immigrants' children should be dealt with in the educational system has entered national debates about education in the form of the following questions:

1 Is there overt discrimination in the form of a deliberate denial of opportunities to immigrant children on grounds of race?

2 Should statistics of immigrant numbers and immigrant performance be kept officially as a basis for educational planning?

3 Should immigrant children be spread evenly through the education system, particularly through a programme of dispersal from the inner city to suburban schools?

4 Do West Indian and Asian children achieve less than their indigenous peers in selection tests and examinations?

5 Do immigrants face special problems in schools or do they have problems because they are part of a large category of disadvantaged children?

6 How can non-English-speaking children be assimilated into the school system?

7 What provision should be made for the education of the children of immigrants in their own language and culture?

8 How should funds be provided to overcome the disadvantages of immigrants and, more widely, of all the 'disadvantaged'?

We shall now record the main points which have been made in the debate around these questions, but before we do that we must make an important preliminary observation. This is that there was no planning at all for the absorption of immigrants' children into the educational system. Had there been, in a society which valued the notions of equality of opportunity and equality of outcome for all of its citizens, then the question would have been how to overcome

162

the manifest disadvantages of the children of immigrants by providing them with the linguistic and other skills necessary for them to compete equally at school, and by giving special consideration to the problems which these children might face as a result of living uneasily between two cultures and as a result of migrating from one social system to another. Instead the problems mentioned arose *ad hoc*, decisions were often taken in panic, and the very way the debate was structured, almost regardless of the answers given to the eight questions, fostered racism.

It is not surprising that the Race Relations Board was not called upon, as the American courts were called upon, to declare practices in education discriminatory, so long as it was necessary under the Act to prove intent to discriminate. Britain had no Little Rocks, where children were denied entry to schools. But the right to an equal education might still be denied if groups of children were faced with a highly selective system without being equipped to compete. What could easily happen without overt or intentional discrimination was that the educational system could be a powerful means of reinforcing and exaggerating social differentiation. A. H. Halsey is surely right when he says that: 'Too much has been claimed for the powers of educational systems for the wholesale reform of societies which are characteristically hierarchical in their distribution of chances between races, classes and sexes' (Halsey, 1972, p. 7).

The issue, as David Smith realized in planning the second PEP survey of discrimination, was not one of intent, but of the consequences of acts and policies which had the effect of producing disadvantage. But if disadvantage existed, it had to be measured, and this involved a prior decision to keep statistics of the numbers and relative facts of children in different categories. On the other hand, in a society in which there was doubt as to whether all children should be treated equally, it was possible to envisage a situation in which the identification of a minority group might well be used as a basis for discrimination. There was thus considerable uneasiness and uncertainty in the way in which educationalists approached this question.

At one point the Department of Education and Science sought to evade the question altogether, arguing that there was no point in collecting immigrant statistics because they did not form the basis of any grant made by the Department of Education and Science (Select Committee on Race Relations and Immigration, 1972b). This suggested a bureaucratic system unguided by any values at all. In fact, however, from 1967 to 1972 the Department of Education did keep statistics, and did so in a way which was deliberately intended to avoid them being used for discriminatory purposes. It defined immigrant children to include only:

1 children born outside the British Isles to parents whose countries or origins are abroad, and
2 children born in the British Isles whose parents lived here for less than ten years (Department of Education and Science, 1967–72).

Thus, after a man and his wife had lived in Britain for ten years it was assumed that no special provision for his children would be necessary, because he would have the rights and the capacity to look after them himself as a normal citizen.

The intention of the DES was laudable but its decision satisfied neither racialists nor liberals. The racialists wanted to play the numbers game and to demonstrate how the schools were being overwhelmed by coloured children, while the liberals wanted the monitoring of relative opportunity to go on for many more than ten years. More immediately, teachers as represented by the National Union of Teachers did not want statistics at all, claiming that 'any attempt to elicit some of the information required as to the country of origin can arouse the deepest resentment and suspicions of racial discrimination, even where no such interest is present' (Select Committee 1973).

On the other hand, the Parliamentary Select Committee recommended in 1972 (Select Committee, 1972b) that a working party be convened to 'formulate statistical requirements' and find some formula by which numbers of immigrants and black children should be recorded.

The Department kept statistics of immigrant children defined in its own limited terms from 1967 to 1972 only. It was at this point that it declared them to be administratively useless. (They may, indeed, have been so, since the record of a figure of 2·1 per cent of the total school population in 1967 rising to 3·3 per cent in 1972 was probably considerably below the actual percentage of coloured children (DES, 1967–72). Several years later, moreover, the past president of the NUT, Mr Max Morris, admitted that he had been wrong to oppose the collection of statistics. All in all this prolonged debate was indicative of a society which was uneasy about its relations with immigrant minorities and was anxious that a potentially ugly political problem should not be too clearly stated.

The issue of 'dispersal' aroused similar ambiguous attitudes. That an argument could be produced for spreading immigrant children around all the schools and preventing incipient segregation was obvious, and there were many liberals on the race issue who argued that Britain should follow the American Supreme Court's view, stated in the case *Brown v. the Board of Education* in 1954, that separate facilities were inherently unequal. Moreover it was clear in Britain, as it was in the USA, that opposition to dispersal came from those who were concerned to keep West Indian and Asian children out of schools in the suburbs. On the other hand, in Britain, West Indian leaders and 'liberals' opposed dispersal on the grounds that the very problem arose only because there was an inadmissible degree of segregation in housing. Bussing the school-children would involve an almost ritual declaration that black children were the cause of educational problems, and that dispersal would break up, or at least weaken, community support which was essential to the children's sense of identity and motivation to succeed. Here, as in the case of the collection of statistics, it was possible to admit that in an ideal world dispersal might help to ensure equality of opportunity, yet to argue that, with a tide of racist opinion moving as strongly as it was, the public display of immigrants as having problems would only lead to punitive action against them.

The question of how well immigrants are achieving in schools is one on which there is still little information. Obviously a first requirement of any possible remedial action is systematic knowledge of the level of performance of West Indian and Asian children in the basic educational skills, and in the various selective and classificatory processes which go on in schools. Hitherto, however, the Department of Education has not undertaken any systematic study of these questions, and such evidence as there is is distinctly patchy and its import uncertain.

Debates about differences in the IQ of different ethnic and other social groups have long been a subject of political controversy in other countries. In South Africa attempts were made in the 1930s to prove that African children had lower IQ scores than their white peers. This led to a systematic scrutiny of the tests used by Biesheuvel (1969) who argued that they were unsuitable for inter-group comparisons. In the USA on the other hand, Klineberg (1935) showed that most blacks scored lower than most whites, and urban blacks lower than urban whites; but urban blacks scored higher than rural whites, suggesting that environmental factors affected the test outcome.

In many tests of supposedly innate performance it would seem that it is the tests themselves that are being tested. Ferron, examining the literature on the subject of racial differences in intelligence between 1936 and 1966, concluded: 'When circumstances are such as to ensure that white and coloured groups share a common way of life and have equal educational opportunities, differences are small or non-existent (Ferron, 1966).

Nevertheless, research into the relative performance and attainment of different ethnic groups has persisted (McFie and Thompson, 1970; Ashby, Morrison and Butcher, 1970).

165

What these studies suggest is that there is nothing approaching proof on hereditary differences in intellectual capacity between ethnic and racial groups, that possibly, as time passed and conditions were equalized, the children of immigrants would do as well as their English classmates, or at very least that there is still much which can be done on the 'environmental' side to improve the immigrant's child's chances.

There are, however, some studies which suggest that there is a problem of West Indian performance (Payne, 1969; Bagley, 1971; and Yule et al., 1975). The Inner London Education Authority literacy survey concluded that Asians were performing at a higher level than West Indians, that underprivileged white children perform at a higher level than West Indian settlers, and 'it is the child from the West Indian background whose needs in terms of basic skills should be given the highest priority' (Little, 1975). Similar conclusions were drawn by the educational priority area surveys (Halsey, 1972), while the report of the Select Committee on the West Indian community (Select Committee on Race and Immigration, 1977) suggested an independent enquiry into the poor school standards of West Indian children and the anxiety felt amongst West Indian parents about many aspects of the educational system.

Rutter's large study in the early 1970s, involving 2,281 Inner London and 1,142 Isle of Wight children, included an intensive study of 100 West Indian children in London (Yule et al., 1975). He noted the anxiety and resentment expressed about West Indian children placed in schools for the educationally sub-normal, the low proportion in selective academic schools and their apparent low level of educational attainment. The results of this study also show UK-born West Indian children performing below the average scores of an indigenous sample of children.

While psychological research was concentrating on measuring low performance, the West Indian political and community organizations were attacking discrimination and, as the central symbol of that discrimination, the categorization of West Indian children as educationally sub-normal.

Coard (1971) addressed the Caribbean Education Association and published his address under the title *How the West Indian Child is Made Educationally Sub-normal in the British School System*, and the issue was kept alive in the journal *Race Today* (1973 and 1975) and in the evidence given to the Select Committee (1973, 1976).

A letter from the DES to chief education officers (DES, 1973) confirmed that there were indeed four times as many West Indian children in ESN schools as their numbers in the total school population might warrant. Why this is so would seem to lie in the complex and unclear procedures for classifying children as educationally

sub-normal and the considerable leeway which this gives for dis-
cretion and the operation of prejudice.

The DES has not yet commissioned any major study of possible
low achievement by West Indian and Asian children. If it did, the
conventional wisdom suggests that both groups of children of immigrants might be shown to be low achievers with the West Indian
children doing less well than the Asians. It is to be expected that if
such a result is arrived at there will be a growth in support for the
notion that Jensen's findings on the intelligence of black Americans
apply to the West Indian child in Britain. Eysenck's book *Race,
Intelligence and Education* (Eysenck, 1971) may be interpreted at its
best as a plea from academic circles that research of this kind should
be conducted.

Those academics who have opposed Eysenck's campaign have,
of course, been accused of being obscurantist and this allegation
has led many to the conclusion that there is something of a conspiracy
amongst academics to conceal the possibility of the hereditary
inferiority of West Indians.

In fact, what has been proved is that in the USA, in a number of
studies of matched groups in which so-called environmental variables
are controlled, black children have consistently achieved lower
scores than whites. It is assumed by many as a result that this means
that environmental factors have been disposed of and that the innate
inferiority of black intelligence has been proved.

We do not accept that the conclusion in that last sentence can be
drawn in the USA, nor that it can be applied to blacks in Britain.
Non-hereditary factors affecting school performance cannot be
reduced to a few crude environmental variables. The motivation
of the West Indian and Asian child to learn in English schools is
affected by a whole set of factors which arise essentially from the
colonial encounter. Until these are understood in their full complexity we will have little knowledge of the way in which 'environment' is affecting performance.

So far no responsible educationalist has attempted to apply the
Jensen-Eysenck analysis in the formulation of policy in Britain. But a
very special type of explanation has grown up. This is that the West
Indian suffers, not because of this or that factor in his environment,
but because of 'disadvantage', a character which he shares with all
other disadvantaged groups. Thus, no particular strategy to improve
the position of West Indians has to be pursued. They will benefit
from a general assault on the problems of the disadvantaged.

The concept of educational disadvantage[1] first emerged from the
Plowden Report (1967) which argued that black and white children
in the inner-city areas of British cities were equally deprived. Thus,
when the Select Committee reported on race and education (Select

Committee, 1973, vol. 1) that 'an immigrant education advisory unit should be set up in the DES', the DES responded by setting up an educational disadvantage unit and and assessment of performance unit. The first of these was to 'influence the allocation of resources in the interests of immigrants, and those identified on the best currently available criteria, as suffering educational disadvantage', while the second was to identify under-achievement and methods of assessment generally. The White Paper on the education of immigrants from the DES (1974) called for the setting up of an information centre, not on immigrant education, but on educational disadvantage. Yet when the minister, Mr Mulley, announced the setting up of the centre, he said it would 'promote good practice in the education of the disadvantaged at all stages, taking into account the distinct needs of ethnic minorities' (Hansard, July 1975).

What immigrants were being asked to accept as a result of these decisions was that any problems that they had would only be solved by an attack on disadvantage which was a quality shared by all immigrants' children with problems and some white children. What was happening could be expressed in tabular form. There are eight potential groups of children in schools:

1	Immigrant children	Disadvantaged	Low achievers
2	Immigrant children	Disadvantaged	High achievers
3	Immigrant children	Not disadvantaged	Low achievers
4	Immigrant children	Not disadvantaged	High achievers
5	Indigenous children	Disadvantaged	Low achievers
6	Indigenous children	Disadvantaged	High achievers
7	Indigenous children	Not disadvantaged	Low achievers
8	Indigenous children	Not disadvantaged	High achievers

All immigrant children with problems (which may not simply be those of low achievement) are lumped together, so that categories 1 to 4 are given the treatment thought appropriate for 5.

Since we have argued that the so-called new poor, deprived and disadvantaged form a special class in British society, which fails to enjoy the full advantages of trade-union protection and the welfare state, it would seem that the classification of all immigrants as part of the disadvantaged means that they are set apart from, and below, the mainstream working class. It may be said that this is unfair since immigrants classified in this way will actually benefit from positive discrimination. It would be, if it was thought by anyone that the policies of disadvantage would work. But this is not what is thought. The problems of the disadvantaged are thought of as intractable, and being placed in this category is almost the opposite of what an immigrant's child needs if he is to have equality of opportunity.

Of course, immigrants do suffer handicaps as immigrants, and their black children suffer handicaps of their own. Amongst these we would identify the problem of language, the problem of cultural identity, and that of the bias which exists in the various selective processes with which they are faced.

The most immediate problem perceived by policy-makers in the early 1960s was the organization of special language classes for non-English-speaking children. A Ministry of Education publication in 1963 contained constructive suggestions for the development of language courses, although Power (1967), in a survey of administrative policies, showed that the DES tended to underestimate the scale of the language teaching required. The most common method of language teaching to immigrant children was in 'withdrawal' classes, but part-time centres and, later, immigrant reception centres were developed by some authorities. Even in the mid-1970s, however, young children of Asian parents still arrive at school with little or no English.

The main focus of policies towards immigrant children during the 1960s was to teach English and to produce materials that could be used by teachers of English as a second language. These policies, of course, applied mainly to Asian and to Greek-speaking Cypriot children. The extent to which West Indian Creole dialect impedes learning has remained a matter for debate (Edwards, 1979).

The mere fact that some provision exists to enable non-English-speaking children to cope with English schools does not, of course, mean that they have equality of opportunity. Language can be learned at various levels. It can be learned as a second language which is not normally a tool of learning; it can be learned so as to cope in a minimal way with the class-room situation; it can be learned so as to enable the learner to pass minimal examinations. Or it can be learned so that it can be used to enable the user to attain his highest possible level of performance. There is no firm evidence on this for the country as a whole, but since the expansion of ESL teaching was conceived of hurriedly, it is to be expected that the first two and possibly the third rather than the fourth will predominate. This language teaching, if not fully carried through to enable pupils to attain the highest levels of its use, may result in a filtering process, whereby most first-generation immigrants at least are able to do no more than obtain minimum educational qualifications. What is surprising in our own experience is the frequency with which Indian boys and girls whose parents know only an Indian language quickly learn to speak fluent English at school. We should beware, however, of generalising from impressive examples. No one knows to what strains these children are at present subject because of language difficulties.

A recent and very interesting development has been the publication in 1975 of a European Economic Community Draft Directive to member states, which suggests that children of migrant workers receive tuition in their mother tongue and culture of origin – in order to ensure the full development of the personality of children situated between two cultures. The Department of Education and Science, however, decided that these proposals did not fit the circumstances of the UK, largely because qualified teachers for the many languages spoken in the UK did not exist. A revision of the draft was made by the EEC in due course which applied the 'mother tongue and culture' clause to EEC migrants only. This is a very significant development. One is often told that the problems of Britain's West Indian and Asian immigrants are no different from those of southern European migrants in the Common Market. Yet, on this crucial issue, what is thought of as a right of a migrant is denied to immigrants to Britain.

The EEC directive immediately raises the second question which we mentioned in speaking of the handicaps of the immigrant child. This is that of cultural identity. Some teachers and educational policy-makers might still subscribe to the doctrine that immigrants must face the cost of their immigration and assimilate to the host culture. This view was encouraged by the Commonwealth Immigrants' Advisory Council which stated in 1964 that 'a national system cannot be expected to perpetuate the different values of immigrant groups' (Commonwealth Immigrants Advisory Council, 1964), but it is now widely accepted that cultural diversity is something which should not only be tolerated but encouraged.

Roy Jenkins seemed to be suggesting the new approach when he spoke in an oft-quoted speech not 'of a flattening process of uniformity' but of 'cultural diversity and mutual tolerance' (Patterson, 1968). This sounds impressive, but to us it serves to indicate the gap which exists between the perception of this problem as it appears to policy-makers and as it appears to West Indians. Jenkins's approach seems to suggest cultural diversity as a pleasant optional extra which all sensible men will appreciate, because it adds quality to the lives of all of us. For the West Indian, however, the assertion of his culture seems essential to his survival and is closely geared into the ethnic and class conflicts which characterize our society.

The West Indian is far from claiming an optional extra when he asks that some way be found of preserving his own cultural traditions and educating his children in them. Like black Americans, West Indians feel that they face a culture within which the achievements of white Europeans are continually asserted, while black men always appear in a degraded role. This is so deeply entrenched in our culture, according to this view, that it has become unconscious. Thus the process of becoming educated for a black child means having to learn to accept an inferior image of himself. The only way he can be saved from this is by being given an alternative education, if not in place of, then in addition to that which is given in the schools.

From this point of view the Asian communities must be objects of envy to the West Indian. Their religious and cultural traditions and organizations are strong, and, even while their children are using school education in an instrumental way, their supplementary cultural education confirms a worthy self-image. Moreover, the host society has learned to recognize the separate Asian religions and the claim which they have to being taught in school. By contrast the West Indian is thought of as having no culture and as having no claim to have his culture taught in schools.

There results a demand for Black Studies which is not at all easily conceded. Multi-culturalism as an optional extra is one thing. Black Studies which are based upon a refusal of the black man to be assimilated, or still worse, upon a culture of Third World revolt, are quite another. As a result, the multi-cultural programmes which have been offered simply do not meet the needs which West Indians feel, and, if that is all the schools have to offer, they are forced into creating their own educational agencies outside the school. It remains to be seen how far the activities of these agencies simply have the effect of confirming a worthy identity in the minds of West Indian children, while permitting social mobility and assimilation on other levels. That is what happens with the Indians and Pakistanis' cultural education, and informally it happens with the regional working-class cultures amongst the English. It is possible, however, that amongst West Indians the very basis of their culture will be one of self-assertion against white society and that this may be a crucial factor in turning the West Indian community into a kind of ethnic class-for-itself.

It is important to recognize that these issues are the most important for politically articulate West Indian leaders. Thus there is a further gap opened up between this community and the political orientations of white liberals. There is in existence amongst teachers an organization called the National Association for Multi-Racial Education which claims to provide:

An organizational framework at both national and local levels for the dissemination and exchange of information, the development of materials, the establishment of projects and discussion forums, and for the planning of direct action on issues of importance in the field of multi-racial education (National Association for Multi-Racial Education, 1975).

There is also an organization called Teachers Against Racism whose name is self-explanatory. But mere multi-culturalism and

171

opposition to discrimination are not enough for the increasingly vocal West Indian teachers, parents and students groups. They want improved teaching which secures success for their children and they want Black Studies. Thus, by the mid 1970s, a Caribbean Teachers' Association, a Black Parents' Movement and a Black Pupils' Movement had all come into existence.

The third handicap which the children of immigrants might suffer is relative lack of success in the various selective processes. Little, if anything, is known about this as yet. No doubt it is a matter with which both the assessment of performance unit and the educational disadvantage unit will be concerned. But enquiries in this field will be difficult because it is a highly sensitive area. The Department of Education as well as the local authorities are likely to be attacked from both sides if they publicly investigate these questions, by the teachers' unions, fearful that they will face a hue and cry in which they are accused of discrimination or prejudice, and, possibly, from racial liberals who might be opposed to any form of racial counting. Certainly we, ourselves, found that both political leaders and administrators were anxious about any investigation in this area. In no way would we suggest that the Labour chairman of the Education Committee was racially prejudiced. She was, indeed, always as helpful and courteous as she could be. But she met us in the presence of officials only and did not offer us a general authorization to enter schools, subject to head teachers' permission, as we had somewhat optimistically hoped. We understood her difficulties in that she was already faced with a potential row over the continued collection of statistics of ethnic origin in the schools. We therefore made our own contacts with sympathetic headmasters.

One primary school which we visited was obviously well equipped to handle immigrant problems. The headmaster, a skilled teacher, was especially concerned with West Indian reading age and deployed a wide variety of reading schemes which could be tailor-made to meet the problems of different children. It was too early, however, to say how successful he was, and it is important to notice that the use of well thought out techniques in a new 90 per cent immigrant school was the sort of thing which was only beginning in the early 1970s. One factor which is likely to affect its success is stability of staffing. In the case mentioned, unfortunately, the well-intentioned headmaster was promoted and moved after two years.

West Indian parents in London are now forming militant organizations concerned about the poor performance of their children. In our survey, reported later in this chapter, we found parents still fairly complacent. The more articulate political leaders amongst the West Indians, on the other hand, tended to turn away from the question of performance in selective tests and to emphasize Black

Identity, Black Studies, and the problem of conflict between black youth and the police. All in all, the question of immigrants' performance in selective tests remains a dark area and little is being done about it as a matter of deliberate policy.

Policy decisions in the educational field are primarily questions about the allocation of money. This is particularly true in the highly decentralized British educational system where basically the Department of Education can decide what to support rather than what should be started. What has happened as far as immigrants are concerned is a new form of additional funding intended to help the overlapping categories of immigrant and disadvantaged pupils.

In the 1964 election the Labour Party undertook to give special aid to local authorities whose areas had high concentrations of immigrants. In general this led to giving extra aid to the local authority for expenditure on all sections of the community (e.g. in housing), but in education it was felt that there were specific identifiable areas in which expenditure on immigrants was justified and could be seen to be justified. Thus Section 11 of the 1966 Local Government Act empowers the Secretary of State to pay grants, in respect of expenditure incurred in the employment of staff, to local authorities, who, in his opinion, are required to make special provision as a consequence of the presence of large numbers of immigrants from the Commonwealth whose language and customs differ from those of the rest of the community.

Authorities with 2 per cent or more Commonwealth immigrants are considered to have prima facie eligibility. The grants were originally paid at a rate of 50 per cent, but in 1969 the rate was increased to 75 per cent. In addition to more teaching staff, Section 11 grants could be used for liaison officers, interpreters, clerical staff, ancillary school staff, social workers and educational welfare officers. In 1975–6, LEAs spent £20 million under Section 11, of which central government contributed £15 million.

A working party of chief education officers prepared a paper in 1976 which claimed that 'the DES, as the central department concerned, has not been directly associated with the LEA's to the extent necessary to achieve the identification of needs, desirable levels of provisions and objectives' and that 'no national policy on ethnic minority education has emerged during nearly ten years in which the Section 11 fund has been in existence' (Community Relations Commission, 1976).

The document also noted that unevenness in the distribution of the fund. Brent, with 24 per cent immigrants on its school rolls, received £6·87 per head of the immigrant population; Nottingham, with 4·5 per cent, received £20·97 per head. The working party suggested a new form of central funding. Reimbursement under this plan would be at a rate of 90 per cent and would cover capital expenditure and overheads as well as staffing.

The second source of funding for areas with large numbers of immigrants was the urban aid programme. This was officially considered as a response by the Labour Government to Enoch Powell's 'rivers of blood' speech in 1968. It was originally intended to fund projects for black and immigrant communities but became a source of funding for a variety of urban projects.

Gavin Weightman, writing in *New Society* on 2 December 1976, noted that 'For nearly seven years, the urban aid programme has fumbled along dispensing alms to inner city bootstrap projects like some vast official charity'.

Again the EEC comes into the picture. Its social fund provides £17½ million for migrant education and applications may be submitted by member governments for such projects as language teaching centres, mother tongue teaching, in-service training for teachers, and education for unemployed school-leavers. Several applications have been made by the British Government, including one of £1,000 for teaching Punjabi at one of Birmingham's immigrant reception centres.

Finally we should note that apart from funds provided specifically for immigrants, they were likely to benefit from funds provided under educational priority schemes for disadvantaged schools, since one of the criteria of disadvantage was the number of immigrants on the roll.

Clearly, then, there was a great deal of *ad hoc* activity, even though the actual financial resources deployed were meagre, to respond to the influx of immigrants into the schools. Undoubtedly these expenditures will have improved educational efficiency generally and education appropriate to immigrants in particular. It can hardly be thought, however, that the scale of the funding or the precision of its application was such that immigrants would attain anything like equality of opportunity. We now turn to look at how these policies worked out on the ground in Birmingham, discussing first the workings of policy and then our own evidence derived from our survey and from interviews.

Education policy in Birmingham

Birmingham's post-war development plan for secondary education was presented to the Council during the period 1945–7 and accepted the three-tier system laid down in the 1944 Education Act: grammar, technical and modern. Serious discussion of the comprehensive issue first began in 1959 when the Education Committee drew up a series of eleven suggestions for discussion – one of which was for the

174

provision of more comprehensive schools in the city. In 1963 the chief education officer was asked by the Council to prepare a report on the future development of primary and secondary education. He considered at this time that the widespread development of comprehensive schools was impractical and suggested an extension of GCE courses to modern schools.

The comprehensive issue became a focus of intense party debate in the mid-1960s, although not along clear-cut party lines. Factions in the Labour Party supported the retention of grammar schools, and factions in the Conservative Party were in favour of comprehensivization. It was debatable whether the comprehensive issue helped Labour to lose the 1966 local election, but when the Conservatives gained control of the City Council in that year, they produced plans for the reorganization of primary and secondary schools in the city, in response to the national government circular 10/65. This plan proposed that twenty-one selective schools be retained for 25 per cent of the city's children, and thirty-five comprehensive schools for the rest.

By the early 1970s the system was still largely based on selection. A quarter of the city's secondary schools were grammar, half were non-selective, and the remainder were bilateral or 'comprehensive'. The difficulties of reorganizing secondary education along comprehensive lines at this time were considered mainly to centre on the different ages and sizes of the secondary schools and the differential resources they offered. By 1972 the City Council had initiated a process of planning the change to comprehensive education, and a working party of education officials and teachers produced a plan whereby from September 1973 selective examinations were to be abolished and secondary schools grouped into eighteen geographical units or consortia. It was intended that within each group of schools the total resources of staff, buildings and materials would be made available to all pupils of secondary age living within the consortium. This scheme was put to the Department of Education and Science in 1973 and half the proposals were turned down by the Conservative minister, Mrs Thatcher. The city re-submitted proposals in 1974, and the new Labour minister approved the consortia plan. In September 1974, nine county secondary schools and ten voluntary aided schools were still selective, but by 1976 only seven voluntary aided 'grammar' schools remained for which 'optional tests' might be taken. The future of these remaining selective schools is still in doubt, despite Section 2 of the 1976 Education Act, which empowers the minister or Secretary of State to require plans for an area or part of an area of an authority to comply with the general requirement of the Act to bring all schools into the comprehensive system without selection by ability.

Within the consortium system each secondary school receives its own intake of pupils, selected on the basis of parental 'choice' between the five or six secondary schools in each consortium. Parents are required to specify three schools of their choice, and some allowance is made for parental preference regarding remaining single-sex schools, denomination, elder children attending the school, and size of the school. The affairs of each consortium are organized by a committee of heads of secondary schools, the district inspector, the principal of the college of further education, and a representative primary school head. Some consortia invite heads of special schools and immigrant reception centres. From April 1974, governing bodies were established for the eighteen consortia to deal with all matters relating to the primary and secondary schools in each consortium. Parents are represented on each governing body and a report by the authority's chief inspector noted that 'communication with parents has also been considerably improved' (Denton, 1975).

One of the major purposes of the consortium system is to work towards a uniform curriculum in the first three years and to share the facilities and resources between schools, so that no child is 'disadvantaged' in terms of taking courses for which his school is not equipped. The chief inspector predicted (1975) that 'consortia will not develop at the same pace or in the same direction. Some consortia, for example, may wish to include Punjabi in the subject option range for older pupils' (Denton, 1975).

All Birmingham primary schools are being offered training, consortium by consortium, in a screening programme to identify children 'at risk' educationally. The programme was developed by the previous special schools' inspector, Mr Tansley (Tansley, 1973), and the procedures were piloted in Lozells schools.

The issue of West Indian children in Birmingham's ESN schools has never been a focus of local activity, apart from sporadic efforts on the part of individual black people. For example, a young West Indian political leader and community worker held a campaign in 1976 to persuade ESN pupils that they were wrongly placed.

The authority has never published figures showing ethnic minority children's attendance at ESN schools. There is reason to believe the total number is proportionate to the percentage of 'non-European pupils' in the total school population, but with an over-weighting towards West Indian pupils (i.e. between 16 and 20 per cent of children in Birmingham ESN schools are 'wholly non-European').

In 1959 there were about 1,000 'coloured' children in Birmingham schools. A survey undertaken in 1960 suggested that white parents did not object to their children being educated with 'coloured' children (Milson, 1961), but the first restrictive Immigration Act of 1962 encouraged many immigrants to send for their dependents, and a 'problem' of large numbers of West Indian and Asian children attending certain schools was officially recognized. The Council's past policy of overall impartiality meant that few positive steps were taken to deal with the problems of immigrant school children – partly for fear of encountering reaction from white parents. However, the initiative was taken elsewhere. Two enterprising teachers produced a series of 'multi-racial' readers for pupils at the Montgomery primary school in Sparkbrook.

Alderman Hall, Conservative spokesman for education, noted in 1962:

> The difficulty which arises is in integrating these children.
> Where the proportion is under 10 per cent assimilation is
> relatively easy. It only becomes a problem when the proportion
> of coloured children gets to the 50 per cent mark (*Mail*, July 12
> 1962).

The chairman of the Education Committee pointed out in 1962 that only twenty-four city schools had more than 10 per cent coloured children and that only 2 per cent of the total school population was coloured.

The idea of dispersal, or 'spreading the children' to suburban schools, was never adopted as a policy by Birmingham Education Authority, although interests as diverse as the *Birmingham Post* and the Indian Workers' Association approved of the idea of dispersal. The Education Committee had discussed the possibility, but after a conference organized by the Birmingham Association of Schoolmasters in 1962, where it was claimed that dispersing children might mean transferring a problem of low academic standards to every school in the city, delegates considered that:

> There would never be enough teachers willing to work with
> backward coloured children, so that it would be most useful to
> concentrate this type of teacher in schools where they would
> come in contact with large numbers of immigrant children
> (Sutcliffe and Smith, 1974, p. 384).

The delegates to the conference concluded that 'racial enclaves had come to stay and coloured immigrants could not be forced to integrate'.

By the end of 1964 some ten or twelve primary schools already had more than one coloured child in three. Two incidents in 1965 provided evidence of a feeling among whites that their children's education was being adversely affected by the presence of large numbers of immigrant children in certain schools. An English teacher at William Murdoch School, Handsworth, resigned because he felt that white children were being held back by immigrant pupils, and he

177

subsequently emigrated to South Africa. In October 1965, white parents of children at Grove Lane Primary School, Handsworth, threatened to withdraw their children if the proportion of coloured children at the school was not reduced. Moreover, Dennis Howell, MP for Small Heath and Under-Secretary of State at the DES, was reported in the *Birmingham Evening Mail* (5 October 1965) as saying that 'Birmingham's policy on educating immigrant children would inevitably lead to segregated schools'.

By 1964 the proportion of coloured school children had risen to 7 per cent of the school population.

A report of the Council's General Purposes Committee in May 1968 noted that the numbers of non-European children in Birmingham schools had risen from 3,500 in 1962 to 15,000 in January 1968, representing 8·7 per cent of the total school population in the city. The forecast that by 1972 the numbers of 'coloured' children in the city's schools would account for 16 per cent of the total school population would appear to have been correct. The report also noted that in January 1967, forty-seven of the authority's schools had more than 30 per cent of immigrant pupils and fourteen schools more than 50 per cent. A quarter of immigrant pupils were found to be in need of special tuition because of their lack of English.

By 1975, when the system of secondary school consortia was begun, the schools with the largest number of pupils of New Commonwealth origin were in the four consortia, CNW1, CNW2, CNW3 and CNW4. The children of the West Indian, Asian and white respondents in the survey of race relations in 'Handsworth' largely attended schools in CNW3 and CNW4. Percentages of 'immigrant' children in each school in these consortia are shown in Table 6.1.

For Birmingham as a whole the percentage of all school children in 1973 who were non-European immigrants was 9·5 per cent, but the percentage of wholly non-European pupils (i.e. those with both parents born in the New Commonwealth) was 17·6 per cent and had risen by 1975 to 18·2 per cent.

Birmingham pioneered one response to the presence of the children of immigrants by setting up a department for teaching English as a second language in 1960. The department does not offer any services specifically for West Indian children unless they have severe language problems. The director was also responsible for the setting up of ATEPO (the Association for Teachers of Pupils from Overseas) in 1962. In 1972 the branches of the National Association of ATEPO merged and became the National Association for Multi-Racial Education. The Birmingham branch of ATEPO, however, refused to join NAME because they considered that the association was dominated by the more militant Teachers Against Racism. However, in 1976 the Birmingham ATEPO became the Society for

TABLE 6.1 *Percentage of 'non-European' children in the CNW1, CNW2, CNW3 and CNW4 consortia in Birmingham*

	January 1975 % of non-European pupils
CNW1	
George Dixon* ⎱	11·74
Stanmore* ⎰	66·03
Ladywood*	52·32
Portland*	59·05
Cardinal Newman R.C.	9·46
St Paul's R.C.	1·41
St Philip's R.C.	0·42
Barford J.I.	62·03
Brookfields J.I.	32·47
City Road J.I.	89·83
George Dixon Junior	42·05
George Dixon Infant	51·20
Nelson J.I.	37·33
Summerfield J.I.	48·80
Oratory R.C. J.I.	3·59
St Edmund's R.C. J.I.	3·78
St George's C.E. J.I.	43·70
St John's C.E. J.I. (B16)	23·86
St Patrick's R.C. J.I.	9·09
CNW2	
Golden Hillock	56·49
Highgate	81·19
Queensbridge	57·16
Lea Mason C.E.*	29·63
St Alban's C.E.	37·87
Anderton Park J.I.	90·25
Arden J.I.	77·46
Chandos J.I.	41·07
Clifton Junior	64·13
Clifton Infant	72·19
Conway J.I.	54·09
Greet J.I.	41·56
Heath Mount J.I.	85·84
Ladypool J.I.	64·96
Lee Bank J.I.	29·74
Montgomery J.I.	59·47
Park Hill J.I.	67·94
Percy Shurmer Junior	61·99

179

TABLE 6.1 *continued.*

	January 1975 % of non-European pupils
Percy Shurmer Infant	82·72
Tindal J.I.	82·64
Christ Church C.E. J.I.	65·02
King David J.I.	10·46
St Anne's R.C. J.I.	1·33
St Catherine's R.C. J.I.	7·46
St John's R.C. Infant	13·65
St Luke's C.E. J.I.	25·22
St Martin's R.C. J.I.	7·94
St Monica's R.C. J.I.	16·93
St Patrick's C.E. J.I.	26·98
St Thomas' C.E. J.I.	23·87
CNW3	
Hamstead Hall*	46·66
Handsworth New Road*	70·56
Handsworth Wood Boys*	87·87
Handsworth Wood Girls*	74·01
Wattville (Holyhead)*	73·93
Handsworth Grammar	14·02
St John Wall R.C.	31·07
Benson Junior*	64·25
Benson Infant*	72·87
Boulton J.I.*	81·10
Cherry Orchard J.I.	12·00
Foundry Junior	47·89
Foundry Infant	60·75
Grestone Junior	8·72
Grestone Infant	9·48
Grove Junior*	94·26
Grove Infant*	92·44
James Watt Junior*	65·70
James Watt Infant*	66·35
Rookery Road Junior*	80·56
Rookery Road Infant*	86·49
Wattville Junior*	70·60
Wattville Infant*	86·25
Wilkes Green Junior*	86·33
Wilkes Green Infant*	88·86
St Augustine's R.C. J.I.	7·51
St James' C.E. J.I.*	68·38
St Michael's C.E. J.I. (B21)	90·80

TABLE 6.1 *continued.*

	January 1975 % of non-European pupils
St Stephen's R.C. J.I.	5·48
St Teresa's R.C. J.I.	6·08
CNW4	
Aston Manor*	60·85
Broadway*	75·76
Duddeston Manor*	19·29
Holte*	55·83
Nechells	26·65
King Edward's, Aston	5·51
King Edward's, Handsworth	9·81
St Chad's R.C.	6·28
St George's C.E.	31·08
Anglesey Junior*	54·81
Anglesey Infant*	69·81
Aston Tower Junior	54·00
Aston Tower Infant	47·61
Birchfield J.I.*	87·81
Burlington J.I.	31·81
Canterbury Cross J.I.	73·45
Cromwell J.I.	26·81
Hampton J.I.	16·66
Heathfield J.I.*	77·57
Lozells J.I.*	35·30
Manor Park J.I.	32·38
Nechells J.I.	41·43
Prince Albert J.I.	85·09
Vauxhall Gardens J.I.	33·77
Welford J.I.*	90·02
Westminster Junior*	91·78
Westminster Infant*	84·01
William Cowper J.I.	32·05
Yew Tree J.I.	42·25
Holy Trinity C.E. J.I.*	76·77
Sacred Heart R.C. Junior	11·27
Sacred Heart R.C. Infant	14·54
St Chad's R.C. J.I.	1·84
St Clare's R.C. Junior*	26·12
St Clare's R.C. Infant	25·60
St Clement's C.E. J.I.	14·63
St Francis' R.C. J.I.	8·76
St George's C.E. Junior*	24·52
St George's C.E. Infant*	26·38

TABLE 6.1 *continued.*

	January 1975 % of non-European pupils
St Joseph's R.C. J.I. (B7)	2·15
St Mary's C.E. J.I. (B20)*	68·30
St Matthew's C.E. J.I.	25·84
St Vincent's R.C. J.I.	6·20

Source: Department of Education, Birmingham.
   *Asterisks refer to the schools mainly attended by the children of our survey population.

the Advancement of Multi-Cultural Education. According to the editorial of the new association's journal, *Contact*, the change of name indicates:

> Changes in emphasis and a broadening of outlook in respect of the needs of our multi-cultural society . . . today there are many children coming into schools who were born in Britain but nevertheless have been brought up in households where they have been exposed to Asian or West Indian cultures and language (*Contact*, vol. 1, no. 1, summer 1977).

In 1970, the *Mail* carried an article criticizing the department (20 March 1970) for not facing up to the real problems of the education of immigrant children. Otherwise, there has been little criticism and the department has become Birmingham's only apparent answer to the problem presented by the presence of black children in the city's schools.

Birmingham Education Authority has kept records of the numbers of all immigrant children entering the city since 1962. Records were also kept on the proportion of all immigrant children (divided into non-European immigrants and European immigrants) in Birmingham schools, and the distribution of these children between different schools. From 1967 to 1972, when the Department of Education required that statistics be collected on the number of 'immigrant' children, totals of numbers of pupils by country of origin for the West Midlands were published in the DES annual statistics. Totals of immigrant pupils (non-European, other immigrants, all immigrants and wholly non-European pupils) were published in the annual volumes of Birmingham statistics between 1966 and 1973 (with a projection to 1975).

After the DES officially discontinued form 7(i) in 1973, the issue of the collection of statistics became a focus of political tension in

Birmingham. Birmingham produced its own version of form 7(i) in January 1974 and head teachers continued to collect information on the country of origin of their immigrant children, and some confusion resulted as to where to classify 'coloured' children born in Britain and the children of 'mixed' parentage. This continued collection of statistics resulted in an article in the *Mail* entitled 'Row over Race Count in Schools' (22 January 1974) which reported that members of the Education Committee were not aware that the city was continuing its own collection of statistics. The education department had continued to collect statistics to January 1975, but since there was continuing opposition from the Birmingham teachers' unions, collection of statistics ceased from that year.

In May 1968 the cost of school building specifically for immigrant children was estimated to be £1,376,235, and the Council considered that 'insuperable problems' would be presented unless special measures were taken to ensure that additional teachers, buildings and money were forthcoming. A report issued at this time by the Council urged central government to refund to local authorities the full additional costs, on both capital and revenue accounts, incurred in respect of immigrants. The Council estimated that in 1968–9 Commonwealth immigrants had 'cost' the city £801,023 (*Birmingham Council Proceedings*, 19 July 1968). Table 6.2 shows the claims made by the city in respect of Section 11, Local Government Act 1966, over the decade 1966–76.

Birmingham has also made annual claims under the urban aid programme. Table 6.3 shows the approvals in 1976 for Birmingham from this source:

TABLE 6.2 *Expenditure, Section 11, Local Government Act 1966*

Actual expenditure (£)	
1966–7	No claim made
1967–8	211,750
1968–9	265,840
1969–70	289,390
1970–1	322,910
1971–2	366,600
1972–3	443,820
1973–4	517,980
1974–5	733,890
1975–6	964,830
Revised estimate 1976–7	1,087,690
Preliminary estimate 1977–8	1,089,030

Source: Department of Education, Birmingham.

183

TABLE 6.3   *List of approvals under urban aid programme 1976 –
Birmingham*

Capital	Cost (£)	Govt Dept	Once only (£)
Intermediate treatment project	14,000 (84,300 p.a.)	DES/DHSS	4,000
Kingsbury Road Annex	18,000 (20,510 p.a.)	DES	
Home–school liaison project	5,000 (4,000 p.a.)	DES	
Floodlit all-weather pitch and playground, Sparkbrook	50,000 (7,160 p.a.)	DOE	
Small Heath law centre	7,500 (36,160 p.a.)	LCD	
Non-capital			
Recruitment and training of ten immigrant non-teaching helps	23,000	DES	
Projects			
Handsworth law centre	32,250	LCD	7,000
Play bus	5,000	DES/DHSS	1,600
St Basil's centre	12,700	DES	
Battered wives project	3,500	DHSS	
Capitation allowance for new immigrant pupils		DES	7,500
'Oliver 68' holiday home		DES	10,000
Handsworth Black Community Worker's project	2,944	HO	2,400
Balsall Heath churches: community councillor	2,800	HO	

Source: Urban Programme Circular 14, Home Office.

The *Post* carried a headline (31 March 1977), 'Immigrant pupils
better off in Midlands – Claim', in which the chairman of the
Education Committee was reported as saying:

> Birmingham is quite consciously and deliberately pouring money
> into immigrant areas; we have recognized the problem and
> dealt with it on a very considerable scale. The result of this
> immense effort has been the provision of a first-rate standard
> of education in Handsworth and elsewhere where there are
> large numbers of immigrants.

The article reported that £2½ million had been spent on school
buildings in Handsworth, but much of this went to the building of a
new Handsworth comprehensive school, with a proposed unit for
special educational treatment.

Apart from the setting up of the department for teaching English as a second language, Birmingham's response to the presence of increasing numbers of immigrant and black children born in the city has been minimal. The education department has preferred to regard black minority children simply as disadvantaged. Since 1967 all 'immigrant' children arriving in the city must report to one of the two registration offices. No head may admit an immigrant child to his school unless the child is registered. A medical examination is given, including blood tests, TB tests, sickle-cell anaemia tests, sight and hearing tests. Primary school age children then attend their nearest school, and non-English-speaking secondary school age children attend one of three immigrant reception centres in the city, for up to three terms.

The 'language problem' of non-English-speaking and poor English-speaking children in Birmingham schools has continued to cause comment in the press. The *Mail* (22 August 1971) carried a story that Asian communities were becoming increasingly 'enclosed' as their children entered school unable to speak English. Another *Mail* report (7 June 1974), 'Pupils' Dialect Barrier', followed the publication of research criticizing the lack of arrangements to teach standard English to West Indian children. An article entitled 'Isolated People' (*Mail*, 12 May 1975) noted that Britain's immigrant communities were becoming isolated from the rest of society.

The *Mail* (27 May 1976) carried a report from the new Tory education chairman that schools in a third of the city's eighteen catchment areas were under pressure from increased numbers of immigrant children, and that the problems of literacy and older children entering schools made the situation more difficult. Birmingham was one of four cities in England selected to participate in A. H. Halsey's action-research project in education priority areas 1969–71. Information was collected from six Birmingham primary schools by a team working from Mount Pleasant Comprehensive School, Balsall Heath. Altogether 46 per cent of the children attending these schools were immigrant children. On the reading tests administered by the project team, 60 per cent of Asian children emerged as 'virtual non-readers', and there were 6–7 per cent more non-readers amongst West Indian children than amongst indigenous children. Although this EPA research was documenting evidence of lower achievement on the part of immigrant children in Birmingham schools, the project report was couched in terms of disadvantaged children generally (Halsey, 1972).

In 1974, the Dutch Van Leer Foundation made funds available for the setting up of a community education project in three Birmingham schools. The three schools chosen were all 'high immigrant' schools, one in Handsworth. The project includes nursery education for under-fives, home-school liaison, work with Asian mothers, and a project to help child-minders.

Two curriculum issues affecting all children in Birmingham schools in the 1970s have been the religious education controversy, and the introduction of Black Studies courses. A working party of church, teacher, and local authority representatives produced in 1974, after four years' work, a new religious education syllabus for Birmingham schools. The syllabus included a study of Hinduism, Sikhism, Judaism, the Muslim faith, Humanism, and a forty-page section on Communism. The issue produced more correspondence in the Birmingham papers than any other educational issue, and became a party political debate.

The syllabus was ruled illegal by barristers retained by the city solicitor because the syllabus did not conform to the definition of a syllabus in the Oxford dictionary. When the Conservatives took control of the City Council, they abolished the religious council which advised Birmingham councillors on religious education, and the Education Committee chairman was reported as saying that the religious council had been influenced by left-wing theologians. The syllabus was a positive attempt to introduce into the curriculum teaching about other faiths and cultures which would presumably have affected all Birmingham school children.

The second curriculum issue has been that of Black Studies. In 1971–2 there was an official reaction to a Black Studies course, which had been incorporated into a Community Studies course at the William Murdoch School in Handsworth. The head of the department and three other teachers taught a Social Education course emphasizing African history and black identity. There were various complaints about this course, including complaints from other teachers at the school, and eventually the chief education officer made a personal visit to the school. He asked for information on the teachers involved and the course was ended. When schools were reorganized a year later, William Murdoch pupils were transferred to Hamstead Hall School, and the pupils of St John Wall R.C. were moved into the William Murdoch buildings. The William Murdoch school ceased to exist. Black Studies has remained an issue in Birmingham schools in that head teachers are wary of the effects of such studies. The *Mail* (20 June 1975) carried a headline, 'Head Hits at Racial Studies', in which an article by the head of Golden Hillock school, Sparkbrook, was reported. The article stressed that Black Studies could aggravate racial prejudice and breed more racial tension. The William Murdoch incident led to the formation of a local Teachers Against Racism group. This group was an active radical group for two years before becoming defunct. The group gave evidence to the Select Committee for the 1977 Education Report

(Select Committee, 1973, vol. 3, p. 776), asking for changes in teacher training, school organization and syllabuses, and school and community contacts. The group felt the religious education syllabus was an important issue in schools.

The achievement and behaviour of West Indian pupils have continued to worry the education department in the 1970s. A DES-sponsored project examining achievement in six Birmingham primary schools in 1974 reported that the test performance of Birmingham immigrant children was below that of immigrant children in other areas. The *Mail* carried a headline on this report, 'Shock Report on Inner Ring School Test Results' (5 December 1974). A working party of teachers and local inspectors set up in 1976 to examine the performance of West Indian children was apparently more hopeful that black children born in the city were achieving better than 'immigrants'.

Heads in the Handsworth area particularly are concerned with the behaviour and identity problems that West Indian pupils present, and a Midlands HMI noted in an interview that 'heads are wary of black power people'. Two educational 'responses' by immigrant communities in Birmingham which have been regarded cautiously by the Education Department are the Asian demand for single-sex schools for their girls, and the setting up of black holiday and Saturday schools. The *Mail* (5 September 1974) carried a report that Asian parents were sending their daughters back to Pakistan rather than send them to mixed schools. The education department was reported as saying, 'We do not discriminate in favour of people with religious preferences.' A report in the *Post* (20 April 1976) noted that Saudi Arabia was offering £100,000 towards the building of two independent Muslim schools in Birmingham. The difficulties experienced by the daughters of immigrant Asian parents are periodically highlighted in the press. A *Mail* report (13 April 1977), 'Problems of Asian Girls in Family Revolt', was followed by a *Post* editorial (18 April 1977), 'Clash of Cultures', noting that:

> One of the problems inherent in immigration, especially from Asian countries, is the clash of cultures that arises when children of incomers seek to adopt the mores of their school colleagues. We have always said that the British-born children of Asians and West Indians have a better chance of integrating than their parents have, and that they are entitled to equal opportunities.

Black holiday schools have been run sporadically in Handsworth, partly as a response to the 1968 Kerner Commission, which reported that releasing school children to idleness in the summer months produced disorders. The 1975 summer holiday school claimed an

187

average attendance of 325 children and was largely funded by the Cadbury Trust, with school buildings and meals provided by the education authority. The 1974 summer school took four themes for the children to explore: Love, Models, Marcus Garvey, and Our Handsworth. The 1975 Easter school sent a letter to parents which noted: 'We have reason to believe that the kind of education our children are receiving at normal school is inadequate and irrelevant to their present conditions and aspirations', and the theme for the Easter school, 'West Indians in Britain', included a note to parents: 'At all times attempts must be made to analyse the sub-culture that is emerging among young West Indians in cities like Birmingham. Be prepared to learn from the youngsters' (letter to parents 27 March 1975).

Survey evidence

In our survey questions were addressed to the householders about their own education and that of their children. None of the immigrant householders interviewed had been born in Britain. The actual distribution of the sample by place of education is indicated in Table 6.4.

The best survey evidence we have of immigrant experience of the British educational system is that relating to the 30 West Indians and 38 Asians who were partially educated in Great Britain. We therefore deal with them first.

Eight West Indians and 15 Asians had started school at some point in the primary system (i.e. before 11), 18 West Indians and 20 Asians had started at secondary school, while 4 West Indians and 3 Asians had had education in England which began after the age of 18.

Eighteen West Indians and 24 Asians had left before the age of 16. The remaining 12 West Indians and 14 Asians had received some

TABLE 6.4   *Distribution of sample by birthplace and place of education*

	West Indian	Asian	British
Born and educated in Great Britain	—	—	400 (100%)
Educated but not born in Great Britain	30 (7·6%)	38 (12·5%)	—
Never in full-time education in Great Britain	365 (92·4%)	267 (87·5%)	—
	395	305	400

form of education after 16 (a relatively high proportion when compared with the whites in the area). Forty-three out of the total of 68 had completed their education at secondary modern or comprehensive school, 2 had attended grammar schools, 14 had gone on to a college of further education or technical college, and one West Indian and two Asians had gone on to university.

So far as qualifications were concerned, only 20 out of the 68 had obtained school qualifications, 8 of these obtaining CSEs, 4 'O'-levels and 5 'A'-levels. Two had degrees, 12 had some form of work qualification, including City and Guild examinations (4), nursing qualifications (3), and apprenticeship (1).

In summary, these second-generation immigrants had entered the school system at various ages and, no doubt, had to face the handicaps of language, culture-shock and a strange school system. Most of them (about 70 per cent) left without any qualifications, but some of the minority who obtained school qualifications, as well as a few of those who did not, went on to further education of some kind.

While there does seem to have been a willingness on the part of these immigrants to stay in education, and there have been a few who have obtained 'A' levels and even degrees, overall one must say that the educational system and the system for training in work has not provided more than a small minority with any sort of proper qualifications.

Of the 68 in this sub-sample, 48 said that they were satisfied with their education, and 13 that they were dissatisfied (the remainder replied 'don't know'). Since the numbers are small and the range of answers varies widely, we record below some of the responses given in answer to the question:

(a) Satisfied
'The type of work I'm doing – it helped – the course was about things I'm doing now at work' (West Indian).
'It helped because I've got to the university now' (Indian).
'Teaching was good. I learned a bit' (West Indian).
'I had as much education as I could manage in the few years I was here (Indian).
'I can read and write, add, take away, I'm not dumb' (West Indian).
'Because when I was in Jamaica I was not doing as well in school as I did when I came here. I had better teaching here. I had every chance to do well' (West Indian).

(b) Dissatisfied
'I wanted to learn more. I only spent short period in this country's school' (Pakistani).
'I was at a much higher standard in India. When I started here

189

the teachers didn't bother to find out what I could do. They are not strict enough and I didn't learn much' (Indian).
'I would have liked to learn more, especially more English' (Indian).
'Probably my fault, didn't take much interest. I wish they had made me take more interest in lessons' (West Indian).

It should be remembered in interpreting these answers that we are referring to adult householders who are now at work. They are also still immigrants, albeit immigrants who came in their childhood. It is quite possible that while they were well-enough satisfied to get through and into jobs, different attitudes might be found amongst their children and younger siblings wholly brought up in England. There is some evidence of this to be found in the small pilot study of youth reported in the next chapter. We also record later in this chapter some evidence of relative satisfaction of these immigrant householders with their children's education.

The majority of our immigrant sample (365 out of 395 West Indians and 267 out of 305 Asians) were born and completed any education they had overseas. They are, none the less, of interest to us, because the kind of education which they had, their skills and their beliefs affect the way in which they themselves affiliate to English society and may well affect the behaviour of their children.

Out of this sub-sample of 365 West Indians and 267 Asians, 6 West Indians and 53 Asians said they had had no schooling whatsoever, and 86 West Indians and 59 Asians had left school at the age of 14 or below. The majority of West Indians, 158, had left school at 15, and a further 109 had stayed on beyond that (84 till 16 only). Amongst the Asians the age of 15 was not the commonest age of leaving school. Of those who stayed on after 14, 23 left at 15, 40 at 16, 21 at 17, 28 at 18, and 42 stayed in full-time education after 18. From these figures it would seem that the Asian community includes a higher proportion of members with no schooling at all (about 20 per cent) than the West Indian (1·8 per cent) but a considerably higher proportion staying in education after 15 (nearly 50 per cent compared with 31·5 per cent). What is surprising about this is that the Asian community is apparently so homogenous within itself and similar to the West Indian community in most of its social characteristics and life-chances in England when their educational backgrounds are so diverse. It could well be that in a generation, class divisions within the Asian community will begin to open up, partly influenced by the educational differences within this population, and that West Indians will remain more homogeneous.

Again, 38·3 per cent of the Asian sub-sample (82) had school qualifications as against 8·3 per cent of the West Indians (30).

190

Forty-seven of these 82 Asians said they had matriculation, 15 that they had FA/FSE,[2] and 6 that they had degrees. Of the 30 West Indians, 6 said that they had school certificates and 17 that they had an elementary or leaving certificate. These immigrants did not, however, take further education courses to any great degree. Only 10 West Indians and 4 Asians were enrolled in full-time or part-time education courses. These figures suggest that there is considerable scope within this population both for using higher skills amongst the Asians more satisfactorily, and for increasing the skills of both groups through further education. It does not seem to be the case that migration is greatly increasing the education and skills of the two immigrant populations.

Respondents were asked whether they had any work qualifications. Most of those who claimed one (116 West Indians and 63 Asians) counted working in a skilled or semi-skilled occupation as a qualification in itself (62 West Indians and 42 Asians). If this category is removed, only 54 West Indian and 21 Asian respondents can be counted as having obtained a qualification while working in Britain. Here again, migration does not seem to improve a man's qualifications and future life-chances.

We must now look at the white population: 328 out of 400 had been to secondary modern or elementary schools and 42 to grammar schools. Only 26 had attended college or university after leaving school. (Eight had gone to technical or commercial colleges, 2 to colleges of music, art or drama, 2 to polytechnics or colleges of advanced technology, 4 to teacher training colleges and 8 to university).

Two hundred and seventy-two had left school under 15, 71 at 15, and 27 at 16. Thus, only 30 out of 400 whites had full-time education after 16 as compared with 26 West Indians and Asians out of 68 who had been educated in this country. On the other hand, 84 out of 400 whites claimed work qualifications (other than merely doing skilled or semi-skilled jobs) as compared with 87 out of 700 immigrants (including both ethnic groups and both those educated overseas and in Britain). It would seem that immigrants more frequently stay on in school while whites are more likely to have obtained work qualifications. This may, however, be a function of the age of the white population, many of whom passed through the schools two decades before the immigrants.

Three hundred and eight of the white British sample said they were satisfied with their education and 80 said that they were dissatisfied. There were a variety of reasons given for satisfaction and dissatisfaction: 34·9 per cent of those expressing satisfaction were saying in one way or another that their education was adequate for their purposes; 34 per cent simply spoke well of their school, the

191

teachers, or the education received, and 22·4 per cent gave an answer comparing the standards of the past favourably with those of the present. On the other hand, about 60 per cent of the 80 expressing dissatisfaction criticized the inadequate standards of the past. (If one looks at the reasons for satisfaction and dissatisfaction together, the vote in favour of the past being better is about 68 to 49).

Three typical white comments on the schools were:

'I could read and write but people now leave at 16 and can't do that. My education was much better than now. Parents don't take the same interest and children watch too much television' (66-year-old retired, skilled worker).

'It was a long time ago, but I can hold my own with my children, one of whom is an accountant' (62-year-old clerk).

'I was being educated in the 1930s and couldn't afford to leave the job I got for more education. A lad had to be "spoken for" to get a job then' (60-year-old retired welder).

Looking at the education of the three groups of adults, we may say that the white British sample look back on their life as a whole and feel that their schools were reasonable. The Asians amongst those educated overseas include a minority with little or no education, and another rather large minority who are educated beyond their present occupational station. West Indians educated overseas have basic schooling and fit into the unskilled, semi-skilled and skilled occupations to an appropriate degree. Amongst the immigrants partially educated in Britain there has been a willingness to go beyond the minimum in education, and there is minority dissatisfaction with the system, and minority 'over-achievement', if staying in education after 15 and then entering unskilled or semi-skilled manual work may be so called.

Although we did not interview children we were able to learn something about them from the survey of adults. We know, for example, that our 395 West Indian respondents had 798 children, our 305 Asians 564 and our 400 white British 164, currently living with them; that 370 West Indian children, 178 Asian children and 70 white British children from amongst these were in the comprehensive consortia, and 12 West Indians, 7 Asians and 11 white British were attending selective schools. Amongst the comprehensive children, 69·6 per cent of the West Indians, 80·6 per cent of the Asians, and 51·2 per cent of the whites were in 'majority immigrant' schools (i.e. schools with more than 50 per cent of their enrolment with both parents born in the New Commonwealth). Clearly, the normal immigrant's child went to an immigrant school, and the white British children in the school went to schools in which they were in a minority. Nothing could show more clearly than this the degree to which 'Handsworth' is an immigrant area. (Compare the ward figures in chapter 3 in which only Soho has an immigrant percentage of as much as 49 per cent.) On the other hand it is always necessary to bear in mind that demographically speaking this is a temporary phenomenon, in that in the long run, as the age structure of the immigrant population changes, they will have fewer children per adult, and that hence, provided the white parents are replaced by other white parents, the immigrant-descended predominance will decrease.

The number of households with children of school age in our sample was 579 (52·6 per cent) as against 512 (47·9 per cent) without. Amongst the West Indians the percentage with children was 71·6, amongst the Asians it was 66·2, and amongst the white British 27·0. Thus, not only are most children in immigrant majority schools, but nearly 85 per cent of the households with children are immigrants. The schools, then, are a matter of great concern to the immigrant community.

Given this fact, and, given a widespread belief that immigrants do not take an interest in their children's schooling, we asked parents whether they had visited the school recently. Some 89·1 per cent of the white British, 79 per cent of the West Indians and 69·4 per cent of the Asians had been recently. About half of those who had been in each group had seen only the teacher. The Asians were rather less likely to have seen the head. About 50 per cent of the immigrant parents who had been, went on a parents' evening. Slightly more of the white British had made a special visit. The differences here are all slight, however, and easily understandable in terms of the relative ease of social intercourse between the different groups on the one hand and the children on the other. They hardly indicate parental disinterest.

On the whole, all groups of parents were satisfied with their children's schooling, but the figure was only 68·5 per cent for the white British, compared with 74·4 per cent for the West Indians and 81·6 per cent for the Asians. On the other hand, 105 out of the 579 parents were dissatisfied, including 50 West Indians, 28 Asians and 27 white British. The 50 dissatisfied West Indians included 11 complaining of 'low standards of education', 11 that 'teaching methods were bad', 8 that 'the teachers were no good', and 8 that 'there was no encouragement to slow learners'. There was a wide range of responses amongst Asian parents, but the most frequent comment was that 'teachers no good' and 'poor discipline'. Thirteen of the 27 white British parents mentioned first that the coloured children impeded progress, or in some other way indicated that the presence of coloured classmates was a problem for their children. Some responses which illustrate these trends are as follows:

193

'Because my children were not accepted for the schools I wanted. Always full up where I wanted to send them' (GB).

'At his last school they went up in ability. Because this school is predominantly black they are moved up in age. Don't get homework and the teachers seem disinterested in this progress' (GB).

'All the attention seems to be centred on coloured children. The few white children are held back' (GB).

'Some of the teachers do not seem well qualified to deal with the children' (WI).

'They are not teaching him things about Britain, only things about our own country, Jamaica' (WI).

'Teaching is different here. In India children are made to learn but here they are not strict enough' (Indian).

'My children have only learned how to draw pictures. They cannot read or write' (Indian).

'They just play in school, not learning anything. He doesn't take to some of the teachers' (WI).

These responses are all interesting, and our own impression after numerous interviews was that the following attitudes were the most characteristic in the three groups.

West Indian parents often felt that British schools were unsatisfactory because they did not fulfil expectations of schools and teachers shaped in the West Indies. Liberal educational methods disappointed those for whom teachers were expected to be relatively authoritarian figures using methods of rote learning now discarded in Britain. Not surprisingly, these methods were blamed for the backwardness of some children.

Asian parents wanted their children to get as much as possible out of their schooling and believed that strict discipline and a nononsense approach were the essential price to be paid for this.

Amongst the white parents the feeling was that the presence of black children stigmatized their schools, and even if they were to accept the view of some teachers and social researchers that there was no proof that the presence of large numbers of black children held their own children back (something which they were not inclined to believe), the fact that they thought that other people thought that it was degrading to go to an immigrant majority school was a sufficient basis for believing that they put their own children at a disadvantage by sending them there.

In explicating these causes of complaint, one should not overlook the fact that the majority of parents in all groups were satisfied. On the other hand, there is reason for looking closely at minority dissatisfaction, because there may well be a tendency for respondents

194

in an interview to say they are satisfied because the expression of dissatisfaction would involve an admission that they had let their children down by living in a poor area with poor schools.

Most respondents in all groups wanted their children to stay on after 16 (see Table 6.5), but the percentage who were willing to see their children leave before 16 was 30 per cent amongst the white British, 15·3 per cent amongst the West Indians and 10·9 per cent amongst the Asians. Similarly, only 53·3 per cent of white British, as against 65·6 per cent of West Indians and 82·3 per cent of Asians, wanted their children to stay on in education after leaving school.

This suggests that Asians value education more, but it should also be pointed out that probably those ethnic groups and social classes who have the highest expectations of job security on other grounds are less dependent upon education. We know of a modern school in another West Midlands city where the headmaster allowed students to stay on an extra year before the school-leaving age was raised, and found that the volunteers were almost entirely Asian. The white boys had moved straight into jobs and apprenticeships which were accessible to them because of their parent's contacts. Getting a job is like getting a house. The secure white natives get rented houses through their personal contacts. The Asians have to rely upon hard cash. The whites set their children up in jobs with people they know. The Asian has to have a certificate. In all of these matters the West Indian is a little more like the white man that the Asian, but because very often he still expects to have the rights of a British citizen and not to be discriminated against, he has not developed the hard-headed reliance on money and certificates of the Asians. Possibly, as a result, he gets the worst of all worlds.

We now turn to the job expectations which immigrant parents have for their sons and, separately, for their daughters. Here the greater belief in the value of formal education amongst immigrants is sometimes taken to imply that they have unrealistic aspirations. Our own evidence seems to go against this view. Of parents, 65·5 per cent of West Indians and 87·0 per cent of Asians gave replies that suggested that they did not know what their sons would do and that they would leave the decision to them. The equivalent figure for whites was only 32 per cent. Amongst those who did specify jobs the social class or occupational distribution was as shown in Table 6.6.

Amongst this minority with definite ideas, Asian parents do aspire for their sons to become professional people more than West Indians or whites, It may be argued that this is unrealistic in view of the much lower proportions in this generation who are in the professions in our sample. It should be remembered, however, that Asian professionals might well have left Handsworth and that, even

195

TABLE 6.5 *Survey of parents' attitudes on children's education*

(a) *Parents' satisfaction with the education their child/children is/are receiving*

	West Indian	Asian	British
	%	%	%
Satisfied	74·4	81·7	68·5
Dissatisfied	17·5	13·9	29·3
Don't know	8·1	4·4	2·2
	100·0 (285)	100·0 (202)	100·0 (92)

(b) *Age(s) at which parents wanted eldest son and/or eldest daughter to leave school and what they wanted them to do after leaving*

(i) *Eldest son: leaving age*

16 and under	15·4	10·9	30·0
17–18	33·0	15·2	35·0
Over 18	9·7	17·7	3·3
Up to him	22·9	37·2	13·3
Don't know	18·9	18·9	18·3
	100·0 (227)	100·0 (164)	100·0 (60)

(ii) *What parents want their eldest son to do after leaving school*

Get a job	12·3	3·7	26·7
Stay on in education	65·6	82·3	53·3
Up to him	13·7	7·9	10·0
Don't know	8·4	6·1	10·0
	100·0 (227)	100·0 (164)	100·0 (60)

(iii) *Eldest daughter: leaving age*

16 and under	12·6	25·0	27·7
17–18	35·3	12·5	27·7
Over 18	9·8	12·5	7·7
Up to her	24·1	31·9	13·8
Don't know	18·1	18·1	23·1
	100·0 (215)	100·0 (144)	100·0 (65)

(iv) *What parents want their eldest daughter to do after leaving school*

Get a job	6·5	6·3	16·9
Stay on in education	71·6	63·8	64·6
Up to her	14·4	11·1	12·3
Get married	—	1·4	—
Don't know	7·4	17·4	6·2
	100·0 (215)	100·0 (144)	100·0 (65)

TABLE 6.6   *Social class of jobs specified by parents in sample choosing jobs for their sons by ethnic group*

	West Indian	Asian	White British
Professional	37 (41·1%)	50 (58·1%)	6 (16·2%)
Intermediate/non-manual	12 (13·3%)	7 (8·1%)	9 (24·3%)
Skilled manual/trades	26 (28·9%)	19 (22·0%)	11 (29·7%)
Other	15 (16·7%)	10 (11·6%)	11 (29·7%)
	90	86	37

in our sample, there is a submerged minority who may be said to be under-employed because of their surplus years of schooling and the number who are matriculated.

Almost a third of the whites and the West Indians wanted their sons to learn a skilled trade. The whites were less likely to expect their children to enter the professions. It is here that West Indian expectations might appear relatively unrealistic, but it should be remembered that the actual number of those aspiring to professional careers for their children (37), is small, and constituted only about 16 per cent of the total of 227 West Indians with children. It could also be argued that these ambitions show the West Indian community to be relatively highly achievement-oriented compared with a somewhat demoralized population of inner-city whites.

Asked about their daughters, 42·2 per cent of the West Indians, 72 per cent of the Asians and 36·8 per cent of the whites made no definite choice. There was no great differences in the percentages wanting their daughters to get a job or stay on in education. The Asian percentage wanting their daughters to stay on was 63·0 per cent compared with the white percentage of 64·6, and a West Indian percentage of 71·6. Those who believe that male chauvinist Asian fathers want their daughters brought out of school and put into purdah would find it difficult to explain the very similar behaviour of the whites!

All respondents wanted a narrower range of jobs for their daughters than for their sons. The most popular choice amongst the white British, amongst whom 21·5 per cent chose secretarial or clerical work for their daughters, compared with 9·3 per cent of West Indians and 7·6 per cent of Asians. Nursing was the most popular choice amongst West Indian parents, 16·7 per cent of them choosing it compared with 9·0 per cent amongst Asians and 9·2 per cent amongst the white British. Nursing, however, was also the most popular choice amongst Asians choosing an occupation, since the great majority of Asians had no clear idea of what they wanted their daughters to do. It would seem that the aspirations of parents for their daughters are all too realistic. The percentages choosing 'doctor' were 2·7 per cent amongst West Indians, 6·2 per cent amongst Asians and 3·0 per cent amongst the white British, and for those choosing 'teacher', 5·5 per cent amongst West Indians, 4·8 per cent amongst Asians and 1·5 per cent amongst the white British.

Immigrant parents were asked about language teaching for their children. Of West Indians 1·0 per cent and 26·7 per cent of Asians said that their children had difficulty in speaking English when they started school. This would suggest that the problem of Creole dialects, frequently mentioned by white educationalists, is not accepted as a problem by West Indian parents who see their children as speaking English perfectly well. In 26 out of the 57 cases in which Asian parents felt that their children had difficulty, they felt that no special effort had been made to help them, and only four Asian parents and one West Indian parent reported that their child had been sent to an immigrant language centre. These figures, of course, represent parents' impressions rather than the objective truth, but clearly there is room for improvement either in the provision of language teaching, or in informing parents what is happening, or both. At present there is a minority of parents amongst the Asians who believe their children are at a disadvantage because of language.

Earlier in the chapter we raised the question of education in the child's culture, and we mentioned the attempts to provide for this inside and outside the school. We did not successfully frame a question about multi-cultural education in schools, but we did ask about attendance at black holiday schools and at the mosque or temple. Only 3 West Indian parents out of 285 had sent their children to the black holiday school, whereas 48 out of 202 Asian parents had sent their children to the mosque or temple. This gives some idea of the total cultural situation. Of the West Indian parents, 64·9 per cent mentioned sending their children to Sunday School, and this answer may, of course, mean sending their children to the Sunday Schools of specifically West Indian sects. We would be inclined, however, to draw the conclusion, disappointing to West Indian political activists, that the attempt to mount a programme of cultural and political education to promote black identity amongst West Indian children has not met with much success.

Head teachers' perceptions of immigrant children

As part of a small study of children moving into special education in Birmingham (Tomlinson, forthcoming), thirty head teachers were asked about their perceptions of the problems West Indian and Asian children in general presented in school. The questions were designed to elicit the cultural beliefs of the heads about the children. There are differing perceptions of the significance schools and teachers attach to cultural and racial diversity, and the kinds of problems that children from different cultural and racial backgrounds might present for schools when they arrive as immigrant children or are born to immigrant parents in Britain. The cultural base of schools in certain areas of the country has changed rapidly over the last twelve years, and children from the dominant culture are often numerically a minority in these schools. The limited research available on the perceptions of teachers about their pupils, once they are working within a changed cultural environment (Brittan, 1976; Giles, 1977), has suggested that teachers tend to operate within a framework of stereotypes, which are reinforced, rather than negated, by the response from the pupils. Brittan, for example, noted that the teachers in her sample perceived West Indian children as of low ability and creating disciplinary problems. Giles found that 'teachers' stereotypes and expectations do influence the way they behave towards West Indian students and have an influence on the interaction process'.

In this research, heads were asked whether West Indian and Asian children had particular problems that might affect their education. Problems of West Indian children mentioned by head teachers are shown in table 6.7. This question elicited a variety of responses from heads, particularly those heads in areas of high West Indian concentration. There was a strong feeling among heads that the learning process was slower for West Indian children, that they lacked the ability to concentrate for any length of time, and that they would tend to under-achieve and be 'remedial'.

The following were some specific answers mentioned by the heads:

'They are bound to be slower. It's their personalities. They lack concentration.'

TABLE 6.7 *Head teachers' views on West Indian pupils*

Learning process slower/poor concentration	9
Language problems/dialect	5
Volatile/boisterous/extrovert	8
Aggressive/troublesome	7
Not keen on education	3
Family problems/working mothers	6
Sickle-cell anaemia	2
Don't have many problems/WI children	8
	48

'I've got a small representative bunch. They are a slow, docile, low-functioning lot.'
'I've had their parents here crying for me to keep their children. They want them to have a good education, but they'll only get CSE. Grade 5.'
'A lot of West Indian children have undoubted difficulty in concentrating for a length of time that we assume to be reasonable.'
'They have the most problems. They are under-performing in comparison with other groups but the potential is there and West Indian parents are concerned.'
'They are slower than the Asian children, not as bright.'

Five heads mentioned the problem of language – the children did not speak standard English or spoke Creole dialects which impeded learning:

'Many of them have a language problem, largely because . . . well, they speak two languages, English and dialect.'
'They have language-dialect problems.'
'West Indian patois is a handicap.'
'We have been saying for years the West Indians have a language problem. I felt the Department for English as a second language had the wrong end of the stick concentrating on Asians.'

Three heads elaborated on their opinion that West Indian children were 'less keen' on education than other groups of children. West Indian children were sometimes unfavourably compared with Asian children:

'They are less keen on education than Asians.'
'It's such a transition for the kids. One minute they are sitting under a banyan tree waiting for breakfast to fall on their heads, the next minute they are in a cold wet place full of walls and cars.'

Eight heads mentioned that West Indian children were more volatile or boisterous than their other pupils and that this could disrupt the normal class-room activity:

'Many of them are extremely extrovert. They tend to be very noisy, which can be upsetting in a class where individual or group work is going on.'
'West Indians are boisterous and less keen on education than Asians. This is well known obviously.'
'The children are mainly born here now but the temperament

of the West Indian child is more volatile, disruptive, easily
stirred.'
'A racial characteristic is that West Indians are voluble. Their
fights look like riots.'

Seven heads also considered that the boisterousness of their West
Indian pupils could become aggression, especially amongst older
pupils. Four of the secondary heads in particular were worried that
their adolescent West Indian pupils might be influenced by Black
Power' groups in their area:

'We are a black power area and it's very dangerous . . . the
black power people destroy kids, especially the less able.'
'They are violent. A "none of you whites are going to tell me
what to do" attitude.'

Three primary heads were quite explicit in their views on the
aggression of West Indians. Two comments were:

'They can get very nasty and aggressive but we try with them.
If I referred every West Indian with temper tantrums I'd refer
them all.'
'I have some who are a danger to other children and to staff.
It's because West Indian parents thump hell out of their kids . . .
they want their kids to grow up to be good citizens, but don't
know how to make it happen.'

The heads in the study were unanimous in their view that West
Indian parents wanted their children to benefit from education and
do well at school. Nevertheless, six heads specifically mentioned
family problems that they felt held the children back educationally.
Three heads mentioned that the West Indian family was 'different'.
Two commented:

'The West Indian family is different. There is trouble for them
when they come over here. Things are not like they are in
Jamaica . . . the West Indian men expect the women to work
and bring up a family.'
'Their home environment is different. The parents are very
strict. My West Indians are co-operative and have bright
children.'

Several heads noted their views on stricter discipline in West
Indian homes, and in one case the head considered that this was
taken to illogical extremes:

'The kid gets the same belting if he drops a fork or robs a bank.'

Two heads complained about working West Indian mothers and
shift working. One said:

201

'The parents are glad their children are getting an education, but they can't give much help . . . they need to stop working shifts and see something of their kids.'

Two heads also mentioned that West Indian children tended to suffer from sickle-cell anaemia. One head answered:

'They don't give special problems. I teach them all to be courteous.'

The secondary school heads in areas with a high concentration of West Indian parents had given a great deal of thought to the problems they considered West Indian children currently presented in their school, and gave lengthy answers. One head had suggested that a meeting of West Indian parents concerned about their children's education should be called, and a committee formed.

Heads were also asked what sort of problems Asian children might have. This did not elicit the lengthy answers that the similar question about West Indian children did. Table 6.8 gives their views. Five heads mentioned that Asians were 'well-motivated to learn' when asked this question, but one said that it was 'a myth that Asians were more interested in education than the West Indian'. The problems which heads considered Asian children presented were largely concerned with language, and with family and cultural differences:

'Their problem is in mastering the language, particularly the idioms and the comprehension. They can usually read well, but their level of understanding is below par . . . it also takes a long time to get over to them that reading is for enjoyment.' 'Most of our Asians can't speak English when they come to school.' 'A lot of the children won't talk – communicate. Where do we go if the child won't talk. But once they get over our stupid English language they usually do well.' 'Language is the main problem, but we have an Asian teacher who can act as an interpreter.' 'I can remember when they came with no English, but now we have the immigrant centres and they come with quite a lot.'

TABLE 6.8 *Head teachers' views on Asian pupils*

Language/communication	7
Family/cultural problems	7
Non-English-speaking mothers	3
Assessment problems	3
None/few here	10
	30

Some comments on the family and cultural differences were concerned with 'good' parental support, which was considered to be carried too far:

'They get good family support but are over-protected.'
'The families have ambitions for the children and give them coaching in the evenings. I don't really approve of that.'

The arranged marriages for girls was mentioned as a problem by two heads, and by and large Asian girls were considered to have more problems of adjustment than Asian boys. One head said:

'I've nothing against people keeping their own culture, but it slows the children at school.'

Non-English-speaking families were considered to be a problem by three heads. One said:

'Our Pakistani parents are mainly peasants from Mirpur. They don't speak English and don't know what's going on.'

Conclusions

We are now in a position to summarize the major conclusions which can be drawn from this chapter, though these conclusions must be tentative, because of the present obstacles in the way of gaining entry to schools to study selective processes and to interview children.

The first and most striking fact is that virtually all immigrant children in Handsworth are already attending or will in due course attend secondary schools in the three comprehensive consortia known as CNW1, CNW3 and CNW4. Most will go to immigrant majority schools, i.e. they will not simply be a minority presenting unusual problems against a background of white British normality. Their problems will be *the* problems of the school. They will be what its educational processes are about.

Prima facie complete comprehensivization would appear to be to the advantage of the immigrant child, since it would mean that he would study in the same buildings as indigenous children and be aware of the opportunities open to them. But there is not complete comprehensivization in Birmingham. There are fee-paying schools and seven selective state schools. Already the fee-paying schools are being used by a surprisingly wide income range of white parents, mainly middle-class, but including some manual workers, to escape the comprehensive system. It seems extremely likely that in heavily immigrant areas the same strategy will be pursued by whites to escape the stigma of having their children educated in black schools. More and more it will be the case that the majority of black children will be educated in black schools.

That this process has not gone very far as yet is shown by the fact that only a handful of our white British respondents' children were in private or even selective schools, but even as things are, the trend is towards segregation. In these circumstances we are still told that, although separate, these schools will offer equal educational opportunities. Of this, three things may be said.

First, this means that Britain is now at the stage reached by the USA at the time of the Plessey *v.* Ferguson judgment of 1896 which sanctioned segregation in the schools, and the fifty-eight years after that judgment proved that separate education was inherently unequal, so that the judgment was revised in 1954. Second, it is clear that with the degree of decentralization and teacher autonomy, there can be no guarantee that something unequal does not go on in the schools, unbeknown to the Department of Education. Third, given the very special problems facing Asian and West Indian children, the schools are bound to be different in their organization and their teaching, and this may well, quite apart from the possible biases of teachers, lead to unequal opportunities for immigrants.

Our information on immigrant background suggests that although the majority of West Indians educated wholly overseas have education up to 15 and little in the way of school qualifications, the Asians are more polarized with 20 per cent without education at all and 50 per cent staying in education after 15 and a minority obtaining matriculation or better.

Moreover, we know that a significant minority of immigrant children in our sample of those educated here are getting more than the statutory minimum amount of schooling. Yet at the present time both groups are clustered in manual jobs and especially in semi-skilled and unskilled jobs. Clearly there must be those who are frustrated themselves and eager that their children should have better opportunities than they have.

Although we cannot say for sure how far these expectations will be frustrated, one thing which does emerge from this research is that the immigrant parents' expectations of the schools and the definition of their children as a problem, both by educational policy-makers and by teachers, produce a situation of misunderstanding at best and direct conflict at worst. The majority of our respondents were naively optimistic about their children's educational chances. Those concerned about the education of the children of immigrants at a national level tended to see them above all as part of the problematic 'disadvantaged' sectors of society, while the head teachers whom we spoke to, speaking from what was probably a more informed and liberal viewpoint than their junior colleagues, were far from confident of their capacity to ensure equality of opportunity for the immigrant child.

So far as our sample of householders is concerned, the movement for multi-culturalism or for studies to promote black consciousness or identity has had relatively little impact. The respondents see the schooling which is available as important for their children, and the West Indians have not responded, to any significant degree, to the opportunity to obtain a 'black' education outside of school. None the less, Asian parents do try to keep their children socially and culturally attached to their own society and the Asian children themselves seem to gain as much as they can from living in two cultures. In the case of the West Indian children, moreover, there may be a very considerable generation gap between migrant parents and their black British children. There is considerable evidence from sources other than the survey that a variety of forms of black consciousness are growing up amongst the young and we shall be concerned with these in the next chapter. Moreover, there are vanguard political movements which are working out their own ideologies and belief systems which they will seek to purvey, if not to the immigrant children, at least to their parents. We shall discuss these organizations in a further chapter on community and political associations.

In each chapter so far we have been concerned with the question of how far immigrants have been assimilated into the working class and how they form an underclass. The relative satisfaction of parents with the educational system suggests that immigrants have been assimilated into the working class. But the segregation of the children, the attitudes of the authorities and the teachers, which have the effect of defining immigrant children as part of the problematic disadvantaged, and the development of new belief systems, especially amongst the young, all point to the development of a distinct class formation amongst the immigrants, both on the level which one may call, in Marxist terms, that of class-in-itself, and on the self-conscious level of class-for-itself.

It is in the schools more than anywhere else that the definitions of social reality are being evolved which will make the social structure of the future. In addition to their normal roles of selecting from and socializing the lower classes, they have now become the places in which the social, cultural and political assimilation or alienation of the immigrants will occur. Of the three institutional sectors of employment, housing and education, our studies in Birmingham have led us to the view that education is the most important, sociologically speaking, though of course what happens in education is determined above all in the political sphere.

Our last word here must concern the differences between West Indians and Asians. Taken all in all, the evidence which we have presented suggests that despite differences of language and religion, the Asians are getting more from the education system than the

205

West Indians. This is in sharp contrast to their relative disadvantage in housing. We may expect, too, that social and political formations amongst Asians will remain distinct from those of West Indians, but it is also possible that the present situation of accommodation amongst Asians, that is of living in British society but not being fully of it, may break down and be replaced by social and cultural organizations which, paradoxically, belong more completely to the society and yet at their heart are in conflict with it. This is a theme to which we shall return in our chapter on community and political organizations.

7 From immigrants to ethnic minority

The populations which we have been discussing as we have presented our survey evidence in the last four chapters, have been, apart from the 400 white British, nearly all immigrants of ten or more years' standing. Most of them are now living in homes of their own, either bought or rented from the Council or a housing association, and they have been in their present jobs for five years or more. There is some evidence that they are satisfied with their housing, the area they live in, the jobs they do, and the schools which their children attend. They are usually members of trades unions and they supported the Labour Party at least up till 1974. One can see, therefore, that some might argue on this fairly superficial evidence that a process of assimilation into British society and, more specifically, into its working class, is taking place.

Such a conclusion, however, would be altogether too facile. The range of jobs occupied by West Indians and Asians, though it does overlap substantially with that of the white British living in the area, is in fact concentrated more in the lower reaches of the occupational system. Though the immigrants may join their unions and even express satisfaction with them, the likelihood is that the Asians at least would be concentrated in 'black workshops' and 'black shifts' doing dirty, tedious and laborious work, relatively cut off from white workmates and, in times of trouble, under-protected by their unions. They work longer hours for the money they earn and do more shift work. Both groups have been cornered in the system of housing allocation and rely upon systems of credit, buying and renting of abnormal kinds (e.g. council mortgages, housing association tenancies). Their houses, apart from the council-built houses which some of them live in, are the worst houses in the city which have not yet been demolished even though they are eligible for, and to some extent have benefited from, improvement grants. Their children go to primary and comprehensive schools which are largely segregated, or are, at least, immigrant majority schools. In these schools they are held back by linguistic and cultural difficulties, to which teachers tend to react in terms of racial stereotypes. The Asians suffer particularly from linguistic handicaps, while the West Indians are educated in a culture which makes a low evaluation of them and probably socializes them into accepting a low self-image of themselves. All in all, therefore, even though the immigrant generation may express satisfaction with its conditions, there are clear differences of life-chances between them and the white British, which would have been even more obvious had we compared them with a sample of whites matched in terms of age structure and levels of economic activity. Such differences of life-chances, if they were sustained over a period, would undoubtedly mean that consciousness of a common identity, common exploitation and oppression, and a common conflict with the host society would emerge and find expression in some kind of ethnic-class-for-itself.

But, if this is true for the immigrant generation it is much more true for its children. Some of these have been educated in Britain, some have been born in Britain, and some have broken with their parents to the extent of leaving home altogether, and, in extreme cases, becoming homeless. Not merely is it the case, therefore, that immigrant class-consciousness will be reinforced with time by the mere repetition of the same experiences, but it will also be related to the consciousness which emerges amongst the young who have rising expectations or new expectations not shared by their parents, and who are likely to be more fiercely frustrated by the experiences of discrimination.

Some idea of the dimensions of this problem can be gained by considering the statistics of age distribution in the immigrant as compared with the total population. As Table 7.1 shows, the immigrant population as a whole is very much younger than the general population and has become more so between 1961 and 1971.

The increase in youthfulness is especially marked in the West Indian and Pakistani population (the latter including Bangladeshis). This is clear from Table 7.2.

The full significance of these figures, however, only becomes apparent when we look at the two populations of immigrants and those born to immigrant parents in Britain. This is shown in Table 7.3.

Obviously there are about 40 per cent of the total 'immigrant' population who are black or coloured British. Moreover, given the age structure of the 'black British', it is obvious that in twenty years' time they will overwhelmingly be the majority of what will still no doubt be popularly and wrongly referred to as the immigrant population.

TABLE 7.1 *Comparison of percentage age structure, 1961, 1966, 1971*

	1961		1966		1971	
Age	All coloured groups	Total population	All coloured groups	Total population	All coloured groups	Total population
Under 15	29	23	34	23	39	24
15–24	16	14	13	14	18	15
25–44	45	26	42	25	31	24
45+	10	37	11	38	12	37

Source: Lomas (1973).

TABLE 7.2 *Percentage age structures for selected groups, 1966, 1971*

	West Indian		Indian		Pakistan		Total population	
Age	1966	1971	1966	1971	1966	1971	1966	1971
0–14	40	51	33	36	24	34	23	24
15–24	11	11	16	18	15	20	14	15
25–44	41⎫	38	40⎫	46	51⎫	46	25	24
45+	8⎭		11⎭		10⎭		38	37

Source: Lomas (1973).

TABLE 7.3 *Percentage age structure of New Commonwealth and British-born coloured population, 1971*

	NC born	Born in UK*	Total
0–4	1·5	37·0	15·7
5–14	12·1	40·5	23·5
15–24	23·4	9·5	17·8
25–44	47·4	7·1	31·2
45+	15·6	6·0	11·7
All ages (thousands)	830·2	555·4	1,385·6

Source: Lomas (1973).
*With one or both parents born in the area of origin.

The point can be reinforced in another way if we look at the population pyramid for the immigrant population in Figure 7.1.

The bulge in the age-group 35–9, the wide base of the pyramid, and the narrow 'waist' in the age-group 25–34, shows how the

209

inflow of new economically active groups was cut off by immigration control and how the replacement of this group of workers must await the ageing of younger groups, landing not from aircraft or ships, but from English schools.

There are, in fact, few differences in the figures for Birmingham as compared with the national population. Nationally, as Table 7.1 shows, immigrants under 25 constituted 57 per cent of the total immigrant population in 1971, while those under 25 in the total population from all ethnic groups constituted 39 per cent. The equivalent figures for Birmingham were 57·3 per cent and 39·8 per cent, while in the four wards of our survey area they were 59·8 per cent and 43·1 per cent.

There is a certain amount of evidence on the attitudes of the young as compared with those of their parents in the immigrant population. Peter Evans's *Attitudes of Young Immigrants* (1971) reported a survey conducted by Marplan for the Runnymede Trust. The Community Relations Commission produced studies of unemployed and homeless immigrant youth (CRC, 1974) (including a sample of employed youth as a control), and a study of the conflicting pressures on Asian youth caught between two cultures (CRC, 1976). The Select Committee on Race Relations and Immigration made the problem of coloured school-leavers the topic of one of its earliest enquiries (Select Committee, 1969). David Beetham made a study for the Institute of Race Relations on *Immigrant School Leavers and the Youth Employment Service in Britain* (Beetham, 1967), and Allen and Smith studied the transition from school to work amongst minority groups in Bradford and Sheffield (Allen and Smith, 1975).

Ideally a study of the attitudes of the youth should include at least three separate samples: (a) those born overseas, but partially or wholly educated in Britain; (b) those born in Britain but living with their parents; and (c) those born in Britain and not living with their parents; with the possibility of further refinements produced by looking at sub-groups within each sample. From this point of view the study of the unemployed and homeless by the CRC is particularly significant, dealing with a group whom, prima facie, one would think were more sharply divorced from their parents' beliefs and attitudes. The study of Asian attitudes also includes some valuable data classified in terms of age on coming to the United Kingdom. Peter Evans's study deals with young people born overseas. The other studies do not present survey data except in relation to the specific problem of employment. With the exception of the CRC study of Asians, all of these studies are to some extent policy-oriented.

We were only able, ourselves, to make a limited study of youth. We had not set out to do so and our budget in terms of time and

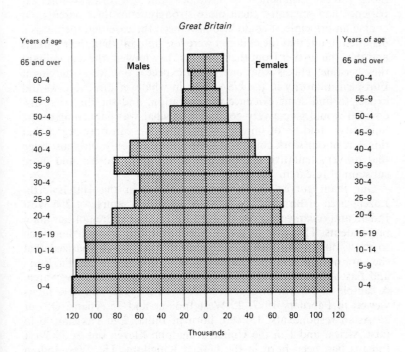

FIGURE 7.1 *Age distribution of the New Commonwealth and Pakistani populations, 1976**

Source: Social Trends, no. 8, 1977, chart 3.17.
* Excluding descendants of mixed marriages.

money did not permit any intensive study. None the less, we were very struck by the gap between the attitudes expressed by the parents on the one hand (which, despite what we said in the second paragraph of this chapter, were relatively conservative and complacent), and those expressed by young people and by the political organizations, especially amongst the West Indians, on the other. So we decided to make at least a pilot study of the attitudes of those young people to whom we had the easiest access. These were the children of householders in our sample who were living at home. It was a useful sample to use because these children and young men and women were not solely British-born and they had not broken with their parents. If, none the less, our data showed increasing militancy amongst this group, this would seem to point to an even more radical disjunction of attitudes amongst those whose experience had separated them more strongly from their parents. Of course, in principle, it could also have been the case that there was a disjunction but that the children were *less* militant than their parents and that the further from their parents they moved, the less militant they became. This is what one would expect if one were studying a European minority in the USA. But, in whatever direction, we did expect to find some evidence of separation, and the direction discovered would give a very good idea of what was happening to the 'minority' children of immigrant parents. We can only regret that this part of our work could reach the pilot stage only and must hope that its very tentative findings will be tested in further and more substantial research.

Our main survey of 1,100 householders in the Handsworth/Lozells area of Birmingham provided us with a sample of 256 West Indian and Asian young people aged 16–21, the children of our main respondents. This gave us a convenient sampling frame from which to draw our young people, although it must be emphasized that they are not the total population of West Indian, Indian, Pakistani and East African Asians in the 16–21 age group in the survey area. A sample of 50, out of a possible 256, 16–21-year-olds were interviewed in February 1977, 25 West Indians and 25 Asians. Of our 25 Asian respondents, 15 were born in India, 3 in Pakistan, 6 in East Africa, and 1 in the United Kingdom. Eleven out of 25 West Indians had been born in the United Kingdom. The West Indian sample included 14 males and 11 females, the Asian sample 13 males and 12 females.

Of those who were not born in Britain, the majority had arrived between the ages of 7 and 14. Fifteen had come with their parents, while 23 joined parents who had preceded them. Before arrival the Asian children had been looked after by their immediate family; the West Indian children had mostly been looked after by a grandparent or aunt. We asked the sample whether they had wanted to come to the United Kingdom or not. Five out of 14 West Indians said that they had and 3 that they had not; 9 out of the 10 Asians that they had and one that he had not. The remainder said that they 'weren't bothered', 'weren't asked', 'were too young to know' or 'didn't know'. The desire to be reunited with the family was offered as the main reason for wanting to come.

We were interested in the amount of education (measured by years of schooling and qualifications) that the children received before coming to the United Kingdom. The majority of our sample born overseas had had their education overseas at a primary level. Only one had a qualification before coming to this country. Thirty-four out of the 38 born overseas had been of school age on arrival. Only 3 had been to a language centre for immigrant children. If the others had had special language teaching they had received it in their ordinary schools. One Indian girl interviewed had arrived in England at the age of 10, and 8 years later had still not attended an English school.

The respondents were asked what reading scheme had been used at a primary level in their schools. Most of them remembered learning to read with the 'Ladybird' series or 'Janet and John'. These middle-class reading schemes have been criticized for their inappropriate presentation of everyday life in Britain to disadvantaged children. They were surely doubly inappropriate to immigrant children. There had been special schemes developed for immigrant children (e.g. the series 'Living Together' which was produced in the Montgomery primary school in Sparkbrook), but surprisingly these had not been used in the teaching of our respondents. One West Indian boy remembered reading *Dick Whittington* and, when asked what job he wanted, replied ironically, 'Lord Mayor.' Another West Indian boy remembered learning to read with *Tom Sawyer*.

The sample were asked whether the teachers in primary school had really helped them to read and write. Most of those attending English primary schools answered 'yes' but 5 West Indians said 'no', and 3 Asian children replied 'don't know'. These are very tiny numbers but, as we shall see in what follows, on most questions the West Indian children were more likely to have had problems with their schooling. There is a certain consistency in these answers which could well be investigated with a larger sample.

All the West Indian children but 5 had left school by 16 and these 5 had left at 17. Amongst the Asians, 5 had left at 17 but 2 had stayed on till 18 with the intention of going to university. The highest qualification obtained in the West Indian sample was CSE, obtained by 14 West Indians who between them passed in 63 papers. Amongst the Asians 11 had 51 CSE passes between them, 4 had 'O'-levels and

213

3 had 'A'-levels. One of those obtaining an 'O'-level was an Asian girl. The remainder getting 'O'-level or 'A'-level passes were Asian boys. There was some resentment amongst West Indians that teachers had not encouraged them to take 'O'-levels when they themselves felt capable of passing them.

Asked the general question whether they thought that their teachers were really interested in whether they got on or not, the children answered as indicated in Table 7.4. This showed that about half of the children did not believe that the teachers were interested in their progress, with a considerably higher proportion feeling this amongst the West Indian sub-sample. Amongst the negative answers were the following:

'They didn't push us to work' (Asian girl).
'They didn't really persevere in explaining things to us' (West Indian girl).
'Some teachers were Army Major types – gave us the cane. I put a chair over the French teacher's head' (West Indian boy).
'The school I was at was a crap school with low standards' (Asian boy).

Those who were prepared to recognize differences between different teachers and different aspects of the system none the less included the following replies:

'Some weren't bothered, they used to give you a book to read and sit smoking through the lesson' (Asian boy).
'After it turned comprehensive they lost interest in us' (West Indian boy).
'Some don't feel well sometimes, or they give up when they see kids messing about and say if you don't want to learn, don't' (West Indian boy).

Clearly there was some recognition by the children of the point often made in studies of the transition from school to work (see Allen and Smith, 1975) that they were being processed through a particular kind of institution which left them ill-equipped for any of the more desirable job opportunities. On the other hand, we would give a false impression if we did not recognize that the majority of Asians, as well as about one-third of the West Indians, did find their teachers committed and helpful, as the following positive replies show:

'They always tried to help in every way' (West Indian boy).
'If you took an interest, they took an interest' (Asian boy).
'They were pleased to see me get through my 'O'-levels. I received extra tuition' (Asian boy).

TABLE 7.4 *Belief in teachers' interest by ethnic group*

	West Indian	Asian
Yes	9	14
No	7	4
Some were/some were not	8	5
Don't know	1	—
Not applicable	—	2

We asked respondents about the careers advice they had received while at school, both from careers teachers and the Youth Employment Service. Forty-one of the 50 said that they had had a careers advice teacher and 31 reported receiving some advice on a future career from him or her, in the form of individual or group sessions. Twelve said that they had never received any advice. It is policy in Birmingham for all school-leavers to have an individual interview with the youth employment officer. Twenty-one out of 25 West Indians and 16 out of 22 of the Asians reported having had such an interview. Four West Indians and 6 Asians had not. (For 3 Asians this question was not applicable owing to their late arrival in the United Kingdom.)

Asked about the value of the advice they had received, only 6 out of 25 West Indians and 5 out of 22 Asians said that it was of value. Fifteen West Indians and 13 Asians who had had advice said that it had not really been helpful. This, of course, could be either due to the inadequacy of the advice or to the real constraints which careers teachers faced in placing coloured young people in employment. The actual answers given by the applicants suggest that the former explanation is correct, however. The children saw the youth employment officer as trying to talk them out of better jobs. (The other side of this coin, of course, is that youth employment officers see immigrant children as having unrealistic expectations.)

Some of the actual answers given were:

'When I had my interview with the careers officer I told him I wanted to go on to study and he kept trying to persuade me to get a job' (Asian boy).

'Because they told me to give up the idea of an electronics job which I wanted to do' (Asian boy).

'They asked what you wanted to do, but did not do anything after that' (West Indian boy).

'I had to fight my way through to get this job' (Asian girl).

'They took up self-judgment. They saw me doing a particular job – a labouring job' (West Indian boy).

215

The outcome of their education and the advice which they received in terms of employment sought is shown in Tables 7.5, 7.6 and 7.7.

The degree of employment and unemployment in Handsworth can be more fully documented (a) from statistics of the numbers of young black unemployed registered at the Handsworth careers office, and (b) the evidence derived from our main sample.

TABLE 7.5 *Type of job wanted by sample by ethnic group and sex*

	West Indian		Asian		Total
	M	F	M	F	
Nursing	—	2	—	1	3
Clerical/office/librarian	1	3	—	3	7
Engineering/mechanical	9	1	6	—	16
Scientific/professional	1	—	5	—	6
Craft	2	1	—	1	4
Other	—	—	—	2	2

TABLE 7.6 *Whether employed. Youth sample by ethnic group and sex*

	West Indian		Asian		Total
	M	F	M	F	
Employed	10	5	9	6	30 (60%)
Unemployed	3	6	—	5	14 (28%)
In full-time further education	1	—	4	1	6 (12%)

TABLE 7.7 *Present employment of sample by ethnic group*

	West Indian	Asian	Total
Shop work/services	—	2	2
Office work	4	1	5
Hospital work	—	2	2
Librarian	1	—	1
Jewellery-makers	1	—	1
Electrical engineering	2	—	2
General engineering:			
Skilled trade	2	3 ⎤	
Semi-skilled	3	5 ⎬	17
Unskilled	1	1 ⎟	
Design engineering/draughtsman	1	1 ⎦	
	15	15	30

Figures for the number of unemployed West Indian and Asian youth in Handsworth from May 1975 to November 1977 are shown in Table 7.8. Since the number of Pakistani and Bangladeshi immigrants in the area is small, the main conclusion to be drawn from these figures is that unemployment affects all groups very severely in August as new school-leavers come on to the labour market, that it affects immigrant groups more than native whites, and that it affects West Indians more severely than Asians.

The distribution of our main sample's children in the 16–21 age-group, numbering 256, between employed, unemployed and college, is shown in Table 7.9. This suggests that our youth sub-sample was probably slightly unrepresentative in not including young unemployed Asian males. On the other hand, the actual high incidence of unemployment in Asian males amongst the children of the main sample may be unrepresentative.

TABLE 7.8 *Unemployed black youth in Handsworth May 1975–November 1977**

		West Indian	Indian	Pakistan/ Bangladeshi	E. African	Others	Total
May	1975	68	11	8	4	—	91
Aug.	1975	259	84	22	—	15	380
Nov.	1975	141	62	6	1	2	212
Feb.	1976	111	28	—	—	—	139
May	1976	121	25	3	5	1	155
Aug.	1976	368	158	22	26	6	580
Nov.	1976			No figures			
Feb.	1977	131	30	3	4	3	171
May	1977	112	19	4	6	5	146
Aug.	1977	375	156	34	21	8	594
Nov.	1977	212	58	22	9	5	306

Source: Manpower Services Commission, Birmingham.
*Figures are for those (i) born in the New Commonwealth or Pakistan, and (ii) those born in the UK with parent(s) born in the New Commonwealth or Pakistan registered at Handsworth careers office (including non-claimants).

TABLE 7.9 *Employment status of main sample's children aged 16–21*

	Employed	Unemployed	College	Total
West Indian, male	62	11	7	80
West Indian, female	46	18	7	71
Asian, male	24	13	18	55
Asian, female	24	23	3	50

So far as the employed amongst our youth sample are concerned, almost two-thirds were employed in some kind of engineering work, e.g. a windscreen repairer at Triplex Glass, an apprentice die-maker, an apprentice design engineer, a welder, an electric motor winder. Ten are employed in the service sector and 9 have apprenticeships involving either day release to college or training on the job. It would seem that although most of these young people left school at 16 with few or no school qualifications, they are by no means confined to the ranks of the unskilled. They have largely reached this position through their own efforts, either by taking further education courses or relying on their own initiative in job-seeking. Seven out of 15 employed West Indians and 13 out of 15 Asians had found their jobs without the aid of the Youth Employment Service or their school's careers teacher. If it is true that the school and Youth Employment Service socialize children from immigrant homes for inferior jobs, it looks as though the children themselves partly make up for this by their own efforts in the labour market, though this tendency is more marked amongst West Indian than Asian youth.

Of the 15 West Indians in employment, 8 had had only 1 job, 6 had had 2, and 1 had had 3. Of the 15 Asians, 10 had had 1, 3 had had 2, 1 had had 3, and 1 had had 4, since leaving school. On the other hand, the Asians were more likely to have been in their present jobs for longer periods of time and the West Indians for short periods. This suggests that the Asians were moving jobs in the earliest stages of their career and then settling down, whereas the West Indians were more likely to have struggled to get a job at all. Obviously the samples here are too small for any but the most tentative conclusions to be drawn. The jobs which respondents had left, however, are interesting. They included those of garment cutter, lemonade bottler, cardboard-box maker, and metal polisher. These were the sort of jobs which young people might take temporarily before settling down to a more permanent job. Three out of the 11 who had left jobs had been made redundant. The other 8 had left of their own accord. It is still the case, however, that the sample were dissatisfied or disappointed by their present job. Answering the question, 'Is your present job the one you wanted when you left school', 12 out of 15 West Indians and 8 out of 15 Asians said 'no'.

Of the 20 who had wanted another job, 13 had made some attempt to get the job they wanted. A West Indian girl had failed to get into the Army, an Asian girl had wanted to be a teacher of the mentally handicapped, and an Asian boy, wanting to be a pilot, had failed an aptitude test. Nine had attended a total of 20 interviews in which they had been unsuccessful. Some of their explanations as to why they did not get the jobs they wanted were:

'I was told I hadn't passed the test. I think I did, but I couldn't argue' (West Indian girl).

'I didn't get the job because of my colour. My white friend got it after they told me it was taken' (West Indian girl).

'I was too well qualified, too skilled for the job' (Asian boy with a City and Guilds qualification).

'They'd write and say that I wasn't suitable' (West Indian boy).

Although they might not have got the job which they wanted on leaving school, our respondents might still be satisfied with the one they did get. Thus, 8 out of 15 West Indians and 12 out of 15 Asians said were satisfied with their present job. Those who were dissatisfied gave replies, including the following, as to why they were dissatisfied:

'It's dirty and hard, it really kills you, it's hot and greasy' (West Indian boy employed as a labourer).

'It's not going to get me anywhere' (Asian girl).

'I fell back on this job' (West Indian boy).

'I've got to be satisfied, though the training isn't sufficient – they exploit us. I may need a job in case Leyland go out of business. Our screws go to Leyland' (Asian draughtsman in a screw factory, who had wanted to be a pilot).

Fourteen respondents were unemployed. These included 9 West Indian boys and 5 Asian girls. Three out of the 5 Asian girls did not intend looking for jobs. R.K. had left school and had been technically unemployed for 5 years. She had told the careers officer that she did not want a job as it is 'not our custom'. She had an arranged marriage and now lives with her extended family. She is an articulate girl with decided views on the position of Indian people in Britain. 'British people', she says, 'don't take any job and work hard like Indian people do so they resent us. My father came in 1966 with nothing but now he has built a business and owns this nice house.'

The following are some of the detailed notes which we made on another five of the fourteen unemployed.

D.K. (Indian girl) had not been able to find a job in the six months since she had left school at the age of 16. She has one CSE. She wanted to work in a chemist's, and had personally applied for a number of jobs, but had not been offered an interview. The Youth Employment Office had been unable to arrange any interviews for her. 'They said there were no vacancies. They didn't really help.' No one else, she said, had helped her in finding a job.

I.P. (Indian girl) had left school at 16 with four CSEs. Her only job, as a temporary copy typist at a local hospital, had been found for her by the employment agency on Soho Road. The job lasted a week, and she had been unemployed for six months when we interviewed her. She was looking for another job as a copy typist and had written after more than ten jobs. I.P. could not remember how many interviews she had had. She believed that colour and lack of experience were the two reasons why she had been unsuccessful at her last interview. 'Because I'm Indian. I phoned and went along, but when I got there they said sorry there's no job.' She was satisfied with the help she had received from both the careers and local employment offices, which had arranged two interviews for her. She had also followed up advertisements at the secretarial bureau and in the *Evening Mail*.

R.J. (West Indian boy) had had four jobs since leaving school at 16 without any qualifications. His first job, welding, had been found through the Youth Employment Office. He had left after six months, having got an offer of a better job, furnace metal making. He had found the job himself. He did the job for two months but left because of the heat. Trouble with the police caused him to leave his next two jobs, furniture spraying for a private firm, and car spraying. Friends helped him to get these jobs, which he had done for about twelve months altogether. When we interviewed him he had been unemployed for three months. He was looking for a job either as a furniture or car paint sprayer. He said he went twice a week to the Youth Employment Office to look for jobs. So far, they had arranged three interviews for him. All three, he said, were for simple jobs, which did not pay very much. He was satisfied with the help he had received from the careers office. 'They are good. If they weren't then people wouldn't bother. But it's blackmail – they can stop your money if you don't try for a job.'

G.P. (West Indian boy) had been unemployed for two and a half years. He had had four jobs since leaving school at 15. The first, as a car body repairing apprentice, had lasted just one week. He had left because of the low pay. He claimed that he was getting £5 for an eleven-hour day. Low wages had also been the reason why he left his next job, working as a packer for a firm making medals, cups and trophies. He worked there for one month. He left his third job, as a metal cutter, after only three days. 'The foreman was getting funny, taking liberties, being cheeky. Don't want to say any more.' G.P.'s fourth job was metal beating for a local firm, which he had left after six months because he had become fed up with it. All of the jobs he had found for himself by walking and looking around. G.P. said he wanted to leave Britain to become a farmer or carpenter in Africa, and had not bothered to look or try to get work. 'Because I know I won't get anywhere – people are just going to look.' (G.P. is a follower of Rastafari and wears his hair in locks.) At the last job the youth

220

employment officer had sent him after, the foreman had told him that he would also have to clean toilets. G.P. thought that they should have got someone else to do that job. The Youth Employment Office, he said, had been no help. 'They sent me somewhere knowing that I wouldn't get the job.'

D.J. (West Indian girl) had no qualifications when she left school at 16 and had been unemployed two months. However, she was not looking for a job as she wanted to go to the local college of further education to take an 'O'-level course in order to train to be a nurse.

This provides us with a further interesting supplement to the job-seeking of the employed.

Six of the young respondents were in further education. One West Indian was at Aston polytechnic taking a diploma in clothing technology. Two Asians were science undergraduates at Aston university and three were attending further education courses studying for 'A'-levels and RSA and City and Guilds examinations.

Of course, the evidence which is offered here is of a very tentative nature. We include it simply to suggest that there may be hypotheses worth investigating further. This small amount of evidence suggests that, given their background and the facilities available to them, the children did reasonably well at school. By no means all of them were satisfied with minimum qualifications. They had higher expectations of employment than careers advisors and youth employment officers thought appropriate, and used their own initiative in doing better than these advisors expected. None the less, they suffered unemployment and found many of the jobs open to them meaningless, boring, heavy or dirty. A good majority of them were seizing any opportunity they had for advancement, though they felt they were discriminated against. Throughout it would seem that the Asians were more self-confident and ambitious than the West Indians, though this did not mean that they were not discriminated against.

Our primary purpose, however, was not simply to describe the pattern of youth employment. It was to find out how far the younger generation had become dissatisfied with their lives or how far they were becoming assimilated into British society. With this in mind we asked them about their perceptions of life in Britain for black people, whether they intended to settle in the area, their friendships, and their perceptions of 'race relations' in Birmingham and Britain, and their understanding of the relationship between black people and the police.

Asked the question, 'How do young people of different ethnic groups get on in this area of Birmingham', 19 out of 25 West Indians and 11 out of 25 Asians thought that there were problems. Two-fifths of adult West Indians and a quarter of adult Asians had given a similar answer to an equivalent question. There was obviously a greater degree of tension in this age-group. Some of the comments made by those who saw problems were:

'I'm called names by white people because I'm black' (West Indian girl).

'White and coloured boys didn't get on in discos and clubs – there's a lot of fighting between black and white' (West Indian boy).

'There is police intimidation, and whites mock Asians' (Asian boy).

'There's all sorts of problems – jealousy, prejudice and no jobs' (West Indian boy).

'Young West Indians cause trouble, but they are stirred up by the National Front' (Asian boy).

'Mr Powell and the media make trouble for us' (Asian girl).

'A few black kids are prejudiced towards whites – there's prejudice in every nation' (West Indian girl).

A minority gave answers including the following:

'Contrary to what's written in the papers about Handsworth, people round here get on' (West Indian boy).

'I've never had any quarrel with anyone, white kids or Asians' (West Indian boy).

'I've never experienced any problems. We get on well at college. I don't know about the adults though' (Asian boy).

Asked about their friends, 20 said they had friends in all groups, and 15 said they had them in the same race or nationality only. They were asked what the main problems facing the young people of the area were, and the answers are given in Table 7.10 (more than one 'mention' was allowed).

By and large the young people perceived unemployment to be the main problem:

TABLE 7.10   *Respondents' view of main problems by ethnic group*

	West Indian	Asian
Unemployment	11	8
Colour discrimination by whites	10	6
Lack of sports or social facilities	2	1
Police	1	—
Black behaviour	3	3
Don't know	4	5
None	—	3

'Jobs are the biggest problem. The young people get hopeless and give up' (West Indian boy).
'You see everyone at the labour exchange' (West Indian boy).

Some respondents saw unemployment to be associated with colour:

'I've had personal experience of going for mechanics' jobs – maybe it was because I'm black that I don't get the job, but I was amazed that I did not hear anything. It's only etiquette to let you know' (West Indian boy).
'The last place I worked the white man interviewed me and his mate said he didn't like blacks and I would not have got the job if it had been up to him' (West Indian boy).

The young people seemed more willing than their parents to mention colour-prejudice/discrimination as a major problem:

'Young black people are underestimated in qualifications, they don't get jobs even if they can do them, everyone thinks this' (West Indian boy).
'Whites are prejudiced, whites don't like you' (Asian girl).
'If you are black some whites won't talk to you. It all comes out in an argument – black this and black that' (West Indian boy).

Six of our respondents mentioned West Indian or Asian behaviour as being problematic:

'They are too strong-headed . . . the kids who wear hats with stripes – they're living in the past, back in slavery – they're stupid. They all want to stick together. I don't know how to explain it – there's nothing wrong with that but I don't like the way they carry themselves. They look dirty with their trousers half way up their legs' (West Indian girl).
'West Indians are uncivilized' (Asian girl).
'Most coloured boys just don't want to work' (West Indian boy).
'Cohesiveness of Indian culture is a bad thing – especially arranged marriages' (Asian boy).
'Asians stick together too much. English people have left the area' (Asian boy).

Although only one respondent mentioned police behaviour as a problem, 15 West Indians and 3 Asians thought police treated black people unfairly. Actual answers to our questions on this point included the following:

'Police try to make trouble for black boys. I've seen this in London as well' (West Indian girl).

'They stop us for nothing . . . and tell us they've studied Karate or Judo' (West Indian boy).
'Police just drive around picking black people up on any pretence' (West Indian boy).

Thirty-eight out of the 50 respondents said they had not had a personal encounter with the police. It might well be the case, of course, that a sample of the UK-born blacks and those not living with parents would have had these contacts more frequently. Even here, 12 had. These included 9 West Indians, 5 of whom said they had been stopped and searched for no apparent reason. As one said:

'It happens all the time. They stop me and search me on the streets for drugs, knives. I got beat up. They bundled me into a police car which was parked on a dark street corner' (West Indian boy).

One boy had had a more serious encounter which he reported as follows:

'I went to Crown Court. They got me in West Bromwich looking in a window and I got pushed around by some police who said they didn't like Handsworth blacks there. I was arrested for abusive language. I kicked his head in and got done for assault. I got probation and deferred sentence. I'm supposed to go down to report tonight. They keep putting us in meat wagons' (West Indian boy).

Twenty said their friends had had trouble with the police. The typical West Indian complaint was being stopped and searched without reason. Friends of three of the Asians had been arrested. One Asian boy said:

'My friend told me he was beaten up to give a statement. I believe him.'

Several of the West Indian boys mentioned their friends as being roughly treated by the police, e.g.:

'They treated my friends as if they were nothing.'
'My friend was stopped by the policemen. He was beaten up and left. They are like vandals walking the streets.'

We shall return to the question of police–immigrant–black relations again in this chapter and the next. Two points are worthy of note here, however. The first is that since our sample consists of young, relatively ambitious people, living with their parents, it is obvious that the source of conflict with the police is by no means confined to homeless black British boys roaming the streets at night.

Indeed, the consistency with which stopping and searching without reason is mentioned suggests that there must be truth in it. And this leads to our second point. This is that police admitted to us that they felt that they had no option but to search West Indian youths in the street if the level of street crime was to be kept down. In the circumstances we can only expect continuing conflict. It is worth noting, moreover, that whereas conflict with the police is thought of primarily as a West Indian problem, a minority of Asian youth also saw the conflict as existing and the police as behaving unfairly.

We were surprised to find, none the less, that a majority of both groups, 14 out of 25 West Indians, and 19 out of 25 Asians, were in favour of more black people joining the police force, a response which suggests that our respondents were by no means opposed to the policing function but to the way in which it was fulfilled. It is interesting to speculate how much would be gained in terms of respect for law and order if black police could be seen, not merely treating black youth fairly, but actually arresting white men.

The actual positive answers given on this point included:

'Black boys would take notice of black police' (West Indian boy).
'They would help communicate with Asian families who can't speak English' (Asian boy).
'West Indians would take more notice of black police' (Asian boy).

There was, however, a minority who were opposed to blacks joining the the force. Typical answers making this point were:

'If they join they will act like their white comrades act. I've seen black police kicking black girls. They get brainwashed' (West Indian girl).
'Black people would think black police are traitors' (West Indian boy).
'Because they are stupid if they do. They'd get themselves killed' (West Indian boy).
'If they joined the police force they'd make enemies among their own colour. They'd feel like an informer on their own people' (West Indian boy).

The summer of 1976 had been particularly bad for race relations in Birmingham. Robert Relf of Leamington Spa, a supporter of the National Front, had refused to comply with a court injunction calling upon him to take down a notice advertising his house as for sale to an English family only, and had been gaoled for contempt. The Front organized a demonstration outside Winson Green prison (near to Handsworth), and there were counter-demonstrations. This was one of many dramas in terms of which racial tensions were played

225

out in Britain during the early 1970s. We felt that it was in terms of their appreciation of, and reaction to, events like these that blacks and whites alike came to define the social reality of race relations.

Twenty-six of our respondents (12 West Indian and 14 Asian) said that the Relf incident had had an effect on race relations. Only 7 West Indians and 1 Asian said that it had not. The following replies were given:

'It caused a lot of upset. He's advertising that he's prejudiced. It made people think it was OK to be prejudiced' (West Indian boy).
'It had a lot of effect. It was boiling up, and it's happening now . . . there will be another summer of trouble' (West Indian boy).
'So many white people have moved out after this incident. Older people here are more frightened and white people won't shop locally' (Asian boy).
'There have been people coming round asking for vigilante groups to be formed and they have been formed' (Asian boy).
'It showed up white hatred for blacks so black hatred for whites increased' (Asian boy).

Those who answered that the Relf incident had had no effect did not necessarily think that race relations were good in the area:

'The trouble between blacks and whites has been going on a long time. I do not think it is anything new' (West Indian boy).
'It was an isolated incident. Problems like that arise in Handsworth. It aggravated things for blacks' (West Indian boy).

One of the general conclusions to emerge from our main survey was the relative satisfaction of first-generation immigrants with their social positions. We therefore asked our respondents whether they were more or less satisfied with their life in Britain than their parents, and Table 7.11 shows their answers. The interesting conclusion here is that most West Indians seem to be becoming less satisfied and most Asians more satisfied. This could mean that the

TABLE 7.11   *Relative satisfaction with life in Britain of youth sample compared with parents*

	West Indian	Asian
More satisfied	8	12
About the same	7	10
Less satisfied	10	2
Don't know parents' views	—	—
Don't know	—	1

West Indians are being rejected and the Asians accepted into British society. Its meaning could also depend, however, on previous causes for dissatisfaction. The Asians might be losing their sense of strangeness through education, while the West Indians, who did not suffer from such a feeling, feel increasingly the pressures of discrimination. These alternative hypotheses deserve further study with a larger sample.

Our own probe as to reasons for satisfaction revealed the following:

'I don't know any other life; they do, so maybe they are less happy than me' (West Indian boy).
'Because I've got qualifications and a good job . . . I haven't got any worries' (West Indian boy).
'It's all I have known. My parents don't understand the way of life here, e.g. customs and marriages' (Asian boy).
'Because I am westernized. Mum and Dad were born in India and would rather go back' (Asian girl).

On the other hand, we received the following typical answers from the increasingly dissatisfied:

'Young people see and understand things more clearly than their parents. They have been too satisfied with life here' (West Indian boy).
'I've grown up in Handsworth. My teenage life has been different to my parents. They know life in Jamaica and are more satisfied here' (West Indian boy).
'I've grown up in Handsworth. My teenage life has been different from my parents. They know life in Jamaica and are satisfied here. I'm not happy. I'd go tomorrow' (West Indian girl).

In our main survey West Indian and Asian respondents were asked whether they were intending to stay in the Handsworth/Lozells/Newtown area, or whether they wanted to move. Of West Indians, 72·2 per cent and 83·6 per cent of Asians said they wanted to stay. Amongst the youth sample only 6 West Indians (24·0 per cent) and 13 Asians (52·0 per cent) wanted to stay. Twice as many West Indians wanted to move as wanted to stay. Their replies included:

'You can't run, it doesn't solve anything. But I'd like to move, move away from the police station' (West Indian boy).
'I'd like to move, but to somewhere similar to Handsworth where there are lots of black people, but a better environment' (West Indian boy).
'Because if I go to a job, as soon as I say I come from

227

Handsworth their faces change. They don't want you there'
(West Indian girl).

It is worth noting that these answers do not imply a simple desire
for a passage to assimilation. Rather, moving is seen as an alternative
strategy to staying for circumventing discrimination and oppression.
We are not talking of West Indians moving more and more into a
society they like. It is possible that young Asians may wish to move
for more positive reasons.

We asked the youth sample whether they intended to go to their
parents' homeland permanently or for a holiday. Thirteen of the
West Indians and 14 of the Asians said 'Yes, for a holiday', but
interestingly, 7 West Indians and no Asians intended to return to
settle. This is at odds with a commonly held view that Asians are our
more temporary settlers. On the other hand, our figures do suggest
that some young West Indians are available as recruits to movements
of a 'black zionist' kind.

We asked the members of this 'half-way' generation what they
thought of themselves as, and received the answers set out in
Table 7.12. It is interesting here to notice, in view of the Government's social survey question currently being piloted asking for
subjective self-identification as white, West Indian, Indian, Pakistani
or Bangladeshi, that few of our 'West Indians' see themselves as
West Indian, and that a fair number of 'West Indians' and 'Asians'
see themselves as British.[1] More immediately we should notice this
group's considerable uncertainty about ethnic identfication.

A topic to which we shall be forced to return both in this chapter
and the next is that of the West Indian religious sect, Rastafari. For
the moment we should notice that Rastafari is well known in
Handsworth and that whites regard it as associated with crime and
black extremism. We asked our West Indian respondents what they
thought of Rastafari's importance. Ten said they thought it im-

TABLE 7.12   *Perceptions* of ethnic identity of youth sample by ethnic group*

West Indian		Asian	
West Indian	4	Indian	16
Jamaican	7	Pakistani	3
British	1	Asian	2
Black British	10	British	3
Black	2	Kenyan	1
Other	2	Don't know	1
Don't know	1		

* More than one mention permitted.

portant, 9 that they did not. Such a response from a sample of this kind, however, does suggest that the movement has made a considerable impact. Some of the answers given on this point were:

'If you look at a black man you always think he should be in Africa. White people used to own the world, then in India they were kicked out, and it will happen in all of Africa.
Rastafarianism is growing with the young people, but it's been sat on; you get jumped on if you got locks' (West Indian boy).
'It helps black people realize their background and culture. It's important for the younger generation. It makes them feel good' (West Indian boy).
'It's important but the way they go about it isn't right. It's good to teach people to be proud of being black though' (West Indian girl).

A number of those who felt that it was not important had very decided views:

'It's just a sect; to me it doesn't serve any real purpose' (West Indian boy).
'To them it's important, to me it's not. You'd be surprised how many black people don't like the movement' (West Indian girl).
'It's rubbish. They're stupid' (West Indian girl).

Some mentioned that the actions of those who called themselves Rastafarians discredited true Rastafarians:

'They're not really Rasta. They give Rasta a bad name. Rasta is peaceful, Rasta likes everyone. (West Indian boy).
'It's just a group of boys. Back in Jamaica Rastafarians don't go round causing trouble' (West Indian boy).
'Quite a few are just troublemakers, but the real Rastas aren't' (West Indian girl).

Interestingly, these answers show a considerable awareness of national political events relating to race. 'Powell', 'Bradford' and 'Blackburn', are all well-understood symbols.
On the other hand there are those who hopefully see mixing and acceptance of blacks as increasing:

'Because people are mixing more. There are lots of British people living in this street; we visit them, they visit us' (Asian girl).
'Haven't heard of any problems. In Handsworth people get on well together' (Asian boy).
'People accept us as part of society' (West Indian boy).
'You see more blacks and whites together. At the clubs blacks and whites mix. They didn't used to' (West Indian girl).

229

The summer of 1976 produced a new series of race dramas nationally as well as locally. There were National Front marches and counter-demonstrations in Bradford and Blackburn as well as Birmingham. In Southall an Asian youth was murdered by white boys. Militant Asian youth began to organize on a national level to protect their communities. We therefore asked our respondents whether they agreed that if black people were physically attacked they should group together to defend themselves. Thirteen West Indians felt that they should and 12 that they should not. Nine Asians felt they should and 14 that they should not.

Amongst the answers of those who felt that blacks should not defend themselves in this way were:

'It does no good. It only leads to more violence' (West Indian boy).
'Should leave it to the police. That's what they are there for' (Asian boy).
'It's obvious you go to the police for help' (Asian girl).

Amongst the minority who thought blacks should defend themselves, however, were these:

'Yes, we should stick together, you've got to show them you're not frightened' (West Indian boy).
'Have to defend themselves. If you're by yourself you're more vulnerable' (West Indian girl).
'We shouldn't lie down' (Asian boy).
'Yes, if they don't get help from the police' (Asian girl).

The state of opinion indicated by these answers would seem to be as follows. The West Indian and Asian youth of Handsworth are conscious of race relations getting worse. They are aware of and angry about racialist attacks on their communities. They are also dissatisfied with the police. Not surprisingly in all these circumstances a minority are ready for organized self-defence and confrontation. But in this sample, at least, the majority still believe in leaving the task of law and order to the police. It would be interesting to compare the answers of a sample of purely black British youth, and of youth not living with their parents, on these points.

A final question related to the future form which race relations should take. One respondent, a West Indian boy, felt that black and white people could not live together. He said that he agreed with Powell: 'Asian and West Indian people should go home.' Amongst the Asians, a significant number of Asian respondents, namely Asian girls, said they did not believe in intermarriage and cultural assimilation: 'I don't believe in intermarriage. We should marry our own kind.'

'People are different, e.g. language and customs. People should live together but there shouldn't be intermarriage' (Asian girl). 'Some families would intermarry and not care about their children. My family has unity and wants to stay that way' (Asian boy).

The majority of respondents, however, felt there should be more racial mixing and greater tolerance:

'There should be more mutual respect between black and white. We are all the same human beings' (West Indian boy).
'We should socialize with one another. I saw a good programme on television showing blacks and whites dancing to a steel band. It looked really good. All together' (West Indian boy).
'Live equally. I would like to see more intermarriage' (West Indian girl).
'We should have equal rights. Colour and language shouldn't make any difference' (Asian boy).
'There should be more integration. We've got to improve standards in school. If things are improved for the younger generation, things would be better' (Asian boy).

This investigation was undertaken as a pilot study for a possible larger study of West Indian and Asian youth in Birmingham, and the researchers are well aware that all they have done is to present the results of a pilot study which should lead to further research. Despite this, the study does permit the discussion of some issues which are currently under discussion at a national level – the education of West Indian and Asian children, their position in the job market, and their relationship to the police – as well as raising wider issues of the position of the children of black immigrants in the class structure and the politics of the United Kingdom.

Two of the pamphlets mentioned earlier (CRC, 1974; Evans, 1971), reporting studies of youth, tell us less than they might have done because they are primarily policy-oriented or concerned with social control. Thus, the CRC's pamphlet on *Unemployment and Homelessness* analyses these problems but tells us little about the social and political attitudes of unemployed and homeless youth. Evans's pamphlet tells us more, but instead of simply recording the degree of militancy, Evans is inclined to balance such evidence by putting into the scales what he calls other more 'heartening' tendencies. He also overestimates the extent to which Asian youth regard themselves as only temporary settlers. Our evidence is that, if anything, they are more settled than the West Indians.

Of greater importance than these pamphlets are the CRC's pamphlet *Between Two Cultures* (1976) and the discussion of West

Indian youth which has been engendered by sensational accounts of West Indian crime by John Brown in his *Shades of Grey* (1977), and, more generally, by the increasing importance of Rastafarianism.

The CRC's study, *Between Two Cultures*, concentrated on Asian youth. Perhaps its most important and central finding is that 50 per cent of Sikh youth, 60 per cent of Hindu, and 63 per cent of Muslims disagree with the statement 'I would like more freedom than my parents give'. Although only roughly one-third of those families from which the samples were drawn are extended families, and two-thirds are nuclear families, the maintenance of kinship ties and cultural traditions and the sealing off of the ethnic group by the banning of intermarriage and cultural integration are strongly supported. Some change in cultural patterns through internal modifications is accepted, but not assimilation. None of these things, however, are shown to be incompatible with an absence of economic or educational ambition, nor with militancy in the face of discrimination. It seems to us that the conclusions are nicely balanced here. The Asians are shown to be conservative in the sense of wanting to conserve their own culture, but they are not mere 'passers through' and will stand up and fight discrimination.

The theme of relations between police and West Indian youth had been a major one in discussions of immigrant problems in Birmingham, and had been central to Gus John's study reported in *Race in the Inner City* (1972). We had not, ourselves, intended to make a study of this question, but since it was increasingly put at the centre of our discussions by West Indian informants, we did make a special point of checking with the police sergeant assigned to immigrant liaison work in the Soho Road police station what the police view of the situation was. We were told:

> That the crime problem in Handsworth was generally
> exaggerated and that the main crimes were robbing and theft
> from the person, both crimes being committed for small amounts,
> though not necessarily with great violence. Many more serious
> crimes against property occurred in other areas.
>
> The police were well in control of the situation. They did not
> regard some of the leaders, whom we had heard referred to as
> trouble-makers, as a problem, and accepted the usefulness of
> the squats, which, in effect, provided homes for the homeless.
> Moreover, when we raised the question of the young men who
> affected Rastafarian 'dreadlock' hair-styles and woollen hats,
> they said they did not regard them as a special problem.

Now it could be that the police were suspicious of us as radical sociologists who might be concerned to write some sort of sensational article which might amplify and exacerbate the problems which they faced, or might comment unfairly on police practice. We would not have treated our interview on this matter as evidence in itself, but for the fact that we were to discover that, three months before, an investigation of crime in Handsworth had been carried out with the collaboration of the police, and it claimed to have received a very different view of the situation from them. The findings of the study were stated in very strong terms in the report itself, and in an even more amplified form in the local and national press.

The first we learned of this investigation was when an article appeared in the *Sunday Telegraph* reporting that Handsworth was being terrorized by a gang known as 'The Dreads', numbering about 200, who were responsible for 'muggings' on a scale which had led to the drafting of extra police into the area as an emergency. The report was said to be financed by the Cadbury Trust and sponsored by the voluntary social work agency, All Faiths for One Race, and to have been carried out by John Brown of the Cranfield Institute of Technology.

On enquiry, we found that neither the Cadbury Trust nor AFFOR had approved the handing of the report to the press. Nor were they satisfied with its contents. The former director of AFFOR, however, did blame much of the misleading publicity which had surrounded the report's publication on the press.

Brown's report, *Shades of Grey* (Brown, 1977), begins clearly enough, and indeed makes the crucial point which has to be made in his opening paragraph:

> Handsworth forms part of the C.1. sub-division of the West Midlands Police, and in terms of crime statistics is unremarkable amongst the twelve divisions of the force. In the first four months of 1977, it ranked tenth in recorded crime, eighth in detected crime, and was the only division with a fall in crime against the same period of the preceding year. Yet in cases of robbing and assault and intent to rob, it led the field, and also ranked fourth in its incidence of thefts from the person.

The actual figures for 'C' division for the twelve months from 1 July 1976 to 30 June 1977, which Brown gives, show that the combined category of robbing and theft from the person produced a total of 215 cases for the whole period. Since these figures would include simple snatching of handbags in the street, they are not remarkable. Unfortunately, Brown does not give the comparative figures for other divisions either for this crime or for others, such as burglary, where other areas ranked higher than Handsworth.

Next, however, the report makes an extraordinary leap. It claims that the crimes concerned are committed:

mainly by a particular group – some 200 youths of West Indian origin or descent who have taken the appearance of the followers of the Rastafarian faith, by plaiting their hair in locks and wearing green, gold and red woollen hats.

Later:

Many of the Dreadlocks, with whom I spoke, in squats, on the streets, in the area housing office, and in the sub-divisional (Thornhill Road) police station, have suffered from the schooling split between vastly different educational regimes in the West Indies – mainly Jamaica – and in Britain, and have records of poor educational attainment. Many also have records of poor family relationships, and have either rejected or been rejected from their homes. Deprived and disadvantaged, they see themselves as victims of white racist society, and, attracted by values and life-styles of alienated Dreadlock groups, drift into lives of idleness and crime, justifying themselves with half-digested gobbets of Rastafarian philosphy.

There follow highly emotive accounts of Brown's experience of incidents in which he accompanied the police on their duties and interviewed the Dreadlocks. On this basis he feels entitled to say that 'for local people and local police the realities of local crime are a good deal more serious than statistics suggest'.

Thus the problem of crime in the immigrant groups has been encapsulated in a very clear, if very misleading image for the British population at large. Coming not long after the disturbances at the Notting Hill carnival, and the rioting at Lewisham and Ladywood engendered by National Front activity, it fitted well into the media image of British society as threatened by a menacing group of strangers.

It is important to notice that Brown offers no proof of the connections between three elements, namely unemployment and homelessness, crime, and affiliation to the Rastafarian movement, and there is, indeed, no study of these relationships of a serious kind. Prima facie, of course, one would accept that the hypothesis (it is no more than that) thrown up by the CRC's report on *Unemployment and Homelessness* is that when there is unemployment and!or homelessness there is likely to be crime and 'alienation' from society. But whereas the CRC suggests a causal relationship running from unemployment and homelessness to crime, the notion of drifting into 'lives of idleness and crime, justifying themselves with half-digested gobbets of Rastafarian philosophy' adds an element of sheer viciousness on the part of 200 or so specific individuals. That note is sustained throughout Brown's report.

234

Of course, there is a problem of crime of specific kinds in Handsworth, and there is a two-way problem of deteriorating relations between West Indian youth and the police. How could it be otherwise if this community suffers, according to Brown, a rate of 25 per cent youth unemployment (though this estimate of Brown's is a purely impressionistic one)? And it is not likely, if a group has no sense of the legitimacy of the white property system or of police authority, that there will be robberies and theft and insolence in dealing with the police? Is it not also to be expected that the forces of law and order should be deployed to protect property and people? What can be questioned is any decision on the part of the police to systematically stop and search and harass groups simply because their life-style is strange and easily recognizable. And, certainly, the Brown pamphlet can only have the effect of directing the police, and any extra-legal group which chooses, to use violence against an easily recognizable minority, while possibly failing to actually prevent the growth of crime.

We shall have to return to Rastafari in another chapter. Here we should be primarily concerned with its popularity amongst, and its affect upon, youth. Ethiopianism is a phenomenon widespread amongst people of the world who have suffered from white political and economic domination. It is readily understandable in that Ethiopia was the only black country to remain unsubdued by European colonialism until the 1930s. Moreover, Ethiopia was a Christian country with a separate Christian tradition from that of the white man, which suggested to mission-educated blacks that they could still be Christian without accepting mere white man's religion.

Rastafari was a branch of Ethiopianism which grew up in the poorer rural areas of Jamaica and suggested a 'black zionist' solution to its members. Originally considered socially and politically dangerous, it gained some respectability in the 1960s and 1970s in an independent Jamaica. In this respectable form it established itself as a religion in Britain.

A more populist vein of Rastafarianism survived, however, amongst poorer immigrants, and this popular version was translated into a more powerful form when it became embodied in reggae music. Meanwhile, the more intellectual amongst West Indian youth established a link between the populist version and the religious version in the form of a highly coherent political philosophy. Some of the young black British and young West Indian immigrants who wore the long Rasta locks in the hair (dreadlocks) and wore woollen hats with the Rasta colours of red, yellow and green, responded to the religion, to the Rasta cues in the reggae, and to the political philosophy. Taken all in all, these sources combined to give them a culture which could unify them in their daily struggle with white society.

235

A *Birmingham Post* report in 1976 included a statement of the Rasta political philosophy by Dennis Deans, a 25-year-old West Indian whose family runs a café and club in Handsworth's Soho Road, together with two other Rastas, Heather Smart and Archie Bailey. They write as follows:

The revelation of Rastafari is the reflection of the true condition of black peoples – material, mental and spiritual. It expresses the degree and severity of our existence within white civilization under a colonialist establishment, our relation to it, and our consciousness of what is to be and will be.

Rastafari teaches that man should cease to deal in corruption and the exploitation of man by man. It believes in the equality of all men in upholding the laws of God. Capitalism has destroyed our past and blocked the road to our future to partake or share in this society with its racisms. Rastafari rejects a racist culture; it is seeking to find that which is black and righteous, that which cultivates the essence and the excellence of man, and our culture . . . we believe in the repatriation of black people to their ancestral black Africa, because without our own history and culture we can never fit into this society. . . . Ultimately, the education of black youths in this country does not include our tradition or history or culture, it does not give us the essential means to identify ourselves or our problems so that we can solve them politically or democratically. And yet we are expected to co-operate and to compete as individuals in a capitalist society.

We are educated to see things from a white man's point of view, in a white perspective, hypnotized in a caricature of fear, shame and pride, only to have our hope and anxiety shattered, when we seek employment or come into contact with the authorities and the police (*Post* 8 June 1976).

We certainly would not claim that Brown's dreaded 'dreads' all know and subscribe to this philosophy. But it is a philosophy which makes sense of their attitudes and behaviour. The authors make a good point when they say:

They (i.e. the crimes of black youth) are seen as crimes organized by the individual to create conflict between blacks and whites. That begs the question – is the black youth who is arrested by the police for an ordinary crime being treated as a political prisoner in view of senior police opinion that the crimes are politically motivated?

The question has renewed force after the publication of Brown's pamphlet.

236

The zionist and revolutionary element in this version of the Rastafari philosophy may be more a matter of rhetoric than of deliberate political intent. There is not likely to be a massive return to the West Indies, let alone Africa. Nor can a black revolution be seriously contemplated. But black youth are in need of a philosophy and a culture which gives them an identity and self-respect in contrast with the degraded self-image which white society imposes on them. This was what first Black Islam, and then the Black Power movement did for the ghettoized descendants of slaves in the USA. The blacks of contemporary Britain are also the descendants of slaves deprived of a culture, even if they have not experienced the degradation of the ghetto to the same extent as the American blacks. It looks as though Rastafari in its British growth and development will provide them at least with the beginnings of a culture of self-respect. It will be resented by paternalists, who do not believe that the Welfare State principle of benefit as of right applies to blacks, and the police and writers like John Brown will see the whole movement as a kind of political crime. But, for the moment at least, it is probably the most important single fact about West Indian society and culture in Britain.

This leads us to a final word about the relation between Asian and West Indian youth and the similarities and contrasts between them. That there are similarities seems clear from the data presented in this chapter and in the substantive chapters about adults which went before. Both groups are deprived in terms of education, employment and housing, and both are conscious to some degree of the inequity of that deprivation. The result is that we may expect to see alliances formed between West Indian and Asian (Sikh, Hindu and Muslim, Indian, Pakistani and Bangladeshi) in the years that lie ahead. Together they will form an immigrant-descended social formation which, if it cannot enter the class system, will figure as an underclass to defend itself.

But there are also crucial differences. If the West Indian is plagued by self-doubt induced by white education, and seeks a culture which will give him a sense of identity, the Asians have religions and cultures and languages of which they are proud and which may prove surprisingly adaptive and suited to the demands of a modern industrial society. We may take Sikhism as a case in point.

Sikhism was founded in the fifteenth century in the Mogul Empire. It was a protestant movement within a Hinduism dominated by an effete Brahman caste. It saw all men as equal and set itself to fight for freedom within the Mogul Empire. It adopted the virile symbols of long hair, the turban, the bangle and the knife, and had an impact in India which belied its small numbers. After the annexation of the Punjab in 1849, the Sikhs came to play their own special role within

237

the framework of the Pax Britannica. They prized education highly and they engaged energetically in commerce, not merely in India but all over the world. Sikh pedlars explored the world on behalf of their people and laid the foundations for the later migrations of the Indian diaspora.

Sikhs have never suffered from the sense of inferiority which plagues West Indians and which most white men assume that all black men have. They experience discrimination, it is true, and they resent it, but this is not the first war for survival that they have won. On the widest level the temple provides a possibility of forming bonds of mutual aid, but more immediately the extended family, on what Le Play called the stem family, provides every individual with security and support.

The family system, which is to a large extent shared with Hindus and Muslims, is not, as many whites imagine, a source of oppression bitterly opposed by young people wanting to 'make it' in British society. It is a means to security even for those who want to 'make it'. Hence, many of the most articulate young Asians believe that it should stay. It gives them precisely that security which the West Indians want to find by creating a culture for themselves. So far as the young turbaned Sikh is concerned, he has a culture to be proud of and one which is far past the stage where it could be dismissed as some sort of delinquency. Sikhs, objecting to having to forsake their turbans for crash-helmets when they ride motor-cycles, are doing something which is symbolically and culturally understandable. Crash-helmets are essential in a world of capitalist individualism; turbans imply a kind of cultural and social solidarity which gives greater protection. (It is of some interest here to note that young West Indians have recently been insisting on wearing Rasta hats in school.)

We have not been able to include in this report anthropological studies of the three Asian religious communities.[2] Each has some similarities of structure and function with the culture and society of Sikhism briefly described above. Each also provides a resource in dealing with British society from an underclass position. These are themes which might well be pursued by urban ethnology along with the more specialized and sometimes antiquarian study of the separate cultures.

A last point which should be repeated here concerns the relationship between Asian immigrant politics and the British political system. The West Indians, as they form Black Power movements, eventually have to face up to the question of the relation between their struggle and that which takes place along a capitalist/socialist dimension. This is a problem which Black Power faces *de novo*. But the political history of the Indian sub-continent has its own indigenous socialist and Marxist dimensions. Hence, one may expect that Asian politics in Britain, which naturally produce divisions between national communities, religious groups, groups affiliated to political parties and factions in the homeland, groups divided by their degree of radicalism in the fight against discrimination, and divisions of generation, may express these divisions in terms of socialist and Marxist politics. At present, young Asians are drawn towards, or at least find it convenient to ally themselves with, British Marxist groups. The interest of this, however, is the uneasiness of the alliance. Trotskyists, for example, might find it convenient to take up Asian causes and gain Asian recruits. The young Asians for their part, needing an organizational basis from which they may oppose both the complacency and conservatism of their elders and the hostility of white society, may find that Trotskyist groups provide them with just that basis. It is unlikely, however, that this alliance would lead to united action on other ideological or political matters of little interest to Asian youth.

We have already begun to talk about organizations which really form the subject matter of our next chapter. What we need to notice here is that youth attitudes, organization and behaviour do play something of a vanguard role for the organization of the community as a whole. If the community does not follow, at least it becomes involved in protecting its young. This is especially true of the social work centres run by immigrants which became a central focus of political activity.

There is one further omission from this chapter which should be mentioned. Some will point out that our pilot study of youth does not have a white sample as a control, and that the characteristics of the groups we have described may simply be those of all the disadvantaged young. To this we would make a twofold reply. The first part of this is that an appropriate matched sample of whites is difficult to find, since the white youth who study in immigrant majority schools face quite special problems distinct from the majority of white youth, and entirely different from those of the immigrants and their young British-born siblings. The second is that most of what we had to say is about attitudes and organization of a culturally specific kind, so that it would be nonsense to ask whether young whites shared these characteristics.

We would like to see a study undertaken of deprived white youth, of white youth from immigrant majority schools, and white youth on the margins of the immigrant areas. At the time of writing, the National Front is busy recruiting youth sections. We believe that a survey of white youth attitudes would suggest that the Front may be successful. We also deliberately depart from sociological objectivity here to say that we hope that we are wrong.

239

8 Race, community and conflict

Sociology, or at least the kind of sociology which underlies the approach of this book, cannot rest content with merely giving an account of the attributes or actions of individuals. Thus, we have, at a number of points in the text, made use of the quasi-Marxist teminology of class-in-itself and class-for-itself, taking this distinction to refer, inter alia, to the way in which a category of individuals sharing a common situation comes to have common beliefs and attitudes and to be organized for action.

In the ideal type of class formation which has dominated sociology in this tradition, the working class in industry forms its own organizations, trades unions, to defend its interests, these then become united into national organizations and are the core around which are formed other organizations which engage in a political conflict. In actual situations this development is less than perfect or complete.[1] Both the industrial organizations and the political formations of which they form the core are imperfect and incomplete in their organization and confused and contradictory in their aims. The description of the working class in any country thus becomes in part a matter of describing empirically the actual organizations which exist both locally and nationally, noting the degree of their separate organization, their aims and their functions, and the relationships of conflict and/or co-operation which exist between organization and organization locally, and between local and national organizations.

In their study of Sparkbrook, Rex and Moore devoted special attention to the function of associations and related these both to 'housing-classes' and to the social groupings formed by the different housing groups. Part of the aim of this study, in these terms, is to consider the relations (a) between housing-classes and classes in the other spheres of resource allocation in order to determine whether, overall, there is a position or set of positions indicative of the formation of an underclass-for-itself, and (b) to show how organizations, particularly at a local level, articulate class interests and help to define the total situation for participant actors.

Elsewhere Rex has written of the functions of associations in the urban 'zone of transition' and has argued that the articulation of class interest is only one amongst several functions which associations perform (Rex, 1973b). The four functions which he mentions are overcoming social isolation, the formation and fostering of belief systems and cultural symbols of all kinds, doing pastoral work amongst members, and acting as a trade union or pressure group on behalf of a clientele in a particular area of resource allocation. The actual organizations which he discerned in Sparkbrook thus performed the function of unions of those with common interests in the housing system, but this union function was partly blurred by the fact that the organizations were also performing the other three functions. One can speak of these other three functions as communal rather than associational, but it should be noted that in any case the notion of class-for-itself involves communal as well as associational ties.

There is a tension between the evidence about individuals gathered through social surveys on the one hand and evidence of associational behaviour on the other. The diffuse and dispersed characteristics of individuals do not of themselves appear to suggest clear common interests, let alone a capacity for clear and concerted action. On the other hand, associations, particularly if they have formal structures, tend to have goals to which all members are committed and which it is the duty of the association's officers or the community's leaders to see are carried out. The gap between these two sets of evidence is closed, however, if it is recognized that associations have not only official leaders and members, but clients and followers. Thus there are often far more individuals who look to the activities and the definition of social reality of organizations for guidance than there are actual members of these organizations. The other side of the same coin is that while survey evidence suggests apathy, the actual dynamic of community development is to be found in the work of organizations.

On the question of the degree of conflict, Rex and Moore suggested in Sparkbrook that it was possible for an association transcending particular interests to come into being and to provide the essential framework within which interaction between the separate conflicting associations could take place. It was held that this community association did not entirely suppress conflict, but that it created a new situation in which, instead of conflicts being fought out by the separate groups to the point of their mutual destruction, they actually achieved more through negotiation and compromise. At the same time the community association itself, apart from this conflict

management function, played an ambiguous and internally contradictory role. It sought both to save individuals from a situation
of individual anomie and group conflict and resocialize them for
participating in a wider society of psychologically secure competing
individuals, and yet to retain individuals in the community who
could play representative and leadership roles within it. On the
whole it tended to emphasize the first of these conflicting roles,
leaving a group of full-time and part-time workers, usually drawn
from outside the neighbourhood, to perform the community social
work functions.

The analysis of Sparkbrook in these terms could be described as
optimistic from the point of view of those who hoped that eventually
racial conflict would disappear. In fact, the title of Rex and Moore's
book was chosen for them by the policy-oriented directors of the
Survey of Race Relations, who were anxious that community would
triumph over conflict. In resurrecting that title for this chapter, we
wish to emphasize that the optimistic analysis no longer holds and
that conflict is triumphing over community.

The first and most obvious point to notice is that there are now
far more immigrant and black minority organizations in Handsworth
than there were in Sparkbrook and that they are far more militant.
The second is that the community organizations are more diffuse
and that they do not articulate very well with the needs and the goals
and the definitions of social reality to be found amongst the ethnic
minorities. The radicalism of these associations lies on a different
dimension to that of the minorities, namely those of class, and of the
left/right division in British politics, and what they are in effect doing
is to socialize the minorities into this other conflict system. That they
fail is an indication of the true degree of overall conflict existing
today between minorities and the native majority, not merely locally
but nationally.

We have considered the possibility of drawing up a table on which
all of the community groups in Handsworth could be classified in
terms of a few simple dimensions, e.g. degree of conservatism or
integrationism *v*. degree of radicalism, and whether political,
religious or social work based, but it has not been possible to do so.
In fact, the white and black organizations have to be looked at in
terms of different dimensions altogether and both vary according
to the extent to which any organization from one group overlaps
with or enters the field of another group.

Thus, if we look at the organizations sponsored from within white
British society to deal with the problems of community, of disadvantage, of race relations and social work, one finds that most of
them are susceptible to pressure to define their problems in three
different ways. At their core they are integrationist organizations and

are bound to be influenced by normal social work doctrines of a conservative kind. That is to say they deal with problem people of all sorts and seek to solve their problems and retain their loyalty to established society. This kind of definition, however, is hard to sustain in Handsworth.

The new social worker feels unable to rest content with this conservative socializing perspective. In one way or another the new type of social worker feels drawn to conflict rather than integrationist perspectives. He seeks not to change his client, but to fight with him against society or against part of society.

Now this was a fairly simple thing to do in the Britain of the 1930s. There were many social workers then who became politicized, and instead of sticking with the idea of soup-kitchens, joined the various radical and socialist groups which were available to fight for a different kind of society. Naturally, moreover, there were some groups which were more radical than others, and attachment to the Communist Party, for example, appeared as a more radical alternative to membership of the Labour Party.

In the post-war period a new situation had emerged. The Labour Party had created the welfare state and the Conservatives, in the early 1960s, had acquiesced in it. This produced the phenomenon which *The Economist* called Butskellism when the Conservative Chancellor, Mr R. A. Butler, retained many of the policies of his predecessor. Groups of the far left, including the Communist Party, and, increasingly after 1956, the New Left and the Trotskyists, insisted that Butskellism was not enough, and went on campaigning for a more radical transformation of the political and economic system. At the same time, if it could be proved anywhere that the existing welfare state system was failing, it could be proved by looking at the 'new poor', the large number, that is, of those who slipped through the net of the welfare state. It was expected, therefore, that one diagnosis of the situation which was faced by the new social workers would be that the system had failed because reformist solutions had been applied, and that the task was to work with and for the victims for a more radical solution.

This identification of an abstract enemy and a very long-term political strategy was unlikely, however, to appeal to those who were up against immediate problems. The black immigrants who formed a large part of the new poor and disadvantaged sections of the population were likely to see the problem as one of white racism, while there would be others who would identify the black immigrants as the cause of their problems. Social workers dealing with problems would be pressed into accepting both of these diagnoses by their clients. Community and social work organizations, therefore, would be in the situation represented by Figure 8.1.

243

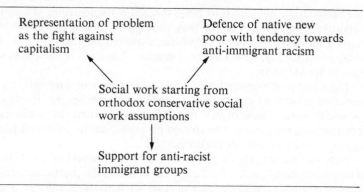

FIGURE 8.1   *Tendencies in white comminity social work*

Not surprisingly, social workers in this situation were uncertain of their role, the more so because many of them were amateurs, or trained workers who had become sceptical of the old expertise but had not found a new one. Very often they ended up using a radical rhetoric but doing normal social work, particularly with and on behalf of native British clients whose problems they could most readily understand. At worst, this produced a kind of implicit racist conservatism, at best, a groping after some new strategy for social work in the new circumstances.

Having seen a surprisingly large number of social workers, young volunteers and others engaged in this work, our first reaction was one of cynicism. It has been said that one of the main achievements of the American poverty programme has been to relieve the poverty of the poverty workers themselves, and we could not help remarking that Handsworth was providing a fair number of former students and student drop-outs with work and with an income, and that they were likely to be uninterested in any diagnosis of the situation which threatened their personal vested interests. We also noted vacillation between the core values and the three alternative value standpoints and strategy represented by Figure 8.1. In the long run, however, we came to realize that only when a more adequate diagnosis of the underlying causes of poverty, disadvantage and racial discrimination is available, will it be possible to establish social work of either a conservative or a radical kind in a sensible way.

Immigrant groups face rather different problems, but it is convenient for our exposition to look at their own equivalent of the social work organizations which we have just been discussing. These are the organizations which arise spontaneously to deal with problems and issues which arise within the immigrant communities. They deal with the stresses and strains which arise in personal relationships owing to migration, with problems of disadvantage in and conflict with the society of the migrant's settlement, and they deal with problems of identity.

There are probably four directions in which actual organizations are pulled away from this core set of activities. First, there is the simplest one of all, namely withdrawal from the society, regarded either as a practical strategy or at least as a utopian ideal. Second, there is the alternative of confrontation and of aggression against the society. Third, there is the active pursuit of integration or at least of peaceful coexistence and accommodation with the society of settlement; and fourth, there is the possibility of allying the group with the radical or revolutionary element in it. Thus, the equivalent diagram for immigrant communities to Figure 8.1 above for social and community work sponsored by the host society is reproduced as Figure 8.2 (a).

In fact, this diagram provides only a general framework for looking at the West Indian and the Asian community and it probably applies less to the Asians than to the West Indians, because it is designed to draw parallels between white and black groups, and the Asians share less with the whites than do the West Indians. None the less, we can specify the way in which the diagram applies to the two communities.

In the case of the West Indian community, all four tendencies are probably to be found, although that which turns on a relationship with white radicalism hardly exists in a pure form. (Rather it is the case that within the third alternative of confrontation and aggression, the question of the relation to the white revolution arises and is discussed.) What is perhaps more interesting, however, is that movements emphasizing black identity need to be placed on our diagram somewhere between practical social work, withdrawal, and

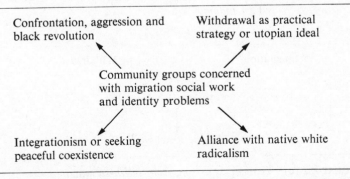

FIGURE 8.2 (a)   *Tendencies of immigrant welfare organizations*

confrontation and aggression. Arguably, movements which have this theme are the most important phenomena amongst West Indians. We should therefore have a sub-diagram like Figure 8.2 (b).

Distinct from black identity groups are those which are concerned with gaining benefits for the group by self-help. This kind of group probably belongs in a different triangle as in Figure 8.2 (c).

In the case of the Asian groups, what one has to notice is that the core activities and all four deviant tendencies are covered within the framework of a group based strongly on kinship, religion and ethnicity. The withdrawal alternative means that kin ties are strengthened as a defensive measure against external threat. The confrontation alternative is closely related as when vigilante and community defence groups are proposed. Alliance with white radicalism takes place through workers' associations which, though they may communicate in terms of socialist and Marxist theory with white groups, are also based upon kin, religious and ethnic structures. Even integration is a strategy pursued by the group as a whole and takes the form of community elites coming to terms with the representatives of the host society. The proper diagrammatic expression of this would show all of the alternatives mentioned but

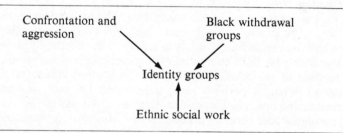

FIGURE 8.2 (b)   *Tendencies arising from identity problems affecting West Indians*

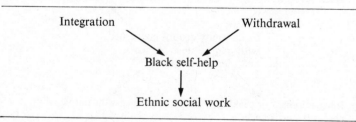

FIGURE 8.2 (c)   *Tendencies arising from self-help reactions affecting West Indian groups*

with the whole encompassed by Sikh, Hindu or Muslim ethnicity, as in Figure 8.2 (d).

In their Sparkbrook study, Rex and Moore made the point that all organizations and associations, whether they saw themselves as pastoral, economic, political, religious or purely social and recreational, tended to fulfil all four of what they regarded as the main functions of associations, viz, overcoming social isolation, the affirmation of beliefs and values, acting as a trade union or interest group, and doing pastoral or social work. If this is true it should be possible to construct another set of diagrams in which the core form is a type of political, religious or social organization (rather than a pastoral or social work one), and to represent the same types of deviant tendency in the case of each. Thus, for example, in the diagram for West Indian religion one would find a place for Rastafarianism at the withdrawal corner of Figure 8. 2(a) or as a black identity group in Figure 8.2 (b), but Pentecostalism, on the other hand, would represent a kind of religious withdrawal, but might also be seen as having to do with a particular kind of adaptation. It seems to belong with the black self-help groups in Figure 8.2 (c).

In trying to relate this study to the study of Sparkbrook with its 'optimistic' analysis of the inter-ethnic conflict there, however, we have emphasized social work as the core activity and have judged all organizations in terms of their performance in the social work area. The Sparkbrook Association did, it is true, fulfil other functions including a political one, but these other functions tended to be subsumed under the notion of social work. In the present, later, and more 'pessimistic' study it would probably be more sensible to give primacy to the political. In fact the reason why the various social and community group-work agencies in both the host society and the ethnic minority communities are so uncertain of their aims is that paternalism and apolitical social work are no longer viable.

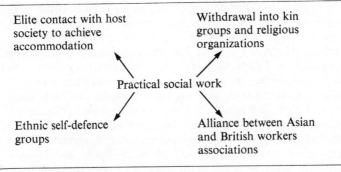

Elite contact with host society to achieve accommodation

Withdrawal into kin groups and religious organizations

Practical social work

Ethnic self-defence groups

Alliance between Asian and British workers associations

FIGURE 8.2 (d)   *Tendencies affecting Asian organizations*

The key activities are really political, or, rather, every group formation and activity has to be looked at in terms of its political role.

The key political concept in the Sparkbrook study was, of course, that of housing-class. Implied in its use was the suggestion that, although the Labour Party was the major organizational means whereby British workers were represented on local councils and were thereby able to affect the allocation of housing, housing questions tended to produce different divisions of interest from those which arose in relation to the labour market. Further it was suggested that most immigrants were in a different housing situation from native workers, with the result that their organizations tended to be not merely ethnic organizations, but the organizations of coalitions of housing-classes. So great, moreover, was the failure of the Labour Party to meet the needs of immigrants in the housing field that there was some possibility that the immigrants might enter the local political arena independently to defend their housing interests. It is now necessary to revise and extend this analysis.

The main lessons which we have derived from the Handsworth study are (a) that immigrants as voters were in fact surprisingly loyal to the Labour Party until 1974; (b) that this loyalty has been weakened in recent times (especially as indicated by the Ladywood by-election of July 1977); and that (c) the core and focus of West Indian political organization has been provided, not by housing-classes in a simple sense, but by local neighbourhood politics, which centre partly on housing, but probably more on the problems of youth and relations with the forces of law and order; while Asian organization has varied between elite negotiation with representatives of white society and other kinds of organization, which, in part, have reference to homeland politics, and, in part, to left-right divisions within British working-class politics.

So far as white politics are concerned, the most important point to be made is that in areas like Handsworth, the voters, although working-class, are alienated from the Labour Party in two directions. On the one hand there are some who for traditional reasons vote Conservative. On the other, there are those whose concern with the problems presented by immigrant neighbours leads them to oppose the party from within, to abstain, to vote Conservative, or in some other way to express their concern with the issue of race in politics.

Again it is useful to sum up these observations in a series of diagrams. First, in Figure 8.3 (a) we set out the picture of mainstream working-class politics. It should be noted that a part of the mainstream working-class political system includes an opposition through which more radical claims may be made inside and outside of Parliament and the town halls. This left opposition includes the Communist Party, the New Left and Trotskyist groups. The first

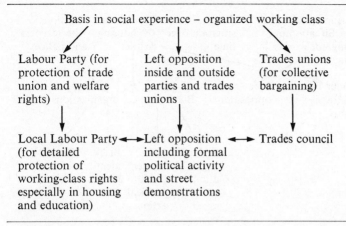

FIGURE 8.3 (a)   *Political structuring of white working class*

and third of these appear within the trade-union movement, while the second and third are to be found especially amongst students. Although they have their allies in the formal Labour Party, they are very much more evident in grass-roots politics, direct action politics and in street demonstrations. They are one of the normal ways in which the pressure of working-class demands affects the Labour Party.

While the organizational means through which the mainstream native working-class man or woman protects his interests in politics arises out of industrial organization in the firms and factories of Great Britain, the organizations formed by immigrants arise from more complex sources. In the case of the West Indians they arise from their position as colonial men and women descended from slaves, from their position as workers, from their position in the housing market and from the misunderstandings and conflicts with teachers in schools and the police in the streets. From these sources there arises a multiplicity of overlapping organizations as well as a relationship to the Labour Party. This we set out in Figure 8.3 (b). This diagram is meant to emphasize that West Indian political action over a number of matters central to the community is not channelled through the Labour Party, even though their situation as workers leads to their normally being supporters of the Labour Party and members of unions. Moreover, there is not a strong connection of any kind between the politics of revolutionary black groups and the left opposition within the Labour movement.

Again, the organizational situation amongst the Asians is different. The need for organization arises from the same sources as it does in

249

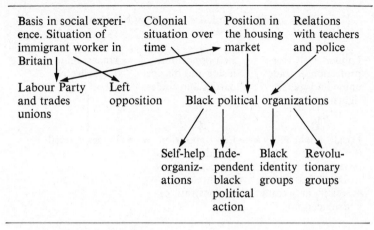

FIGURE 8.3 (b)   *Political structure of West Indian community*

the West Indian community, but the Labour movement as a whole, and kinship, play more important roles in meeting the needs of the Asians in all areas of interest. Thus we have the situation set out in Figure 8.3 (c). Obviously the Asian workers' associations are all-important here, but these organizations relate to elite negotiations with the host community, to Labour politics and to left politics, while at the same time dealing directly with a number of issues in community politics.

Finally we must consider the situation of the white workers in the inner city. They are either members of the mainstream working class (often retired), or they are members of the 'new poor' or 'lumpenproletariat'. All of them live in underprivileged housing. Thus we have the situation in Figure 8.3 (d). The important point to

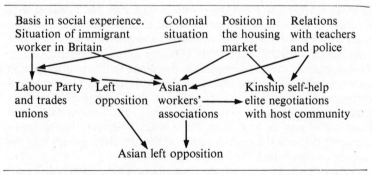

FIGURE 8.3 (c)   *Structure of Asian political organization*

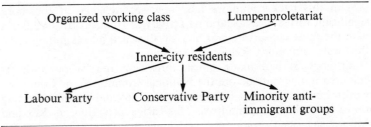

FIGURE 8.3 (d)   *Structure of inner-city white political organization*

notice here is the difference between the organizational forms amongst these inner-city residents and those amongst the mainstream working class. One should perhaps notice that on local issues connected with schools and housing, as well as on the national issue of immigration control, support for the Conservatives and the far right increases.

These various forms of political organization and behaviour are paralleled by the forms of organization in the religious sphere. Here the inner-city whites are divided between Anglicanism and orthodox Non-conformity. The West Indians, while they might be Anglicans, Methodists or Baptists too, also belong to Pentecostalist and Holiness churches, which may involve some kind of withdrawal into religious experience yet which encourage an individual self-discipline, and Rastafari which is supportive of political alienation from British society. The various Asian religions also help to maintain a separate cultural identity and some of them are undoubtedly supportive of social mobility and of commercial activity. All of these religions have political importance and serve to confirm Richard Niebuhrs' contention that the sources of religious differentiation are as much social as theological, but we would add that together they help to define the class system of the inner city and are sensitive indicators of the full complexity of that system.

Our principle starting-points in this theoretical comment on the organizational situation in Handsworth have been the study of social and pastoral work amongst the various groups and the politics and religion of those groups. What we have sought to show is that the total situation is comprehended neither in terms of the theory of social work nor the new community social work. It is not comprehended by the normal range of working-class political organization, even when that is extended to take in the groupings and groupuscules of the far left. Finally there is a range of belief systems here which lend themselves to a class analysis, but one which has to go beyond that which is normal in the sociology of the relations between the Christian denominations and social class.

251

With this background we may now record some of the more significant forms of associational activity in Handsworth. We begin with the most conservative agency of all which affects immigrants, the local Community Relations Council.

Birmingham had made official provision for liaison with its coloured immigrants before the National Committee for Commonwealth Immigrants came into existence in 1965 and began the setting up of local liaison committees. This earlier provision, as Rex and Moore suggested, could only be understood as arising from a colonialist mentality on the part of the Council. The liaison officer appointed was an ex-colonial policeman and he had neither independence from the Council nor effective responsibility to the immigrant community. Hence, when the first liaison committee was set up in conjunction with the NCCI there was actually a strengthening of contact with the immigrant community and there was greater independence from the City Council. In due course this became the local Community Relations Council.

The work of the Community Relations Commission and its associated councils has been well discussed and criticized by Hill and Issacharoff (1971). They saw the councils as doing little more than act as agencies for the co-option of immigrant elites and as in no way capable of making an immigrant voice heard in the city halls. The Birmingham Community Relations Council has been no exception to this. It is, as such councils go, quite good at its work, but its work is defined in essentially paternalistic terms, and it is hardly in a position to fight against discrimination.

The present community relations officer is David Chakravati, a Sri Lankian described by the *Birmingham Post* as a 'benevolent 58 year old barrister, who took a degree at Cambridge, worked in the Ministry of Food and at Unilever, who has now reached the top of the Midlands race relations tree.'

There are eight full-time officers who advise the City Council on all matters affecting immigrants and who are now expected to encourage self-help schemes. One of these officers, however, a West African, Bill Assam, was highly critical of the whole idea of self-help schemes, which he called 'a dangerous misconcept' (Assam, 1976), and went on to write: 'Blacks in Britain are in a desperate posiiton. They are not second but third class citizens. For anybody to propose such grandiose schemes as a Black Chamber of Commerce, a Black Centralized Accountancy Service etc. is totally unrealistic.'

Here, at least, was one officer who saw as entirely unrealistic the apparent belief in the Community Relations Commission that blacks were playing a significant part in business, when in practice they seemed more like a group lower than the working class. It is doubtful whether such a view will carry much weight, however. Although the

West Indian Federation is represented on the council, its voice can carry very little weight either. The other members of the local council tend to be drawn from Asian elites or from whites who, while they have often been very actively involved in activities designed to oppose discrimination and to promote better race relations, are hardly likely to push the council in a radical direction. Many West Indians and some Asians are openly cynical about the Community Relations Council, even though they find it worthwhile to be represented on it and are concerned about the views which any immigrant who is a member of the council puts forward on their behalf. The Asian communities, who have a more immediate problem of doing public relations on behalf of their communities and their culture, and who are concerned with managing a system of pluralistic accommodation, have more interest in the council's work.

The Community Relations Council does not fit very easily into any of the diagrams which we have set out above. It embodies most of the values of conservative social work organizations, but in a peculiar form which is appropriate to dealing with immigrant problems. Its stance is paternalistic and excludes completely those political deviations which we suggested created stresses in most social work organizations. These stresses and strains tend to be displaced and to lead to struggles to enhance, not the power of minority organizations to influence the commission and its councils, but rather the career prospects of its minority staff.

The paternalism of the Community Relations Council is so obvious that radical alternatives are bound to arise. The most threatening will be those which are set up by minorities for minorities. Before we turn to look at these, however, we should notice that there has also been official government support for its own sort of radicalism as an alternative to the Community Relations Commission. This kind of radicalism identifies the problems of the immigrant minorities as the problems of the new poor in the inner city, and proposes that they be dealt with as a special new kind of administrative problem or as part of the political struggle against capitalism. Generally speaking, governments have not been willing to look at the problems of immigrant minorities from a radical perspective, but they have increasingly been inclined to license highly radical approaches to the inner city.

The clearest development in this direction was the setting up by the Labour Government in 1969 of the Community Development Projects. These had as their brief the identification of the problems of areas of social stress and the formulation of policies to deal with them. Inevitably the projects came up with diagnoses and solutions which were embarrassing to local government, but this they were meant to do. In this way, so it seemed to Labour Party leaders, the basis

253

would be laid for extending the scope of the welfare state into difficult areas.

It is generally thought, by those who opposed them and by those who supported them alike, that the Community Development Projects clashed with the Government and were closed down because they were too radical. This is, indeed, true. With their final pamphlets (CDP, 1976 and 1977), especially the one entitled *Profits Against Houses*, they moved towards an extreme Marxist perspective, arguing that housing problems as such could not be solved within the context of capitalism. What is often overlooked, however, is that the CDP as a whole had little to say about the specific hardships and discrimination faced by minorities. It was small comfort to the members of these minorities to be told that their only salvation lay in a revolution which young radical social workers wanted, but which both Labour and Conservative governments regarded as unacceptable. This was another version of the problem which we noted in our chapter on education where we saw the official response to minority problems as one which subsumed them under the more general problems of the disadvantaged (though here, of course, we are discussing more radical options).

There was no Community Development Project in Handsworth. There was one in neighbouring Saltley, which shared most of the characteristics of the CDP generally, including a general stance of radicalism coupled with an ambiguous stance on immigrant questions. There were, however, a number of interrelated 'new social work' agencies financed by charitable trusts and manned largely by young volunteers and amateur social workers. The most important of these were the curiously named All Faiths for One Race, and the Westminster Endeavour for Liaison and Development. In many ways these expressed the same philosophy and the same stresses and strains as the Community Development Projects.

All Faiths for One Race came to be housed in the Lozells Social Development Centre on Lozells Road in 1974. There it came to be connected with a number of other agencies and was recognizable as the equivalent in its importance to the Sparkbrook Association described in Rex and Moore's study. The Lozells Social Development Centre was described by the *Mail* (9 June 1976) as 'one of the city's unofficial social work agencies'. But it was more than this. It was a place in which the more radical type of white community worker exchanged ideas with others like himself and where perspectives on race, disadvantage and the inner city were formed.

AFFOR was started in 1971 to 'realise brotherhood in the relations between people of different colours, creeds and cultures in Birmingham and throughout the world'.

Its first chairman was a distinguished liberal theologian, Professor

254

John Hick, editor of *The Myth of God Incarnate*. Its name and its sponsorship in fact suggest a highly important enterprise which sees religious creeds, including the Christian one, not as unifying but as potentially divisive factors, and sets itself to find common ground amongst them which will make unity and co-operation in a multi-racial society possible.

This high aim, however, was hardly evident in the day-to-day activities of AFFOR. There were clubs to be run, people's immediate social problems to be dealt with, newspapers to be edited, demonstrations and political campaigns to be planned, and delicate relations with various outside groups to be attended to. In fact, in June 1976 the *Mail* reported that the Charity Commission had investigated AFFOR's finances and its charitable status was called into question. Earlier, in its 1972–3 annual report, AFFOR had written: 'We do not apologise for the controversial aspects of AFFOR's activities. All who know the realities and problems of race relations know that its work is inherently controversial.'

The first director of AFFOR, John Plummer, took the organization of opposition to racist movements, and case work with individuals who were not getting justice from the local authority, as central issues. AFFOR also worked on the settlement of Ugandan Asians, undertook a study of child-minding in the area and started a play-group and, after the building firm of Wates had donated money to start a library, employed a full-time education officer. John Plummer resigned as director in 1975 to study for a law degree. He also became an active supporter of International Socialism (later the Socialist Workers' Party), and was continually criticized by the Birmingham press. In 1975 the *Mail* (10 October) wrote, 'Is there no end to the social conscience of Mr John Plummer', and accused him of believing, 'If you won't do as I demand you must be wrong and evil'. Subsequently, Plummer was found guilty of a minor offence in connection with the anti-Relf demonstrations outside Winson Green prison. By 1976 the *Mail* had decided that 'the centre at Finch Road, Lozells [i.e. the Lozells Social Development Centre], is emerging as a base for political activists in the city'. After John Plummer, AFFOR was directed by Geoff Wilkins, who had worked on the resettlement of Ugandan Asians, and then by Clare Short, a former senior civil servant who had been secretary to Mr Alex Lyon, a junior minister, who claimed that he had been sacked by the Prime Minister for 'sticking up for the blacks'.

Clearly AFFOR was an organization set up for, and to some extent engaged in, work amongst black immigrants. It also participated in campaigns against racism. But if we were to place it on our diagram we would place it much more in the corner of radical white politics. John Plummer's orientation towards International Socialism was not unique amongst AFFOR workers, and there was a disinclination to define immigrant minority problems as distinct from others amongst the poor and disadvantaged.

We were not surprised to find, in fact, that though AFFOR set itself up as the main organization dealing with immigrant problems, it was not seen as such by any of the immigrant groups. In fact, we were warned by one such organization that if we occupied an office in the Lozells Social Development Centre it would positively harm our chances of gaining the confidence of West Indians. On the other hand, we found AFFOR deeply suspicious of our own investigation because it was not oriented towards remedial action.

WELD began in 1968 'as an attempt by teachers at the Westminster Road School, Handsworth, to find a form of education which related to the needs of the area more closely than did conventional education' (*New Society*, 14 August 1975).

In 1971 premises were obtained at the old New Trinity School and the LEA eventually paid the salaries of two teachers to work there full-time. Community action with local residents has been an integral part of WELD's activities. Two idealistic young teachers initially ran a play-group and a shop, but activities have now expanded to seven pre-school sessions a week, two youth club nights, an Asian dramatic society, painting and woodwork classes for adults, and work with ESN children. Two afternoons a week 'disturbed children' from a local school attend the centre. In general, WELD is engaged far more directly in community and social work activity than AFFOR and becomes less involved in politics.

WELD has also become connected with the implementation of housing and inner-city policy. One of the housing associations gave advice there. The group was connected with the Housing Advice Liaison Group and had a research worker from the Centre for Urban and Regional Studies at Birmingham university attached to it. The centre has had urban aid grants, and is heavily used for placements of polytechnic and college students taking diplomas in community education. In 1974 a series of lectures on urban renewal, with city officials invited to speak, was held at Westminster Endeavour Liaison Development (WELD) in collaboration with the Workers' Educational Association.

A more radical group than WELD was an Action Centre in Villa Road. This was run by a group of ex-university students who occupied a house in the area. The Action Centre sold Marxist and feminist literature and gave housing and other advice. One of the women workers organized a claimants' union branch, but this collapsed when she left. The group claimed that they had a lawyer available to give advice. According to one of the group members, the idea was to live in the area, know it, and help the residents, He claimed that the group wanted to avoid becoming regarded as community leaders. One or two of the members of this group were extremely hostile to our research and, far from assisting us in any way, actively discouraged members of the local community from talking to us. This opposition was no doubt in part based upon the natural opposition of community workers to research not related to immediate action projects, but may also have rested upon an ideological basis. It is indicative of the fact that white radical groups were radical only in terms of English politics, that, because we were posing wider Third World issues, we were looked on with suspicion. For them, our race relations orientation did not fit with the rationale of their work which was defined much more in terms of radical social work and grass-roots community politics.

In approaching West Indian organizations we were aware that we would encounter difficulties of a different kind. The most important single difference between Handsworth in 1974 and Sparkbrook in 1964, and in Birmingham as a whole between those dates, is the growth in the militancy of the West Indian organizations. In Sparkbrook, Rex and Moore found nothing but accommodating leaders, and they make reference to an even more acquiescent leadership in Winson Green. It is tremendously important, therefore, to notice that, even though the established immigrant residents of Handsworth appear relatively complacent, organizations do now exist which provide more militant definitions of the social and political situation.

The oldest organization still operative is the West Indian Federation. This organization is hard to pin down and its committee men rather than its membership seem to exercise influence. None the less, it is an organization whose officers sit on the Community Relations Council and one whose politics are at least important in bringing significant political leaders to the fore. One such was James Hunte, who was president until 1968, was then defeated, but returned for a period in 1974. James Hunte, however, came to have an importance and a sphere of influence outside of the federation, and the federation itself made little impact on politics.

The most militant of Handsworth's black groups in terms of a rejection of paternalist and integrationist policies, and a willingness to accept black–white confrontation, is the Afro-Caribbean Co-ordinating Committee (later known as the Afro-Caribbean Self-help Organization). This group will not discuss its goals with white researchers. It dates back to 1966 when several black teenagers, influenced by a growing black awareness in the world and the race riots in the USA, met to discuss black people's problems in Handsworth. They established a study group to read black-oriented literature and accepted Pan-Africanism as an ideology. The belief that the black man's future is in Africa and that he has no future in

257

England has led to four visits to Africa by members of this group, and another delivered a paper at the sixth Pan-African Congress in Dar-es-Salaam. The group is especially responsive to events in southern Africa.

Initially this group was organized as a para-military political unit with members holding posts of Minister of Defence, Minister of Information and so on. Gus John, during his research in Birmingham in 1970, considered the group to be 'the most progressive organization in the area, well prepared for any eventuality like riots, and in a position to mobilize the masses if necessary' (John, 1972).

In 1970 the *Evening Mail* sent a white female reporter to interview the group and she was refused entry. It then claimed that it came under the surveillance of the security forces and that on one occasion a special branch officer pulled a gun and threatened the group members. When another young West Indian leader, Sebastian Godwin, was shot in Hall Road in 1974, the group claimed that 'the police and the army surrounded the ACSHO base to find out whether the gunman was sheltering there'.

ACSHO originally occupied a small house but later moved to a larger house in Heathfield Road in which they are establishing a library and a nursery. At various times the group has produced a newspaper, first called *Harambee*, then *Paw*, then the *African*. A 1974 edition of the *African* pointed out that 400 years in captivity in the western hemisphere has prevented people remembering their origins: 'We must emphasize an African awareness amongst ourselves here in the West in order to develop in the same gear as our brothers and sisters on the continent' [i.e. Africa].'

The group deliberately kept in touch with African affairs in South Africa. It was addressed by Herbert Chitepo of the Zimbabwe African National Union and a speaker from the South African Pan-African Congress. It also heard a representative of the MPLA in Angola, although it made its own political position clear by making the white woman from the Angola Solidarity Committee wait outside.

This identification with African affairs was coupled with an interest in Black America and an attempt to model its own actions on those of the Black Panther Party. In parallel with the Black Panthers, ACSHO drew up a ten point programme including two which were 'to develop a black political party' and 'to promote black business co-operatives'.

The activities of this group and its mythological representation of events in terms of actual open warfare may seem to whites somewhat bizarre. If, however, one takes the view that the structures which have to be transformed if the black man is to liberate himself are the structures of colonialism, their rejection of the relatively simple politics of European class struggle in favour of an alliance with the Third World Revolution makes a lot of sense. Myths, as Sorel saw, have a crucial structural political importance and, as we see it, the ACSHO is likely to have wider and wider appeal if racial divisions deepen and paternalistic reformist, and simplistic Marxist solutions to the black man's plight are seen to fail. Groups such as this do not merely help to define the position of the underclass and to turn it into a class-for-itself, but they associate that underclass with the structural transformation of capitalist and colonial society which is going on in the Third World. For those of us who hold that this process is fundamental to the understanding of contemporary politics – more fundamental than the revolution of the working class in the advanced countries – the option opened up by the ACSHO is more important and less utopian than any other on offer in Handsworth today.

The organizer of ACSHO is Beanie Brown, who is one of a group of young men who systematically began to educate themselves in black political history and political thought in the mid-1960s. Others include Sebastian Godwin, who has been active in a number of situations of confrontation with the authorities, and Maurice Andrews and John Benjamin, two black social workers who became associated with the Harambee House project.

Godwin is not a man who can be labelled as belonging to one group rather than another. He seems to have had a hand in nearly every militant activity being pursued by any black group. He regards the ACSHO as consisting of 'black brothers'; he refers to the Rasta brothers, extending the term Rasta to include most of the militant young, and he regards himself as one of the founders of Harambee House. He has also been to Africa and has visited both Dar-es-Salaam and Mozambique, whose politics he discusses with perception and intelligence.

Having read Huey Newton's biography, *Revolutionary Suicide*, with approval, Godwin is inclined to see his own encounters with authority as akin to those experienced by the Black Panther leader. He was shot in the stomach by another black man over what is variously described as a personal and a political dispute. He, too, claims that the British Army became involved on this occasion. In 1975 he began attending the West Bromwich College of Technology. Eight weeks after starting his course he was president of the Students' Union. In 1976 he alleged that there was racialism amongst college lecturers and that they were intimidating students. A lecturer at the college was reported as saying that Godwin had been responsible for a series of disruptive incidents, including assaults on lecturers. The lecturer said that he was a 'Black Power devotee'. The students eventually voted to displace him as president after he had been expelled from the college. In 1977 he applied for a place at Warwick university, but after a second special interview with the registrar present he was not admitted.

In May 1976, Godwin was again in the news when he helped some West Indian squatters to move into a house on Hamstead Road. In June 1976 he was reported as being charged with an assault on a security officer in the Birmingham Central Library. Finally, in July 1977, he was jailed after an incident in the social security office in which he was alleged to have used threatening behaviour.

To the press, Godwin appears as a figure part menacing and part absurd. It is important, therefore, to point out that while others theorize and teach, he acts, and that to young black men who have bad relations with teachers and the police, his acts of defiance and his courage in pursuing his conflicts to the point of imprisonment are bound to be impressive. The fact that we think he exaggerates the injustices which he personally suffers is irrelevant. He is simply using his own life to dramatize the position in which most young blacks see themselves. It is difficult to predict the future of such a man. What one can say is that there will be others like him, if, as seems likely, blacks take to a position of militant confrontation.

The Harambee organization encompasses a black community workers' group, a housing association, and a number of other projects, e.g. the Marcus Garvey pre-school project and the Handsworth black summer school. The organization took the opportunity of presenting itself through the BBC's 'Open Door' television programme and a reviewer noted: 'The programme was not intended as an exercise in the promotion of racial harmony or as an exposé of the virtues of life in a multi-racial society, but as a portrayal of the concept of a self-help for the black community.'

According to one of the workers:

'The ideology of the organization can be summed up as "Harambee" which means working together. This belief system is influenced by Pan-Africanism, African socialism, and parts of the black power philosophy. It is believed that though conditions of black people are influenced by what happens in Africa, in this way black people can carve out for themselves a decent existence in Handsworth'.

The organization began when a group of black social workers who were particularly concerned with the problems of homelessness amongst black youths met in 1972. Through grants obtained from the Cadbury Trust, the British Council of Churches, and the CRC, and the leasing of a large house from the Council, a hostel for homeless youth was set up in Hall Road. Later other houses in Hall Road were acquired and turned into self-contained flats for ex-Harambee residents. A shop and advice centre was opened in Grove Lane in 1974, legal advice being given by qualified lawyers, who would also represent black youngsters in court. The original Harambee building is due for demolition and the hostel is now (1977) about to move into a new building acquired with money from charitable trusts.

Harambee workers told us:

'The organization now represents black people in all areas of their lives. It is also committed to community development. However, it has learned from experience the operation of the vicious circle of poverty among black ex-colonial people in an urban ghetto. The association would now like to set up its own workshop to train young people to produce goods in 'non-capitalistic conditions.'

The Harambee organization is particularly concerned with education. The first black summer school was held in 1970, and by 1974, Easter and summer schools were well established, permission being given by the education authority for local schools to be used. The workers are concerned that many 'black children leave school with a "failure syndrome" ' as though they have been conditioned to expect failure in their undertakings. In this respect, the 'educators have failed in their role', according to a report on the summer school of 1975.

This report goes on to criticize the white-biased curriculum and the lack of conviction of young blacks that hard work brings rewards: 'Even before they leave school they display the symptoms of alienation. They baffle their teachers at school and infuriate their parents.'

The schools have been funded by the Cadbury Trust, and staffed by the Harambee workers, black teachers and volunteer parents. The curriculum taught is a basic subject curriculum, but oriented to 'giving a truer and fairer account of historic and cultural events'. The programme is supplemented by educational trips; for example, the 1974 summer school celebrated the birthday of Marcus Garvey by a trip to Colwyn Bay. At the 1974 summer school a theme relating to black people was chosen each week. For example:

Theme: Models.
Every day of this week an admired modern leader will be
chosen and reasons given for the choice, e.g.
(1)   Julius Nyerere – humility
(2)   Mohammed Ali – sacrifice
(3)   Shirley Chisholm – female achievement

The aim of the summer schools is to give a sense of pride and identity to black children.

The organization also concerns itself with pre-school children, since 'literature on Handsworth shows how deprived black children in the area are during their most formative pre-school years'. A pre-school project is currently being formulated with the aim of setting up a black nursery.

The Harambee organization's third interest in education is running a Black Studies course for young people at the hostel. This is a sophisticated programme drawing on texts from Fanon, Cleaver, Carmichael, Paton, Segal, Nkrumah, Nyerere, Heskovits, M. G. Smith and C. L. James.

The Harambee workers feel that the City Council has always regarded their organization as a threat. We were told: 'The city politicians have tried to use the big stick to force the association to alter its policies.'

In 1976 an urban aid grant was offered to the association on condition that all property bought by the organization be in the name of the local authority.

The interesting thing about the Harambee group is that, although it is led by men who educated themselves in black thought, along with Beanie Brown and Sebastian Godwin, it combines its political perceptions with practical action. It could be pointed out that this parallels the position of those Black Panther leaders who, when they gave up the idea of revolutionary confrontation, took to social work. This, however, is misleading. The Harambee leaders are not concerned with black–white confrontation for its own sake; nor are they men who have sold out. The revolutionary change which they seek is one which restores the black man's sense of his identity and dignity. Helping homeless youths and running summer schools are constructive parts of a general and sometimes militant programme directed to this end. It seems likely that men like Maurice Andrews[2] and John Benjamin will have an important part to play in representing their community when they complete their law degrees.

Another significant leader of West Indians in Handsworth is James Hunte, who has on two occasions been president of the West Indian Federation in Birmingham. He is not conflict-oriented in that he believes in 'humanity and the brotherhood of black and white', but he believes in black self-help, organized around a variety of issues. He came originally from Barbados, and served in the British Army in Malaya, where he was in prison for a short time for political activity among the Malays. For some time he worked as a door-to-door canvasser for the Christadelphian Church. He works with an Arab lieutenant, Mr Sayeed, from his home in Leonard Road.

The most important issue which Hunte took up was the case of pyramid selling and the Holiday Magic scandal. According to the *Birmingham Post* (23 April 1975), an American, Gary Yancey, formed a company called Apollo UK Ltd and recruited people in

Birmingham to sell non-existent cleaning products. He also recruited former employees of Golden Chemical Products to help him. At the same time, a cosmetic firm, Holiday Magic, had been recruiting people as agents to sell their products. The agents of a number of banks and finance companies arranged loans and second mortgages for people to buy positions in the sales organizations for between £800 and £1,000. When pyramid selling was made illegal, one of the finance companies at least, namely that of Julian Hodge, expressed their willingness to redress the injustice done to the victims. James Hunte, meanwhile, formed an action group and negotiated with the banks and finance companies to cancel debts that individuals had incurred. Yancy, the original pyramid seller, was arrested by Fraud Squad officers, but jumped bail and returned to the USA. Hunte's action group organized meetings and marches to protest about the scandal.

At a meeting in Birmingham Town Hall, September 1975, Hunte claimed that his association had reached agreement with the Hodge and UDT finance groups to write off millions of pounds in debts, but that about forty finance companies were involved. According to the *Mail* (30 September 1975), 'top level talks will be opened in Whitehall tomorrow in a new bid to help Midland victims of pyramid selling'. John Lee, Handsworth's MP and the action group's legal adviser, met the Minister of State for Prices and Consumer Protection and the *Mail* reported (8 July 1975) that 'Caribbean governments are expected to press Whitehall for changes in the law to compensate families in debt after borrowing cash from pyramid-selling companies'.

James Hunte has attempted to work within the framework of the Labour Party – he stood for selection as a local Labour candidate – but in August 1977 he stood as an Independent candidate in the Ladywood by-election, polling 336 (2·2 per cent) of the vote. At one point in the campaign he was approached by the Labour Party and asked to stand down as it was feared that he would take votes away from Labour. In May 1977, Hunte was reported in the *Mail* as suggesting that a lump sum of two years' advance payment of state benefits should be made for youths who wished to return to the West Indies. ('Cash call for West Indians to go home', Mail, 2 May 1977). The following week, under the headline 'Alarm at payouts to go home plan' (Mail, 13 May 1977), Hunte was criticized by other black organizations for his suggestion.

Hunte has also been a controversial figure within the West Indian Federation. He was president in the 1960s and, although he claimed to be president again in 1976, a member of the management committee said, 'Mr. Hunte is a self-styled President, he was originally appointed by the committee as a publicity officer in a voluntary

263

capacity' (*Post*, 2 November 1976). A later report (*Post*, 2 February 1977, 'Split West Indian group has two leaders') noted that the association had splintered. A job creation scheme at the federation had been abandoned because the young people involved were not turning up for the work.

Hunte is particularly interesting in that he is not one of the group which educated itself in black thought. He is not in fact an ideologist at all, but a natural politician, sensitive to the issues which affect the man in the street. That is his strength. But his lack of a systematic political philosophy is also a weakness. Because he depends so much on his personal appeal, any sign of personal weakness on his part is likely to be seized upon by his enemies and opponents. It is not for us to judge his personal strengths and weaknesses in this study. All that we can say is that in the pyramid selling campaign at least he was particularly successful, and that leadership by men with Hunte's flair of this issue-oriented kind will make an important contribution to the future. He has also explored the electoral option which is open to West Indians and has established himself, as no one else has, as someone to be negotiated with by the Labour Party.

All of the leaders we have mentioned so far have been, relatively speaking, militants, and their emergence in the last ten years is one of the key phenomena in Handsworth. It is unfortunate that we could not ask the respondents to our survey to give their opinions on these men, but to do so would have appeared as an attempt to use the survey to meddle in community politics. Had we done so, however, we believe that, despite the cautious conservatism of our respondents, we would have found considerable respect for all of these individuals for seeking in one way or another to assert black community power and more generally the dignity of the black man.

It would be a mistake, however, to suppose that this more aggressive style of organization and leadership was the only kind to be found in Handsworth. There were also groups like the Faith, Confidence and Finance Club which coupled ideas of saving and self-help with the idea of racial harmony. There was also a group known as the Jamaican Community Service Group set up by a representative of the Jamaican High Commission, and a number of groups concerned about education. Most of these turned their backs on militancy and continued the style of organization which had been evident in Sparkbrook in 1964.

There is, of course, also a religious dimension to the community life and organization of the West Indian community. The majority of West Indians claimed to be members of a Christian denomination, and there was also the phenomenon of Rastafarianism, which, as we have seen, spread far beyond the confines of the formal Rastafarian churches. According to our survey, 17 per cent of the West

Indian respondents went to Pentecostal churches, 37 per cent went to the Methodist or Baptist churches and 22 per cent claimed to be Church of England. Retrospectively we felt that we should have made some finer distinctions here (as between Pentecostalist and Holiness churches for example),[3] and we should have either included Rastafarianism as one of the religions or asked a question about it. None the less, the actual religious situation is reasonably well revealed by our researches.

There are a number of Pentecostal churches in Handsworth and they provide a focus for a feeling of solidarity for the congregations. The First United Church of Jesus Christ, Apostolic Church of God, in Beaudesert Road, has a congregation of about 250 people, mainly children and people over 35 – the congregation dress up in their best clothes and take part in an enthusiastic, spontaneous service, playing tambourines, and testifying or preaching if the spirit moves them. The New Testament Church of God in George Street, Lozells, has about 190 members. The pastor, Mr Thompson, says his church began spontaneously in Jamaica as a desire to return to an 'original church'. The headquarters of this church is now in Tennessee, USA, and a European headquarters is in Germany. He thinks the West Indians have brought their own religion to England, and although he does not approve of Black Power he said there were connections between his church and the church in Africa. His church functions as a self-help organization, 'tithes' are collected and money is lent to people to buy property. The Church of God of Prophecy in Peel Street has a congregation of about 220 including children. Funds are being collected to build a new church. This church again has a spontaneous service, accompanied by tambourines and electric guitars, in which 'audience participation', is invited.

Some 37 per cent of our West Indian respondents attend Baptist or Methodist churches. Astbury Memorial Methodist Church in Handsworth had a congregation of about 150, with rather more West Indian than white people, although the minister and the choir are white. A black man does take the collection, however. Cannon Street Memorial Baptist Church has about a third of the congregation black, two-thirds white. The black people are mainly women, and the choir is mixed. The minister at this church is critical of the Pentecostal churches and the Jehovah's Witnesses. The Methodist church on Villa Road has developed a 'neighbourhood centre' and runs a youth club and play-group. The Rev. Michael Ward, minister of this church, offered a room to our research project in 1974.

Despite Birmingham's Nonconformist traditions, the Church of England has always made better church provision. There are four large C of E churches in the survey area, dating back to the days of Handsworth as a respectable middle-class suburb. Although 74 per

265

cent of our white respondents and 22 per cent of our West Indian respondents claimed to be C of E, the churches are not very well attended. Hunters Road Catholic Church, the largest Catholic church in the area, is well attended, mainly by Irish people, but by only about a dozen black people.

We may, of course, conclude that the relatively large affiliation to the Anglican church especially, and to some extent to the Methodist and Baptist churches, is a sign of conservatism and conformity, and there can be little doubt that the percentage of the total West Indian community who attend these churches is an index of such conformity. It is important, however, to notice the minority who are members of the less orthodox Pentecostalist and Holiness churches and the pervasive influence of Rastafarianism, not merely amongst its own members, but in the spread of its ideas to those who are members of other churches, to those who are members of none, and particularly to the young.

Pentecostalism is a phenomenon common amongst poor, exploited and black peoples. It involves a turning away from the world to the cultivation of an intense religious experience (possession by the Holy Spirit). Although it involves the idea of an after-life, in which the present fortunes of the rich and the poor, the wicked and the good, are reversed, this very idea serves to make life tolerable on this earth, and the consequence of belonging to the Pentecostal church might well be acquiescence of the poor and the exploited in their present condition.

On the other hand, it should be noted that in all the Pentecostal churches we have encountered, other elements enter which make for the strengthening of resistance to racial injustice. In the first place, it should be noted that these churches belong to the West Indians themselves. For many they provide a secondary structure of group life beyond the family of the utmost importance. Moreover, the church's pastors are put in an important position of leadership. It may well be that these organizations lack a militant direction, but organization and leadership of this kind make militancy possible in a way in which it would not be without such churches, and if the church provides for what Parsons calls collectivity-integration it also provides for what he calls ego-integration. The central principle of Methodism, that is a methodical moral discipline, is shared by many of the Pentecostalist and the Holiness churches, and it is precisely this discipline which may save the immigrant worker from the moral disintegration which might otherwise follow from his immigration and his sufferings in a strange land.

It was precisely the shop-front churches in the USA which saved American blacks from moral disintegration in the ghetto. The Pentecostalist churches may well do the same in Britain. But just as in the USA the Black Muslims stepped in to provide something more, namely a religion which was not a white man's religion at all, but one which they could call their own and which emphasized the dignity of blackness, so Rastafarianism in its religious form may provide the something more for Britain's West Indians. Apart from the more general cultural manifestations of this religion mentioned in the last chapter, there is a formally organized centre of the church near to Handsworth in the more respectable area of Erdington, and it can be expected to grow in influence. Thus the growth in political organization which we noticed earlier is also strengthened by and anchored in religious development. The Rastafarianism emphasis on the notion that Jamaican people have been in captivity for 400 years and that white institutions are the institutions of Babylon has immense political significance.

In their Sparkbrook study, Rex and Moore noted that while the West Indian community produced organizations with committees, the Asian community could be mobilized through kinship and through patron-client relations. This is still largely true, and such organizations can be very effective indeed. But there are formal organizations of a political kind which operate in all three national Asian communities. From our point of view the most important is the Indian Workers' Association.

An organization known as the Indian Workers' Association was first established in Coventry in 1938. A Birmingham branch of what later developed as a national organization was set up in 1958. The IWA handles a variety of immigrant problems, but, to a greater degree than other Asian organizations, it is also concerned with the open, rational and deliberate fight against racialism and racial discrimination.

Right from the beginning, according to Dilip Hiro, 'the leadership of the IWA consisted of two main groups; the moderate entrepreneurs and the political radicals' (Hiro, 1971). The moderates stressed social welfare work, whereas the radicals advocated trade-union and political activities. The organization in 1958 was broad-based enough to contain both groups. There were, however, also other differences arising from the Sino-Russian split amongst Indian Marxists and from the splits in the Indian Congress Party. The Birmingham branch, under the leadership of a Marxist, J. Joshi, took the Chinese side in the Russian-Chinese split, but never had any doubt about the importance of activity in the labour and trade-union movement and, broadly speaking, in support of the left opposition within that movement.

At one point after the Powell speech in 1968, Joshi was one of those who supported a national Black People's Alliance founded at a conference in Leamington Spa, but later he came to regard such

267

activity as diversionary. The IWA was concerned to defend Indian workers' rights but to defend them within the trade-union movement. Thus, even the industrial disputes at the Mansfield Hosiery Works and the Imperial Typewriter works in the East Midlands did not lead to the formation of separate Indian unions. Members of the IWA also played their part in the British Labour and Communist Parties.

One other activity in which the IWA engaged was in marches, demonstrations and other activities designed to oppose racism. In the Midlands, especially, this meant participation in demonstrations against Powell and, more recently against Relf, the National Front and the Klu Klux Klan. In a number of cases it involved collaboration with the Socialist Workers' Party and the International Marxist Group. IWA members did not hesitate to collaborate on these occasions, probably because the fight against racism appeared too important to their leaders for such activities to be opposed on sectarian grounds. It is possible, though, that the readiness of the Trotskyist groups to sponsor such activity as well as their opposition to immigration control won them some support amongst younger Indians.

We were not able to find out from Mr Joshi the actual size of his membership. We believe that it is not more than 200–300, but its influence, of course, stretches beyond this. On the other hand, however, we should not ignore the importance of continuing patron–client relationships between Asian businessmen and the rest of the population. Such elite Asians sit on the Community Relations Council and are primarily concerned to iron out cultural difficulties and some material problems so as to make pluralism and peaceful coexistence possible. In Southall this type of community leadership, which existed within the Indian Workers' Association, as well as outside of it, was seriously challenged after the murder of a Sikh boy, but an equivalent development had not occurred in the Midlands.

One development which did occur was the intervention of an Asian candidate in the Ladywood by-election on behalf of the Socialist Unity Party, the political organization of the International Marxist Group. The fact that this candidate, Raghib Ahsan, gained nearly 600 votes, was more successful than the Independent West Indian, James Hunte, and very much more successful than the Socialist Workers' Party candidate, suggests that he must have had strong support amongst Asian workers. It seems likely that if this kind of support can be maintained, a new type of organization may arise to challenge both the IWA and the elite Indian leadership. It should be noted, moreover, that Ahsan's campaign was exceptionally militant, involving direct attacks by his members on the National Front even during the count before the result was announced. The fact of the matter is that such aggressive behaviour does not seem

268

to have lost Ahsan support. It may have gained him some. There is no doubt that the Indian community, particularly its younger members, are increasingly willing to fight racism and the National Front, and, most interesting of all, to do it in conjunction with the West Indians. In a more recent Midland event, a demonstration against racist attacks on West Indian youth in Wolverhampton, Asians played an important part.

We have mentioned the importance of the social work function. There are, of course, an immense number of problems associated with immigration and with the maintenance of Asian customs and Asian religion. These are dealt with continually by all the Asian associations. A recent development of some importance in Handsworth is the opening of an Asian resource centre.

The Asian Resource Centre is run by a very articulate Indian in his late twenties, Ranjit Sondhi. Before becoming the only full-time worker at the centre, he had spent four years working as a community worker at the Villa Road Action Centre. One of the main reasons for setting up the Asian Resource Centre, according to Sondhi, was that very few Asians used the Action Centre, although, he says, more started to come in for advice. It was generally felt by those doing community work in the Asian communities in the area that a centre was needed to focus these efforts. A committee was convened, and it was decided to establish the Asian Resource Centre. The ARC, according to Sondhi, is modelled on Harambee. The centre opened in February 1977, and is now in its third premises. Apart from Ranjit Sondhi, all the workers are volunteers.

The ARC is mainly financed by the Cadbury Trust, which has given a grant of £8,000 for two years. The British Council of Churches, he says has promised £2,000, and the Commission for Racial Equality is considering financing the centre.

The aims of the centre are:

1 To provide advice, information and assistance to the most culturally and materially disadvantaged Asians in the area
2 in order to enable them to become more active on their own behalf;
3 in order to enable them to claim their rights;
4 in order to enable them to become 'first-class citizens'.

According to Ranjit Sondhi, the ARC differs from the traditional neighbourhood groups in that it attempts to involve people in solving their own problems. At an advice session (weekdays between 1 p.m. and 6 p.m.) those who have come in with problems sit round a table discussing each individual's problems and offering solutions. This, he says, has an educative effect; everyone learns from the problems and experiences of others.

269

The centre deals with a whole range of problems – employment, housing, immigration, cultural and personal. During an afternoon spent at the centre by David Hearnden, the following people and problems were dealt with:

1 A Pakistani family whose move to a new council house had been delayed.
2 A Bangladeshi man who wanted a form filled in which required him to prove that he was legally married for the purposes of a National Insurance claim.
3 A Pakistani man wanting a sickness benefit claim form filled in.
4 A Pakistani man with a tax rebate form he wanted filling in.
5 A Bangladeshi man who wanted to evict a fellow Bangladeshi man from his council house in Wednesbury. The tenant's wife and six children had arrived from Syhlet only a few months before, and he needed the room for them. This was a sensitive issue. He had asked the other man to go, but he would not. It was suggested that he try asking him to go once more before going to a solicitor, and one of the other 'clients' offered to go round and speak to the man.
6 A tax problem.
7 Another tax form to be filled in.
8 A Pakistani man with problems concerning his life insurance.
9 A query about a bill from a solicitor for the conveyancing on the sale of a house.
10 A Pakistani who was not happy about the council property he had been allocated in Aston.

People come from as far away as Wolverhampton, says Sondhi, with their problems. After the advice session, the centre is taken over as an Asian youth club.

Besides its welfare function, says Ranjit Sondhi, the ARC also has a political role to play – 'to raise the political consciousness of local Asian people'. Past leadership had been 'mediocre'; this was largely due to the existence of 'conservative forces necessary for the maintenance of the extended family system and all that goes with it'. Asians recognize that they are living in a hostile society, but many older Asians had withdrawn from the 'struggle' against discrimination. The ARC at the moment is mainly involved in solving problems within the Asian community, but in two or three years' time he suggests the centre will become more politically active in the community as a whole.

He describes relations with the IWA as being very good – the IWA encourages the welfare work of the centre. However, he regards the CRC in Birmingham as a 'waste of time'. They are, he says, totally alienated from the people they are supposed to represent.

Of Asians in our survey, 41 per cent said they were Sikhs, and Sikhism seems to be a strong religion in Birmingham. The largest Sikh temple in the Midlands, the Guru Nanak Gurdwara, is situated in Smethwick High Street, and some people from our survey area go there. Other people go down to the Graham Street Gurdwara, near Hockley, which is a temple for the Ramgarhia Sikhs. Mr Dharsam Singh Bhogul, a past vice-president of the CRC, is a Ramgarhia Sikh who attends the Graham Street temple. He has written a pamphlet on Sikhism, published by AFFOR. There are several other Sikh temples in Handsworth, housed in converted Methodist churches which are colourfully painted in blue, pink and gold. Business and money transactions take place in the Gurdwara, and Gurdwara politics are, in fact, very complicated. There are factions between the temples, and within the temples which while being a cultural and integrative force, are also a conflict area among the Handsworth Sikhs.

In our survey, 32 per cent of Asians said they were Hindu. There is a Hindu temple right in our survey area, the Shri Geeta Bhawan Madir, situated in a converted school in Heathfield Road, opposite Mayfield ESN school. The temple's secretary, Mr Bhardwaj, is a teacher at Wattville comprehensive school, (now the new Handsworth comprehensive). Those following the Hindu religion do not appear to see the temple in the same light as the Sikhs. Several people stressed that one can worship in the home and they are not dependent on a temple. There is a young Hindu association centred on the Heathfield Road temple. There is also a Vedic Centre in West Bromwich, with a 'centre' at a house in Dawson Road, Handsworth. The Vedics are followers of Arya Samag, a teacher who led a breakaway movement from Hinduism.

Of our respondents, 18 per cent (59) said they were Muslim, 42 of those being Pakistani. The Muslims come most into contact with Birmingham City Council as a pressure group, since the education of their children often conflicts with Western educational standards. In particular, the issue of single-sex schools has worried the Muslim community. The Pakistan Government had been approached by a group of Muslim businessmen in Birmingham to help pay for a Muslim school and the *Post* reported (20 April 1976) that Saudi Arabia was planning to give £100,000 towards the building of two Muslim schools in the City. The Education department has not been particularly enthusiastic over the idea of Muslim schools. An education official was reported in the *Post* (20 January 1975), as saying that the city planned a comprehensive system of education. However, the Race Relations Board had agreed that setting up a Muslim school would not be unlawful.

271

The issue of providing mosques for Birmingham Muslims to worship in has always been problematic. Planning permission was granted in 1962 for the building of a large Mosque in Balsall Heath, and a Mosque Trust was set up. Eventually the mosque was built and Dr Mohammed Nasim, Chairman of the Trust, has emerged as a spokesman for Birmingham's Muslim community. Birmingham planning officers have served enforcement notices on several Mosques which had been set up in private houses. 'Mini-mosques' in Holly Road and Frederick Road, Handsworth, were both served with notices. A report in the *Mail*, 'Storm over Mini-Mosques' (15 July 1976), warned of 'health hazards', noisy prayer sessions and car-parking difficulties. Other issues on which the Muslim community have clashed with city officials are 'child brides' and the slaughtering of Halal meat. There are various factions within the Muslim community making for conflict.

Of the seventy-three 'sects' in Islam, the Sunni and Shia are best represented in Birmingham. There is a small but determined group, the Ahmadiyya sect, which was declared a 'non-religion' by President Bhutto in Pakistan in 1974. The 'leader' is Mr Dard who lives in our survey area but works in Balsall Heath as a home–school liaison teacher. He is writing a thesis on the sect for a degree at Birmingham university.

Bangladeshi people also appear to be increasingly unwilling to attend the same mosques as Pakistani people, and separate mosques are being developed.

The high percentage of our total sample who said they were either Sikhs, Hindus or Muslims is indicative of the lively part which religion still plays in the lives of immigrants. It also means that the problems and conflicts facing the community are not simply problems of social and cultural breakdown. If anything, they are the opposite. It is the very intensity of social control exercised by the religion and culture of the Asian communities which leads to conflict. Thus, in the belief of the police at least, whereas the principal conflict presented by the West Indian community is violence by young people in the streets, the principal problem presented by the Asian community is conflict arising from the imposition of authority in the family and, not infrequently, conflict within the Sikh temples themselves.

We have given a picture in this chapter so far of the failure of paternalism in the form of the Community Relations Commission, of the radicalization of social work, mainly in an orthodox, European Marxist form, and of the growing militancy amongst the two major ethnic groupings. It remains to be said that this militancy is matched by the increase in expressions of racial hostility amongst the whites of the inner city, and in particular by the growth of the National Front.

Much of the Front's activity in the West Midlands has concentrated on elections. Since the 1974 general election, they have contested the Walsall North, Stechford and Ladywood by-elections. At the general election in October 1974, the Front contested four out of the twelve seats in Birmingham; viz. Erdington, Handsworth, Perry Barr and Yardley. It polled less than 5 per cent of the vote in each constituency; in Handsworth the Front's candidate, John Finnegan (a car worker living in Castle Bromwich who joined the Front in 1973), won 838 (2·8 per cent) of the 30,377 votes. At the local elections in May 1976, the Front contested thirteen out of the thirty-nine wards. In four wards, Fox Hollies, Kingstanding, Perry Barr and Saltley, Front candidates succeeded in pushing the Liberal candidates into fourth place. In the Handsworth ward, however, the Front's candidate, J. Colley, polled no more than 200 out of 6,319 votes (3·2 per cent).

Its election meetings and marches have often resulted in violent clashes between police and anti-fascist demonstrators. The *Birmingham Evening Mail* described the street battle between police and demonstrators outside Boulton Road School, where the Front's candidate in the Ladywood by-election was holding a meeting, as 'the worst riots seen in Birmingham for years' (*Mail*, 16 August 1977).

The Front has not confined its activities to electioneering. At its conference on 15 October 1977, the setting up of a National Front youth organization was announced. According to the West Midlands regional organizer, Mr Keith Jowsey (*Birmingham Post*, 29 August 1977), the Front had begun recruiting school children from the West Midlands into the youth organization in August 1977. 'We will get our young members already in the party to push the National Front at school, and distribute leaflets.'

The Front has also been active in the trades unions. A letter in the *Birmingham Evening Mail* (29 August 1974), from a Mr E. E. Evans of the National Front Trades Union Group, West Midlands, claimed that approximately half the National Front membership in Birmingham and the Black Country were, in fact, trades unionists, and that in places shop-stewards, branch secretaries and whole branch committees were members of the Front.

A *Mail* article (14 August 1974). 'On the Home Front', noted that the Front's activities in Birmingham were run by a nine-man committee. Two brothers were prominent, John Finnegan, who stood as National Front candidate for the Handsworth constituency at the general election in October 1974, was chairman, and Tom Finnegan, a works manager at an Erdington factory, was secretary. (A third brother stood at National Front candidate in Perry Barr at the local election in May 1975.) The Birmingham organizer was an insurance broker in Handsworth, who was a former member of the Monday Club. His experience of living in Handsworth had attracted him to the Front.[4]

The article claimed that the Front had no more than 200 members in the city. The Front's office in Stoney Lane, Balsall Heath, was opened in late 1974.

What this chapter seems to suggest is that, whatever comfort those who wish to see growing multi-racial harmony may draw from the evidence of a stable and established working-class immigrant community, there is evidence of growing racism in the white community matched by a growing lack of confidence in white goodwill and increasing militancy amongst immigrants. We do not see that this line of development will be arrested unless or until decisive action is taken with the support of all major political parties to stop racial incitement, to attack racial discrimination, and to give West Indian- and Asian-descended men and women a secure sense of citizenship. We do not, however, accept the view that this cannot be done or that it is in the interests of British capitalism to see such racial conflict develop. Immigrants are playing their part in the workforce and in the economy. The escalation of racial conflict can only stand in the way of their continuing to do so. The main problems lie in British party politics and in the fact that it now looks as though the electoral advantage to be gained from 'opposing immigration' and thereby appearing to be against the black population is overwhelming.

9 Working class, underclass and Third World Revolution

What we set out to do in the empirical studies reported in this book was to discover something of the relationship between West Indian and Asian immigrants, and their children and the class structure (or class struggle) in British Society. We wished to see how far they appeared, from what we could discover of their employment, housing and educational histories, to have attained the same position as other working-class people, and how far they identified with or participated in working-class organizations. The concept of underclass was intended to suggest the alternative possibility, namely that these minorities were systematically at a disadvantage compared with working-class whites and that, instead of identifying with working-class culture, community and politics, they formed their own organizations and became in effect a separate underprivileged class. The third term in our title, however, draws attention to the possibility that this underclass need not be seen as simply having negative qualities, namely those which follow from being left out of the native working class, but might be thought of as presenting, within the content of British politics, a wider political conflict, arising from the restructuring of a formerly imperial society.

To state briefly at the outset the conclusions which we propose to spell out in more detail in this chapter, what we shall argue are the following points:

1 That, although there is some considerable overlap between the experience of West Indians and Asians and their white working-class neighbours, this is not sufficient to justify the expectation that within, say, a generation, the minorities will have been absorbed into and have equal rights with the working class.

2 That the differences between the minorities and the working

275

class are not simply quantitative but qualitative and structural, with the immigrant situation being characterized by a different kind of position in the labour market, a different housing situation, and a different form of schooling.

3 That during the period of immigrant settlement, while the immigrant minorities have tried to adjust to British society and have established their own security in it to the extent of having obtained regular employment and their own housing, they have also been stigmatized as an unwanted and threatening element in that society.

4 That the question of the absorption of immigrant minorities into the working class has been settled against absorption, with the native working class rejecting black immigrants and uniting with other indigenous classes against them.

5 That the immigrant minorities have been forced in this situation to begin organizing themselves for self-defence, developing their own political strategies separately from those of the working class.

6 That this process of organization takes a different form in the two minority communities: in the Asian communities it takes the form of defensive organization within which individuals may aim at capital accumulation and social mobility; in the West Indian community it may take the form of withdrawal from competition altogether with emphasis upon the formation of a black identity, even though a small minority might achieve, and a larger might continue to aspire towards, assimilation.

7 That the conflicts with British society in which immigrants and their children find themselves engaged may come to be understood in terms of a wider perspective of the readjustment of classes, groups and segments, which occurs with the collapse of the imperial social structure. For the West Indians this is clearest in that their ideologies will emphasize an end to the period of captivity which they believe their people to have suffered. For the Asians it may involve a reconsideration of the rather more favourable position which they have had within the empire, and, particularly, whether they could still find themselves a role as 'the Jews' of post-imperial society.

The underlying theme which runs through all of these points is that of increasing polarization in the relation between the West Indian and Asian minorities on the one hand and the British cultural, social and political organizations on the other. It may therefore be asked whether our perspective is not simply a utopian one, in Mannheim's sense of that term, as referring to a social science perspective which emphasizes and thereby promotes change and instability. Possibly it is. It certainly is an ideal typical exaggeration of present trends. But the opposite of such a utopia is an ideology which emphasizes not only the stability but the essential justice of present arrangements. We believe that when our utopian view is set alongside the ideological one, it gives a truer account not merely of the present state of affairs, but of the long-term trend in race relations.

We do not believe it is our job as sociologists to predict a happy ending to the story which we have told. That is the essence of ideology and it is characteristic of the way in which most politicians talk about race relations in Britain. What we may do, however, is to consider the effect on white people, who do not wish to support an unjust racial order, of reading what seems to be a pessimistic assessment of realistic prospects of change. We conclude, therefore, with a consideration of what might be done, not simply to arrest or resolve the conflicts which exist, but actually to resist the injustice of the present order of things by white Britons. In doing this we make it possible to suggest acceptable programmes of adaptation to the minorities who will continue to live here.

When we look at the survey data which we have gathered, we can see how, if analysis remains on a superficial level, it could be argued (a) that differences between ethnic minorities and the native working class are not all that great, and (b) that there is a prospect of them diminishing. The argument would probably run as follows:

1 While there are more native whites in managerial and white-collar jobs than there are coloured immigrants, and a higher percentage of coloured immigrants in semi-skilled and unskilled jobs than there are native whites, there is none the less a considerable overlap and it is to be expected that in time this overlap will become complete.

2 Immigrants are overwhelmingly members of trades unions and express satisfaction with them, and also show their identification with the native working class by their overwhelming support for the Labour Party.

3 While they have had to wait their turn for publicly provided rented housing and have not been able to afford to buy expensive suburban housing, they have not been left without houses, but have first been helped in special ways, as for instance through local authority mortgages or through the flats provided by housing associations, and, more recently, as they have become qualified, they have been allowed to move into council-built houses.

4 Far from being denied schooling, their children have been able

277

to enter a system which is becoming increasingly egalitarian, and, if help in overcoming handicaps (e.g. lack of language and other skills) has had to be provided without adequate preparation, it has been provided none the less with especially allocated government funds and it is getting better all the time.

According to this optimistic view, present disadvantages of immigrants will be overcome in two ways. One is that a series of policies have been initiated to help those who suffer from multiple disadvantage, and because of these programmes immigrants are unlikely to enter that 'tangle of pathologies' or the 'cycle of deprivation' which has affected American blacks. The other is that the new Commission for Racial Equality has as its brief, not merely the legal overcoming of racial discrimination, but the prevention of all those acts which lead to *de facto* disadvantage regardless of any question of intent. The differences in life-chances which we have shown to exist would be precisely the sorts of differences which the CRC's activity should overcome within a generation.

Anyone who has dealt with problems of race relations in Britain over the past twenty-five years will know that this optimistic picture can only lead to ideological self-delusion. Yet there are many politicians and policy-oriented sociologists who believe it. Indeed, believing in it is the hallmark of the Fabian and liberal race relations industry which has grown up in Britain as well as of those sociologists who wish to put political argument to one side and to get on with the business of piecemeal social reform. Inevitably, too, it is this view which is represented as the liberal one to be counterposed to that of the racists. In what we say, by way of expressing doubt about how far the immigrants are being assimilated, we will certainly be thought of as troublesome, and no doubt we shall be called 'moral nihilists' as one of us was for trying to inject some realism into the debate about immigration in the 1960s. We believe, however, that any real long-term understanding as well as any long-term peace depends precisely on an appreciation of the conflicts which presently exist.

Looking at the data which we have provided in a non-superficial way immediately reveals that West Indian and Asian immigrants not merely do worse than whites in quantitative terms but that they may be thought of as living in different labour markets, in different kinds of housing situation and in different types of school from comparative whites. Moreover, it is to be noted that since our survey data compare the minority householders with some of the most disadvantaged whites, the differences which we note are actually smaller than they would be if we had compared the immigrants with a group of whites matched for age and rates of economic

278

activity, and that, since our sample consisted of fairly long-established immigrants, it is quite possible that they were the immigrants who had achieved more. In short, the differences to which we now refer underestimate the disadvantage of immigrant ethnic minorities and are the more significant for that.

The percentages of West Indians and Asians in our Handsworth sample who are in white-collar employment are 9·6 per cent and 5·1 per cent respectively as against 30 per cent whites. In a national sample, Smith found the figures for Asians to be slightly higher than this and for East African Asians to be higher still, but his figure for whites was 40 per cent. On the other hand, in our sample the percentage of West Indians and Asians in semi-skilled and unskilled work is 44·1 per cent and 38·7 per cent, and that of whites 27·4 per cent. Here Smith gives lower percentages for all groups except Pakistanis, but the gap between white and black workers is still wide.

In Handsworth it is fair to say that about half of the non-white population are employed in semi-skilled and unskilled manual work and less than 10 per cent in white-collar jobs, whereas only about a quarter of whites are in the low-skill groups and a third in white-collar jobs. That already suggests a considerable difference despite the overlap. If one then looks at industrial and occupational differences, one finds that the West Indian and Asian populations are more concentrated in labouring jobs and in hot and dirty industries, and are poorly represented in professional, scientific and administrative jobs. Both West Indian and Asian workers had to work extra hours to earn the same as white British workers, and were also more likely to be on shift work. According to Smith, unemployed rates amongst immigrants went down steadily in the years after immigration so long as employment levels were high, but rose relative to those of whites in times of higher unemployment. In 1976 we found that about 19 per cent of our immigrant samples and 13·5 per cent of our white British sample were unemployed, and noted that although they formed under 10 per cent of the workforce in Birmingham, immigrant workers constituted 20 per cent of the unemployed.

These figures may not confirm that there is a completely dual labour market situation with whites gaining internal appointments and promotions in protected jobs and the immigrants getting what jobs they can in the open market. But they are consistent with the notion of two kinds of job situations with whites predominant in one and blacks in the other. In fact, the degree of apparent overlap may be deceptive and case studies of actual employment might well show that in each industrial, occupational, skill and social class category, the actual job situation of the black is less desirable and secure than that of the white.

So far as change in the system is concerned, we have noted that there are barriers to promotion in the first generation and to social mobility for the second generation. The kinds of promotion hoped for by blacks are those which involve only entry into more skilled (but often only semi-skilled) work. Even here it seems difficult for Asians to break out of the replacement labour black workshop situation and possibly for West Indians to gain their fair share of the more skilled jobs. So far as promotion to supervisory and managerial jobs is concerned, it is virtually non-existent. There is also little sign that the British-educated children of immigrants are doing much better. Although they show initiative and often find their jobs without the aid of the Youth Employment and Careers Advisory Service, they are not very much better off, if at all, than their parents in terms of the class of work done, and their levels of unemployment may well be higher (though the data here is somewhat impressionistic).

Identification of immigrant workers with the trades unions and Labour Party remains strong, despite the poor record of both in handling immigrant cases. Recent events have shown, however, that immigrants may find independent ways of defending themselves in the industrial and political fields, at least in order to compel white workers' organizations to take notice of them, but possibly to remain independent. Amongst the young, the main focus of identification is rarely the labour movement at all, but much more a cultural and black revolutionary consciousness.

In housing it seems clear that the white authorities are torn between two discriminatory policies. One of these is the segregation of the black immigrant population in the least desirable housing, and here they are positively helped to find homes. The other is to disperse them so that their unwanted presence may be put more or less out of sight. There is a long history of discriminatory policies of both these kinds in Birmingham, and, though the local authority has agreed to changes in its system of housing allocation, it is too early to say whether anti-discriminatory policies are really likely to be sustained.

The characteristic situation of the immigrant used to be that of the so-called twilight zones, where they lived in multi-occupied lodging-houses together with the city's down-and-outs. Now, as urban redevelopment has run its course and as the process of family completion and settlement has been carried through, the black population finds itself heavily concentrated in the second ring of development and identified in the public mind as part of the pathology of the inner city. This inner city is thought to have essentially intractable problems, but two strands are confused even in the attempts which are made to deal with these problems. One is that of helping the black population to attain equality and overcome their problems through increasing employment and improving the environment. The other is that the visible concentration of blacks is considered to be the problem, and that, as economic and environmental improvement occurs, the blacks should somehow be made to disappear, so that the old white working-class and lower middle-class areas can be restored to their former glory.

The concentration of the black population has produced in both of the two minorities a defensive consciousness. Amongst the actual immigrant generation this shows itself in fear of dispersal and loss of communal support. Amongst the young it may express itself in movements to control their own territory in the streets of places like Handsworth, and to make their collective presence felt in the city centre itself. A place like Handsworth becomes the stage-set for the perpetual drama of the confrontation between West Indian youth and the forces of law and order, or of the White Babylon.

Educationally the immigrant child suffers from the fact that the quality of opportunity which the system appears to offer is in fact a well-disguised system of inequality. That it is an unfair system for whites is a favourite theme of British educational sociology, but in the immigrant majority school it is acutely so in different ways for the two ethnic minority groups.

For the West Indians there are undoubtedly cultural problems of an acute kind. This may seem paradoxical in that they do after all share British culture to an extent that non-English-speaking Sikhs and Hindus do not. But that precisely is the problem. What the West Indian child is always called upon to do is to dance to someone else's tune and to celebrate a culture in which he and his people are systematically downgraded. Moreover, it may well be more difficult for him when that culture is offered to him through a liberal pedagogical regime, which his parents might have expected for him at home. At all events, such evidence as there is suggests that West Indian children do not do well in formal examination situations. Our own small amount of evidence in our pilot youth study confirms a picture of the typical West Indian child as aiming at most at getting CSEs rather than GCEs and of generally coming to believe that the school system has little to offer him. This should not, of course, be taken to mean that some West Indian children do not take 'O'-levels and 'A'-levels and go on to university. But the odds appear to be stacked against them, and the irresponsible discussion of Eysenck's book which is taken to have proved genetic negro inferiority, rather than only poor test performance by American blacks, appears to offer a deterministic hereditarian explanation of the relatively low success rate.

Asian children have less trouble in school. In so far as they surmount the language problem which many immigrating children have

281

had to face, they seem to be moving ahead of the West Indians and doing at least as well as white children in the same schools. In this they are greatly aided by two factors. One is that they have a degree of security in that their culture has not been destroyed. The other is that the outsider attitude which their parents have towards their country of settlement goes along with a strongly instrumental attitude towards education. Their problems may, however, arise at higher levels. We mentioned one odd case of a boy who wanted to be a pilot, and, of course, he is not typical. He may, however, be a symbol of the young Asian who wants to enter a most exciting and interesting profession, but finds himself in a system where he is directed, for instance, to making screws. It is worth noting here that even amongst the older immigrant generation, there are a considerable number of educated men who are employed as labourers. They, themselves, must experience frustration. But they do this for their children. If their children also succeed educationally but cannot enter the better jobs, their energies and intellectual ability are almost certain to be diverted into radical politics.

One tentative idea which does emerge from our evidence on householders educated in England and our small pilot youth study, however, is that however frustrated young West Indians and Asians may be in school, in the employment advice and opportunities which they receive and in the jobs which they get, they do take opportunities for further education, and they do make their own efforts to improve their job situation. In part this redeems their total situation. In part it may make it worse, in so far as their aspirations are frustrated.

One can imagine that despite this pessimistic account of the life-chances of black immigrants in Britain, there are still those who would argue that, given time, the children of the immigrants will, in the main, be absorbed into the working classes and that some – perhaps especially at first the Asians, because of their culturally sanctioned patterns of motivation and their aptitude for business – will move into the professional and commercial middle classes. We would admit that there is a case, albeit a somewhat tenuous one, of this kind which can be argued.

The kind of process which this envisages, however, posits not merely a decrease in the quantitative variation of life-chances, but also an actual social, structural and cultural alliance of groups. What one actually sees, however, at this level (the level of class-for-itself as opposed to class-in-itself) is not merely quantitative variation of life-chances, or even only cultural diversity, but rather an increasing polarization between the vast majority of whites, including especially the working class, and the West Indian and Asian immigrant and British-born black communities. No understanding of the likely development of race relations in Britain is possible which does not take note of this fact and explain it.

The first empirical observation to be made on this level is that long before the immigrant communities began to show even the slightest tendency towards militant organization, the reaction of the British electorate to their presence was negative and hostile. Even had the conclusion of *Colour and Citizenship* (Rose *et al.*, 1969), that the British people as a whole were relatively tolerant, been justified (and it is clear from the criticisms of Bagley (1970) and Lawrence (1974) that it was highly questionable), the actual development of political events showed that electoral opinion was increasingly hostile to black immigration.

Rex and Moore argued somewhat optimistically that had the Government taken action against discrimination quickly enough, the absorption of immigrants might well have occurred within a relatively short period of time, and that the actual conflicts which developed did so simply because discrimination isolated the immigrants in pathological situations in which they were both visible and problematic. There may have been something in this argument, but, as the diaries of R. H. S. Crossman show, the tide of anti-immigrant feeling was already running too strongly by 1964 for it to be likely that any party concerned with winning elections would do anything other than swim with it.

The long chronology of events in British race relations need not be rehearsed here in any detail. We need only recall that R. A. Butler reluctantly capitulated to the demand for immigration control in 1962; that none the less the Smethwick campaign of 1964 showed that the controllers were not satisfied; that, although Hugh Gaitskell promised to repeal the Butler Act and Harold Wilson called Peter Griffiths a Parliamentary leper, the Labour Party in fact tightened up on immigration control; that in 1968, the myth of full British citizenship for categories of people like the East African Asians was abandoned; that Powell showed in the same year that there was no platform more popular in British politics than an anti-immigrant one; and that subsequently each new attempt to tighten immigration control only led to more extreme demands, with the additional complicating element that an anti-immigrant party emerged on the right which threatened the party system itself.

The feelings which politicians diagnosed as being the feelings of their white constituents were spread widely across the country. Powell's first major anti-immigration speech was, it is true, made only three or four miles from Handsworth. But his message was as eagerly received in Bournemouth as in Birmingham. We found, on the other hand, that among the white residents of the inner city there was, in addition to the general sense of wrong shared by large sections of the white electorate, a more particular complaint, that they had been called upon to bear an undue share of the new white man's burden.

What is most noticeable about our survey evidence of responses of black and white to our questions about the problems of the neighbourhood is their striking asymmetry. West Indians, and still more Asians, regard Handsworth as a good place to live in, and nearly half the West Indians and two-thirds of the Asians thought the races got on well. Amongst the whites, on the other hand, approximately 60 per cent saw the problems of the area as simply due to the presence of coloured people or to physical deterioration which they associated with their presence. Moreover, no less than 62 per cent said that they saw race relations as involving problems. Those blacks who felt their future was assured in Handsworth and in Britain might almost literally be said, therefore, to be living in a fool's paradise.

In the general election of 1964, the white voters in our sample voted for the Conservatives, as much as they did for Labour, even though they belonged within a working-class culture, and at local elections half of them had voted Conservative. The upsurge of support for the National Front was not yet reflected in the voting intentions of our sample, but the fact that the Front's candidate in the Ladywood by-election received a fifth of the number of votes cast for the successful Labour candidates should be a sufficient indication that it is gaining support.

As to the Front itself, there can be little doubt that, in so far as it sticks to the immigrant issue, it will get a ready response. It has succeeded already in producing a reaction from the main party leaders and from responsible newspapers to the effect that they must bring the immigration issue into the open and campaign on it, to prevent the growth of the Front. Thus it functions as a pace-maker in the development of 'anti-immigrant' and 'anti-black' policies.

There have, of course, been ex-Nazis associated with the Front and its policies are sometimes overtly racist. We would underestimate its importance and the danger which it represents to the black population, however, if we were to see it merely as the party of the lunatic fringe. It is unlikely that a party which called for the suspension of Parliamentary democracy and trade-union rights, or which suggested racist conspiracy by Jews or black people on a world scale, would, for a moment, be taken seriously. But it was possible for the young man who became the National Front candidate in Ladywood to have been converted to the Front, because he believed that the Conservatives had betrayed their trust by letting in the Ugandan Asians.

This is by no means to suggest that either the assertions of fact or the policies of the National Front are based upon a valid analysis of Britain's immigration problem. In fact, the hopes which they raise in the minds of many working people that the immigrants are the actual cause of the social and economic hardships which they suffer, are ludicrously misleading. But they have produced a response, first in the electorate and then amongst politicians conscious of their electoral importance. The question is why the 'threat' of coloured immigration can loom so large in the public mind. Superficial explanations of this threat are that it is because capitalists foster racism in their own interests as a means of dividing the working class, and that the degree of working-class racism varies with the degree of unemployment. Neither of these explanations seem to us to be adequate.

Business interests have not been in the forefront of the campaign for immigration control at all. The campaign was one which developed in the Conservative Party and was carried on by politicians like Enoch Powell, who saw themselves as speaking for national rather than business interests. Capitalists on the whole have been interested in having cheap labour available but have been prepared to accommodate themselves to immigration control and to the acceptance of discriminatory practices, if the presence of immigrant workers cost them more in terms of bad labour relations than it benefited them by cutting the wage-bill. Moreover, we have certainly not seen any large-scale diversion of business funds into support for bodies like the National Front, paralleling business support for Hitler in the 1930s. It is conceivable that in times of extreme crisis and revolutionary challenge such a course might appeal to some more reactionary businessmen, but there is no reason to suggest that such a crisis or revolutionary challenge exists at the present time.

So far as the relationship between racism and the threat of unemployment is concerned, it has to be pointed out that the campaign for immigration control and against coloured immigrants was mounted successfully at the very time that Harold Macmillan made his famous electoral speech using Truman's phrase 'you never had it so good'. Subsequently, far from it being the case that racism has ebbed and flowed with the trade cycle, the tragic truth is that while racism flows it rarely ebbs. Each time a definition of the situation less favourable to immigrants has been put forward, it has come to be part of the renewed wisdom which is taken for granted in later debates. Thus some statements made by Powell and regarded as extreme in 1968 are now the common currency within both major parties. Economic prosperity would not alter this even though it is true that immigrants might be used as a scapegoat by politicians in times of increasing unemployment.

We believe that white political behaviour and class formation cannot be adequately explained simply in terms of the immediacies of the present British economic situation or by looking at events in the British Isles in isolation from the rest of the world. We do see a

285

process which can be called class formation, it is true, but the social system within which it occurs is the social system of the British Empire, including its Indian, African and West Indian dominions, and stretching back in time over a period of 400 years.

It is a curious fact about much of what passes as Marxist discussion of race relations in Britain that it leaves out any serious discussion of the process of labour exploitation on which the whole system depends, and that it treats the organized working class in Britain as though it could be understood simply as the innocent victim of capitalism. Surely a Marxist analysis should recognize that the whole development of British industrial capitalism depended upon a process of capital accumulation in India and the West Indies, and that in later times the capacity of British capitalism to meet the costs of the welfare state rested, at least in part, upon the unequal trade which Britain was able to carry on with the rest of the world. So far as we are concerned we do not ultimately care whether we are called Marxists or not. We simply believe that a serious sociological analysis of race relations problems must rest upon a concept of the social structure of empire and of the class formations which occur within it.

The question of the social structure of colonialism is one which Rex has discussed elsewhere (Rex, 1970; UNESCO, 1977). Here all that needs to be said is that the social structure of contemporary Britain emerged from a historic process in which a variety of forms of colonial social structure came into being. Each of these had its own system of classes, estates, castes or other social formations, and any of the social positions involved made the position of a British factory worker seem enviable. To be the descendant of a slave in a stagnant Jamaican economy or a peasant or pedlar in India, Pakistan or Bangladesh, was a miserable existence indeed, and it was inevitable that some of the more ambitious amongst them would seek an existence in the advanced industrial countries, either permanently, or as a means of accumulating capital.

But complementary to the roles of the ultimate slave or peasant were the roles of those who as capitalist entrepreneurs, as overseers and managers, as missionaries, soldiers and administrators, actually ran the empire. The individual and cumulative experience of these roles helped to shape the basic British belief system about colonial men and women. Some actually loved the people whom they taught or administered in a paternalistic way. Others brutally exploited and oppressed them. But in any case they came to regard them as inferior. Built into the culture of a competitive metropolitan society, therefore, was the notion that some sort of caste barrier must be preserved between white men and black colonials if white men were not to be destatused. Indians and West Indians were good enough people in their place, but their place was not Handsworth, Birmingham.

We are especially concerned that we should not be represented here as saying that racist beliefs are simply an archaic survival and that they have nothing to do with the economic and political basis of society. What we are saying is that the British Empire over the past 400 years is the economic and political basis of our existence. It is unlikely that the mere coming of political independence since 1945 for most of the former colonial territories could overcome the fearful sense of threat and competition with which British men and women faced the people of Empire.

At the outset of our study, we did not fully realize the importance for British politics of what we have just been saying. Had we done so, we might have asked probing questions of our white respondents about their existence of and perceptions of Empire, and particularly of West Indians and Asians, although there are ethical problems here in that such questioning in a social survey might well have served to reinforce attitudes which we ourselves regard as dangerous. But in any case we are aware of the limitations of such studies of attitudes and beliefs. What is far more important is the political culture and the belief systems which exist in a city like Birmingham. This was, of course, the very place where Joseph Chamberlain made a populist appeal which combined the notion of reform at home with support for imperialism abroad. It would be possible and it would be important for a social historian to trace the sorts of belief systems which were generated in Chamberlain's day and the degree to which they have been changed or perpetuated with the coming into being of new social movements and new centres of political power.

British people, we are saying, were likely to respond to the arrival of West Indians and Asians as fellow-workers and neighbours with many fears and anxieties arising from these belief systems; and because the fears and the anxieties and beliefs were not brought out into the open, they responded with hostility and aggression, and, building on the obvious physical and cultural differences between themselves and the new immigrants, came to accept new beliefs to justify this hostility and aggression. This analysis is one in which we follow Myrdal (Myrdal et al., 1969). We also follow him in his notion of a cumulative principle whereby the existence of racist beliefs, once they are established, leads to discrimination, and this discrimination produces conditions which further justify the beliefs. Thus the British image of the West Indian, Indian or Pakistani is not now simply that of a colonial savage, but additionally of a man in the ghetto, or a young man in trouble with the police.

The belief systems which do operate are to some extent held in check by what is thought respectable or morally permissible to say. Thus Rex and Moore argued that the hostile attitudes towards immigrants which were felt in 1964 were not expressed because they were in conflict with other moral belief systems and ideologies. The significance of the Powell speech was that it seemed to make the expression of these attitudes permissible. Thereafter, too, a number of those who could be thought to have a certain moral influence over such matters either made statements or failed to make statements in such a way as to reinforce anti-immigrant attitudes. Amongst these, for example, we would mention the judges who lectured young blacks convicted of crimes while imposing exemplary sentences on them, or insisted on the rights of free speech of men like the National Party councillor, who, after the Southall murder of an Indian boy, had said, 'One down, a million to go.' We would also mention those who arranged religious and documentary television programmes, so structuring the debate as to present immigrants as a threat and a problem, and comedians who came more and more to rely upon jokes which were damaging to minorities as their stock in trade. Even statements by men like Archbishop Coggan, who intended, no doubt, to insist upon the rights of immigrants who are already here, appeared to throw ecclesiastical authority behind demands for more severe immigration control (see note 3 to chapter 2), the more so when his remarks were compared with those of his predecessor who had actually regarded the debate about control as one which was potentially damaging to immigrants.

The process which we are describing here suggests that, far from hostile attitudes and beliefs about immigrants and black men becoming less widespread and less entrenched as the memory of Empire faded, they actually came to take a new form as the arrival of colonial immigrants seemed to threaten the privileged position of native British workers, and in this new form the hostile beliefs and attitudes in question came to be sanctioned by the highest moral authority.

If a kind of class formation develops amongst working-class and lower middle-class British against the colonial intruders, and if this conception of a class interest has some foundation in the social structure of a capitalist empire, it is only to be expected that similar formations will occur amongst the immigrants themselves. The nature of this formation, however, is complex and differs between the minority ethnic groups and between generations.

So far as the Asians are concerned, the British Empire has provided a structure within which they have been able to play a variety of roles to their own profit, which are quite distinct from those of the poor peasants who were at the basis of the Empire, or the coolies, who for ninety years after the emancipation of slaves manned sugar, tea and rubber plantations around the world. Some came to act, themselves, as the foot-soldiers of Empire and wherever, under the umbrella of imperialism, there were commercial opportunities to exploit, Indian traders took them. They played their part in the commercial development of East Africa, Mauritius, Malaysia, Fiji, Guyana and many other countries. Naturally, though the pedlars and traders were a class apart from the coolies and peasants, there were coolies and peasants who graduated into commerce.

Asians from the Indian sub-continent have become adept at living in the diaspora, of being in a society yet not being completely of it, of not fussing too much about discrimination or lack of political rights, but making the most of their opportunities to accumulate capital by manual work and by trade. Despite Max Weber's characterization of Hinduism as other-worldly mysticism, a number of Asian groups, such as Gujerati Hindus, Punjabi Sikhs and the Muslim Ismaelis who settled in East Africa, have shown great aptitude for business, and there are also many who have successfully entered the professions.

The natural social and political resources of such groups have been, as we saw in the last chapter, the extended kinship group, the workers' association, and patron–client relations. All of these groupings have participated to some extent in elite negotiation with British society, not raising fundamental and difficult political questions, but trying to manage a situation of cultural pluralism within which economic opportunities may be pursued. They have been prepared to go very far in compromising with the host society to keep those opportunities open.

We cannot feel absolutely sure that a substantial part of the Asian community may not come to have what we have called a Jewish future in Great Britain. That is to say, we can envisage the possibility of some of those who are now accumulating capital while working long hours in foundries or factories investing that capital in their own commercial and industrial enterprises and achieving economic success, while remaining culturally separate and not pressing too strongly for political recognition. It might even be the case that some Asians will identify with the middle class and start voting Conservative (though there is no evidence of this amongst Asians in Handsworth, as yet).

Two crucial changes, however, have occurred in the Asian community, which may stand in the way of this kind of development. One is the fact that because they prize education as an instrument to success, their children have come to develop new aspirations. The other is that their community has come under attack.

It seems hardly likely that a generation of Asian youth who have grown up and been educated in British schools will continue to accept the position of a pariah people who, if they are successful, will be channelled into the professions and into commerce without trying to claim political rights. What is most likely to happen is that they will still rely upon their ethnic community as a resource for success in education and in business, but that they will also accept various British associations and British culture patterns, becoming, as it were, completely culturally bilingual.

Both the young Asian men and women and their parents, however, are increasingly aware that their interests are threatened by the debate about immigration control. Moreover, they are a proud people who are used to organizing in the face of attack. Such a response is certainly to be expected from Sikhs and Muslims, given the history of their religion, and workers' politics – to which, as we have often pointed out in this study, Indians are long accustomed – provides for the possibility of radical Marxist politics, whether Communist, Maoist or Trotskyist.

There is a strong commitment to law and order in the Asian communities. Indeed, some Sikhs have been accused of expecting the police to enforce their own domestic and communal customs, but, if law fails to give adequate protection, they will take what action is necessary. After the Southall murder, Asian leaders were forced by their own communities to call on the Prime Minister demanding protection. Younger members of the community, however, saw this as a token action only and increasingly demanded action against racism. Street demonstrations against racism have, on important occasions, always seen Asian workers' representatives and Asian youth represented amongst the marchers, and recently in Wolverhampton, after a confrontation had occurred between West Indian youth and the police, Asians joined the West Indians in the subsequent anti-racist march.

The other spheres in which Asian action is likely to become more militant are trades unionism and politics. Generally Asians have been far more active in the trade-union field than West Indians. What they have begun to achieve is a state of affairs in which the unions have had to take them seriously because they are capable of taking independent action. They are beginning to have their own shop-stewards and may well be forced by their younger English-speaking members to break down the virtual colour bars which were shown to exist in the Mansfield Hosiery and Imperial Typewriter cases.

In politics there is already a considerable history of Asians standing as independents, or as minority party candidates, in local and in national elections, as well as of pressure groups influencing both the Labour and the Conservative Parties. The Ladywood events show that such campaigns can be very militant indeed.

For the moment, the cultural bilingualism of the Asian communities enables them to keep two separate options open. One is that of participation in British politics in its own idiom in terms of Conservative, Liberal, Labour or Marxist. The other is to reflect the divisions within Indian politics. It is not surprising that amongst other things the leader of the Indian Workers' Association in Birmingham should be a Maoist. That ideology enables him to have a position in both local and international or Third World politics. It could be the case that in the long run it will be the international dimension which becomes the predominant one, and through that changes in the Third World will be projected into Asian politics in Britain.

The spirit and style of West Indian class and political organization is quite different from that of the Asians. From the outset they have nothing to gain from accepting discrimination and adopting a pariah role. They are overwhelmingly working-class people whose ancestors were forced into accepting British culture along with their servitude. They do, therefore, speak English and are better equipped to obtain employment as individuals than the Asians. But they are conscious of failure in the educational system, conscious of discrimination in employment and housing, conscious of a conflict of their children with the forces of law and order, and conscious of racist attacks directed against them.

Some West Indians will gain acceptance into the working class, and their numbers may be more than the token contingent who now gain admission to working men's clubs, to the position of shop-steward and into football and other sports teams. But it is quite evident that many will not and that for them the quest for a black identity and alternative base for political action will become all-important.

We have seen that, from the point of view of organization, the focus of West Indian political and class activity is not primarily the Labour movement. In fact, those West Indians who have been active in the Labour Party have often been regarded as token blacks at best and Uncle Toms at worst. The real focus of activity is in community and political groups and the churches. There is an intermediate position which has been effectively occupied by James Hunte involving, first, pressure within the Labour Party, and then an electoral challenge from outside. But more important long-term growth points may be the various black identity groups, the Rastafarian religion and culture, and other organizational and cultural forms which may succeed them.

Whatever else may be said about these groups, they are not simply groups of irrational extremists. Nor are they lacking in sociological understanding. For what they are seeking is to obtain acceptance for the following propositions:

1 that the true class position of the black immigrant from the

West Indian islands is only understood if it is recognized that he is part of a people who were taken into captivity;

2 that captivity meant not only slavery but cultural castration;

3 that if he is to regain his manhood, the West Indian must assert that he is proud to belong to an African culture;

4 that, since this culture cannot be fully recaptured he must start building it anew, though a first step in this direction must be a denial of the culture which has been imposed upon him; and

5 that the revolution of the Third World, and particularly the African part of it, is his revolution and one which with he should be identified in every way.

This revolutionary black consciousness appeared in many ways and had effectively displaced simple working-class consciousness amongst West Indians in Handsworth. Not merely the political articulate leaders, but the uninstructed youth identify freely with black and Afro fashions and symbols, and one quite astonishing event which passed almost without notice, because it was peaceful, was an African Liberation Day rally in Handsworth Park in the summer of 1977 attended by some 4,000 people, and organized by the local black leaders in conjunction with the South African Pan-African Congress.

Of course it must be recognized that this kind of revolutionary class-consciousness is not incompatible with alternative orientations amongst the black leadership. It is not without significance that the contact with Africa which was established was with the Pan-African Congress and not with the mainstream African National Congress which was more socialist (and Moscow-oriented). A Black International including Pan-Africanists and their allies might well emerge, which puts black liberation before anti-capitalism and socialism. Moreover, it was clear enough in Birmingham that black leaders saw multi-cultural education as an area in which Black Studies could develop without any overtly socialist content. Some of them were very sympathetic to a proposal for a multi-cultural education resource centre which was canvassed by a visiting American professor in 1977 and 1978, even though he was strongly committed to the idea of the creation of a black middle class.

The actual situation here is complex .One layer of potential West Indian leaders had already been creamed off into salaried positions with the Commission for Racial Equality. Quite possibly those who remained, being human, would not reject opportunities for their own personal advancement and would attempt to define the goals of their movement in terms of the creation of a separate, black, social status pyramid with scope for a black middle class. Even if this turns out to be the case, however, we should still insist that the black political movements will remain separate from working-class movements, and that its ultimate structural source is to be found in the social structure of Empire and Third World liberation movements. It is these which make possible the present initiatives of the black leadership and, in the long run, it seems likely that new and more radical leaders will emerge.

The notion of the creation of a black social pyramid should not be seen as one which negates our conception of a revolutionary underclass. No doubt there will be class tensions within the West Indian community as there will be in the Asian. But in the case of both communities the organization of the minority society, policy and economy has to be defended against attacks from the indigenous political organizations in the land of settlement, and there is little sign that there will be any effective assimilation of the aspirant West Indian and Asian middle classes either to the white British middle class or to the established and incorporated working class. These groups will be forced to be radical, if only in self-defence.

We cannot imagine that the pressures which are driving immigrants in this direction will abate in the future. In fact, a point has already been reached at which the British political parties are hard put to see what they can do beyond what has been done already to show that they are against coloured immigration. In these circumstances Powell has reminded the leaders of the parties that the principal source of recruitment for the black population is the birth of black British children, and that a reduction of numbers can only be achieved by repatriation. Most recently he has suggested that a million people should be induced to accept repatriation. To the right of Mr Powell there are others who will take the argument further and urge compulsory segregation and repatriation. It is because they see where the logic of this argument leads that in their different ways the two minority communities have become militant.

It is not our job to provide our book with a happy ending. We set out to analyse with the aid of empirical data the class position of the immigrant. We conclude that it is likely that the minority communities will develop forms of self-help and self-defence in this society and that they will increasingly interpret their experience from a Third World point of view, looking to a change in the balance of power and resources between rich and poor nations as a means to their own liberation.

To say this, however, is to leave the white readership of our book dumfounded, and we would therefore like to conclude by mentioning what the minority of British people who do not want this polarization to occur can do in this situation. First, there is the question of what can be done to arrest the vicious cumulative spiral of escalating racism. Second, there is the question of what to do if it is not arrested.

The only thing which can be done now to arrest the spiral of racism is to call a halt to the present competition between the parties to win support from people thought to be infected by racism, by actually facing up to the changes consequent upon the collapse of Empire. This could be achieved without the emergence on the racist right of the National Front, or something worse, as a major political force, because there are still traditional party loyalties in Britain and it is difficult for a fourth party to break into politics. Then, with a truce achieved, it should be possible to address the question of overcoming discrimination and disadvantage as well as, most important of all, of developing the sort of social and educational policies which will enable the known black British population to have their place either as individuals or as groups within the society as a whole. It was quite absurd to suppose that nearly a million settlers from the former colonies could be absorbed into Britain peacefully if no preparation was made for their arrival. Now that they are here, even though it is late in the day, policies for a multi-racial, multicultural society must be developed.

Within this framework, the hypothetical whites who want to avoid polarization and yet achieve justice could very well occupy themselves with improving the services which help minorities to cope with British society and attempting to explain to the white population something of the history and the culture of the peoples who have come to Britain to stay.

Probably one of the major spheres in which worthwhile work can be done is that of multi-cultural education. The plain fact is that, although they have an Asian and West Indian descendent community of a million and a half people living amongst them, very few English people have any but the most distorted view of Indian and Afro-West Indian history. Even racial liberals have been taught that Indian and African civilizations were inferior. Multi-cultural education could be devoted to showing on the one hand that, although they were very different from our own, if properly understood these civilizations merit our respect, and on the other that our own involvement with them was essentially an exploitative one. Such education need not be aimed at inducing guilt in the British people and their children. If it was so aimed it would fail. What it should aim at doing is to encourage the English child to accord to the civilizations of India and Africa the same respect that he accords to that of France. It is, after all, much more important that he should understand these civilizations than that he should learn French history. Even though we are members of the Common Market, there are not a million and a half Frenchmen living here.

294

We do not want to suggest, however, that the educational sphere is the only one in which tough-minded racial liberals might work. At every point within the various allocative systems where there is injustice to be righted, there is political work to be done. There is a fight to be carried on in trades unions to see that black workers are adequately protected and that the unions do not become defence organizations for a white aristocracy of labour. There is work to be done in housing advice centres, not merely helping individuals to improve their chances within a discriminatory system, but to change that system. And within the educational system there are dozens of selective processes which could operate in a discriminatory way, unless the problems of West Indian children are really understood, instead of being dismissed in terms of a series of stereotypes. All of these things could be tackled with energy and determination in a society committed to overcoming racial polarization and enabling immigrant minorities to have equal social rights.

In the more likely event of increasing polarization, however, there will be no obvious framework within which to work. In those circumstances the hypothetical white to whom we refer will have a simple choice of deciding whose side he is on. The cause of the West Indian- and Asian-descended populations in those circumstances will not be a hopeless one. They will be able to use help, even though they must rely ultimately only on self-help, in building up their resources, keeping contact with their homelands and fighting and negotiating while in Britain to be treated with the justice which they believe to be their due. The more white British there are engaged in this work the less likely it is that the conflict will become a purely racial one.

The one thing which appears to us to be unlikely as a result of our study is that somehow the escalating 'anti-immigrant' tone of our policies can be ignored, and that, if only the immigrants will accept that, they will be given their rights. The time for such paternalism is past, and increasingly the young black British know that it is past. The choice is really between effective political organization on their own behalf and mindless violence and despair.

Appendix 1 Sociology, theory, typologies, value standpoints and research

John Rex

This book is intended specifically as a sociological study of race relations and, though it is intended for an audience wider than one consisting of professional sociologists, it does aim at the same time to make a contribution to a longer-term sociological understanding of the questions that it raises than are of immediate political significance. It is also hoped that by bringing sociological insights and understanding to bear additional illumination may be provided, over and above that provided by lay commentators, to the political argument itself.

We cannot, however, offer a simple cut and dried formula as to what constitutes a specifically sociological analysis. There is no simple concept of a scientific approach to questions such as these which we could support. Like Myrdal, one of our greatest forerunners in the race relations field, we recognize that the relationship between social science value judgements and politics is complex. On the other hand, we also face a particular intellectual conjuncture which Myrdal did not, in which any conception of a discipline of sociology at all tends to be swept away. Since the student disturbances of 1968 and the race riots in the USA which roughly coincided with them, there has been a tendency to deny the very existence of sociology, especially in the field of race relations, and to substitute for it an activist politics. Questions as fundamental as the nature of facts, of what constitutes the social, of criteria of truth in social research, and of the separability or otherwise of academic study and political action, are now very much in the air, and it sometimes seems hard to define any secure foundations for sociological work.

Despite all these difficulties, however, we do not feel that we should simply accept a lowering of standards and surrender to unreason either amongst students and colleagues or amongst political activists in the race relations field. We do not believe that there is something which can specifically be called 'sociological study', and we write within a tradition of thought which derives most especially from Max Weber and which has definite, though sometimes complex views on all of the fundamental questions such as the nature of the sociological subject matter, the importance of change, of conflict and value judgments, the theoretical status of the micro and macro social structures and entities to which sociologists refer, the kinds of proof and certainty which we can expect in social science, and the relationship between sociologists' theories and constructs and those employed in common-sense, in ideology and in myth.

In the first place we find it necessary to set aside two views of the task of the sociologist in the field of race relations which are widely held and which provide convenient oversimplifications for those anxious to 'get on with the job'. The first of these is that race relations research is simply concerned with the monitoring of racial discrimination in a simple, quantitative way. The second is that sociology is essentially an inductive science seeking to discover the laws of human behaviour by empirical study and generalization.

The key notion in the monitoring concept of social science is that of disadvantage in the distribution of 'life-chances'. This is, in fact, what has normally been thought to be the task of social science in England. In the Fabian tradition of the London School of Economics, a main task of sociology was seen as that of monitoring the life-chances of children with parents of different occupational levels, showing particularly the extent to which the children of manual workers were capable of mobility or were permanently at a disadvantage with regard to their own employment, their income and their education, compared with the children of non-manuals (see Glass, 1954). It seemed natural enough, therefore, that, at the time of the passing of the second and third Race Relations Acts, a similar type of study should be carried out into the relative life-chances of parents of different races or ethnic groups.

We would in no way wish to deny the immediate political importance of studies of this kind. Within British society they have provided essential arguments for liberals, egalitarians and socialists seeking to undermine class domination by promoting social mobility and, in the field of race relations, far from denying the importance of such studies, we would heartily commend the work of David Smith on behalf of Political and Economic Planning in the second survey of racial discrimination reported in his book *Racial Disadvantage in Britain* (Smith, 1977). This latter work introduces new refinements of measurement and a sophistication in assessing the significance of such measurements which has raised this type of social science to a new high level. None the less, a sociologist must ask further questions about the overall significance of such studies, and, in answering them, must go beyond them to questions of a more difficult structural kind.

In social mobility studies the questions which came increasingly to be asked were: What is meant by social class? Why does mobility from one class to another matter? Why are such factors as income, educational attainment or occupational category to be taken as indicators of class? And, why is it thought important that children from one class should be able to enter another, particularly if the socialization process to which they are subject *en route* makes them indistinguishable from their new class peers? Answering these questions clearly depends upon some theory of the nature of the structures called classes and the relations between them. These questions, moreover, pose others about the epistemological status of the class concept and about the sorts of evidence necessary to prove what we say about class.

At first sight it might seem that the question 'What do you mean by different racial or ethnic groups?' is a simpler one than that which asks 'What do you mean by social class?', but only a slight consideration of the matter will show that studies of racial discrimination, like studies of class mobility, only have meaning because it is assumed that there should be no significant difference between people of different racial or ethnic parentage, just as it is assumed that all children should have equal claims to social mobility. Built into this is the notion that social recognition of race is a pathological state of affairs. It is surely both possible and necessary in this case to go on to ask what the nature of the group structures is which prevents the operation of a state of perfect mobility.

In any case the concept of discrimination assumed that all men should or do desire the same goods to satisfy their needs. This, however, is the case in very few societies. Far more, normally, different groups socialize their members into having different needs including the need to remain a member of one group and to resist any attraction which they might feel to join another group, which may be conceived of as alien or even as the enemy. Though it is true that minorities, and especially ethnic minorities, might fight to attain goods and services which are denied to them, those goods and services may have special meanings to them in terms of their own scale of values, as for example when Asian parents in Britain seek equal opportunities in education for their children in England with a view to that education being used wholly within the Asian community in Britain or the homeland. Prior, then, to simple studies of life-chances, there clearly must be some understanding of the groups to which men belong and the values which determine their choices and actions as a result of this belonging. Just as a theory of classes and class relations is presupposed in ordinary mobility studies, so a theory of race or ethnic relations is presupposed in studies of racial disadvantage. At a more complex level, moreover, as our first chapter shows, there has to be a theory of the interpenetration, overlap and conflict, between class structures and race relations structures. This is essentially the level on which we have analysed our data and conducted our argument. It therefore becomes important that we should give due consideration to the ontological and epistemological status of statements about class systems and race relations systems.

We are unlikely to be helped in this matter by the second view of the task of sociology which we wish to criticize. This is the view of sociology as an inductive science seeking to discover empirical laws. Actually very few sociological theorists actually hold this view, but it is still common amongst empirically-oriented social researchers who see it as their task to test hypotheses about the relationship between independent and dependent variables and to accord to their findings the status of laws. In fact, the relationships thus discovered can very rarely be generalized except with the aid of a huge *ceteris paribus* clause when it is quite clear that other things are never likely to be equal. The attempt to divorce measurable attributes of sample populations from the specific structures within which they occur always fails, because these attributes are structurally located and mean nothing taken by themselves. What is necessary is not simply generalization of the attributes but comparative study of the structures. Once again, therefore, we are led to the need to study types of structure.

Even with this said, however, there is another kind of complaint about this conception of a scientific sociology which must be considered. This is its inherent determinism. It is assumed that once a generalization has been made, what we are asserting is that things could not have been otherwise, and this on the basis of a limited and specifically located set of observations only. At most, the changing of social reality is conceived in terms of what Popper called piecemeal social reform. We understand a causal sequence, and having understood it we alter the cause in order to alter the effect. What is missing from this type of approach, however, is the insight, at the time of any empirical observation, that, although things are as they are, they could have been otherwise. It is this insight which leads many sociological theorists to counterpoise to postivist social science the notion of social science as critical theory (a term which we should not allow to be appropriated simply by the Marxist Frankfurt school).

Clearly what these critical observations on the limitations of monitoring and of positivist social science point to is the need for two things. One is some understanding of the meaning of structures of social relations as entities which consist of more than simply the attributes of individuals or things. The other is that such structures should not be conceptualized in such a way as to preclude the possibility of social change. There are a number of ways in which a sociology which takes account of these two points might be developed. For our part we find the most valuable starting-point for understanding what is involved in them in the writings of Max Weber. This by no means implies that we think Weber resolved all the problems involved in the development of a structural sociology. It does imply that he faced up to them fully and was prepared to accept the ultimate limitations of social science without rejecting it as worthless or impossible.

Since the main point which we are making is that sociology has to give an account of social structures thought of as operating in the world and affecting men's behaviours, it is also important to point out that this by no means involves turning our backs on empirical data. Such data may be used with imagination and insight to suggest typical patterns of action, constraints on action and, indeed, social structures. More importantly, however, once we are capable of justifying our structural concepts it is possible, by describing and quantifying the actual behaviour of individuals, to see how far they depart from the ideal typical forms implicit in our structural concepts. What we wish to do is to develop ideal typical structural constructs referring particularly to classes and similar structures which are *relevant to our empirical material* and, having done this, to compare these ideal structures with our observations of actual behaviour. In order to deepen our understanding of what this involves we must turn to a sociology of the kind suggested by Max Weber and explore some of the difficulties involved in it.

All statements about social relations must go beyond what is available to us in the evidence of our senses. We simply cannot see social relations even in the sense in which we see physical objects. In the case of physical objects, of course, sensory experience of the same objects varies, but by imposing mathematical categories on our experience and devising agreed measuring instruments we arrive at an agreed conception of a shared and inter-subjective world. The first difficulty in the way of talking about social objects, however, is that we do not appear to have the equivalent of the mathematics and measuring instruments which are necessary to make a shared and inter-subjective social world possible.

Now the Kantian view which influences so much the methodological thinking of Max Weber is that we come to have a belief in a shared inter-subjective world of physical objects subject to law-like regularities and causes, because we impose categories on the world in the course of perceiving it and reasoning about it. The problem with the human and social world is whether there is any set of *a priori* categories which can command universal assent in a similar way. If there were it would be as legitimate to speak of social structures and their law-like behaviour as it is to speak of a world of nature. In neither case would our assertions rest solely upon experience. Rather they would combine the evidence of observation with a grounding in *a priori* categories needing no further justification.

The quest for a sociological *a priori* was bound sooner or later to be raised within the neo-Kantian school of which Weber was a part, and it was, indeed, specifically raised by Georg Simmel in his essay *How is Society Possible?* in which by asking a question analogous to Kant's 'How is Nature Possible?' he drew attention to the possibility of a science of human affairs logically analogous to the sciences of nature. As soon as he asked this question, Simmel saw difficulties in the analogy, with which we shall deal in a moment. Generally, however, the attempt to elaborate the notion of the *a priori* led either to highly formalistic analysis of the elements of elementary actions, as in the work of Znaniecki and Parsons, or to sweeping generalizations about the interaction of sub-systems within a system such as we find in the work of the later Parsons as well as in some of the more theoretical recent forms of Marxism. In the one case the attempt leads to triviality, in the other to systematically codified dogma.

Weber is the most interesting of the founders of modern sociology in that, while he started with the elementary 'geometry' of social actions and social relations in the manner of Simmel, he went on from this to build up systematically the structural concepts or sets of structural concepts in terms of which he believed the major social structures in any institutional sphere could be analysed. So, for example, he developed sets of concepts for the analysis of different structures of economic production, of authority systems, of religious organizations and, not least, of classes, status groups and ethnic communities. The problem we have to face, since we are concerned to consider the operation of structures of this kind in Birmingham, is that of their epistemological status and what is actually necessary to the proof of statements which refer to them.

Weber's own view, which he was inclined to state in an exaggerated form, was that, far from being given in observation, these structural concepts were theoretical fictions only, useful for heuristic purposes, but having no independent ontological status.

Hegelian and Marxist critiques of Weber have argued that this emphasis upon the fictional status of ideal types is inherently absurd and that it is the inevitable consequence of the adoption of a Kantian epistemology (see, for example, Lukàcs 1971). Instead of making an initial philosophic assumption of a division between subject and object, between reason and experience, between the *a priori* and experience, they argue that we ought to see each of these pairs as united in nature and history. Hegelian philosophy thus begins with

301

the development of the categories of thought in history. Marx begins with the development of the world through the action of human labour upon it. There are as many ways of categorizing the world as there are forms of thought for Hegel and forms of labour for Marx. The only way out of this relativism to is look to the future in which alienated forms of thought and labour have been transcended and the perfect philosophy or the perfect society brought into being.

The implication of this view for Weber's structural ideal types is that they are inherently limited by the class position of the social scientist who puts them forward. They do not simply come out of the air; nor do they have *a priori* validity. The same would be true of all other forms of consciousness excepting one. That one, according to the Marxist philosophy of history, is the class perspective of the proletariat. If it is true that the whole history of mankind is the history of the overcoming of alienation in the labour process, then the thought categories of the class which finally carries through that transcendence may be held to have more than a passing validity. Thought is inseparable from practice and the thought forms of the proletariat are to be accepted not because they have a timeless *a priori* validity but because they are part and parcel of the world transforming labour process.

Clearly the difficulty with this view is that it starts by making precisely the kind of metaphysical assumptions which Kantian scepticism would disallow. Because of this, those who claim to derive the truth about society from the consciousness of the proletariat have usually been able to use this justification for saying exactly what they like. Of course, it is a colossal assumption to accept that the historically located and specifically structured class which Marx calls the proletariat should have the universal time-transcending role assigned to it. But worse than this, all those who have professed these views have in fact professed themselves dissatisfied with the fruits of proletarian knowledge and have suggested that proletarian thought needs redemption from another consciousness which comes to it from outside. In due course, however, even the consciousness of the vanguard party which becomes substituted for proletarian consciousness by Lenin becomes suspect, and at that point those who wish to maintain the notion of a privileged consciousness which will finally assert itself in history are left with nothing to say but that they wish to use categories which transcend the immediate observed world which positivism reveres and provide the basis for criticism. In Lukàcs's *History and Class Consciousness* we start with the thought forms of the proletariat. In Lenin's *What is to be Done?* (Tucker, 1974) we are offered the privileged consciousness of the vanguard party. Finally, in the work of the Frankfurt school we are offered the privileged consciousness of the professors.

Of course, this particular discussion is usually thought to be concerned with the way in which we can extract a political and moral imperative from history, but it is important to notice that the forms of consciousness of which these Hegelianized forms of Marxism speak are the central answer of Marxism to the neo-Kantian quest for a sociological *a priori*. In the case of Weber, not the abstract categories of thought but the structural ideal types in terms of which he seeks to understand social life are at issue. What Marxism does is to substitute for these sociological constructs a metaphysic of labour. The subsequent attempt of Marxists to discuss the relationship between labour and thought, being and consciousness, basis and superstructure, is only an extension of this metaphysic. For our part, whatever be the weaknesses of Weber's notion of his types as fictions or the neo-Kantian notion of the sociological *a priori*, we are not prepared to abandon sociology for metaphysics in this way. The problem then is whether there is any other way in which the relation between sociological types and the empirical world can be established.

Simmel, in fact, moved away from a Neo-Kantian perspective almost as soon as he answered his question 'How is society possible?' for he very quickly came to accept what was to become almost the central tenet of American phenomenological sociology, namely that the concepts in terms of which we think about society and which make society possible are not the concepts purely of sociologists but the concepts of participant actors themselves. As he says:

> There is a decisive difference between the unity of science and the unity of nature. It is this: In the Kantian view (which we follow here), the unity of nature emerges in the observing subject exclusively; it is produced exclusively by him in the sense materials, which are in themselves heterogeneous. By contrast the unity of society needs no observer. It is directly realised by its own elements, because these elements are themselves conscious and synthesizing units. . . . Societal unification needs no factors outside its own component elements, the individuals (Simmel, 1959, p. 338).

Thus it seems that, whatever the status of the constructs which sociologists make to comprehend society, they have competitors. The members of that society are sociologists too. One is tempted to say that they are amateurs. But a case can be made and indeed has been made strongly in recent years that they are the real professionals. The really important question, however, is what the relation is between the observed actors' constructs which these actors use in their day-to-day construction of social reality and the concepts used by sociologists. Whereas before, as we saw, we were concerned with Weber's problem which was to show that there was any connection at all between his ideal types and the 'world out there', we now discover that there are theories and constructs out there which threaten to displace sociological typology and theory altogether.

Alfred Schutz specifically addresses himself to the question of providing a philosophical underpinning for Weber's methodology. But he does so by subjecting Weber's concept of ideal types to a new and strict condition, namely that the ideal type constructs should be understandable by, and acceptable to, the actors themselves. Schutz calls this the postulate of adequacy, which he defines as follows:

> Each term in a scientific model of human action must be constructed in such a way that a human act performed within the life-world by an individual actor in the way indicated by the typical construct would be understandable to the actor himself as well as for his fellow-men in terms of commonsense interpretations of everyday life. Compliance with this postulate warrants consistency of the constructs of the sociologist with the constructs of commonsense experience of the social reality (Schutz, 1967, p. 44).

Here at least there is a suggestion that sociological constructs need not be arbitrary, nor should they have only an *a priori* grounding. It seems that what is suggested is that these concepts should be grounded in the empirical world. Unfortunately this is an exaggeration. The 'empirical' reality which is referred to here is only one stage closer to the world of things in themselves, and there is surely just as much of a possibility that these actors' constructs will be erroneous as that those of the observing sociologist should be so. Indeed, the case could be put that since the sociologist is a trained observer, his observations and conceptualizations should command more respect. More than this, however, some Marxist writers, who have always felt it necessary to raise the question of the possible false consciousness of the working class, have suggested that it is possible to go beyond *a priori*, theoretical or actors' constructs, to give an account of the world as it actually is. Thus, for example, one of the most sociologically sensitive of recent Marxists, Lucien Goldmann, writes:

> The weakness of phenomenology seems to us to lie precisely in the fact that it limits itself to a comprehensive description of the facts of consciousness. . . . The real structure of historical facts permits, however, beyond the conscious meaning of those facts in the thought and intentions of the actors, the postulate of an objective meaning which often differs from the conscious meaning in an important way (Goldmann, 1969, p. 32).

Now Weber would agree with at least part of this assertion. He would claim that there is a difference between the kind of consciousness implicit in his ideal types and that in the constructs and the meanings which occur in the participant actor's consciousness. The question is whether this difference means that the sociologists' constructs are in some way superior and, even more, whether they can be said to be 'objectively' grounded in the world as it actually is.

There are several reasons for holding that sociologists' concepts are superior. For one thing they are capable of giving a larger view than those of the observed actors. These actors, after all, are concerned with the immediacy of the social relations within which they work, and do not necessarily see the way in which small-scale structures form parts of, or sometimes conflict with, structures of a larger kind. Second, the practical business of social life does not permit a segregation of the cognitive, affective and evaluative aspects of our reactions to events, so that participant actors' concepts might well be subject to cognitive distortion. Finally, the sociologist subjects his concept to two kinds of testing; on the one hand considering their empirical applicability, on the other arguing about them and possibly arriving at a consensus about them with his colleagues. It is by these means that sociologists claim to arrive at 'objective meaning which differs from conscious meaning in an important way'. Clearly, however, the objectivity is limited and one can understand the view of contemporary phenomenological sociologists that the objectivity of these constructs does violence to what is called the indexicality of the concepts of everyday life, that is to say their essential inseparability from the contexts in which they occur.

One reading of the Goldmann text quoted above, which we cannot allow however, is that which claims that we can have direct access to real structures which lie behind the appearance of events. This form of essentialism or, as it is sometimes called, realism, has recently become surprisingly popular amongst Marxists of structuralist persuasion. Rejecting the notion of any kind of sociological *a priori*, they claim to have a scientific way of understanding social reality, and this scientific way seems to allow the acceptance not merely of common-sense terms about social action and social relations, but terms which refer to social systems as wholes and which describe particularly the relations between various human activities and the mode of production. Such metaphysical speculation is interesting enough, but when it claims to have the validity of science, if often becomes little more than dogma.

It would seem that this is not the view of methodological realism in science which has recently been defended by Keat and Urry. They suggest that realism and positivism have certain common features:

First, the idea that scientific theories must be objectively assessed by reference to the empirical evidence. This evidence is such that all scientists who are competent, honest, and lacking in perceptual deficiencies can agree upon it, though not necessarily with total certainty. Second, there is the idea that there are 'objects' in the broadest sense of the term, which exist independently of our beliefs and theories about them. In other words there is some commitment to a theory of truth in which there is a clear dichotomy between the 'world' and the various attempts that we may make to describe and explain it correctly (Keat and Urry, 1975, p. 44).

These modest claims are far more acceptable than those made by some who say they accept the realist view, and they seem to us to be both acceptable and a necessary correction to Weber's own scepticism and his claim that his concepts are mere fictions. We suggest that the whole exercise of precisely defining concepts, of refining them in the course of historical studies, of arguing about them, and then applying them again as yardsticks against which reality can be measured, has significance only on the assumption that these conceptualizations correspond in some albeit unproven way to reality 'out there'. If this be realism, we would wish to modify Weber's claims about his methodology, so that it conforms to realism's standards, yet we would still claim that the emphasis which Weber places on the distance between these concepts and the real world does provide a salutary warning against the dangers of metaphysical dogmatism.

We should now note, however, that Schutz, whom we discussed above, is only concerned with the relation between the world of social science and the world of common sense, while writers like Keat and Urry are only concerned with the definition of social science. Sociologists, however, have another and more difficult problem, namely that of the relationship between their theories and the theories of some of the actors whom they observe. These are the intellectuals, ideologists and myth-makers in the community of actors who themselves attempt to construct social reality not merely on the level of day-to-day social transactions, but in terms of relatively large-scale entities and processes.

Alvin Gouldner has recently written an extremely interesting account of the nature of ideological thought, which, though it does emphasize the limitations and inadequacies of ideological thinking, is one of the clearest recent accounts of its social function. Amongst other things, Gouldner makes the following point:

Ideologies weaken traditional structures by refocussing the vision of everyday life and, specifically, by calling to mind things that are not in normal evidence, not directly viewable by the senses,

306

not in the circumference of the immediate. .... One cannot, for example, see a 'class' or a 'nation' or a 'free market', but the ideologies of socialism, nationalism and liberalism bring these structures to mind. In doing so, they provide a language that enables interpretations to be made of some things that may be seen and heard within the immediate. ... Ideologies permit interpretations of everyday life that are not possible within the terms of everyday life's ordinary language: an argument between workers and foremen, may now, for example, be interpreted as intensifying 'class struggle' (Gouldner, 1976, p. 42).

It would seem that the claims which Gouldner is making here for ideology overlap to a considerable degree with the claims which we have made for Weber's sociology, and we shall have to ask whether there are none the less not important differences between the two types of thought. Before we do this, however, it will be convenient to note that a similar degree of overlap has been noted between Weber's concept of the ideal type and certain concepts used by Sorel. H. Stuart Hughes draws attention to Sorel's

characterization of historical 'myths' and in particular the syndicalist myth of the general strike as 'pictures of battles' which were alone capable of arousing the inert mass of mankind to concerted action; and the more paradoxical assimilation of this thinking in terms of myth to the methodology of modern science (Hughes, 1959, p. 165).

Sorel's more general notion is that of 'diremption' which, he says, aims

to examine certain parts (of a situation, a series of events or the like) without taking into account all the ties which connect them to the whole, to determine in some manner the character of their activity by isolating them (Hughes, 1959, p. 173).

Hughes goes on to suggest that, although 'superficially considered, the myth would seem to be a special kind of diremption', it was both more and less than such a conceptualization:

It was more because it was not just a methodological abstraction: it was a 'complex of pictures' rather than a single element taken in isolation. Hence it reflected reality at more than one point. Moreover a myth was a non-logical irrational affair; for that very reason it approached closer to the 'fluid character of reality' than did the logically ordered abstractions that social theorists usually devised. Finally it was what human beings acted upon – a merely logical abstraction left them cold; in this sense also it possessed a kind of reality. On the other hand the

307

myth was less than a normal diremption in that it was less susceptible to empirical control . . . (the former) were to be constantly subject to change and correction as circumstances and the knowledge of the observer also changed. Myths, on the other hand 'were autonomous, perfect in themselves, and should not be tampered with'. . . . The result was a kind of sociological mysticism (Hughes, 1959, p. 175).

Turning first to Gouldner's characterization of ideological thought, we should say that in the respect in which he writes in the passage quoted earlier, there is no difference between the ideological conceptions of which he writes and the structural and group concepts used in sociology. Both, it may be said, invent or create the larger group structures of the public realm which are not normally thought of by the ordinary man in the street. Both attempt to be systematic and precise forms of discourse in contrast to the open-endedness or indexicality of everyday speech. And both become the sociological means of interpretation through which the interaction between individuals is seen as moved by changes in social structures which are more than simply the sum of individual sctions.

These similarities appear, however, because in the quoted passage Gouldner is emphasizing the cognitive aspects of ideology. In fact, however, it is characteristic of ideological thinking that it does not separate out cognitive from affective or evaluative reactions to events. Moreover, far from simply being concerned with describing, analysing or explaining the world, ideology sets out both to prescribe the future and to change the world. In this sense, Marx's eleventh thesis on Feuerbach's 'Hitherto philosophers have merely interpreted the point is to change it' represents the very charter of ideological thinking.

Of course, one should mention that we are not using the term 'ideology' here in the sense in which it is used by Marx. Marx confines the term to thinking, which, while pretending to be scientific, posits a changeless and law-like world and thereby plays down the possibility of change. By contrast he represents his own thinking as scientific. Karl Mannheim (1954), moreover, accepted Marx's definition of ideological thinking, but called Marxian thinking utopian in that it posited nothing but change and thereby destabilized the world in the course of describing it. What we are doing here is referring to Mannheim's ideology and utopia collectively as forms of ideological thought, and suggesting that there are ways of describing and analysing the social world which are neither utopian nor ideological (in Mannheim's sense) and which have some claim to the title 'scientific'. In practice we believe that many Marxists do not always accept the special activist and pragmatic attitude to social thought referred to in the eleventh thesis and actually accept a view of science far more like our own.

The threefold distinction between science, ideology and utopia is important to make and we do want to insist on the separateness of sociological analysis from all ideological forms. With this said, however, we should also be willing to recognize with Mannheim that the distinction which can so readily be made on the level of the intent of the theorist is more difficult to sustain when one considers the content and the style of this reasoning. Mannheim spoke of the lie in the soul and suggested that since thought itself was subjected to social causation, and because our basic conceptualization and even our standards of truth were distorted by our interests and our social location, there could be no such thing as objective social science. Ultimately we would accept this, but we would also follow Mannheim in suggesting that there are social locations from which it becomes possible to look reflexively at one's own situation and minimize the degree of cognitive distortion in one's thought.

Finally, on the question of ideological thought, however, having insisted that distinctions can be drawn, we should now go back to Gouldner's emphasis on the positive aspects of ideology and suggest that because there are precise cognitive elements in such thought, it is always possible for sociologists in their quest for structural hypotheses and types to turn to conceptions which have been put forward originally in ideological contexts. This is, as it were, the reverse of Schutz's postulate of adequacy. It is also the reason why, in many Communist countries today, sociology of a kind flourishes as academics claim to be subjecting Marxist hypotheses to empirical testing.

The use of myths as a source of sociological hypotheses is another matter, at least, if we take the term in its Sorelian sense. The crux of the matter here is that, although it makes a claim to talk about the world, the purpose of the myth is not cognitive at all. It is a set of images which cannot and should not, according to the myth-makers, be broken down and analysed. The sole purpose in putting forward a myth is to mobilize a collectivity and prepare it for action. The task of a sociologist is to take the myth as datum, or as a symptom of underlying reality, and then to seek to describe sociologically the collectivity which it (the myth) seeks to integrate and to mobilize. The description of the structure and functioning of the collectivity would then, of course, include reference to the myth.

Before we proceed to other aspects of the problem of concept formation and empirical work in a sociological study, it will be as well to stop for a moment and relate the above somewhat abstract discussions to our own concrete focus of interest. We are confronted with large-scale complexes of social interaction. We record data

309

about people and about groups, and we study statements about the policy intentions of those in authority, those subject to that authority and those resisting it. But, because we are not methodological individualists in any crude sense which suggests that the only reality consists of the actions or behaviour of individual men and women, we do also want to explain such behaviour in terms of the operation of social structures and groups and the interaction between these. For this purpose we develop such concepts as class and underclass.

Quite obviously concepts such as these, developed in the way in which they are in our first chapter, do draw heavily upon the concepts which are used by the more politically articulate members of the immigrant and native-born communities. In talking to men who had already assessed their own situation with the ideas of Garvey and Fanon we had little difficulty in finding some common intellectual ground, and our own concepts have been shaped by trying to bring them into relation to these ideas. To that extent we were fulfilling the requirements of Schutz's postulate of adequacy. But even here we had continually to be careful because our purposes were not the same as those of our discussants. Quite naturally they were concerned to go beyond a mere definition of social reality to put forward ideas which would evaluate experience, organize the emotions of their fellows and prepare them for action. They were thus inclined to be critical of a sociological study which in some respects at least claimed to be value-free. What they did not normally understand or accept was that it was possible, while pursuing such a sociological objective, none the less to recognize the validity of their enterprise.

In formulating this sympathetic view of ideology, and indeed of myth, there are, however, points at which we have to draw the line and dissociate our views from those of some of our respondents. We have encountered amongst people in our research area, amongst students and participants in race relations affairs nationally, and amongst so-called radical sociologists and black sociologists internationally, those who mistake the process of myth-making for sociology and who would demand of us that as a mark of our good faith we assent to propositions which we know to be untrue. Thus, while we are quite clear that racialist practice and racist theory are now deeply institutionalized in British society, we do not have to assent to the view that the police are systematically poised for attack on the black community, or even, as one of our informants told us, that the British Army had moved into Handsworth in order to have a man killed. These are manifest distortions and untruths which one can understand as part of the way in which the underclass is recruited and mobilized. It is unfortunate that the picture of the world which they create is one which is sometimes dignified with the name of radical black sociology. In fact, a radical perspective on politics requires precisely the capacity amongst some political leaders to transcend myths like these and understand more objectively the structure and dynamics of their situation so as to be better able to control it.

We have spoken so far as though, despite a stance of epistemological scepticism, we are to some extent prepared to accept the methodological realists' case, and to claim that what we are doing by more or less complex procedures is to describe the structures of race, class and ethnic group relations in the area of our study. But the structural concepts which we use are not simply related to reality as descriptive statements and they are not unambiguous. This is not a guilty admission that in the long run we should give up our sociological perspective, however. Rather it involves the simple recognition of the methodological subtlety of what we have to do.

The first point to be noticed is that our structural ideal types are used, not as descriptions, but as yardsticks. For example, if we speak of 'the working class' we would be positing a state of affairs in which a large number of people were socially linked to each other through organizational and other forms, were all conscious of certain shared experiences, and conscious of belonging together as well as being readily available for united political action. In fact, everyone knows that the term is used more generally than this, however. The term is not abandoned altogether because a particular group of workers exist who are not particularly class-conscious and are not members of anything. The concept still remains useful because it is a relevant yardstick against which the actual states of relatedness and consciousness in a particular population can be measured.

It is noteworthy that although the term 'working class' is in fact a highly problematic one in the ways just mentioned, it has become part of the normal political vocabulary of Britain and of Western Europe. We would also judge that it is more than a mere myth term. Unlike such terms, it can be explicated and used as a criterion of measuring empirical reality.

Terms and concepts which refer to 'yardsticks' and 'criteria of measurement', then, are not descriptions. But this does not mean that they have no relation to empirical reality. A term like 'working class', however it is explicated, is a relevant term for analysing large bodies of data because it focuses on aspects of social life which are crucial and problematic. Some other term like, say, the 'community of saints' would not be relevant because there would be little achieved by measuring the extent to which a given population measured up to this standard. In this sense we may sometimes speak loosely and say that there is a sense in which the working class exists or is real but the community of saints is not.

In the area in which we are working, however, there are special

311

problems and special features of interest precisely because common usages of terms like 'social class' and 'stratification systems' have broken down. As we saw in chapter 1, the situation of colonial black ethnic minorities cannot be adequately captured in terms of these more standard ideal types. This is why we have tried to use our imagination and to see whether the term 'underclass' could be developed so as to take account of the new and more complex reality. In fact we believe that much of the most creative work in sociology has consisted in conceptual development of this kind. It is a central part of what Glaser and Strauss were getting at when they found it necessary to write their book, *The Discovery of Grounded Theory* (Glaser and Strauss, 1968.)

One thing which will be apparent in our study is that we have by no means refrained from using survey data. In fact a very large part of our total resources of money, time and energy were spent in conducting a survey, coding, processing and analysing data. What is the significance of this?

Contrary to what is often said in critiques of the survey method, we did not think that, taken overall, the method of gathering information distorted reality or that the meaning of the data was coded out of existence. Much depends in the use of survey material on how scientistic, in the bad sense which we take that term to have, the attitude of the sociological analyst who looks at such data takes. There seemed to us to be three important uses to which the survey material could be put.

In the first place, in the process of coding we received a great deal of counter-intuitive information which led us to refine our ideal types or to devise new ones. In discussing the problem of ideal typical yardsticks above we have found it convenient to illustrate our argument by reference to the concepts of class and underclass and these terms recur again and again in our text. In practice, however, such terms, even if they were wholly clear in themselves, would provide only the crudest general framework for our study. All along the line we are discussing more complex and subtle structures and processes, many of which occurred to us as we made our way through the often surprising, although repeated answers to our questions. Our experience moreover is, we believe, a general one. If one looks at a body of structural theoretical hypotheses such as is contained, for instance, in Robert Merton's *Social Theory and Social Structure*, it is clear that very few of his most interesting structural concepts are derived from ideology or from grand theory. Most of them have arisen in the course of coding humdrum data and asking questions about its significance. To take an even more extreme example, many of the interesting discoveries and insights of ethnomethodology have surely been derived from the task of trying sensibly to interpret survey data.

A second point which is sometimes made against survey data is that they break up information about meaningful action into bits and so distort its true nature. Given our Weberian perspective, we naturally enough sympathize with this criticism. But the criticism is not so much of the form of the data as of the ways in which they are interpreted. We have not, on the whole, considered our data in terms of variables mechanically related to each other. We have been probing for meanings, and even where we have used forced choice questions we have realized that the interpretation of the answers is by no sense given in the form of the questions, and that this process of intepretation had to be done when we have the tables of figures before us. Our purpose becomes even more clear when we add that we included many open-ended questions in our survey and that even when we coded these so as to make quantitative comparisons we could, and did, still go back to the questionaires to allow particular individuals to 'talk to us'.

In some ways a long and complex questionnaire is a little life history in itself, and we may claim that what we did, following Thomas and Znaniecki, was to study 1,100 life histories. If, however, we had simply asked 1,100 people to write or tell us their life histories the task would have been a lifelong one, the individual auto-biographers would not have dwelt on many of the points which were of interest to us, and in allowing a totally free form of expression we would have sacrificed the possibility of comparability. Obviously in using the survey method we lost something and we fully recognize the arguments brought by Cicourel and others against the survey method. For all that, however, our own initial participant interaction with our respondents, the tough-minded determination of the professional interviewers provided for us by a commercial survey organization, and finally, sitting and coding 1,100 questionnaires largely by ourselves, did, we believe, enable to to get at what is, after all, the final underpinning of any attempt to describe social structure: meaningful accounts of people's lives. Although most of the chapters are organized topically, therefore, we believe that they can be read, not as data on housing, employment, education and so on, but as the accounts of these lives and the structures which interrelate one life and another.

Finally and most obviously, because as we have said, ideal types are not descriptions but yardsticks against which historical and empirical reality can be measured and compared, the data which we have produced enable us to measure the extent to which the behaviour of these populations actually approximates any of the polar points which are set out in our ideal types. The ideal type which provides the main framework of our research is set out in chapter 1. A rereading of that chapter will show that although it takes the form of a series of ideal types, these types themselves serve to suggest a whole number of researchable questions. The survey data on the one hand and the many other research findings which we made during studies of official data, interviews with policy-makers, social participation and so on, on the other are answers to the research questions posed there.

One final point which may be made is this. One can imagine a state of affairs in which sociology is already possessed of well-established ideal types nearly sufficient to provide an approach to any research area. In this case the task would be simple. We would simply have to ask how far, according to the data collected, empirical reality departed from the standards suggested in our idealized and ideal typical world. We would say that the conceptual vocabulary with which Weber has provided us already goes quite far in this direction. But we certainly found that we were changing and refining our ideal types all the time and that there was in a true sense of the word a dialectical relationship between our theorizing and our fact-finding. We would at least say in retrospect that we wonder whether this process is not of the essence of sociological research and whether a research which began with an already established lexicon of ideal types would not stifle the kind of imagination which is essential to the research process.

We must now turn to the final set of questions which arises from the ambiguities surrounding the nature of ideal typical sociological concepts. These are those which concern the meaningfulness, the instability, the proneness to conflict, and the relevance to moral and political issues of sociological concepts. Unfortunately it is all too common today for sociologists to assert that their sociology is critical, non-value-free or reflexive, and having done so to abandon any attempt to conform to the sorts of standards of reasoning and proof which are characteristic of scientific thought. We do not want to be involved in sheer propaganda of this sort. It therefore becomes important for us to indicate the more limited senses in which our own sociology departs from the normal naturalistic paradigms.

Our own starting-point is to be found in Weber's first definition of a social relationship. What he says is:

> The term social relationship will be used to denote the behaviour of a plurality of actors insofar as, in its meaningful content, the action of each takes account of that of others and is oriented in these terms. The social relationship thus consists entirely and exclusively in the existence of a probability that there will be a meaningful course of social action – irrespective for the time being of the basis of that probability (Weber, 1968, p. 26).

It has often been pointed out that in this definition Weber is attempting to reconcile the traditions of both *verstehen* and positivism in social science, and clearly the rather questionable second sentence of the definition seems to give too much to positivism by implying that the existence of social relations is in some simple sense verifiable. For our purposes, however, we may leave this question aside and note the implications of the notion that 'the action of each takes account of that of the others'.

The importance of this assertion is that social relationships are thought of as doubly contingent, to use Talcott Parson's term. That is to say that although a social relationship in the fullest sense of the term cannot be said to exist unless two separate actors do actually fulfil the stipulations of the definition, there is always the possibility that while one will, the other will not. Weber, unlike Parsons, seems to leave open this possibility. For Parsons the term 'social relation' or 'social relationship' is virtually restricted to the situation in which there is total mutuality and compliance between the actors concerned; Weber keeps open a wide range of possibilities of conflict. These have been systematically developed by Rex elsewhere (Rex, 1973a).

Of course, Weber does go on to discuss the case in which mutuality of orientation exists, and this concept is essential to his subsequent development of concepts referring to larger-scale structures. But the basis of the probability of actions occurring which is referred to in the second part of the definition above is to be found simply in the fact that 'action, especially social action which involves a social relationship, *may* be guided by the belief in the existence of a legitimate order' (Weber, 1968, p. 31, our italics). So long as nothing more is said here than 'may be guided', stable social relations, the basic elements of all social structures, are themselves seen to be highly contingent phenomena. More than this, it should be remembered that the notion of the action of one actor 'taking account of' the action of another is even more sweeping in scope than the notion of orientation to a legitimate order. This taking account of may refer only to one actor calculating the statistical probability of another's behaviour and, to speak colloquially, betting on it. Such action is all that is assumed in all types of ecological studies and in economics. Sociology simply cannot be confined to the study of systems of social relations governed by a normative order as the tradition which runs from Durkheim to Parsons suggests. This has a number of implications.

In the first place, because social relations must be thought of as inherently contingent and unstable things, it is wrong to forget this when going on to a more complex level of analysis and talking about social systems. This is why Weber, who knew of systems theory primarily in its organicist forms, argued that such theories were

315

useful only for preliminary orientation and that all group concepts, indeed, must be verified or unpacked in terms of the actions out of which they were constituted.

If this is done, one consequence is that sociologists are likely to have a different approach to social change. The positivistic approach, which assimilates all the objects of its study to the phenomenal world of natural science, is to speak of dynamic laws or of laws of social change. In the sphere of race relations, for example, this would involve using something like 'the race relations cycle', as described by Park, as an explanatory principle. If the contingency of social change is grasped then it becomes important not merely for historical but for sociological explanation to think not of law-like change, but of events. This is why we have found it necessary, in setting up an account of the race relations situation in Britain, to begin by giving precisely such an account of events. It is in the nature of an event that, although it was so, it could have been otherwise.

We have already seen that concepts like 'working class' are ideal types only. We should now note that the variation of actual situations from the norm indicated by the type might involve conflict on the part of an actor with the expectations which other actors have of him. The account of the evolution of what Marx, using Hegelian language, calls the evolution from class-in-itself, is essentially an account of the elimination of these conflicts and a conscious participation in a stable class organization by its members. We are implicitly considering such conflicts every time we draw attention to the failure of particular individuals to conform with the ideal type of 'class' or 'underclass'. More important than this, however, is the fact that we do not pass beyond the level of class analysis to the level of systems analysis at all. We believe that the only consequence of attempting to apply such systems analysis is to conceal conflicts, and that this is something which would normally only be done by sociologists who were implicitly looking at matters from the point of view of the authorities.

The notion of looking at the same situation from a number of different points of view, however, serves to relate this work to another important tradition in the methodology of sociology which runs particularly from Max Weber, through Karl Mannheim, down, in the study of race relations, to the work of Gunnar Myrdal. Weber saw that, faced with the flux of events which confronted the social scientist and which was in principle infinite, the sociologist had to begin his study by selecting from these manifold events those which were important for study, and that the criterion for so doing should be 'relevance for value'. Mannheim saw that all social science tended to ideologize events by emphasizing their stability or to utopianize them by emphasizing their inherent tendency to change. Thus there

was in Europe, for example, the possibility of bourgeois and proletarian social science. Finally Myrdal, asked to discover the facts or
the truth of the American race relations situation in 1939, said that
there were no simple facts or truth and that the relationships which
might be discovered could only be deemed 'necessary' in the sense
that they were necessary from a particular point of view.

It is unfortunate that what is most often remembered about
Myrdal in the study of race relations in the USA is that he decided
to study race relations there in terms of what he called the 'American
dilemma', that is in terms of the departure of the social reality
brought into being by political practice from certain norms set out
in the American constitution. A later generation who were less than
impressed with the clarity or importance of the norms of the constitution then tended simply to dismiss Myrdal as someone whose
consensual liberalism was irrelevant in a situation marked by rising
conflict. In fact, however, Myrdal was well aware that the relationship he was discussing could be looked at from the perspective of
conflicting groups. In the following passage, for example, he quite
explicitly emphasizes the importance of conflict perspectives in the
sociology of race relations:

> Relevance is determined by the interest and ideals of actual
> persons and groups of persons. There is no need of introducing
> value premises which are not actually held by anybody.
> Within the circle of relevance so determined a still more narrow
> circle of significance may be taken to denote valuations which
> are held by substantial groups of people or by small groups
> with substantial power (Myrdal, 1969, p. 157).

This has been very much our own perspective in this study, though
the question is perhaps not quite as simple as Myrdal's reference to
value premises would suggest. We do attempt to make a structural
analysis of tendencies to the formation of classes and similar groups,
and these concepts are derived in part from systematic sociology and
not simply in terms of structures which we see as relevant to ends
which we or some of our respondents happen to value. But clearly it
is the case that in deciding to make certain structural concepts
central we have decided to organize our material in a particular way.
This is what we were doing in our first chapter when we saw the
structure of the immigrant community as pulled on the one hand to
conforming with the needs of the society and culture of the homeland,
and on the other to absorption in the society, politics and culture of
the native-born working class. Clearly this is one amongst several
structural emphases which could have been made in such a study.

There is none the less a certain openness in our study. In setting up
three separate structures as reference points we implicitly leave it to

317

our readers to decide which of these is to be given most emphasis. Our own emphasis is probably towards saying that immigrant minorities should maintain their independence of the organizations and structures of the working class until they can have full and equal participation with other workers, but that at the same time they should be able to preserve their cultural identity and their links with the homeland. What we have to say, however, should be of interest to those who look forward to total absorption of the minority into the British class structure as well as those who maintain a zionist perspective which suggests that all structures and actions should be judged by their effect on the possibility of an eventual dignified return to the homeland. It is also possible that our conclusions might be of interest to those who do actually want to maintain a system of unequal racial stratification. It is in the nature of sociology that this should be the case.

Finally, since many of our sociological readers in Europe and the USA are likely to be influenced by the critical theory of the Frankfurt school, it might be useful here to say something of the relationship of the kind of sociologizing which we are doing to the three types of discipline discussed by Jurgen Habermas (Habermas, 1972). These, of course, are analytic-empirical science, hermeneutic, and critical-emancipatory science, and the injunction of the Frankfurt school seems to be that it is the third sort of science which we should be doing.

Now we have some sympathy with Habermas's point of view because he is, like Weber, deeply influenced by the ideas of Kant. On the most crucial point at which he goes beyond Kant, moreover, we would agree with him. It does seem to us to be true that the natural science which deals with the phenomenal world is something which arises because of man's *interest* in controlling the world. Again it is clear that the hermeneutic tradition has as its interest the increase of understanding of texts, of cultures and people. Clearly, too, it is possible to posit intellectual disciplines based upon other interests such as emancipation.

We would disagree with Habermas where he suggests that the sort of sociology which Weber does is confined to the analytic-empirical or the hermeneutic tradition. It must be quite clear from what we have said in this chapter that Weber's view of sociology has a much more complex and fruitful relationship to the various categories of thought and action set out in Kant's philosophy.

As we have seen, what Weber was concerned with, as was also the case with Simmel, was to find an appropriate equivalent in sociology to the *a priori* categories of natural science. But unlike some other writers who returned to Kant, Weber did not simply create categories which would in effect assimilate the study of man to the study

318

of nature. That surely was what Parsons must have been doing when he sought to apply the general systems theory of Henderson to the reconceptualization of his categories of action. What Weber did, on the other hand, was to produce categories which had relevance, not merely to the world of scientific necessity, but to the world of moral freedom. The groups and other structures which he discusses are never merely 'things' or 'systems', they are networks of social relations which may or may not rest upon a belief in a legitimate order. That is to say, men may allow the social and the normative to determine their conduct or they may not, a point which reminds one immediately of Kant's world of moral freedom. As Rex has put the matter in an earlier book: 'The paradox of sociology lies precisely in this, that though we are compelled by forces external to ourselves, these forces are none the less made by men and can be changed by men' (Rex, 1973a).

If, then, Weber's sociology and the sort of sociology which we are proposing cannot be pigeon-holed as analytic-empirical or as hermeneutic, how does it relate to the third type of social science, the critical-emancipatory. Certainly there may be some parallel. What Habermas suggests is that the exemplar of this new type of study is psychoanalysis, in which the analyst gives the patient an account of his behaviour which the patient accepts as valid, and he goes on to argue that there is an equivalent socio-analysis which would have as its purpose the de-ideologization of the world. Thus far, it would seem that we are speaking about something very similar. Habermas, however, goes beyond this in a manner which one would expect from the standpoint of the critical theory of the Frankfurt school, and it is here that we would distinguish our conception of sociology from his critical-emancipatory science.

In the case of the psycho-analysis, what is involved is not simply valid understanding and explanation. Psycho-analysis is also therapy. To understand truly is to be liberated from one's fantasies and delusions. But understanding of social fantasies and illusions is surely a different matter. Such understanding cannot lead to emancipation unless an imperative to a certain kind of action is taken as given in the structural analysis. If the maxim of psycho-analysis is 'Ye shall know the truth and the truth shall make ye free', that of a socio-analysis is surely 'Ye shall know the truth and thereby become conscious of the source of your alienation and oppression'. It is not perhaps surprising that Habermas himself was eventually forced to dissociate himself from student activists who thought that his sociological analysis must commit him to a course of political action. Some thought that in the last analysis Habermas could be charged, as Marx had previously charged Feuerbach, with wanting only a thought revolution.

For our part we would not regard that charge as particularly damaging. To assume that our role as sociologists gives us an entitlement to political leadership is simple arrogance, which fails to recognize that political change is the task of those who suffer political oppression. Like Habermas, we do not accept that sociology should rest content, as the simpler forms of positivist sociology do, with simply describing the world as it is, subject to some kind of scientific law. We see the world we are describing as continually subject to change. But we cannot extract any imperative for our sociological studies. What we can envisage are alternative structural futures – e.g. assimilation, the emergence of an underclass, social and cultural separatism in the case of immigrant minorities – and having indicated what these futures are, leave it to actual historical agents to change them. Our sociology is certainly critical and we would want it to give insight to the oppressed. But emancipation is something which involves moral choice and resolve. We can, and indeed we do wish to make that choice, but it would simply make our sociology less clear if we failed to realize that this sort of choice was a separate act from our sociological analysis.

Finally, we may perhaps comment on the notion that sociology should be what Gouldner calls 'reflexive.' Gouldner, it seems to us, is so much influenced by Mannheim, as we are, that it would be unlikely that we should disagree with him very much. Some of those who have taken up the notion of reflexive sociology, however, have gone on to do nothing but the sociology of sociology and sociologists. While we have tried already to make our own social position and perspective clear, we also believe that our work should have some content. What we present here, we hope, is a self-consciously reflexive sociology of race relations in Birmingham.

Appendix 2 Research methodology

This study has not been conceived in terms of some simple and unitary research design. It has attempted throughout to present an argument at once theoretical and empirical and to back that argument with data gathered by whatever methods seemed appropriate. Of considerable importance has been the massive amount of data about a sample survey population, gathered for us with great skill and competence by National Opinion Polls. But while we have found such data immensely illuminating and productive of many counter-intuitive insights, ultimately the interpretation of that data itself has depended upon information and insights derived from other sources. Although one of us could claim to be one of the earliest critics of sociology's preoccupation with hard data,[1] we believe that survey data of the kind which we have presented here is an immensely valuable instrument for the generation of theoretical insights and for the refinement of ideal types of social action and social relations. On the other hand, had we merely sat in our office and waited for the data to come in, we could hardly have known what it was about. To have that understanding we had first to go out and spend about two years worrying councillors, local government officials and community leaders, and gathering in official documents of all kinds, in order to tease out the exact nature of our empirical problem.

So far as actual fieldwork was concerned then, three different kinds of work were undertaken:

1 Unstructured interviewing of 300 policy/decision-makers and community 'leaders'.
2 Structured interviewing of 1,100 heads of households including a main sample of 300 white British, 300 Asians and 300 West Indians, and a further sample of 100 white British and 100 black council tenants.

3 Structured interviewing of a small sample of Asian and West Indian youth – children of respondents in our main sample.

Unstructured interviewing took place throughout the whole period of the project, 1974–7, and provided a continual source of information in helping us to understand the policies which affected black and white people in the survey area. Approximately 300 unstructured interviews were conducted. These were as follows:

1	Local government officials/teachers/social workers/police, etc.	110
2	Councillors/MPs.	15
3	Community activists (white).	39
4	Community activists (black).	43
5	High commissioners/consuls.	5
6	Official bodies, e.g. CRC/RRB/Department of Employment/Inner Area Study/churches/temples.	48
7	Miscellaneous. NAME meetings/TAR meetings/ National Front marches/local festivals, etc.	18
8	Observation days – housing visitors/schools, etc.	22
		300

Cuttings were kept for the period 1974–7 from the Birmingham newspapers, the *Post* and the *Mail*, the minutes from the monthly Birmingham Council meetings were acquired, 1974–8, and the Birmingham Statistics Office provided assistance with local census material. The issues covered by the main survey questionnaire were largely generated by the informal interviews.

The survey

The 'Handsworth' area of Birmingham, comprising parts of the Soho, Sandwell, Handsworth and Newtown wards, was chosen for a survey because it contains enumeration districts with the largest number of New Commonwealth citizens in Birmingham, and also because it included West Indians and Asians living in the same area. Information concerning the proportion of New Commonwealth citizens down to enumeration districts was obtained from a study of Birmingham Small Area Statistics, 1971 census. (Also see Map in chapter 3, p. 76).

The main sample

Our main sample was a quota sample drawn from 128 contiguous enumeration districts which were the ones with the highest concentration of New Commonwealth immigrants and New Commonwealth-descended residents in the four wards. Within each enumeration district we drew a sample of our respondents in proportions equivalent to the proportions in that enumeration district using the formula:

Number of Asian/ West Indian/British interviews $=$ $\dfrac{\text{Number of WI/Asian/ British in e.d.}}{\text{Number of WI/Asian/ British in all e.d.s}}$ $\times$ Size of ethnic sample

The actual numbers for each group in all 128 enumeration districts were:

White British	39,480
West Indian	6,520
Asian	7,582

Thus, as an example of the number of interviews calculated according to the above formula, the number of Asian interviews for Newtown ward, enumeration district 1, was:

$$\frac{51}{7,582} \times 300 = 2\cdot017$$

Possible biases in the main sample
The selection of 128 e.d.s from the four wards on the basis of degree of immigrant concentration meant that we left out those native whites and immigrants living in areas of lower concentration. This may have involved some bias, but the bias is essentially the same as that which was involved in selecting Handsworth as an area of study in the first place. What we wished to study were precisely the characteristics of immigrants and natives living in an area of high immigrant concentration.

Quota sampling within e.d.s was forced upon us by the real constraints under which we had to work. To have generated a suitable sample using random sampling techniques would have involved expenditure of time and money on recall visits which was far beyond our means.

Despite the inherent limitation of quota sampling, however, we did achieve a measure of geographical dispersion in our interviews by drawing on all 128 e.d.s, and there is some reason to suppose that the biases within each group were not of the grosser sort to which quota sampling is thought to be subject. Quota sampling might have produced few shift workers and an over-representation of retired people if interviews had not been planned at different times and the numbers checked against other sources.

Thus we did obtain a fairly large number of interviews with shift workers, and the large number of retired whites was roughly that suggested by census figures. It should also be noticed that prolonged interviews of an hour or so's duration, conducted often in the evenings or at weekends with householders in their homes, are not subject to exactly the same degree of criticism as a quota sample of individuals selected hurriedly and interviewed briefly on the street.

The council house sample

In addition to the main sample, a further sample consisting of a list of 100 white and 100 West Indian and Asian tenants on the Newtown estate was provided by the Birmingham Corporation Housing Department. Since West Indians and Asians constitute only about 10 per cent of the population of the estate, they were obviously over-represented in this sample, but this did not affect the main purpose of the sample which was precisely to compare the characteristics of white and black council tenants.

Subsequently it was decided to combine the council house sample for the different ethnic groups with the main samples for each of the groups. Strictly speaking, any such use of the combined sample would over-weight the percentage of immigrants who had council houses, and, in so far as they had special characteristics, bias the aggregated sample. The combined samples were not used in our analysis of the housing fate of different groups, but we still had to decide whether to weight our tables for other characteristics to allow for the inflated proportion of West Indians and the relatively low proportion of whites in the council house sample. (There were only five Asians amongst the 100 black tenants.) We found, however, that a comparison of weighted and unweighted tables presented only slight variations and we therefore simply presented unweighted tables A further study by Peter Ratcliffe (1979)[2] presents weighted and unweighted tables.

The sample was designed by the research team. The questionnaire was designed in collaboration with NOP Market Research Limited, who organized the interviewing, both at the pilot stage in April 1976 and in the final survey carried out between May and June 1976, and delivered 1,100 completed questionnaires to us for coding, data processing and analysis.

Interviewers were instructed to interview the following people:

1 'White' people born in Great Britain (England, Scotland, Wales, excluding Northern Ireland).
2 'West Indians'. Black people born in ex-British Caribbean territory. (It was expected that the majority of West Indians would come from Jamaica, Barbados, Trinidad and Tobago.)
3 'Asians'. Coloured people born in the Indian sub-continent, India, Pakistan (east or west) and Sri Lanka. Also people born in East Africa whose origin lay in the Indian sub-continent.

The birthplace of those respondents actually interviewed was as follows:

1 British	400	Great Britain
2 West Indian	331	Jamaica
	15	Barbados
	1	Trinidad and Tobago
	48	Elsewhere in West Indies
3 Asian	243	India
	42	Pakistan
	10	Elsewhere in Asia (e.g. Sri Lanka)
	10	East Africa

The structured interviewing was principally concerned with respondents' experiences in housing, employment and their own and their children's education. In addition, questions were included in the interview schedule dealing with the migration experiences of the West Indian and Asian respondents, and all respondents were asked about their perceptions of the local area and its problems.

A draft questionnaire was piloted in April 1976 by National Opinion Poll interviewers, twelve of whom were responsible for interviewing for the main survey, which was carried out between May and June 1976.

Some consideration was given to the possibility of employing ethnically matched interviewers. Research in the USA had indicated that apparently more 'accurate' answers are achieved by interviewers of the same ethnic group.[3] Black Americans apparently gave more 'socially acceptable' answers to white interviewers than to black interviewers. However, we do not think that American experiences can necessarily be generalized to apply to Britain. A survey in 1974 attempted to match interviewers to ethnic groups – articles appeared in the black newspapers *Grassroots* and *West Indian World* 'warning' black people that this was happening and recommending that black people did not respond to black interviewers at all. We decided to interview West Indian respondents with white interviewers and as an experiment to use Asian interviewers to interview part of our Asian sample, and be available as interpreters if necessary. In all, 105 interviews were undertaken by Asian interviewers and 200 by white interviewers; there was no apparent difference between the level and type of response achieved.

On average the interview lasted between one and one and a half hours. In many cases where a respondent who fitted the quota controls was not available when the interviewer called a recall was made at a convenient time. Interviewers were also asked to record the ethnic origins of non-responses. Interviewing was mainly carried out in the evenings and at weekends, and therefore was not biased towards retired and non-working heads of households.

The editing and coding of the survey data was undertaken by the whole of the research team, with the assistance of temporary coders. The data was analysed using the Statistical Package for the Social Sciences (SPSS) version 5 on the Burroughs 6700 Computer at Warwick university, with the assistance of Mr Peter Ratcliffe.

Youth survey

As the main survey progressed, the need for research concerning the problems of young people – the children of immigrants – became apparent. The economic recession of the mid 1970s was particularly affecting young black people and there was growing concern about the relationships between young black people and the police. It was therefore decided to undertake a small-scale study of West Indian and Asian young people between the ages of 16 and 21 in the main survey area. The respondents were drawn from a sampling frame of 259 young people, this being the total number of young people in the age-group 16–21 who were the children of respondents in the main survey.

An interview schedule was prepared and 50 young people were interviewed by the research team in February 1977. Out of the West Indian respondents, 11 were born in the United Kingdom and 14 in the West Indies. Out of the 25 Asians, 15 were born in India, 3 in Pakistan, 6 in East Africa and 1 in the United Kingdom. Twenty-seven boys and 23 girls were interviewed. The analysis of this small survey was done manually. The Birmingham Youth Employment Office provided information on 26 out of the 50 as a cross-check on some of the employment and careers advice data.

Notes

Chapter 1 Class analysis and colonial immigrants

1 The crucial work here is of course Mannheim's set of essays *Ideology and Utopia* (Mannheim, 1954). Too often Mannheim has been represented by Marxists as assigning to the consciousness of the so-called free-floating intellectuals the privileged position which Lukács assigned to the proletariat in his *History and Class Consciousness* (Lukacs, 1971).

2 See Durkheim (1933). This is not to say that Durkheim represented the conservative tradition of anti-Enlightenment writers. There are interesting veins of liberalism and socialism in his work. But both liberalism and socialism are ideologies which arise in the striving of men towards some natural overall unity based upon the division of labour. Durkheim expects that in the long run the divisions of labour in industrial society will promote individualism and mutual dependence within a context of social order.

3 There is hardly any need here to rehearse this debate. The perspective of structural-functionalism is best represented in Talcott Parsons, *The Social System* (Parsons, 1951), and in Talcott Parsons *et al.*, *Theories of Society* (1961). Among the criticisms which have been directed at Parsons are Dahrendorf's essay, 'Out of Utopia' (reprinted in his *Essays in the Theory of Society* (Dahrendorf, 1968)), C. Wright Mills's *The Sociological Imagination* (1959) and David Lockwood's 'Some Reflections on the Social System', *British Journal of Sociology*, June 1956, vol. 7.

4 This perspective goes back to Park's conception of a race relations cycle. It was used by writers such as Sheila Patterson in her *Dark Strangers* (Patterson, 1965) and by Michael Banton in his *The Coloured Quarter* (Banton, 1955). There are, however, more sophisticated theoretical elements in Banton's usage of this framework, deriving from Simmel's concept of the stranger. Banton has usefully classified his views in a note in *Race* (Banton, 1973b).

5 This usage is less central in American sociology precisely because the use of 'wave-after-wave' of immigrant labour made the ethnic group

far more important and prevented the overall development of social classes.

6 Marx's class analysis undergoes considerable development including *inter alia* a philosophical conception expressed in his *Critique of the Hegelian Philosophy of Right* (see Tucker, 1972), a sociological and political conception expressed in *The Communist Manifesto* and the political writings of the early 1850s (Marx and Engels, 1962), and a philosophical and economic conception based upon the notion of surplus value in *Capital*.

7 We refer here to Weber's *Economy and Society* (Weber, 1968, vol. 2, ch. 9). The chapter on social class in the first volume actually confuses social class, social status and social mobility, or, rather, attempts to combine them to arrive at a more complex composite model. This model is notoriously unsatisfactory as was Marx's incomplete attempt to conceptualize class in the third volume of *Capital*.

8 It is this tradition which has characterized much of the work of the London School of Economics (see Glass, 1954), although the concepts of social disadvantage and restricted social mobility on which they were based also involved an implicit protest against the British status order, and, even more strongly, an identification of the egalitarian case with Marxism. For a recent development of this tradition see Westergaard and Resler, *Class in a Capitalist Society* (1975).

9 The term 'underclass' occurs in our text for the first time at this point. It is a term derived from the Swedish which was used by Gunnar Myrdal to describe the situation of the 'unemployed and gradually unemployable persons and families at the bottom of a society, in which, for the majority of people above that level, the increasingly democratic structure of the educational system creates more and more liberty . . . at least over the course of two generations.' In using the term here we use it in a different sense because (a) the normal social pattern which we assume is not that of 'liberty' so much as welfare guaranteed by class politics, and (b) what we want to point to is the situation of immigrant minorities, who do not share in this welfare deal, but who, instead of forming an inert or despairing social residue, organize and act in their own 'underclass' interests, often relating themselves to colonial class positions. In a narrow, Weberian sense, we may speak of class and underclass in each of the allocative systems, such as employment, housing and education, but class and underclass formation takes place across all of these sectors. Like Baran and Sweezy, who see the immigrants and American blacks as fulfilling a psychological function as a scapegoat group, we see it as part of the definition of the immigrant situation that the immigrants are stigmatized, but we resist the notion that they are an inert mass characterized by a ghetto mentality or a culture of poverty (see Myrdal, 1964, and Baran and Sweezy, 1966).

10 It is really of some interest to note that the period during which the tripartite system of secondary education was established and tested and then partially rejected in favour of comprehensivization was also the period in which West Indian and Asian settlement in Britain

occurred. Some would say that this was a prime example of immigrants acting as a barium meal which helped to show up the inequalities of English society. Apart from the unpleasant, even racist, overtones of this metaphor, we would wish to point out that the educational system was grappling with two problems, of inequality and selection, overlaid on one another. The first was that of class inequality, the second that of inequality between white and black.

11 There is little reason to regard the actual reports and recommendations of the Parliamentary Select Committee on Race Relations and Immigration as constituting objective sociological analyses. Its members were, after all, party politicians drawn from political parties which, as the next chapter shows, worked all too often in terms of racist assumptions. None the less in an essentially paternalistic situation, the evidence offered by those who had contact with immigrant groups provides information not to be found elsewhere. Just as Marx learned much about the English working class from the reports of factory inspectors, so the Select Committee can be regarded as an important if partial source of evidence on the state of Britain's immigrant minorities in the 1960s and 1970s.

12 A recent work which grasps clearly the potential role of the ex-colonial immigrant to the metropolis is Hugh Tinker's *Race, Conflict and the International Order* (1977). We see that work as involving a valuable ideal typical overstatement of this point. It does none the less act as a reference point against which our data should be measured. The way in which immigrant class formation in Britain articulates with the Third World Revolution is discussed in the final chapter.

Chapter 2 British political ideologies and the race question

1 The term 'ideology' is used here to refer to theories and images of society which 'idealize' certain aspects of reality (i.e. represent the *status quo* falsely as conforming with some central value). This represents a special usage within the more general usage of Karl Mannheim who uses the term to refer to all theories which misrepresent reality in order to stabilize it. The matter is complicated by the fact than in Mannheim's work liberal and socialist thought appears as 'utopian', as using social thought to accelerate change rather than to stabilize society. But the fact is that the same theories which may be utopian when applied in the European context are used as ideologies when applied to the Empire.

2 The following is a full list of the publications from which this chronology is drawn:

Banton, Michael, *Racial Minorities*, London, Fontana, 1973.
Birmingham Post and Mail cuttings, 1950–72, Birmingham Central Library – Local Studies department.
Birmingham Post and Mail cuttings, 1972–7, Warwick University Library – records.
Department of Employment, Unit of Manpower Studies, *The Role of Immigrants in the Labour Market*, London, Department of Employment, 1976.

329

Dhondy, Mala, 'The Strike at Imperial Typewriters', *Race Today*, vol. 6, no. 7, July 1974.

Dummett, Ann, *Citizenship and Nationality*, London, Runnymede Trust, 1976.

Evans, Peter, *Publish and be Damned*, London, Runnymede Trust, 1976.

Foot, Paul, *Immigration and Race in British Politics*, Harmondsworth, Penguin, 1965.

Foot, Paul, *The Rise of Enoch Powell*, Harmondsworth, Penguin, 1969.

Griffiths, Peter, *A Question of Colour*, London, Leslie Frewin, 1966.

Hiro, Dilip, *Black British, White British*, Harmondsworth, Penguin, 1971.

Humphrey, D., and Ward, M., *Passports and Politics*, Harmondsworth, Penguin, 1974.

Lawrence, D., *Black Migrants, White Natives*, London, Cambridge University Press, 1974.

Patterson, Sheila, *Immigration and Race Relations in Britain 1960–67*, London, Oxford University Press, 1969.

Peach, Ceri, *West Indian Migration to Britain*, London, Oxford University Press, 1968.

Prem, Dhani, *The Parliamentary Leper – a history of colour prejudice in Britain*, London, Metric Publications, 1965.

Rogaly, Joseph, *Grunwick*, Harmondsworth, Penguin, 1977.

Rose, E. J. B., *et al.*, *Colour and Citizenship*, London, Oxford University Press, 1969.

Official publications (all published in London by HMSO):

Colonial Office, *Jamaica: Annual Report for 1946*, 1949.

British Nationality Act, 1948.

Commonwealth Immigrants Act, 1962.

Immigration from the Commonwealth, Cmnd 2379, White Paper, 1965.

Race Relations Act, 1965.

Department of Education and Science, *The Education of Immigrants*, circular 7/65, 1965.

Commonwealth Immigrants Act, 1968.

Race Relations Act, 1968.

Select Committee on Race Relations and Immigration, *The Problems of Coloured School-leavers 1968–9*, 1969.

Select Committee on Race Relations and Immigration, *Housing*, 1971.

Immigration Act, 1971.

Select Committee on Race Relations and Immigration, *Police/Immigrant Relations*, 1972.

Select Committee on Race Relations and Immigration, *Education 1972–3*, 1973.

Pakistan Act, 1973.

Select Committee on Race Relations and Immigration, *Employment*, 1974.

Home Office, *Immigration Rules: Commonwealth Citizens*, Cmnd 5715, 1974.

Department of Education and Science, *Educational Disadvantage and the Educational Needs of Immigrants*, Cmnd 5720, 1974.

Select committee on Race Relations and Immigration, *The Organiza-tion of Race Relations Administration*, 1975.

Home Office, *Racial Discrimination*, Cmnd 6234, 1975.

Department of the Environment, *Race Relations and Housing*, Cmnd 6232, 1975.

Race Relations Act, 1976.

Select Committee on Race Relations and Immigration, *The West Indian Community*, 1977.

Department of the Environment, *Inner Area Studies*, final reports, 1977a.

Department of the Environment, *Policy for the Inner Cities*, Cmnd 6845, White Paper, 1977b.

3 Archbishop Coggan's words on this point were, 'There must be a clearly defined limit to the numbers of those allowed into this country. There are signs that our present legislation needs looking into on this point', *Birmingham Post*, 12 July 1976.

4 The full Ladywood by-election result was:

Labour	8,227
Conservative	4,402
National Front	888
Liberal	765
Socialist Unity	534
J. Hunte (Ind.)	336
Socialist Workers	152
Reform	63
Other independent	46

5 The result of this first PEP survey was reported in Daniel, 1968. A follow-up some seven years later was reported in Smith, 1977.

6 Mr Maurice Foley, the junior minister concerned with race relations, was in fact carrying out enquiries with a view to the formulation of an adequate policy, but the White Paper based on the work of Mr Herbert Bowden's Cabinet committee was published long before these enquiries were complete.

7 The first PEP survey was used in this way. John Rex served on its supervisory committee, not because he believed that further 'scientific' proof of discrimination was necessary, but because the then chairman of the Race Relations Board made it clear that survey data of this kind would strengthen Roy Jenkins's hand in the Cabinet.

Chapter 4 Black immigrants at work

1 Figures refer to employment complaints (other than those wholly dealt with by industry machinery) disposed of between 1 January 1975 and 30 June 1976, and refer to complaints under Sections 3(1)(a), 3(1)(b), 3(1)(c), 4 and 12 of the 1968 Race Relations Act. (See Report of the Race Relations Board, 1975–6, Table 6.)

Chapter 5 Black immigrants and the housing system

1 Amongst the most important discussion of the concept are the following: Haddon (1970), Lambert and Filkin (1971), Lambert,

Blackaby, and Paris (1975), Ward (1975), Pahl (1969 and 1970), Davis and Taylor (1970), Bell (1977), Richmond (1973), Pickvance (1976), and Clarke and Ginsborg (1975).

Haddon suggests that Rex's use of the concept emphasizes type of housing actually occupied to the exclusion of access to housing. Lambert and Filkin argue that the concept rests upon the notion of a unitary scale of values which does not hold in reality. Ward, and Davis and Taylor, both emphasize that housing stress might not lead to ethnic conflict, while Davis and Taylor also place emphasis upon the profit motive amongst immigrant landlords. Richmond argues on the basis of attitude studies that Rex's implied prediction of an association between inferior housing position and racist attitudes is not borne out by observation.

Pahl re-states the theory to emphasize what he calls the class of 'those who must rent' and connects this debate with the work of Manuel Castells. Pickvance suggests that Rex's use of the concept escapes some of Castells's strictures on urban sociology in general. Lambert, Blackaby and Paris connect their work with that of Castells by arguing that the system of housing queues is part of the ideological state apparatus which mystifies social reality. Bell, reviewing the work of Rex and Castells amongst others, asks of a system of housing class conflict, 'Who is exploiting who?'

The best analysis of the theoretical and methodological problems involved in the use of the concept is to be found in Ward's thesis.

Rex has replied to some of these writers in *Race* (Rex, 1971) and in the *Australian and New Zealand Journal of Sociology* (Rex, 1977).

2 In fact, all the recent evidence on owner-occupation by immigrants in the inner-city reinforces our conclusion that there is a class of those who 'must buy' which is actually less privileged than Pahl's class of those who 'must rent'. See *New Community*, vol. 6, nos 1 and 2, winter 1977–8, especially the articles by Smith and Karn.

3 Karn's position has now clearly changed. In her *New Community* article she speaks of the coloured population 'progressing towards a monopoly of the areas of worst housing in the city' and says that 'for the most part their housing in these areas is owner-occupied'.

4 See the report of the Department of the Environment's inner-city team in Small Heath entitled *Unequal City* (Department of the Environment, 1977c).

5 It should be noted that, although these averages are well below the overcrowding level of 1.5 persons per room, statistical minorities were living above that level. Analysis of these distributions will be reported by Peter Ratcliffe in a separate volume.

Chapter 6   Black immigrants, schools and the class structure

1 The best documented study of disadvantage in education is, of course, A. H. Halsey, *Educational Priority* (1972) in five volumes. Although the focus of volume 1 is on disadvantage in general, the volume of statistics (volume 2) shows clearly that West Indian and Asian children are less successful in a number of tests of educational achievement.

2 FA/FSE are Indian qualifications, intermediate between matriculation and a bachelor's degree.

Chapter 7   From immigrants to ethnic minority

1 The question being piloted by the OPCS in 1978 was quite surprising. It seems that the decision to try it resulted from the high refusal rate produced by a question on parents' birthplace. But that question had been asked at a time when the Government was restricting the rights of non-patrials. The new question asks respondents to declare whether they are white or, as though this was an alternative, come from different countries or groups of countries. It seems clear that this question will include all white immigrants whether from Europe, or from the Commonwealth, with the British, while any other choice of answer will identify the respondent as 'non-white'. The justification of this cannot be that the Government is interested in ethnic self-identification as our Table 7.12 shows. It can only be based upon the assumption that there is a colour bar in Britain, even though those who drew up the question might see the advantage of these statistics as lying in the possibility of checking on whether non-white British are being treated equally.
2 Independent studies of the Pakistani community in Sparkbrook have been carried out by our colleague Pervaiz Nazir and will be reported in other publications.

Chapter 8   Race, community and conflict

1 The methodological and theoretical problem of the relation between ideal typical constructions and ideologies is one of the major themes of the extended excursus on method and theory in Appendix 1.
2 In fairness to Mr Andrews we should like to point out that he expressed doubts about our research at its outset and, on hearing an account of part of it when it was completed, said that he saw us as working within the assumptions of white racism.
3 A serious study of West Indian religious organizations is being undertaken by the Rev. Roswith Gerloff, and we learned something of the complexity as well as the rationality of West Indian religion from her. The publication of her theology thesis will, we believe, open up and clarify the whole question of the social functions of these churches.
4 There was a split in the National Front in the Midlands at the end of 1976 and a number of leading members, including the Finnegans, whose involvement in the movement was based upon local populism rather than on a doctrinaire acceptance of its ideologies, parted company with it.

Appendix 2   Research methodology

1 Aaron Cicourel in his *Method and Measurement in Sociology* (1964) refers to Rex's *Key Problems of Sociological Theory* (1961) as containing a 'lucid discussion of differences in the substantive foundations of social theory and research' (p. 225). That same perspective still in-

forms this study, even though its argument builds upon survey data, amongst other sources. The use of open-ended questions and the interpretation of 'bits' of data in terms of meaningful sequences of action have, we believe, helped us to transcend the limitations which the coding process and measurement by fiat usually involve. Moreover, in our last three chapters, when we talk of the various forms of class and group-consciousness amongst immigrants, we are looking, not merely at the attributes of individuals, but at the way in which those individuals are constructing and describing their own social world.

2 P. Ratcliffe, *Black Immigrants in Birmingham*, Routledge & Kegan Paul, forthcoming.

3 H. Schuman and J. M. Converse, 1971, 'The Effects of Black and White Interviewers on Black Response 1968', *Public Opinion Quarterly*, 35, 1971.

J. A. Williams, 'Interviewer – respondent – inter-action', *Sociometry*, vol. 27, 1964.

D. O. Price and R. Searle, *Some Effects of Interviewer Respondent Inter-action on Responses in a Survey Situation*, American Statistical Association, 1961.

The questionnaire and the data from the survey are being deposited with the Data Bank at Essex University.

Bibliography

ALLEN, SHEILA, and SMITH, CHRISTOPHER (1975), 'Minority Group Experience of the Transition from Education to Work', in *Entering the World of Work – Some Sociological Perspectives*, ed. P. Brannen, London, Department of Employment, HMSO.

ALTHUSSER, LOUIS (1971), *Lenin and Philosophy and Other Essays*, London, New Left Books.

ASAAM, WILLIAM (1976), 'Self-help: Analysis of the Concept', *CRC Journal*, vol. 4, no. 4, April.

ASHBY, B., MORRISON, A., and BUTCHER, H. (1970), 'The Abilities and Attainments of Immigrant Children', *Research in Education*, no. 4, London.

BAGLEY, CHRISTOPHER (1970), *Social Structure and Prejudice in Five Boroughs*, London, Institute of Race Relations.

BAGLEY, CHRISTOPHER (1971), 'A Comparative Study of Social Environment and Intelligence in West Indian and English Children', *Social and Economic Studies*, vol. 20, no. 4.

BANTON, MICHAEL (1955), *The Coloured Quarter: Negro Immigrants in an English City*, London, Cape.

BANTON, MICHAEL (1973a), *Racial Minorities*, London, Fontana.

BANTON, MICHAEL (1973b), 'The Stranger Hypothesis', *Race*, vol. 15, no. 1, July.

BARAN, PAUL, and SWEEZY, PAUL (1966), *Monopoly Capital: An Essay on the American Economic and Social Order*, New York, Monthly Review Press.

BEETHAM, DAVID (1967), *Immigrant School Leavers and the Youth Employment Service in Birmingham*, London, Institute of Race Relations Special Series.

BELL, COLIN (1977), 'On Housing Classes', *Australian and New Zealand Journal of Sociology*, vol. 13, no. 1.

BELL, DANIEL (1960), *The End of Ideology*, Chicago, Free Press.

BEVERIDGE, WILLIAM (1944), *Full Employment in a Free Society: A Report*, London, Allen and Unwin.

335

BIESHEUVEL, S. (1969), 'Psychological Tests and Their Application to Non-European Pupils', *Year Book of Education*, London, Evans.

Birmingham Broadside (1976), 'Leyland – Black Car Workers Hit by Racial Discrimination', *Broadside*, no. 5, December 1976–January 1977.

BOLT, CHRISTINE (1971), *Victorian Attitudes to Race*, London, Routledge & Kegan Paul.

BOSANQUET, NICHOLAS, and DOERINGER, PETER (1973), 'Is There a Dual Labour Market in Great Britain?', *Economic Journal*, vol. 83.

British Nationality and Status of Aliens Act, 1948, London, HMSO.

BRITTAN, ELAINE (1976), 'Multi-Racial Education 2. Teacher Opinion on Aspects of School Life – Pupils and Teachers', *Educational Research*, vol. 18, no. 3.

BROWN, JOHN (1977), *Shades of Grey: Police-West Indian Relations in Handsworth*, Cranfield, Cranfield Police Studies.

BURGESS, TYRELL (1968), *Matters of Principle, Labour's Last Chance*, Harmondsworth, Penguin.

BURNEY, ELIZABETH (1967), *Housing on Trial: A Study of Immigrants and Local Government*, London, Oxford University Press.

CASTELLS, MANUEL (1977), *The Urban Question*, London, Arnold.

CASTLES, STEPHEN, and KOSACK, GODULA (1973). *Immigrant Workers and the Class Structure*, London, Oxford University Press and Institute of Race Relations.

CENTRAL STATISTICAL OFFICE (1977), *Social Trends*, no. 8, London, HMSO.

CICOUREL, AARON (1964), *Method and Measurement in Sociology*, New York, Free Press.

CITY OF BIRMINGHAM (1968), General Purposes Committee Report in *Birmingham City Council Proceedings*, 19 July.

CITY OF BIRMINGHAM (1973), *A New Plan for the City. First Stage. Report of Survey: Employment and Industry*, Birmingham City Council.

CLARKE, SIMON, and GINSBURG, NORMAN (1975), *The Political Economy of Housing*, paper presented to CSE Conference, London, March.

COARD, B. (1971), *How the West Indian Child is Made Educationally Subnormal in the British School System*, London, New Beacon Books.

COLONIAL OFFICE (1948), *Jamaica: Annual Report for 1946* (58–1–22–46), London, HMSO.

COMMISSION ON INDUSTRIAL RELATIONS (1971), *Birmingham Aluminium Casting (1903) Company Limited, Dartmouth, Auto Castings Limited, Midland Motor Cylinder Company Limited*, report no. 4, London, HMSO.

Commonwealth Immigrants Act, 1962, London, HMSO.

Commonwealth Immigrants Act, 1968, London, HMSO.

COMMONWEALTH IMMIGRANTS' ADVISORY COUNCIL (1964), *Third Report* (Cmnd 2458), London, HMSO.

COMMUNITY DEVELOPMENT PROJECTS (1976), *Profits Against Houses: An Alternative Guide to Housing Finance*, London, CDP.

COMMUNITY DEVELOPMENT PROJECTS (1977), *Gilding the Ghetto: The State and the Poverty Experiments*, London, CDP.

COMMUNITY RELATIONS COMMISSION (1974), *Unemployment and Homelessness*, London, CRC.

COMMUNITY RELATIONS COMMISSION (1975), *Wednesday's Children*, London, CRC.

COMMUNITY RELATIONS COMMISSION (1976), *Between Two Cultures: A Study of relationships between Generations in the Asian Community in Britain*, London, CRC.

CONSERVATIVE POLITICAL CENTRE (1975), *Towards a New Citizenship*, London, CPC.

COX, OLIVER CROMWELL (1948), *Caste, Class and Race*, New York, Doubleday.

CROSSMAN, RICHARD (1975), *The Diaries of a Cabinet Minister*, vol. 1, London, Hamish Hamilton and Cape.

DAHRENDORF, RALF (1959), *Class and Class Conflict in Industrial Society*, London, Routledge & Kegan Paul.

DAHRENDORF, RALF (1968), *Essays in the Theory of Society*, London, Routledge & Kegan Paul.

DANIEL, WILLIAM (1968), *Racial Discrimination in England*, Harmondsworth, Penguin Special.

DAVIS, JON GOWER, and TAYLOR, JOHN (1970), 'Race, Community and No Conflict', *New Society*, no. 406, 9 July.

DEAKIN, NICHOLAS, ed. (1965), *Colour and the British Electorate 1964*, London, Pall Mall Press.

DEAKIN, NICHOLAS (1969), 'Race and Human Rights in the City', in *Urban Studies*, vol. 6, no. 3. November.

DEAKIN, NICHOLAS (1970), *Colour, Citizenship and British Society*, London, Panther Books.

DEEDES, WILLIAM (1968), *Race Without Rancour*. London, Conservative Political Centre.

DENTON, B. (1975), 'The Development of Consortia', *Trends in Education*, no. 2, June.

DEPARTMENT OF EDUCATION AND SCIENCE (1965), *The Education of Immigrants*, circular 7/65, London, HMSO.

DEPARTMENT OF EDUCATION AND SCIENCE (1967–72), *Statistics in Education*, annually, London, HMSO.

DEPARTMENT OF EDUCATION AND SCIENCE (1973), *Educational arrangements for immigrant children who may need special education*, circular letter, London, HMSO.

DEPARTMENT OF EDUCATION AND SCIENCE (1974), *Educational Disadvantage and the Educational Needs of Immigrant Children*, Cmnd 5720, London, HMSO.

DEPARTMENT OF EMPLOYMENT (1972), *Report of a Committee of Inquiry into a Dispute Between Employees of the Mansfield Hosiery Mills Limited, Loughborough, and their Employer*, London, HMSO.

DEPARTMENT OF EMPLOYMENT, UNIT OF MANPOWER STUDIES (1976), *The Role of Immigrants in the Labour Market*, London, Department of Employment.

DEPARTMENT OF THE ENVIRONMENT (1968), *Old Houses into New Homes*, Cmnd 3602, London, HMSO.

DEPARTMENT OF THE ENVIRONMENT (1975), *Race Relations and Housing: Observations on the Report on Housing of the Select Committee on Race*

Relations and Immigration, Cmnd 6232, London, HMSO.

DEPARTMENT OF THE ENVIRONMENT (1977a), *Inner Area Studies: Liverpool, Birmingham and Lambeth: Summaries of Consultants' Final Reports*, London, HMSO.

DEPARTMENT OF THE ENVIRONMENT (1977b), *Policy for the Inner Cities*, Cmnd 6845, London, HMSO.

DEPARTMENT OF THE ENVIRONMENT (1977c), *Unequal City. Final Report of the Birmingham Inner Area Study*, London, HMSO.

DHAYA, BADR (1973), 'Pakistanis in Britain: Transients or Settlers', *Race*, vol. 14, pp. 246–77.

DHONDY, MALA (1974), 'The Strike at Imperial Typewriters', *Race Today*, vol. 6, no. 7, July.

DOERINGER, PETER, and PIORE, MICHAEL (1971), *Internal Labour Markets and Manpower Analysis*, Lexington, Mass., Heath.

DUMMETT, ANN (1976), *Citizenship and Nationality*, London, Runnymede Trust.

DURKHEIM, ÉMILE (1933), *The Division of Labour in Society*, Chicago, Free Press.

EDWARDS, V. (1979) *The West Indian Language Issue in British Schools*, London, Routledge & Kegan Paul.

EVANS, PETER (1971), *Attitudes of Young Immigrants*, London, Runnymede Trust.

EVERSLEY, D. (1964), 'Industry and Trade 1500–1880', *Victoria County History of Warwickshire*, vol. 7, London, Oxford University Press.

EYSENCK, H. (1971), *Race Intelligence and Education*, London, Temple Smith.

FERRON, O. (1966), 'The Test Performance of Coloured Children', *Educational Research*, vol. 8, no. 1.

FISHER, T. L. (1975), 'The WELD Experiment', *New Society*, vol. 33, 14 August.

FOOT, PAUL (1965), *Immigration and Race in British Politics*, Harmondsworth, Penguin.

FOOT, PAUL (1969), *The Rise of Enoch Powell*, Harmondsworth, Penguin.

GILES, RAYMOND (1977), *The West Indian Experience in British Schools*, London, Heinemann.

GLASER, BARNEY, and STRAUSS, ANSELM (1968), *The Discovery of Grounded Theory: Strategies for Qualitative Research*, London, Weidenfeld & Nicolson.

GLASS, DAVID, ed. (1954), *Social Mobility in Britain*, London, Routledge & Kegan Paul.

GLASS, RUTH (1960), *Newcomers*, London, Allen & Unwin.

GOLDMANN, LUCIEN (1969), *The Human Sciences and Philosophy*, London, Cape.

GOULDNER, ALVIN W. (1976), *The Dialectic of Ideology and Technology*, London, Macmillan.

HABERMAS, JURGEN (1972), *Knowledge and Human Interest*, London, Heinemann.

HADDON, ROY (1970), 'A Minority in a Welfare State Society: Location of West Indians in the London Housing Market', *New Atlantis*, vol. 2, no. 1.

HALSEY, A. H. (1972), *Educational Priority, vol. 1, Educational Priority Areas, Problems and Policies*, London, HMSO.

HATCH, STEPHEN, and THOMPSON, DOROTHY (1958), 'Discussion: The Welfare State', *New Reasoner*, vol. 1, no. 4.

HEINEMAN, BENJAMIN (1972), *The Politics of Powerlessness*, London, Oxford University Press and Institute of Race Relations.

HILL, MICHAEL, and ISSACHAROFF, RUTH (1971), *Community Action and Race Relations. A Study of Community Relations Committees in Britain*, London, Institute of Race Relations.

HIRO, DILIP (1971), *Black British, White British*, Harmondsworth, Penguin.

HOBHOUSE, LEONARD TRELAWNEY (1951), *Morals in Evolution*, London, Chapman & Hall.

HOME OFFICE (1965), *Immigration from the Commonwealth*, Cmnd 2739, London, HMSO.

HOME OFFICE (1974). *Immigration Rules: Commonwealth Citizens: Statement of Change for Control on Entry*, Cmnd 5715, London, HMSO.

HOME OFFICE (1975), *Racial Discrimination*, Cmnd 6234, London, HMSO.

HOME OFFICE (1977), *British Nationality Law, Discussion of Possible Changes*, Cmnd 6795, London, HMSO.

HOUSING ADVICE LIAISON GROUP (1973), 'Allocation, Priorities and Housing Management. Some Observations on the Present Housing Situation in Birmingham', paper sent to Director of Housing, Birmingham City Council, by HALG.

HUGHES, H. STUART (1959), *Consciousness and Society*, London, MacGibbon & Kee.

HUMPHRY, DEREK, and JOHN, GUS (1971), *Because They're Black*, Harmondsworth, Penguin.

HUMPHRY, DEREK, and WARD, MICHAEL (1974), *Passports and Politics*, Harmondsworth, Penguin.

Immigration Act, 1971, London, HMSO.

JACOBS, JANE (1962), *The Death and Life of Great American Cities*, London, Cape.

JOHN, AUGUSTINE (1972), *Race in the Inner City*, London, Runnymede Trust.

KARN, VALERIE (1967), a note on 'Race, Community and Conflict: A Study of Sparkbrook', *Race*, vol. 9, no. 1, July.

KARN, VALERIE (1978), 'The Financing of Owner Occupation and its Impact on Ethnic Minorities', *New Community*, vol. 6, nos 1 and 2, winter 1977–8.

KEAT, RUSSELL, and URRY, JOHN (1975), *Social Theory as Science*, London, Routledge & Kegan Paul.

KIERNAN, V. G. (1969), *The Lords of Human Kind; European Attitudes Towards the Outside World in the Imperial Age*, London, Weidenfeld & Nicolson.

KLINEBERG, OTTO (1935), *Negro Intelligence and Selective Migration*, New York, Columbia University Press.

KUPER, LEO, ed. (1975), *Race, Science and Society*, London, Allen & Unwin for UNESCO Press.

LAMBERT, JOHN, BLACKABY, ROBERT, and PARIS, CHRISTOPHER (1975),

'Neighbourhood Politics and Housing Opportunities', paper presented to the Centre for Environmental Studies' Urban Sociology Conference, 'Urban Change and Conflict', held at York University, January.

LAMBERT, JOHN, and FILKIN, CAMILLA (1971), 'Ethnic Choice and Preference in Housing', final report to the Social Science Research Council on the pilot research project, London, Centre for Urban and Regional Studies (unpublished).

LAWRENCE, DANIEL (1974), *Black Migrants, White Natives: a Study of Race Relations in Nottingham*, Cambridge University Press.

LAYTON-HENRY, ZIG, and TAYLOR, STAN (1977), 'Race at the Polls', *New Society*, vol. 41, no. 777, 25 August.

LESTER, ANTHONY, and DEAKIN, NICHOLAS, eds. (1967), *Policies for Social Equality*, London, Fabian Society, Fabian Research Series.

LIPSET, SEYMOUR MARTIN (1960), *Political Man*, London, Heinemann.

LITTLE, ALAN (1975), 'The Background of Under-achievement in Immigrant Children in London', in G. K. Verma, and C. Bagley, *Race and Education across Cultures*, London, Heinemann.

LOMAS, GILLIAN G. B. (1973), *Census 1971. The Coloured Population of Great Britain*, London, Runnymede Trust.

LUKÁCS, GEORG (1971), *History and Class Consciousness*, London, Merlin Press.

MCFIE, J., and THOMPSON, J. (1970), 'Intellectual Abilities of Immigrant Children', *British Journal of Educational Psychology*, vol. 40, London.

MCPHERSON, CRAWFORD B. (1962), *The Political Theory of Possessive Individualism*, Oxford, Clarendon Press.

MANNHEIM, KARL (1954), *Ideology and Utopia*, London, Routledge & Kegan Paul.

MARSH, PETER (1967), *The Anatomy of a Strike: Unions, Employers and Punjabi Workers in a Southall Factory*, London, Institute of Race Relations.

MARSHALL, THOMAS H. (1950), *Citizenship and Social Class*, Cambridge University Press.

MARX, KARL (1972), 'Contribution to the Critique of Hegel's Philosophy of Right, Introduction', in Tucker, 1972.

MARX, KARL, and ENGELS, FREDERICK (1962), *Selected Works*, London, Lawrence & Wishart.

MERTON, ROBERT (1957), *Social Theory and Social Structure*, Chicago, Free Press.

MILLS, CHARLES WRIGHT (1959a), *The Power Elite*, New York, Oxford University Press.

MILLS, CHARLES WRIGHT (1959b), *The Sociological Imagination*, New York, Oxford University Press.

MILSON, FRED (1961), *Operation Integration: An Enquiry into the Experience of West Indians Living in Birmingham, with Particular Reference to Children and Young People*, Birmingham, Westhill College.

MINISTRY OF EDUCATION (1963), *English for Immigrants*, no. 43, London, HMSO.

MINISTRY OF HOUSING AND LOCAL GOVERNMENT (1969), *Council Housing Procedures and Priorities*, London, HMSO.

MYRDAL, GUNNAR (1964), *Challenge to Affluence*, London, Gollancz.

MYRDAL, GUNNAR, et al. (1969), *The American Dilemma: The Negro Problem and Modern Democracy*, New York, Harper & Row.

NATIONAL ASSOCIATION FOR MULTI-RACIAL EDUCATION (1975), *Policy Statement*.

PAHL, RAYMOND, ed. (1969), *Readings in Urban Sociology*, London, Pergamon Press.

PAHL, RAYMOND (1970), *Whose City?*, London, Longman.

Pakistan Act, 1973, London, HMSO.

PARIS, CHRIS, and BLACKABY, BOB (1973), *Research Directions in Urban Sociology: Neighbourhood Associations and Housing Opportunities*, working paper no. 16, Centre for Urban and Regional Studies, University of Birmingham.

PARSONS, TALCOTT (1951), *The Social System*, Chicago, Free Press.

PARSONS, TALCOTT (1954), *Essays in Sociological Theory*, Chicago, Free Press.

PARSONS, TALCOTT, et al. (1961), *Theories of Society: Foundations of Modern Sociological Theory*, New York, Free Press.

PATTERSON, SHEILA (1965), *Dark Strangers: A Study of West Indians in London*, Harmondsworth, Penguin.

PATTERSON, SHEILA (1968), *Immigrants in Industry*, London, Oxford University Press for the Institute of Race Relations.

PAYNE, J. (1969), 'A Comparative Study of the Mental Ability of 7 and 8 Year Old British and West Indian Children in a West Midlands Town', *British Journal of Educational Psychology*, vol. 39, London.

PEACH, CERI (1968), *West Indian Migration to Britain*, London, Oxford University Press.

PICKVANCE, CHRISTOPHER (1976), *Urban Sociology: Critical Essays*, London, Tavistock.

PLOWDEN REPORT (1967), *Children in their Primary Schools*, London, HMSO.

POWER, J. (1967), *Immigrants in School*, London, Council and Education Press.

PREM, DHANI (1965), *The Parliamentary Leper – A History of Colour Prejudice in Britain*, London, Metric Publications.

Race Relations Act, 1965, London, HMSO.

Race Relations Act, 1968, London, HMSO.

Race Relations Act, 1976, London, HMSO.

REX, JOHN (1961), *Key Problems of Sociological Theory*, London, Routledge & Kegan Paul.

REX, JOHN (1968), 'The Race Relations Catastrophe', in Burgess, 1968.

REX, JOHN (1970), *Race Relations in Sociological Theory*, London, Weidenfeld & Nicolson.

REX, JOHN (1971), 'The Concept of Housing Class in the Sociology of Race Relations', *Race*, vol. 12, no. 3, London. Reprinted in Rex, (1973b).

REX, JOHN (1973a), *Discovering Sociology*, London, Routledge & Kegan Paul.

REX, JOHN (1973b), *Race, Colonialism and the City*, London, Routledge & Kegan Paul.

REX, JOHN (1974), *Sociology and the Demystification of the Modern World*, London, Routledge & Kegan Paul.

REX, JOHN (1977a), 'New Nations and Ethnic Minorities', in UNESCO, 1977.

REX, JOHN (1977b), 'Sociological Theory and the City – A Response to Some Recent trends in Australian Urban Sociology', *Australian and New Zealand Journal of Sociology*, vol. 13, no. 3.

REX, JOHN, and MOORE, ROBERT (1967), *Race, Community and Conflict*, London, Oxford University Press and Institute of Race Relations.

RICHMOND, ANTHONY (1973), *Migration and Race Relations in an English City: A Study in Bristol*, London, Oxford University Press for the Institute of Race Relations.

ROGALY, JOSEPH (1977), *Grunwick*, Harmondsworth, Penguin.

ROSE, E. J. B., *et al.* (1969), *Colour and Citizenship: A Report on British Race Relations*, London, Oxford University Press.

SAVILLE, JOHN (1957), 'The Welfare State', *New Reasoner*, vol. 1, no. 3.

SCHUTZ, ALFRED (1967), *Collected Papers, I, The Problem of Social Reality*, The Hague, Martinus Nijhoff.

SELECT COMMITTEE ON RACE RELATIONS AND IMMIGRATIONS 1968–9 (1969), *The Problems of Coloured School-Leavers*, vols 1–4, London, HMSO.

SELECT COMMITTEE ON RACE RELATIONS AND IMMIGRATION (1970), *Control of Commonwealth Immigration*, vols 1–2, London, HMSO.

SELECT COMMITTEE ON RACE RELATIONS AND IMMIGRATION (1971), *Housing*, vols 1–4, London, HMSO.

SELECT COMMITTEE ON RACE RELATIONS AND IMMIGRATION (1972a), *Police/Immigrant Relations*, vols 1–3, London, HMSO.

SELECT COMMITTEE ON RACE RELATIONS AND IMMIGRATION (1972b), *Statistics of Immigrant School Pupils*, London, HMSO.

SELECT COMMITTEE ON RACE RELATIONS AND IMMIGRATION 1972–3 (1973), *Education*, vols 1–3, London, HMSO.

SELECT COMMITTEE ON RACE RELATIONS AND IMMIGRATION (1974), *Employment*, vols 1–2, London, HMSO.

SELECT COMMITTEE ON RACE RELATIONS AND IMMIGRATION (1975), *Organization of Race Relations Administration*, vols 1–3, London, HMSO.

SELECT COMMITTEE ON RACE RELATIONS AND IMMIGRATION (1977), *The West Indian Community*, vols 1–3, London, HMSO.

SIMMEL, GEORG (1959), 'How is Society Possible?', in Kurt, Wolff, *Georg Simmel 1858–1958*, Columbus, Ohio State University Press.

SMITH, BARBARA (1964), 'Industry and Trade 1880–1960', in *Victoria County History of Warwickshire*, vol. 7, London, Oxford University Press.

SMITH, DAVID (1977), *Racial Disadvantage in Britain*, Harmondsworth, Penguin.

SMITH, DAVID (1978), 'The Housing of Racial Minorities – Its Unusual Nature', *New Community*, vol. 6, nos 1 and 2, winter 1977–8.

SOREL, GEORGES (1961), *Reflections on Violence*, London, Collier-Macmillan.

SUTCLIFFE, ANTHONY, and SMITH, ROGER (1974), *History of Birmingham, vol III, Birmingham 1939–1970*, London, Oxford University Press.

TANSLEY, A. E. (1973), 'Special Educational Treatment in Schools', *Review*, no. 15, summer.

TAWNEY, RICHARD H. (1964), *Religion and the Rise of Capitalism*, Harmondsworth, Penguin.

TINKER, HUGH (1977), *Race, Conflict and International Order*, London, Macmillan.

TOMLINSON, SALLY (forthcoming), 'Decision-making in Special Education with Some Reference to Immigrant Children', Ph.D. thesis in preparation, University of Warwick.

TUCKER, ROBERT (1972), *The Marx-Engels Reader*, New York, Norton.

TUCKER, ROBERT (1974), *A Lenin Anthology*, New York, Norton.

UNESCO (1977), *Race and Class in Post-Colonial Society*, Paris.

Victoria County History of Staffordshire (1967), vols 1–2, London, Oxford University Press.

WARD, R. (1975), 'Residential Succession and Race Relations in Moss-Side, Manchester,' Ph.D. thesis, University of Manchester.

WARNER, WILLIAM LLOYD (1942), *The Status System of a Modern Community*, New Haven, Yale University Press.

WEBER, MAX (1968), *Economy and Society*, 3 vols, New York, Bedminster Press.

WEDDERBURN, DOROTHY (1965), 'Facts and Theories of the Welfare State', in *Socialist Register*, II.

WEIGHTMAN, GAVIN (1976), 'Urban Aid', *New Society*, vol. 38, no. 739, 2 December.

WESTERGAARD, JOHN, and RESLER, HENRIETTA (1975), *Class in a Capitalist Society*, London, Heinemann.

YULE, W., *et al.* (1975), 'Children of West Indian Immigrants, II, Intellectual Performance and Reading Attainment', *Journal of Child Psychology and Psychiatry*, vol. 16.

343

Index

Routledge Social Science Series

Routledge & Kegan Paul   London and Boston

68–74 Carter Lane London EC4V 5EL
9 Park Street Boston Mass 02108

Contents

Authors wishing to submit manuscripts for any series in
this catalogue should send them to the Social Science Editor,
Routledge & Kegan Paul Ltd, 68–74 Carter Lane,
London EC4V 5EL

● *Books so marked are available in paperback*
All books are in Metric Demy 8vo format (216 × 138mm approx.)

International Library of Sociology

General Editor   John Rex

GENERAL SOCIOLOGY

Barnsley, J. H. The Social Reality of Ethics. *464 pp.*
Belshaw, Cyril. The Conditions of Social Performance. *An Exploratory Theory. 144 pp.*
Brown, Robert. Explanation in Social Science. *208 pp.*
● Rules and Laws in Sociology. *192 pp.*
Bruford, W. H. Chekhov and His Russia. *A Sociological Study. 244 pp.*
Cain, Maureen E. Society and the Policeman's Role. *326 pp.*
Gibson, Quentin. The Logic of Social Enquiry. *240 pp.*
Glucksmann, M. Structuralist Analysis in Contemporary Social Thought. *212 pp.*
Gurvitch, Georges. Sociology of Law. *Preface by Roscoe Pound. 264 pp.*
Hodge, H. A. Wilhelm Dilthey. *An Introduction. 184 pp.*
Homans, George C. Sentiments and Activities. *336 pp.*
Johnson, Harry M. Sociology: *a Systematic Introduction. Foreword by Robert K. Merton. 710 pp.*
Mannheim, Karl. Essays on Sociology and Social Psychology. *Edited by Paul Kecskemeti. With Editorial Note by Adolph Lowe. 344 pp.*
  Systematic Sociology: *An Introduction to the Study of Society. Edited by J. S. Erös and Professor W. A. C. Stewart. 220 pp.*
Martindale, Don. The Nature and Types of Sociological Theory. *292 pp.*
●**Maus, Heinz.** A Short History of Sociology. *234 pp.*
Mey, Harald. Field-Theory. *A Study of its Application in the Social Sciences. 352 pp.*
Myrdal, Gunnar. Value in Social Theory: *A Collection of Essays on Methodology. Edited by Paul Streeten. 332 pp.*
Ogburn, William F., and **Nimkoff, Meyer F.** A Handbook of Sociology. *Preface by Karl Mannheim. 656 pp. 46 figures. 35 tables.*
Parsons, Talcott, and **Smelser, Neil J.** Economy and Society: *A Study in the Integration of Economic and Social Theory. 362 pp.*
●**Rex, John.** Key Problems of Sociological Theory. *220 pp.*
  Discovering Sociology. *278 pp.*
  Sociology and the Demystification of the Modern World. *282 pp.*
●**Rex, John** (Ed.) Approaches to Sociology. *Contributions by Peter Abell, Frank Bechhofer, Basil Bernstein, Ronald Fletcher, David Frisby, Miriam Glucksmann, Peter Lassman, Herminio Martins, John Rex, Roland Robertson, John Westergaard and Jock Young. 302 pp.*
Rigby, A. Alternative Realities. *352 pp.*
Roche, M. Phenomenology, Language and the Social Sciences. *374 pp.*
Sahay, A. Sociological Analysis. *220 pp.*
Urry, John. Reference Groups and the Theory of Revolution. *244 pp.*
Weinberg, E. Development of Sociology in the Soviet Union. *173 pp.*

FOREIGN CLASSICS OF SOCIOLOGY

●**Durkheim, Emile.** Suicide. *A Study in Sociology. Edited and with an Introduction by George Simpson. 404 pp.*
Professional Ethics and Civic Morals. *Translated by Cornelia Brookfield. 288 pp.*
●**Gerth, H. H.,** and **Mills, C. Wright.** From Max Weber: *Essays in Sociology. 502 pp.*
●**Tönnies, Ferdinand.** Community and Association. (*Gemeinschaft und Gesellschaft.) Translated and Supplemented by Charles P. Loomis. Foreword by Pitirim A. Sorokin. 334 pp.*

SOCIAL STRUCTURE

Andreski, Stanislav. Military Organization and Society. *Foreword by Professor A. R. Radcliffe-Brown. 226 pp. 1 folder.*
Coontz, Sydney H. Population Theories and the Economic Interpretation. *202 pp.*
Coser, Lewis. The Functions of Social Conflict. *204 pp.*
Dickie-Clark, H. F. Marginal Situation: *A Sociological Study of a Coloured Group. 240 pp. 11 tables.*
Glaser, Barney, and **Strauss, Anselm L.** Status Passage. *A Formal Theory. 208 pp.*
Glass, D. V. (Ed.) Social Mobility in Britain. *Contributions by J. Berent, T. Bottomore, R. C. Chambers, J. Floud, D. V. Glass, J. R. Hall, H. T. Himmelweit, R. K. Kelsall, F. M. Martin, C. A. Moser, R. Mukherjee, and W. Ziegel. 420 pp.*
Jones, Garth N. Planned Organizational Change: *An Exploratory Study Using an Empirical Approach. 268 pp.*
Kelsall, R. K. Higher Civil Servants in Britain: *From 1870 to the Present Day. 268 pp. 31 tables.*
König, René. The Community. *232 pp. Illustrated.*
●**Lawton, Denis.** Social Class, Language and Education. *192 pp.*
McLeish, John. The Theory of Social Change: *Four Views Considered. 128 pp.*
Marsh, David C. The Changing Social Structure of England and Wales, 1871-1961. *288 pp.*
Mouzelis, Nicos. Organization and Bureaucracy. *An Analysis of Modern Theories. 240 pp.*
Mulkay, M. J. Functionalism, Exchange and Theoretical Strategy. *272 pp.*
Ossowski, Stanislaw. Class Structure in the Social Consciousness. *210 pp.*
Podgórecki, Adam. Law and Society. *About 300 pp.*

SOCIOLOGY AND POLITICS

Acton, T. A. Gypsy Politics and Social Change. *316 pp.*
Hechter, Michael. Internal Colonialism. *The Celtic Fringe in British National Development, 1536–1966. About 350 pp.*
Hertz, Frederick. Nationality in History and Politics: *A Psychology and Sociology of National Sentiment and Nationalism. 432 pp.*

Kornhauser, William. The Politics of Mass Society. *272 pp. 20 tables.*

Laidler, Harry W. History of Socialism. *Social-Economic Movements: An Historical and Comparative Survey of Socialism, Communism, Co-operation, Utopianism; and other Systems of Reform and Reconstruction. 992 pp.*

Lasswell, H. D. Analysis of Political Behaviour. *324 pp.*

Mannheim, Karl. Freedom, Power and Democratic Planning. *Edited by Hans Gerth and Ernest K. Bramstedt. 424 pp.*

Mansur, Fatma. Process of Independence. *Foreword by A. H. Hanson. 208 pp.*

Martin, David A. Pacifism: *an Historical and Sociological Study. 262 pp.*

Myrdal, Gunnar. The Political Element in the Development of Economic Theory. *Translated from the German by Paul Streeten. 282 pp.*

Wootton, Graham. Workers, Unions and the State. *188 pp.*

FOREIGN AFFAIRS: THEIR SOCIAL, POLITICAL AND ECONOMIC FOUNDATIONS

Mayer, J. P. Political Thought in France from the Revolution to the Fifth Republic. *164 pp.*

CRIMINOLOGY

Ancel, Marc. Social Defence: *A Modern Approach to Criminal Problems. Foreword by Leon Radzinowicz. 240 pp.*

Cain, Maureen E. Society and the Policeman's Role. *326 pp.*

Cloward, Richard A., and **Ohlin, Lloyd E.** Delinquency and Opportunity: *A Theory of Delinquent Gangs. 248 pp.*

Downes, David M. The Delinquent Solution. *A Study in Subcultural Theory. 296 pp.*

Dunlop, A. B., and **McCabe, S.** Young Men in Detention Centres. *192 pp.*

Friedlander, Kate. The Psycho-Analytical Approach to Juvenile Delinquency: *Theory, Case Studies, Treatment. 320 pp.*

Glueck, Sheldon, and **Eleanor.** Family Environment and Delinquency. *With the statistical assistance of Rose W. Kneznek. 340 pp.*

Lopez-Rey, Manuel. Crime. *An Analytical Appraisal. 288 pp.*

Mannheim, Hermann. Comparative Criminology: *a Text Book. Two volumes. 442 pp. and 380 pp.*

Morris, Terence. The Criminal Area: *A Study in Social Ecology. Foreword by Hermann Mannheim. 232 pp. 25 tables. 4 maps.*

Rock, Paul. Making People Pay. *338 pp.*

● **Taylor, Ian, Walton, Paul,** and **Young, Jock.** The New Criminology. *For a Social Theory of Deviance. 325 pp.*

SOCIAL PSYCHOLOGY

Bagley, Christopher. The Social Psychology of the Epileptic Child. *320 pp.*

Barbu, Zevedei. Problems of Historical Psychology. *248 pp.*

Blackburn, Julian. Psychology and the Social Pattern. *184 pp.*

5

●**Brittan, Arthur.** Meanings and Situations. *224 pp.*

Carroll, J. Break-Out from the Crystal Palace. *200 pp.*

●**Fleming, C. M.** Adolescence: Its Social Psychology. *With an Introduction to recent findings from the fields of Anthropology, Physiology, Medicine, Psychometrics and Sociometry. 288 pp.*

● The Social Psychology of Education: *An Introduction and Guide to Its Study. 136 pp.*

Homans, George C. The Human Group. *Foreword by Bernard DeVoto. Introduction by Robert K. Merton. 526 pp.*

● Social Behaviour: *its Elementary Forms. 416 pp.*

●**Klein, Josephine.** The Study of Groups. *226 pp. 31 figures. 5 tables.*

Linton, Ralph. The Cultural Background of Personality. *132 pp.*

●**Mayo, Elton.** The Social Problems of an Industrial Civilization. *With an appendix on the Political Problem. 180 pp.*

Ottaway, A. K. C. Learning Through Group Experience. *176 pp.*

Ridder, J. C. de. The Personality of the Urban African in South Africa. *A Thematic Apperception Test Study. 196 pp. 12 plates.*

●**Rose, Arnold M.** (Ed.) Human Behaviour and Social Processes: *an Interactionist Approach. Contributions by Arnold M. Rose, Ralph H. Turner, Anselm Strauss, Everett C. Hughes, E. Franklin Frazier, Howard S. Becker, et al. 696 pp.*

Smelser, Neil J. Theory of Collective Behaviour. *448 pp.*

Stephenson, Geoffrey M. The Development of Conscience. *128 pp.*

Young, Kimball. Handbook of Social Psychology. *658 pp. 16 figures. 10 tables.*

SOCIOLOGY OF THE FAMILY

Banks, J. A. Prosperity and Parenthood: *A Study of Family Planning among The Victorian Middle Classes. 262 pp.*

Bell, Colin R. Middle Class Families: *Social and Geographical Mobility. 224 pp.*

Burton, Lindy. Vulnerable Children. *272 pp.*

Gavron, Hannah. The Captive Wife: *Conflicts of Household Mothers. 190 pp.*

George, Victor, and **Wilding, Paul.** Motherless Families. *220 pp.*

Klein, Josephine. Samples from English Cultures.

1. Three Preliminary Studies and Aspects of Adult Life in England. *447 pp.*

2. Child-Rearing Practices and Index. *247 pp.*

Klein, Viola. Britain's Married Women Workers. *180 pp.*

The Feminine Character. *History of an Ideology. 244 pp.*

McWhinnie, Alexina M. Adopted Children. *How They Grow Up. 304 pp.*

● **Myrdal, Alva,** and **Klein, Viola.** Women's Two Roles: *Home and Work. 238 pp. 27 tables.*

Parsons, Talcott, and **Bales, Robert F.** Family: Socialization and Interaction Process. *In collaboration with James Olds, Morris Zelditch and Philip E. Slater. 456 pp. 50 figures and tables.*

SOCIAL SERVICES

Bastide, Roger. The Sociology of Mental Disorder. *Translated from the French by Jean McNeil. 260 pp.*

Carlebach, Julius. Caring For Children in Trouble. *266 pp.*

Forder, R. A. (Ed.) Penelope Hall's Social Services of England and Wales. *352 pp.*

George, Victor. Foster Care. *Theory and Practice. 234 pp.*
Social Security: *Beveridge and After. 258 pp.*

George, V., and **Wilding, P.** Motherless Families. *248 pp.*

●**Goetschius, George W.** Working with Community Groups. *256 pp.*

Goetschius, George W., and **Tash, Joan.** Working with Unattached Youth. *416 pp.*

Hall, M. P., and **Howes, I. V.** The Church in Social Work. *A Study of Moral Welfare Work undertaken by the Church of England. 320 pp.*

Heywood, Jean S. Children in Care: *the Development of the Service for the Deprived Child. 264 pp.*

Hoenig, J., and **Hamilton, Marian W.** The De-Segregation of the Mentally Ill. *284 pp.*

Jones, Kathleen. Mental Health and Social Policy, 1845-1959. *264 pp.*

King, Roy D., Raynes, Norma V., and **Tizard, Jack.** Patterns of Residential Care. *356 pp.*

Leigh, John. Young People and Leisure. *256 pp.*

Morris, Mary. Voluntary Work and the Welfare State. *300 pp.*

Morris, Pauline. Put Away: *A Sociological Study of Institutions for the Mentally Retarded. 364 pp.*

Nokes, P. L. The Professional Task in Welfare Practice. *152 pp.*

Timms, Noel. Psychiatric Social Work in Great Britain (1939-1962). *280 pp.*

●   Social Casework: *Principles and Practice. 256 pp.*

Young, A. F. Social Services in British Industry. *272 pp.*

Young, A. F., and **Ashton, E. T.** British Social Work in the Nineteenth Century. *288 pp.*

SOCIOLOGY OF EDUCATION

Banks, Olive. Parity and Prestige in English Secondary Education: a Study in Educational Sociology. *272 pp.*

Bentwich, Joseph. Education in Israel. *224 pp. 8 pp. plates.*

●**Blyth, W. A. L.** English Primary Education. *A Sociological Description.*
1. Schools. *232 pp.*
2. Background. *168 pp.*

Collier, K. G. The Social Purposes of Education: *Personal and Social Values in Education. 268 pp.*

7

Dale, R. R., and **Griffith, S.** Down Stream: *Failure in the Grammar School.*
108 pp.

Dore, R. P. Education in Tokugawa Japan. *356 pp. 9 pp. plates.*

Evans, K. M. Sociometry and Education. *158 pp.*

●**Ford, Julienne.** Social Class and the Comprehensive School. *192 pp.*

Foster, P. J. Education and Social Change in Ghana. *336 pp. 3 maps.*

Fraser, W. R. Education and Society in Modern France. *150 pp.*

Grace, Gerald R. Role Conflict and the Teacher. *About 200 pp.*

Hans, Nicholas. New Trends in Education in the Eighteenth Century.
278 pp. 19 tables.

● Comparative Education: *A Study of Educational Factors and Traditions.*
360 pp.

Hargreaves, David. Interpersonal Relations and Education. *432 pp.*

● Social Relations in a Secondary School. *240 pp.*

Holmes, Brian. Problems in Education. *A Comparative Approach. 336 pp.*

King, Ronald. Values and Involvement in a Grammar School. *164 pp.*

School Organization and Pupil Involvement. *A Study of Secondary Schools.*

●**Mannheim, Karl,** and **Stewart, W. A. C.** An Introduction to the Sociology of Education. *206 pp.*

Morris, Raymond N. The Sixth Form and College Entrance. *231 pp.*

●**Musgrove, F.** Youth and the Social Order. *176 pp.*

●**Ottaway, A. K. C.** Education and Society: An Introduction to the Sociology of Education. *With an Introduction by W. O. Lester Smith. 212 pp.*

Peers, Robert. Adult Education: *A Comparative Study. 398 pp.*

Pritchard, D. G. Education and the Handicapped: *1760 to 1960. 258 pp.*

Richardson, Helen. Adolescent Girls in Approved Schools. *308 pp.*

Stratta, Erica. The Education of Borstal Boys. *A Study of their Educational Experiences prior to, and during, Borstal Training. 256 pp.*

Taylor, P. H., Reid, W. A., and **Holley, B. J.** The English Sixth Form.
A Case Study in Curriculum Research. 200 pp.

SOCIOLOGY OF CULTURE

Eppel, E. M., and **M.** Adolescents and Morality: *A Study of some Moral Values and Dilemmas of Working Adolescents in the Context of a changing Climate of Opinion. Foreword by W. J. H. Sprott. 268 pp. 39 tables.*

●**Fromm, Erich.** The Fear of Freedom. *286 pp.*

● The Sane Society. *400 pp.*

Mannheim, Karl. Essays on the Sociology of Culture. *Edited by Ernst Mannheim in co-operation with Paul Kecskemeti. Editorial Note by Adolph Lowe. 280 pp.*

Weber, Alfred. Farewell to European History: *or The Conquest of Nihilism. Translated from the German by R. F. C. Hull. 224 pp.*

SOCIOLOGY OF RELIGION

Argyle, Michael and **Beit-Hallahmi, Benjamin.** The Social Psychology of Religion. *About 256 pp.*

Nelson, G. K. Spiritualism and Society. *313 pp.*

Stark, Werner. The Sociology of Religion. *A Study of Christendom.*
Volume I. *Established Religion. 248 pp.*
Volume II. *Sectarian Religion. 368 pp.*
Volume III. *The Universal Church. 464 pp.*
Volume IV. *Types of Religious Man. 352 pp.*
Volume V. *Types of Religious Culture. 464 pp.*

Turner, B. S. Weber and Islam. *216 pp.*

Watt, W. Montgomery. Islam and the Integration of Society. *320 pp.*

SOCIOLOGY OF ART AND LITERATURE

Jarvie, Ian C. Towards a Sociology of the Cinema. *A Comparative Essay on the Structure and Functioning of a Major Entertainment Industry. 405 pp.*

Rust, Frances S. Dance in Society. *An Analysis of the Relationships between the Social Dance and Society in England from the Middle Ages to the Present Day. 256 pp. 8 pp. of plates.*

Schücking, L. L. The Sociology of Literary Taste. *112 pp.*

Wolff, Janet. Hermeneutic Philosophy and the Sociology of Art. *About 200 pp.*

SOCIOLOGY OF KNOWLEDGE

Diesing, P. Patterns of Discovery in the Social Sciences. *262 pp.*

●**Douglas, J. D.** (Ed.) Understanding Everyday Life. *370 pp.*

●**Hamilton, P.** Knowledge and Social Structure. *174 pp.*

Jarvie, I. C. Concepts and Society. *232 pp.*

Mannheim, Karl. Essays on the Sociology of Knowledge. *Edited by Paul Kecskemeti. Editorial Note by Adolph Lowe. 353 pp.*

Remmling, Gunter W. (Ed.) Towards the Sociology of Knowledge. *Origin and Development of a Sociological Thought Style. 463 pp.*

Stark, Werner. The Sociology of Knowledge: *An Essay in Aid of a Deeper Understanding of the History of Ideas. 384 pp.*

URBAN SOCIOLOGY

Ashworth, William. The Genesis of Modern British Town Planning: *A Study in Economic and Social History of the Nineteenth and Twentieth Centuries. 288 pp.*

Cullingworth, J. B. Housing Needs and Planning Policy: *A Restatement of the Problems of Housing Need and 'Overspill' in England and Wales. 232 pp. 44 tables. 8 maps.*

Dickinson, Robert E. City and Region: *A Geographical Interpretation* *608 pp. 125 figures.*
The West European City: *A Geographical Interpretation. 600 pp. 129 maps. 29 plates.*
● The City Region in Western Europe. *320 pp. Maps.*
Humphreys, Alexander J. New Dubliners: *Urbanization and the Irish Family. Foreword by George C. Homans. 304 pp.*
Jackson, Brian. Working Class Community: *Some General Notions raised by a Series of Studies in Northern England. 192 pp.*
Jennings, Hilda. Societies in the Making: *a Study of Development and Re-development within a County Borough. Foreword by D. A. Clark. 286 pp.*
●**Mann, P. H.** An Approach to Urban Sociology. *240 pp.*
Morris, R. N., and **Mogey, J.** The Sociology of Housing. *Studies at Berinsfield. 232 pp. 4 pp. plates.*
Rosser, C., and **Harris, C.** The Family and Social Change. *A Study of Family and Kinship in a South Wales Town. 352 pp. 8 maps.*

RURAL SOCIOLOGY

Chambers, R. J. H. Settlement Schemes in Tropical Africa: *A Selective Study. 268 pp.*
Haswell, M. R. The Economics of Development in Village India. *120 pp.*
Littlejohn, James. Westrigg: *the Sociology of a Cheviot Parish. 172 pp. 5 figures.*
Mayer, Adrian C. Peasants in the Pacific. *A Study of Fiji Indian Rural Society. 248 pp. 20 plates.*
Williams, W. M. The Sociology of an English Village: *Gosforth. 272 pp. 12 figures. 13 tables.*

SOCIOLOGY OF INDUSTRY AND DISTRIBUTION

Anderson, Nels. Work and Leisure. *280 pp.*
●**Blau, Peter M.,** and **Scott, W. Richard.** Formal Organizations: *a Comparative approach. Introduction and Additional Bibliography by J. H. Smith. 326 pp.*
Eldridge, J. E. T. Industrial Disputes. *Essays in the Sociology of Industrial Relations. 288 pp.*
Hetzler, Stanley. Applied Measures for Promoting Technological Growth. *352 pp.*
Technological Growth and Social Change. *Achieving Modernization. 269 pp.*
Hollowell, Peter G. The Lorry Driver. *272 pp.*
Jefferys, Margot, *with the assistance of Winifred Moss.* Mobility in the Labour Market: *Employment Changes in Battersea and Dagenham. Preface by Barbara Wootton. 186 pp. 51 tables.*

Millerson, Geoffrey. The Qualifying Associations: *a Study in Professionalization. 320 pp.*

Smelser, Neil J. Social Change in the Industrial Revolution: *An Application of Theory to the Lancashire Cotton Industry, 1770-1840. 468 pp. 12 figures. 14 tables.*

Williams, Gertrude. Recruitment to Skilled Trades. *240 pp.*

Young, A. F. Industrial Injuries Insurance: *an Examination of British Policy. 192 pp.*

DOCUMENTARY

Schlesinger, Rudolf (Ed.) Changing Attitudes in Soviet Russia.
2. The Nationalities Problem and Soviet Administration. *Selected Readings on the Development of Soviet Nationalities Policies. Introduced by the editor. Translated by W. W. Gottlieb. 324 pp.*

ANTHROPOLOGY

Ammar, Hamed. Growing up in an Egyptian Village: *Silwa, Province of Aswan. 336 pp.*

Brandel-Syrier, Mia. Reeftown Elite. *A Study of Social Mobility in a Modern African Community on the Reef. 376 pp.*

Crook, David, and **Isabel.** Revolution in a Chinese Village: *Ten Mile Inn. 230 pp. 8 plates. 1 map.*

Dickie-Clark, H. F. The Marginal Situation. *A Sociological Study of a Coloured Group. 236 pp.*

Dube, S. C. Indian Village. *Foreword by Morris Edward Opler. 276 pp. 4 plates.*

India's Changing Villages: *Human Factors in Community Development. 260 pp. 8 plates. 1 map.*

Firth, Raymond. Malay Fishermen. *Their Peasant Economy. 420 pp. 17 pp. plates.*

Firth, R., Hubert, J., and **Forge, A.** Families and their Relatives. *Kinship in a Middle-Class Sector of London: An Anthropological Study. 456 pp.*

Gulliver, P. H. Social Control in an African Society: a Study of the Arusha, Agricultural Masai of Northern Tanganyika. *320 pp. 8 plates. 10 figures.*

Family Herds. *288 pp.*

Ishwaran, K. Shivapur. *A South Indian Village. 216 pp.*

Tradition and Economy in Village India: *An Interactionist Approach. Foreword by Conrad Arensburg. 176 pp.*

Jarvie, Ian C. The Revolution in Anthropology. *268 pp.*

Jarvie, Ian C., and **Agassi, Joseph.** Hong Kong. *A Society in Transition. 396 pp. Illustrated with plates and maps.*

Little, Kenneth L. Mende of Sierra Leone. *308 pp. and folder.*

Negroes in Britain. *With a New Introduction and Contemporary Study by Leonard Bloom. 320 pp.*

11

Lowie, Robert H. Social Organization. *494 pp.*
Mayer, Adrian C. Caste and Kinship in Central India: *A Village and its Region. 328 pp. 16 plates. 15 figures. 16 tables.*
  Peasants in the Pacific. *A Study of Fiji Indian Rural Society. 248 pp.*
Smith, Raymond T. The Negro Family in British Guiana: *Family Structure and Social Status in the Villages. With a Foreword by Meyer Fortes. 314 pp. 8 plates. 1 figure. 4 maps.*

SOCIOLOGY AND PHILOSOPHY

Barnsley, John H. The Social Reality of Ethics. *A Comparative Analysis of Moral Codes. 448 pp.*
Diesing, Paul. Patterns of Discovery in the Social Sciences. *362 pp.*
●**Douglas, Jack D.** (Ed.) Understanding Everyday Life. *Toward the Reconstruction of Sociological Knowledge. Contributions by Alan F. Blum. Aaron W. Cicourel, Norman K. Denzin, Jack D. Douglas, John Heeren, Peter McHugh, Peter K. Manning, Melvin Power, Matthew Speier, Roy Turner, D. Lawrence Wieder, Thomas P. Wilson and Don H. Zimmerman. 370 pp.*
Jarvie, Ian C. Concepts and Society. *216 pp.*
Pelz, Werner. The Scope of Understanding in Sociology. *Towards a more radical reorientation in the social humanistic sciences. 283 pp.*
Roche, Maurice. Phenomenology, Language and the Social Sciences. *371 pp.*
Sahay, Arun. Sociological Analysis. *212 pp.*
Sklair, Leslie. The Sociology of Progress. *320 pp.*

International Library of Anthropology

General Editor Adam Kuper

Brown, Paula. The Chimbu. *A Study of Change in the New Guinea Highlands. 151 pp.*
Lloyd, P. C. Power and Independence. *Urban Africans' Perception of Social Inequality. 264 pp.*
Pettigrew, Joyce. Robber Noblemen. *A Study of the Political System of the Sikh Jats. 284 pp.*
Van Den Berghe, Pierre L. Power and Privilege at an African University. *278 pp.*

International Library of Social Policy

General Editor Kathleen Jones

Bayley, M. Mental Handicap and Community Care. *426 pp.*
Butler, J. R. Family Doctors and Public Policy. *208 pp.*
Holman, Robert. Trading in Children. *A Study of Private Fostering. 355 pp.*

Jones, Kathleen. History of the Mental Health Service. *428 pp.*

Thomas, J. E. The English Prison Officer since 1850: *A Study in Conflict. 258 pp.*

Woodward, J. To Do the Sick No Harm. *A Study of the British Voluntary Hospital System to 1875. About 220 pp.*

International Library of Welfare and Philosophy

General Editors Noel Timms and David Watson

● **Plant, Raymond.** Community and Ideology. *104 pp.*

Primary Socialization, Language and Education

General Editor Basil Bernstein

Bernstein, Basil. Class, Codes and Control. *2 volumes.*
  1. *Theoretical Studies Towards a Sociology of Language. 254 pp.*
  2. *Applied Studies Towards a Sociology of Language. About 400 pp.*
Brandis, W., and **Bernstein, B.** Selection and Control. *176 pp.*
Brandis, Walter, and **Henderson, Dorothy.** Social Class, Language and Communication. *288 pp.*
Cook-Gumperz, Jenny. Social Control and Socialization. *A Study of Class Differences in the Language of Maternal Control. 290 pp.*
● **Gahagan, D. M.,** and **G. A.** Talk Reform. *Exploration in Language for Infant School Children. 160 pp.*
Robinson, W. P., and **Rackstraw, Susan D. A.** A Question of Answers. *2 volumes. 192 pp. and 180 pp.*
Turner, Geoffrey J., and **Mohan, Bernard A.** A Linguistic Description and Computer Programme for Children's Speech. *208 pp.*

Reports of the Institute of Community Studies

Cartwright, Ann. Human Relations and Hospital Care. *272 pp.*
●   Parents and Family Planning Services. *306 pp.*
   Patients and their Doctors. *A Study of General Practice. 304 pp.*
● **Jackson, Brian.** Streaming: *an Education System in Miniature. 168 pp.*
Jackson, Brian, and **Marsden, Dennis.** Education and the Working Class: *Some General Themes raised by a Study of 88 Working-class Children in a Northern Industrial City. 268 pp. 2 folders.*
Marris, Peter. The Experience of Higher Education. *232 pp. 27 tables.*
   Loss and Change. *192 pp.*

Marris, Peter, and **Rein, Martin.** Dilemmas of Social Reform. *Poverty and Community Action in the United States. 256 pp.*

Marris, Peter, and **Somerset, Anthony.** African Businessmen. *A Study of Entrepreneurship and Development in Kenya. 256 pp.*

Mills, Richard. Young Outsiders: *a Study in Alternative Communities. 216 pp.*

Runciman, W. G. Relative Deprivation and Social Justice. *A Study of Attitudes to Social Inequality in Twentieth-Century England. 352 pp.*

Willmott, Peter. Adolescent Boys in East London. *230 pp.*

Willmott, Peter, and **Young, Michael.** Family and Class in a London Suburb. *202 pp. 47 tables.*

Young, Michael. Innovation and Research in Education. *192 pp.*

●**Young, Michael,** and **McGeeney, Patrick.** Learning Begins at Home. *A Study of a Junior School and its Parents. 128 pp.*

Young, Michael, and **Willmott, Peter.** Family and Kinship in East London. *Foreword by Richard M. Titmuss. 252 pp. 39 tables.*

The Symmetrical Family. *410 pp.*

Reports of the Institute for Social Studies in Medical Care

Cartwright, Ann, Hockey, Lisbeth, and **Anderson, John L.** Life Before Death. *310 pp.*

Dunnell, Karen, and **Cartwright, Ann.** Medicine Takers, Prescribers and Hoarders. *190 pp.*

Medicine, Illness and Society

General Editor W. M. Williams

Robinson, David. The Process of Becoming Ill. *142 pp.*

Stacey, Margaret, *et al.* Hospitals, Children and Their Families. *The Report of a Pilot Study. 202 pp.*

Monographs in Social Theory

General Editor Arthur Brittan

●**Barnes, B.** Scientific Knowledge and Sociological Theory. *About 200 pp.*

Bauman, Zygmunt. Culture as Praxis. *204 pp.*

●**Dixon, Keith.** Sociological Theory. *Pretence and Possibility. 142 pp.*

●**Smith, Anthony D.** The Concept of Social Change. *A Critique of the Functionalist Theory of Social Change. 208 pp.*

Routledge Social Science Journals

The British Journal of Sociology. *Edited by Terence P. Morris. Vol. 1, No. 1, March 1950 and Quarterly. Roy. 8vo. Back numbers available. An international journal with articles on all aspects of sociology.*

Economy and Society. *Vol. 1, No. 1. February 1972 and Quarterly. Metric Roy. 8vo. A journal for all social scientists covering sociology, philosophy, anthropology, economics and history. Back numbers available.*

Year Book of Social Policy in Britain, The. *Edited by Kathleen Jones. 1971. Published annually.*

Printed in Great Britain by Unwin Brothers Limited
The Gresham Press Old Woking Surrey
A member of the Staples Printing Group